Ethnography as Christian Theology and Ethics

T&T Clark Studies in Social Ethics, Ethnography, and Theology

Over the last half century, there have been numerous calls for Christian theology and ethics to take human experience seriously—to delve into particular economic, sociopolitical, racial-ethnic, and cultural contexts from which theological and moral imagination arises. Yet actual theologies that draw upon descriptive-rich, qualitative methods—methods that place such particularity at the center of inquiry and performance—are few and scattered. **T&T Clark Studies in Social Ethics, Ethnography, and Theology** is a monograph series that addresses this gap in the literature by providing a publishing home for timely ethnographically driven theological and ethical investigations of an expansive array of pressing social issues, ranging from armed conflict to racism to healthcare inequities to sexuality/gender and discrimination to the marginalization of persons with disabilities. The scope of the series projects, taken together, is at once global and intensely local, with the central organizing conviction that ethnography provides not only information to plug into a theology, but a valid and vibrant way of *doing* theology.

Ethnography as Christian Theology and Ethics

A Fully Revised 2nd Edition

Aana Marie Vigen and Christian Scharen

t&tclark
LONDON • NEW YORK • OXFORD • NEW DELHI • SYDNEY

T&T CLARK
Bloomsbury Publishing Plc
50 Bedford Square, London, WC1B 3DP, UK
1385 Broadway, New York, NY 10018, USA
29 Earlsfort Terrace, Dublin 2, Ireland

BLOOMSBURY, T&T CLARK and the T&T Clark logo are trademarks
of Bloomsbury Publishing Plc

First published in Great Britain 2024

Copyright © Aana Marie Vigen & Christian Scharen, 2024

Aana Marie Vigen & Christian Scharen have asserted their right under the Copyright, Designs and Patents Act, 1988, to be identified as Author of this work.

Cover design: Ben Anslow
Cover image © Wil Gafney

All rights reserved. No part of this publication may be reproduced or transmitted in any form or by any means, electronic or mechanical, including photocopying, recording, or any information storage or retrieval system, without prior permission in writing from the publishers.

Bloomsbury Publishing Plc does not have any control over, or responsibility for, any third-party websites referred to or in this book. All internet addresses given in this book were correct at the time of going to press. The author and publisher regret any inconvenience caused if addresses have changed or sites have ceased to exist, but can accept no responsibility for any such changes.

A catalogue record for this book is available from the British Library.

Library of Congress Cataloging-in-Publication Data

Names: Vigen, Aana Marie, editor. | Scharen, Christian, 1966- editor.
Title: Ethnography as Christian theology and ethics / [edited by]
Aana Marie Vigen & Christian Scharen.
Description: Fully revised 2nd edition. | London; New York: T&T Clark, 2024. |
Series: T&T clark studies in social ethics, ethnography and
theology; vol. 4 | Includes bibliographical references and index.
Identifiers: LCCN 2024008698 (print) | LCCN 2024008699 (ebook) |
ISBN 9780567710468 (HB) | ISBN 9780567710451 (PB) |
ISBN 9780567711482 (ePDF) | ISBN 9780567710475 (ePUB)
Subjects: LCSH: Christianity and culture. |
Ethnology–Religious aspects–Christianity. | Christian ethics.
Classification: LCC BR115.C8 E847 2024 (print) | LCC BR115.C8 (ebook) |
DDC 261.5–dc23/eng/20240511
LC record available at https://lccn.loc.gov/2024008698
LC ebook record available at https://lccn.loc.gov/2024008699

ISBN: HB: 978-0-5677-1046-8
PB: 978-0-5677-1045-1
ePDF: 978-0-5677-1048-2
ePUB: 978-0-5677-1047-5

Typeset by Deanta Global Publishing Services, Chennai, India
Printed and bound in Great Britain

To find out more about our authors and books visit www.bloomsbury.com
and sign up for our newsletters.

To Nancy L. Eiesland (1964–2009), beloved teacher and mentor, with my enduring gratitude—Christian Scharen

With abiding love and profound gratitude for David Clifford Vigen (1933–2019), Kathryn Louise Voss Vigen (1934–2022), L. Warren Strickler (1928–2019) and Joan Oren Strickler (1926–2024); and again and always to Alison and Benjamin Gabriel, my family, for the infinite joy and grace you embody and for keeping me grounded in the particular—Aana Marie Vigen

And in honor and loving memory of the indomitable Rev. Dr. Melissa D. Browning (1977–2021)

Melissa with Olivia, Chicago Teachers Union Protest, 2013—photo by Wes Browning, used by permission

Contents

Foreword *Traci C. West* ix
Drawing from the Wells of a Feminist Theologian, Ethicist, and Community Mobilizer: Reflections on the Life, Works, and Legacy of Rev. Dr. Melissa Browne Browning (1977–2021) *Emily Reimer-Barry and Damaris Parsitau* xv
Preface: Blurring Boundaries xxvi

Part I Prolegomena

1 What Is Ethnography? 3
2 The Ethnographic Turn in Theology and Ethics 32
3 Critiques of the Use of Social Science in Theology and Ethics 49
4 Theological Justifications for Turning to Ethnography 61

Part II Exemplars

5 A Conversation between the Researcher and the Research Assistant on Ethnographic Praxis *Elina Hankela and Clementine Nishimwe* 81
6 Ethnography and Crucified Bodies: A Liberationist-Incarnational Approach *Sunder John Boopalan and RC Jongte* 95
7 A Trauma-Ridden Body Lifted High: Eschatological Imagination in a Public Square *Hee-Kyu Heidi Park* 111
8 Theodicies at the Border: Grasping with Evil in the Lives of Indonesian Female Migrant Workers in Singapore *Lailatul Fitriyah* 127
9 Fieldnotes from the Gardens: Methods, Ethics, and Rants *Nicole Hoskins* 143
10 The Curious Case of the Swedish Woman: Ethnographic Reflexivity and Accountability in Transnational Feminism *Sara A. Williams* 156

11 Qualitatively Studying Evangelical Whiteness: Excerpts and
    Experiences *Nicole Symmonds*   170

12 Inhabiting the Aftermath of Firearm-Caused Violence: Guns and the
    Practice of Vigil Keeping *Michael Grigoni*   183

13 Making Lemonade with Substitute Sugar: Toward an Ethics of
    Receptivity *AnneMarie Mingo*   198

Part III Method

14 Benedictions: For Those Willing to Give Ethnography a Try   217

Bibliography   233
Contributors   250
Index   253

Foreword

Traci C. West

The boldness of the thinkers gathered here in the Second Edition of *Ethnography as Christian Theology and Ethics* reminds me of certain similar legacies of bold thinkers who preceded them. Charting vastly differing routes, they each creatively engage ethnographic methods of inquiry, Christian religious faith and ethics, and issues of unequal social power. These researchers shake up our perceptions of whose knowledge we truly need and how we should gather and analyze its significance. As I think about the riskiness of participating in such intellectual boldness, even if it is just as readers of their texts, I can't help wondering: how do you prepare to have some of your most foundational assumptions about learning unsettled?

Legacies of Pioneering Boldness Need to be Remembered

When Zora Neale Hurston (1891–1960) traveled in 1927 from her New York City academic base of Barnard College and the influential mentorship of Columbia University's anthropology professor Franz Boas to her childhood hometown of Eatonville, Florida, how had she been prepared to do her research there? In the world from which she started out, she was the first Black student to racially integrate what she described as Barnard's "sharp white background."[1] She lived in predominantly Black Harlem and had connected with its thriving and publishing Black intellectual community in the New Negro movement. But she was also surrounded by racist local store policies that did not allow their Black customers—the majority of their customers—to try on hats or dresses when deciding on a purchase, or to use the public toilets. On her way from Harlem to Florida, she journeyed deeper into the land of southern Jim Crow racial segregation at a time when the occurrence of lynchings by white Christians was at the height of their frequency and visibility in public spaces. All of these contextual realities could have helped to prepare her by providing knowledge of the stunning breadth and variations of both white racism and expressions of Black communal life. Hurston made the trip to conduct some of the first research interviews by any Black scholar that documented the folk ways and Christian religious beliefs expressed in everyday southern rural Black community life.

---

[1] Zora Neale Hurston, "How Does It Feel to Be Colored Me," *The World Tomorrow*, May 1928 in Zora Neale Hurston and Cheryl A Wall, *Folklore Memoirs and Other Writings* (New York: Library of America), 1995.

In addition to the contextual influences, as she was heading to Florida on that 1927 research trip, Hurston's own grit, inventiveness, and intellectual ambitiousness must be counted as part of her preparation. The combination of her onerous financial instability, navigation of racial and gender discrimination alongside the limitations in her academic training on how to ask research questions to her Black community must have evoked some nervous thoughts during her travel southward. Hurston's research focused on Eatonville, incorporated as an all-Black town in 1886 where she had grown up. Her choice of this setting meant that she had to design an approach based on outsider methods and understandings of race and culture taught by Boaz but also clearly informed by the insider's perspective she brought. With no scholarly road map of a range of participant–observer approaches, I am speculating that she may have had some self-doubts about exactly how she would gather the communal Black self-knowledge she sought. Ultimately, she did indeed craft an extremely inventive methodological approach.

When she died in her late sixties, Hurston was impoverished, extremely ill in a Florida county public welfare nursing home, and buried in an unmarked grave. She had published seven major books of folklore studies as well as fiction representing Black communities across the south and abroad, along with plays, poetry, short stories, and well over fifty nonfiction essays and journalism articles. She endured tremendous hardship throughout, having had to work as a domestic, a cook, a librarian on a US air force base, and navigate paternalistic and controlling white benefactors. Yet she managed to locate her knowledge-seeking projects in local community sites in several national contexts. Her transnational research during the 1930s included the study of Yoruba-based Black religious practices with research trips to Haiti and Jamaica. As Hurston documented everyday language and habits of Black community members, her writing featured sharp critiques of patriarchal Christian colonial impacts on Black women as well as celebratory accounts of Vodou and African-based spiritualities.

When I think of precedents of the scholarly boldness found in this Vigen/Scharen volume that exemplify how ethnography, particularly the work of Hurston, constitutes a project of Christian ethics, none other than the scholarship of Katie Cannon immediately comes to mind. In her pioneering 1988 construction of Christian social ethics, *Black Womanist Ethics*, Katie Cannon concentrated on Hurston's ethnographic method. Cannon explained how Hurston's research showcased the moral wisdom found in Black folklore. "In order for Zora Hurston to collect the much desired folklore," Cannon argued, "she had to shed the superficial vestiges of privilege and voyeur status and stand in solidarity with the group of people who sat on the steps of Joe Clarke's store, exchanging lies and telling stories with the best of them."[2] Cannon's analysis reveals the risk-taking enterprise of incorporating ethnographic material such as Hurston's in Christian ethics. It is a daring intellectual move in an initial construction of womanist ethics. Cannon illustrates how Hurston's documentation of and participation in rural, southern Black people's everyday exchange of lies and stories in the shared communal space of a small-town general store can provide a needed resource in the formulation of Christian social ethics.

[2] Katie Cannon, *Black Womanist Ethics* (Atlanta: Scholar's Press, 1988), 146.

For Cannon, Hurston's method crucially involved the ethics of not only valuing everyday thoughts and imaginations but also solidarity as a guiding principle in such an experientially engaged research design. Cannon emphasized how Hurston developed the methodological skill of shedding "superficial vestiges of privilege." As Cannon pointed out, Hurston taught the evolution of her method by admitting to making costly mistakes when she first started conducting interviews. After realizing her mistakes, Hurston made the conscious choice to engage in a more participatory style of interacting with interviewees.[3] Again, valuable lessons for Christian ethics can be found in the researcher's transparent revelations about her own dynamic process of learning within an isolated local community, uniquely undervalued by the broader society. Cannon's formulation defied traditional conceptions of communal Christian ethics as something that is most notably evidenced in the ways in which communities hold fast to timeless, static truths. Instead, incorporating ethnography makes it possible to perceive the strengthening of communal ethics through the communal bonds of trust and relatedness that collective imagination and invented narratives dynamically transmit.

Ethnography as Christian ethics in Cannon's study of Hurston radically embedded the meaning of Christianity within the folk language arts, belief systems, and sociopolitical experiences of the people. Starting in the 1920s, Hurston's research of US religion mainly depicted the complexity of Christian theology and practices in southern Black rural community life. It was almost always with ironic and paradoxical storytelling that her fiction featured Black Christian pastors, Hebrew Bible scriptural characters, or Black women's prayer lives. As Cannon notes, Hurston showcased Black collective wisdom specifically in their discernment of discrepancies "between professing Christian learnings and practicing a religious faith."[4] For Cannon, Hurston's ethnographic folklore accounts documented the moral capacity of Black communities for resilience, fortitude, and action to resist relentless subjugating white supremacist assaults.[5] Note that Hurston's conservative racial politics could never fit within Cannon's liberationist vision of Christian ethics that attended so directly to the tasks of dismantling white supremacy. But it seems as if the boldness of Hurston's ethnographic research of Black Christianity, religion, and social life sparked boldness in Cannon's expansion of the resources, methods, and content of Christian ethics in her conceptualization of womanist frameworks and imagining. For Christian ethics, ethnographic research can supply resources for the daring inclusion of dismissed Black moral worth and dignity, that is, for doing ethics in ways that one is otherwise unprepared.

Vigen and Scharen's *Ethnography as Christian Theology and Ethics, Second Edition* falls within the same genre of audacity exhibited in Cannon. Subjectivity, specifically shared subjectivity, is one specific example of it that I find throughout the chapters. By subjectivity, I refer to lived habits that reflect what the mind, body, and spirit know

---

[3] See Cannon, *Womanist Ethics*, 104; Zora Neale Hurston, *Dust Tracks on a Road: An Autobiography* (New York: J.B. Lippincott, 1971), 174–5.
[4] Cannon, *Womanist Ethics*, 137.
[5] Ibid., 145.

about selfhood and how to navigate social reality.[6] With a range of defiant strategies, the authors consider what kind of research is needed in Christian ethics and theology in order to craft deeper understandings of the subjectivity of certain community members. Several of the chapters also include probing investigations of their own subject position in the research and habits of knowing. We find out what happens if one intentionally seeks out what kinds of conscious knowing can be jointly shared in relation to certain demoralizing social realities and how that activity inhabits Christian theology and ethics.

There is a sharpness I welcome here in the repeated undermining of coercive whiteness. In many cases, the authors destabilize how whiteness has saturated the academic study of religion and the social sciences with a tendency to standardize a distant, opaqueness surrounding the social identity of those in dominant positions of social and/or academic power who are engaged in research. Collectively, the authors disobey entrenched academic models of, for instance, Global North and West, white researchers and theologians hiding their subjective white racialized biases and interests while reflexively configuring members of nondominant racial and ethnic groups as monolithic, simplistic objects of study.

Practicing Shared Subjectivity Contributes Risks and Vibrancy

The bold risks and vulnerabilities of identifying shared subjectivity across so many intellectual, religious, sociopolitical, and global divides by the authors in this *Ethnography as Christian Theology and Ethics* text must not be taken for granted. Their willing exposure of the difficulties in the fissures they cross and divulge can be too acquisitively seized by us, their readers, and treated as if we are greedily consuming entertainment media, or coldly appraising the sufficiency of their vulnerability on a competitive academic scale. Shared subjectivity is trickier than it sounds. Though committed to it, I remember, for example, the degree to which I was unprepared for its demands when I initially talked with leaders in Johannesburg, South Africa.

It was in the early twenty-first century at the beginning of my research on race, religion, and gender violence with activists there. The activist leaders I met were staff members of a nongovernmental organization with a renowned, highly regarded reputation of working to end the targeting of Black lesbians for rape and murder. I was not conducting an interview, just a preliminary meeting to help me prepare for later ones, and start to understand the activist context of the antiviolence movement in Johannesburg. Very soon after we sat down around a table in the warm outdoor air just a short distance from their office entryways, I felt it. The awkwardness of actually creating a sense of shared subjectivity related to my project crept in.

---

[6] I am informed by the formulation of subjectivity by feminist critical theory scholar Teresa De Lauretis in Teresa De Lauretis, *Alice Doesn't: Feminism, Semiotics, Cinema*, Vol. 316 (Bloomington: Indiana University Press, 1984), 182.

The two leaders of this Black lesbian-centered antiviolence organization welcomed me but also stared at me with questioning eyes even after I had briefly introduced my project, interests, and commitments. I had been clear that I strongly supported gender justice movement work back home and globally. But after my opening, I could sense that they remained curious and a bit uncertain about who I was and seemed to want to know something more personal about me. We discussed the particularity of the targeting of Black lesbians and of the masculine gender expressions of most of the lesbians who were so brutally victimized. The Black lesbian selves of the anti-violence activist leaders were inescapably part of the dynamics of our exchange. I also noticed their almost imperceptible wince and slight drawing back from me when I mentioned my Christian seminary teaching background. Christians, including US-based Black evangelicals, were responsible for fueling terror, hate, and violence against them. It was not clear what kind of sharing was needed in that moment. Should I have described the queerness of my own heterosexuality-partnered bisexuality in my opening? Should I have given details of my activism against Christian anti-LGBTQI hate, discrimination, and violence in my own US church context and political witness back home? I did not want to risk lengthy self-disclosures that took up too much space by reinforcing US American experience as dominant and center, thereby stifling rather than opening up sharing among us.

At the conclusion of our long conversation that day, I turned to head out to the street to call my taxi. One of the leaders warmly smiled and lightly pulled my arm, asking me to wait a moment. After opening a closet with piles of supplies and shirts, the smile became a delighted grin as she handed me the gift of a black T-shirt with "feminist" on the front and "Stop the War on Women's Bodies" on the back. Fragile trust building had begun between us in a language of political fierceness that my own US Black feminism shared. The exchange seemed to signal movement toward solidarity. At the same time, her expression of agency in that charitable gesture from an African to a US American seemed to also demonstrate a shared knowledge of racist paternalism between and within our national contexts that needed interruption. As I reflect back on that meeting, I now realize how little awareness I had beforehand of exactly what I would need for the co-creation of the antiviolence social ethics knowledge that I had envisioned would emerge.

Yet, I believe that the risks involved in embracing such uncertainty are crucial to the process of learning and are part of why I need this adventurous collection of chapters so much.

Starting with the core structuring of *Ethnography as Christian Theology and Ethics*, the ideas here irrigate any hardened, desiccated inclination to retreat to safety. The discussion of method in the opening chapters cocreates a fresh notion of shared subjectivity in their relationship to the later chapters that challenge, illustrate, and depart from that framing. Throughout, rebelliousness can be found in how their Christian ethics and theology craft ethnographic queries that cross boundaries of disciplines, researcher and subject, religious traditions and practices, nation-state and ethnic origins, and many more conventional divides in the politics of belonging. The chapters consistently refrain from a search for commonalities that force erasure of authentic conflicts of interest and inequalities of status and access to resources and power, or require uniformity across global spaces. Instead this work demands expansiveness of thought and practice with a capacity to grasp contingency, interdependence, and the impacts of irreducible historical injustice.

Legacies such as barrier-breaking folklore ethnographer Zora Neale Hurston and Christian ethicist innovator Katie Cannon's mining of Hurston's work, as well as the brazen vision of the authors in this book demonstrate how to radically develop ethnographic learning and knowing in Christian ethics and theology.

Their boldness beckons.

Drawing from the Wells of a Feminist Theologian, Ethicist, and Community Mobilizer: Reflections on the Life, Works, and Legacy of Rev. Dr. Melissa Brown Browning (1977–2021)

Emily Reimer-Barry and Damaris Parsitau

Introducing a Fearless Pioneer

The Rev. Dr. Melissa Brown Browning squeezed a lot of living into forty-three years. A Christian activist intellectual, practical theologian, feminist ethicist, ordained Baptist minister, anti-death penalty advocate, community organizer, world traveler, partner, mother, teacher, friend—she worked to build bridges of understanding, foster structures of justice and accountability, and teach her students strategies for community organizing and practical theology that would transform relationships and foster flourishing. This brief tribute will introduce readers to her notable publications while giving her friends the opportunity to explain the huge loss we feel as we grieve her passing.

Melissa Brown grew up in Georgia, immersed in the Bible and eager to learn more about God's plan for her. Her passion for African studies began as an undergraduate student at Gardner-Webb University where she earned a Bachelor of Arts in Religious Studies with a minor in African Studies. She met Wes Browning there and when they married Melissa Brown became Melissa Browning. Melissa went on to earn an MDiv from Baylor and a PhD from Loyola University Chicago. She built her skills in fieldwork with training from Maryknoll Institute of African Studies in Nairobi, Kenya, and with the strong support of her faculty mentors at Loyola University Chicago, notably Aana Marie Vigen, Susan Ross, and Patricia Beattie Jung, and her fieldwork mentor in Tanzania, Pauline Gasabile. Browning built relationships with African scholars across the continent through her participation in conferences of the Circle of Concerned African Women Theologians, African Association for the Study of Religions (AASR), and the work of Africa Exchange. In what follows, we will identify the key contributions Melissa made to the field of Christian ethics, with a focus on ethical method.

An Overview of Melissa Browning's Scholarly Publications

Melissa was not afraid to ask big questions in her scholarly work. Many of her research questions arose from real-life situations in which she found herself in a predicament where she witnessed human suffering and sought both to *think theologically* about that suffering and *work creatively* to alleviate it. Catholic theologian Edward Schillebeeckx, OP, explained in his own work that human suffering has a "critical and productive epistemic power" and that suffering enables us to imagine another way forward. Suffering provides a counterpoint to flourishing, a "negative contrast experience," that is a foil to a life of communal justice. Witnessing injustice gives rise to a protest: *this should not be*. Then, the witness engages in discernment to determine the appropriate response.[1] Melissa's scholarly work reflects her theological and professional journey as she chose to put herself in the company of suffering people, witness complex injustices, and write about appropriate Christian responses.

An early study she conducted in Nairobi, Kenya, when she was affiliated with the Maryknoll Institute of African Studies,[2] enabled Melissa to observe the survival strategies of street children. Her analysis began with description, contextualized to examine the social factors that contribute to the precarity of street children's dangerous lives. In the struggle for survival, "morality and faith are always present, yet are redefined."[3] Melissa drew on data from Amnesty International, the Consortium for Street Children, Human Rights Watch, and activists on the ground in order to describe street children in three different categories: children of the streets, children on the streets, and children for the streets.[4] While all street children experience vulnerability as neglected children, they experience different degrees of danger that Melissa wanted to account for in her analysis. The suffering of street children was found to be in contrast to the rhetoric of "blessing" and "life" that permeates African cultures and traditions.[5] Melissa explained that the goal of her fieldwork was to "allow children to speak their stories in the hope that their stories would provide a path for street children to be reintegrated into the systems of community from which they had been separated."[6] Toward this end, Melissa describes the faith narratives of Rose Wambui, Teresia Nambura, and Kimathi Kimaru, and then analyzes them through the lenses of Christianity, African traditions, and structural violence. With her characteristic empathy for her informants, she explains the need to reject any so-called morality that would fail to understand the constraints street children endure. For example, naming stealing or nonmarital sexual activity as wrong without bothering to place oneself in

---

[1] Kathleen McManus, OP, *Unbroken Communion: The Place and Meaning of Suffering in the Theology of Edward Schillebeeckx, OP* (Lanham, MD: Rowman & Littlefield, 2003).
[2] The website of the Maryknoll Institute of African Studies is https://mias.edu/.
[3] Melissa Browning, "Morality on the Streets: An Examination of the Beliefs and Moral Practice of Street Children in Light of Christianity and African Traditional Religions," in *Ethnography as Christian Theology and Ethics*, ed. Christian Scharen and Aana Marie Vigen, eds. (New York: Continuum, 2011), 142–60 at 143.
[4] Ibid., 145–6.
[5] Ibid., 147.
[6] Ibid., 149.

their shoes perpetuates shame-based discourse instead of an ethic of solidarity and community. Melissa explains:

> When seeking out morality within the context of life-sustaining actions, we again ask the question of whether these children, at the edge of desperation, are behaving in life-sustaining or life-destroying ways. It is evident that these children are seeking to sustain life and looking for ways to make life strong, even if the end result of their action is immoral. Within this perspective, their morality should be judged on their intentions. This does not excuse their life-destroying actions, but it understands why they behave the way they do and provides an avenue for reconciliation. In order to be effective reconcilers of street children, we must not only teach them what not to do, but must empower them to find different and better ways to make life strong. We cannot ask them not to steal if we will not teach them how to earn money and we cannot ask them not to sniff glue without bringing enough food to satisfy their hunger.[7]

Here, and elsewhere, Melissa's method moved from listening to her informants to advocating on their behalf. The reader learns about the reality of another and is challenged to act instead of absolving oneself of responsibility.

Melissa turned her attention to abstinence education in two articles for *Theology and Sexuality*. In the first, Melissa argued that proposals to "end AIDS in Africa" through sexuality education focusing on abstinence were misguided and harmful because they failed to take into consideration the economic, gender, and social inequalities that fueled the HIV epidemic.[8] Her scathing postcolonial critique of US foreign policy and white Christian imperialism demonstrates that she was concerned about racist and capitalist motives behind some of the West's "answers" to the AIDS crisis. At the same time, Melissa draws on liberation theology, including Black and womanist theologies, feminist theologies, and African theologies, to construct a way forward that envisioned abstinence as a liberating space because "in the face of HIV and AIDS, creativity is needed more than prohibition, equality is more urgent than charity, and agency cannot be sacrificed for abstinence."[9]

Melissa's second article on abstinence for *Theology and Sexuality* described fieldwork with a dance and drama team charged with promoting abstinence among teenagers in the US context, both in school and church settings.[10] While in this context the scripts were less about preventing AIDS and more about promoting purity, Melissa noted the prevalence of patriarchal dynamics within the performance scripts as well as the gender norms of the teams in the informal interactions she observed.[11] For example:

---

[7] Ibid., 158.
[8] Melissa Browning, "HIV/AIDS Prevention and Sexed Bodies: Rethinking Abstinence in Light of the African AIDS Pandemic," *Theology and Sexuality* 15, no. 1 (2009): 29–47.
[9] Ibid., 45–6.
[10] Melissa Browning, "Acting Out Abstinence, Acting Out Gender: Adolescent Moral Agency and Abstinence Education," *Theology and Sexuality* 16, no. 2 (2010): 143–61.
[11] Ibid., 151–2.

The performers in the drama performed typical gender roles. [Girls] were carrying the laundry while the boys were standing on the side of the street. The boys were cast in the role of "player" while the girls were on the receiving end of their advances.... The male characters talked frequently of sexual conquests and of their sexual needs.... The performance asked young men to delay sexual pleasure to avoid STDs while it asked young women to delay sex to make oneself a more attractive future mate.[12]

Melissa explains that the gender scripts embedded in the abstinence education show did not challenge traditional gender roles but rather reinforced them. And in this way, they disempowered young women while baptizing male domination in sexual relationships. Melissa named this as very problematic. As she charts a better way forward, Melissa relies on feminist and queer scholarship to advocate for a sexual education that is truly "subversive" of traditional Christian gender norms, norms which reinscribe patriarchy. This subversive education would mean that abstinence, when taught, is taught "not as an end in itself, but as a means to an end," in the service of life and love.[13] Melissa dreams for "a queering of abstinence education" whereby binaries of male/female, masculine/feminine, gay/straight, yes/no, and virgin/slut are cast aside in favor of a responsibility ethic rooted in human dignity and relational justice.[14]

Melissa's contributions to the field were also notable in the way that she fostered community among colleagues and led academic collaborations, like the one where we first worked together. We became her friends because of our shared interests in global feminist theologies and participated in collaborative research in Nairobi, Kenya, for three weeks in the summer of 2009 with seven other colleagues.[15] In the summer of 2009, women theologians from the United States and Kenya lived and worked together in Nairobi in a collaborative project that included fieldwork with vulnerable populations in the region. Melissa advocated for fieldwork with women by women so that we could "hear and honor" women's voices for the church and the academy. Melissa led this small circle of young upcoming theologians to reflect the theme of listening as ethnography. As we read texts and deeply listened to each other's stories and experiences, we became aware of the power of stories as ethnography. This experience changed Damaris's academic life trajectory as she began to learn how to employ ethnographic methods. Listening to stories also helped us understand issues more contextually, and Damaris reports that this experience launched her career as a religious ethnographer.

---

[12] Ibid.
[13] Ibid., 159. Here Browning is drawing on the work of Patricia Beattie June in "A Case for Sexual Fidelity," *Word and World* 14, no. 2 (Spring 1994): 115–24.
[14] Ibid., 157, 160.
[15] The Global Feminist Theologies project was funded by Wabash Center for Teaching and Learning and Loyola University Chicago. Participants included Melissa Browning, Edith Chamwama, Eunice Kamaara, Sussy Gumo Kurgat, Sister Anne Nasimiyu-Wasike, Emily Reimer-Barry, Susan Ross, Elisabeth Vasko, and Jeanine Viau. Melissa D. Browning, Edith Chamwama, Eunice Kamaara, Sussy Gumo Kurgat, Damaris Parsitau, Emily Reimer-Barry, Elisabeth Vasko, and Jeanine Viau. "Listening to Experience, Looking Towards Flourishing: Ethnography as a Global Feminist Theo/Ethical Praxis," *Practical Matters Journal* (March 1, 2010), http://practicalmattersjournal.org/?p=1172.

Melissa encouraged us not only to focus on what we were learning as scholars but on what we could give back to the community. Part of the collaborative research project involved undertaking a service project in Nairobi and the Rift Valley Province that had just experienced the worst postelection violence crisis in 2007. As we drove to visit communities living in the internally displaced camps, we all came face-to-face with the raw impact of the postelection violence on women and girls who had been displaced from their homes and communities. While undertaking this service project at the camps in Naivasha and Gilgil in Nakuru County, we came face-to-face with unimaginable pain and suffering like we have never witnessed before. We listened to women and girls narrate harrowing stories of abuse and loss, as well as generational trauma in stories of legacies of gender and sexual-based violence, loss of family members, homes, and properties. Melissa led us on ways of being in solidarity and in community with these women and communities even as we struggled to comprehend the scope of the injustice and pain. "Ethnography can help researchers to explore the complex contexts of women's experiences, so that researchers can begin to understand what is going on, what is at stake, and what prevents women from flourishing," Melissa wrote at the conclusion of that project.[16] Listening to these stories was painful and life changing. After listening to women's narratives and stories of pain, hope, and survival, Damaris resolved to research and work with women by documenting their stories and experiences in a bid to give them voice and agency and center them in her work. While this collaborative service project led to a number of joint publications for Damaris and Melissa, Damaris took away two things: theology and social justice, and community engagement. Melissa was an indefatigable social justice advocate who worked on a wide range of social justice issues including women's rights to dignity and flourishing.

As a feminist theologian and ethicist, Melissa was keen to understand the roles of culture and patriarchy in the oppression of African women and girls. The works of the Circle of Concerned African Women Theologians deeply influenced not just her reading of African theological and religious conversations but also influenced her to deeply understand and unpack how the combined legacies of capitalism, colonialism, and Christianity intersect with African culture and patriarchy to negatively impact the lives of women and girls. She believed that these three forces worked together with culture and patriarchy to make African women even more vulnerable than before. This is reflected in her monograph *Risky Marriage*.

Melissa's monograph, *Risky Marriage: HIV and Intimate Relationships in Tanzania*, centers on the experiences of married women in East Africa in order to better understand why marriage is a risk factor for HIV infection and what interventions would be most appropriate and life-giving.[17] Melissa noted that since Christians are in the "business" of marrying people, they should develop a theology of marriage that advances the flourishing of married women.[18]

The fieldwork at the heart of Melissa's research in *Risky Marriage* included eight months of participatory action research in Mwanza, Tanzania, under the dual

---

[16] Ibid.
[17] Melissa Browning, *Risky Marriage: HIV and Intimate Relationships in Tanzania* (Lanham, MD: Lexington, 2014). Reviewed by Jeanine Viau, *Religious Studies Review* 47, no. 3 (September 2021): 366–7.
[18] Ibid., 1.

sponsorship of a local church and Melissa's academic institution. Twelve married women met together to discuss marriage, relationships, and HIV and AIDS, and they collaborated on other shared projects as part of their co-learning and mutual support.[19] Melissa's research tacks back and forth between the "particular" of her informants' stories and social, historical, and theo-ethical analysis that offers greater context to interpret her informants' stories. A key part of this analysis is Melissa's description of how colonialism, capitalism, and missionary Christianity worked together to disempower women: "Colonialism created systems where women were dependent on men, as work for pay became men's work, centralized in the cities. Christianity reinforced this through the concept of women's submission."[20] Melissa explained in detail how practices of hidden polygamy, dowry/bridewealth, land inheritance, child marriage, female circumcision, widow inheritance, and male infidelity contributed to the unhappiness of her informants' lived experiences even as these practices were sometimes defended as natural or traditional in their cultural framework.[21] In this way, she challenges the authoritative voices of African scholars such as Kenyan theologian John Mbiti, whose classic text *African Religions and Philosophy* has shaped the field of African studies, by surfacing the concerns her informants raised about their own experience of dehumanizing violence and strategies for survival in their marriages. A noteworthy example can be found in the second chapter, in which Melissa cites Mbiti's defense of male infidelity:

> It is in fact an expression of friendship and hospitality to let a guest spend the night with one's wife or daughter or sister. It is not the act in itself which would be "wrong" as such but the relationships involved in the act: if relationships are not hurt or damaged, and if there is no discovery of breach of custom or regulation, then the act is not "evil" or "wicked" or "bad."[22]

Melissa writes: "The women in this study did not believe Mbiti's suggestion was possible. They were all deeply hurt by their husband's infidelities."[23] At the same time, Melissa repeats throughout that it is not her goal to "paint a picture of African women as weak or as victims," noting that "the women in this study showed strength and resilience in the face of insurmountable obstacles."[24] When the women in the participatory action research study were invited to brainstorm about metaphors for fidelity, the one the group agreed was most helpful at the end of the conversation was that of a fence, "such as those that surround traditional homesteads throughout East Africa. The fence around the homestead marks off the boundaries of the home. It is not built to keep neighbors out but to keep those within safe."[25] By creating an opportunity for married women to come together to speak about their shared experiences and

---

[19] Ibid., 2.
[20] Ibid., 15.
[21] Ibid., 17, 21–9, 79–95, 135–80.
[22] Ibid., 25.
[23] Ibid.
[24] Ibid., 43.
[25] Ibid., 151.

to envision a better way forward, Melissa was able to record their authentic vision for a marriage that would bring flourishing and safety for everyone involved, which provides a counterpoint to Mbiti's description, rooted as it is in male domination even within the traditional household.

Melissa's constructive vision of a healthy and just theology of marriage begins from the testimony of her informants' lives and their dreams for a better way forward. It is also deeply rooted in the principles of African religion and culture that the women themselves found most life-affirming: community, life and health-affirming, and a safe space that includes power sharing.[26] Melissa builds on the work of African feminist theologians who for decades had been critically evaluating cultural traditions, engaging in feminist biblical hermeneutics in an African key, and seeking ways to affirm gender equality while remaining authentically African. Key interlocutors included Musa Dube, Mercy Amba Oduyoye, Isabel Apawo Phiri, Sarojini Nadar, Beverley Haddad, Denise Ackermann, Esther Mombo, Anne Nasimiyu-Wasike, Musimbi Kanyoro, Teresia Mbari Hinga, Nontando Hadebe, and Teresa Okure. From this rich engagement, Melissa articulates a revised theology of Christian marriage that includes gender equality, mutual concern, and fidelity. She explains that Christian leaders should conduct an assessment of everyday practices (rituals, mahari/bridewealth, property laws, sexual education, responses to domestic violence, separation and divorce) in order to care for those most vulnerable and transform practices that are unjust.[27]

Risky Marriage has been adopted in both undergraduate and graduate classes for students pursuing studies in feminist theology, pastoral theology, and health care ethics. Melissa also shared her research with church groups and students both through in-person and virtual presentations after the book was published. One of Emily's last memories of Melissa is her "Zoom" visit to Emily's HIV and Christian Ethics students at the University of San Diego in Fall 2020, in which students asked Melissa about her research methods and some of the unique challenges of fieldwork. One question in particular stood out: a young woman asked Dr. Browning if it was hard to be "objective" when hearing such traumatic stories from her informants. Melissa answered, with a laugh, saying objectivity was one of the rules she was happy to break, and went on to explain why she thought that a better ethical principle to pursue in fieldwork was truth-telling. This led to a discussion about how she built genuine relationships of friendship and mutual support with her informants, why she cared about them and their families, and how that motivated her to "get their stories right—to be honest and accurate—to tell the truth."[28] Reflecting on her answer afterward in conversation with Wes, we believe that this captures what made Melissa such a competent scholar. Wes noted that Melissa was always able to juggle her curiosity, objectivity, and compassion in ways that did not taint her research. The women she worked with trusted Melissa to get their stories right, and they were comfortable being vulnerable with her because they knew that others might benefit from hearing their stories. They could trust Melissa to bring something positive out of their pain.

---

[26] Ibid., 135–81.
[27] Ibid.
[28] Zoom dialogue, THRS 332 students (University of San Diego) with Melissa Browning and Emily Reimer-Barry. September 30, 2020.

Melissa's advocacy for women's flourishing continued to be a theme in her scholarship after her book was published. She worked behind the scenes as a series editor for the Social Ethics, Ethnography, and Theology series at Bloomsbury/T&T Clark, work that enabled her to encourage other scholars to pursue ethnographically driven theological and ethical investigations on a wide range of social issues.[29] She and Emily co-wrote an article on women's voices in Christian ecclesial communities, with a special focus on the "prophetic" voices of women religious communities in the US context who advocated for social welfare programs after their praxis of accompaniment of the marginalized.[30] And Melissa wrote with courage and conviction about the cruelty of state executions in Georgia, and especially about her students' advocacy for Kelly Renee Gissendaner, who was put to death by the state of Georgia on September 30, 2015.[31] Melissa often shared the hashtag #kellyonmymind through social media and taught her students and colleagues how to blend learning, teaching, and activism in their campaign for justice and mercy in 2015. Melissa's untimely cancer diagnosis interrupted her final writing project, a manuscript for Fortress Press entitled *Navigating Dystopia: How to Understand Injustice, and then Start Changing the World*. This project would have combined her growing experience in asset-based community development, engaged pedagogy, and Christian social activism.

Major Themes in Melissa Browning's Work

Engagement with African Women

From her undergraduate years to her time as a professor, Melissa's scholarly work reflected a deep learning from African Christian women, especially from the Circle of Concerned African Women Theologians and the AASR. Melissa's fieldwork training at Maryknoll and her familiarity with African traditional religions prepared her to amplify the voices of African women in her own work. Attention to her method shows that Melissa was very aware that her own positionality shaped her voice, and that she could be written off as an "outsider" or disregarded as a white woman unconcerned for the real suffering she witnessed; Melissa was careful to privilege the voices of African scholars and to link critiques of patriarchy to critiques of Western colonialism when appropriate. In this way, her arguments could be heard and have a greater impact within the academy and church in African contexts.

Melissa also deeply contributed to religious and theological conversations in Africa through her engagement with the AASR in Africa and its diaspora where Damaris now serves as its first female president. Melissa played a substantial role in the association for many years, serving with dedication and integrity. This included serving on the

---

[29] Series editors now are Todd D. Whitmore, Aana Marie Vigen, Traci C. West, and AnneMarie Mingo. For more information, see https://socialethicsethnographytheologies.com/.

[30] Melissa Browning and Emily Reimer-Barry, "Preaching, Sexuality, and Women Religious: Listening to Prophetic Voices at the Margins of Religious Life," *Theology & Sexuality* 19, no. 1 (2013): 69–88.

[31] Melissa Browning, "Teaching on the Streets: Engaged Pedagogy after an Execution," *Perspectives in Religious Studies* 46, no. 4 (Winter 2019): 449–56.

Executive Committee as Assistant Secretary General and Webmaster (2010–15), for which her husband Wes generously provided technical expertise and web support and continued to do for several years following the conclusion of Melissa's tenure. As Asst. Secretary General, Melissa served meritoriously and in many instances did the "heavy lifting," always with grace, cheerfulness, and selflessness. In fact, Melissa and Wes provided tremendous support to the AASR by housing and updating the AASR website for a very long time.

Listening

Melissa's fieldwork focused on listening as a theological praxis. Justice is part of this because she was especially concerned with giving attention to vulnerable voices and creating safe spaces for people on the margins to share their lived experiences of God, life, and the church. A key piece of this is intellectual humility. This means that Melissa was keenly aware of the limits of her own knowledge and social location and was eager to learn about life from other people's perspectives. In terms of epistemology, she was good at asking of herself and her students, "How do I know what I know? How is my knowledge conditioned by my status and social location? Who should my conversation partners be so that I can better understand the complexity of this issue from multiple perspectives?" An example of this recognition can be found in the introduction of her book. Note her honest self-disclosure as she told readers:

> A common saying among foreigners who have lived in Africa opines that "Once you live in Africa, the continent is forever a part of you." It is for this reason that I felt compelled to write on HIV outside of my own cultural and geographical context. After working and studying in Kenya and knowing many people there who were living with HIV or AIDS, I wanted my research to be a response that honored their lives. And as a person living between two worlds, as an American living in Kenya, I was troubled by the responses of Western Christian churches that sent mission teams to lead abstinence crusades or preach stigmatizing sexual ethics in foreign pulpits. It was first hand encounters with some of these sermons and crusades that made me realize that more intercultural theo-ethical work was needed on HIV and AIDS. While I believe I have something to say, I know the words I speak from my own experience and carry with them the baggage of my own particular culture, education, and privilege.[32]

Melissa's focus on listening enabled her to attend to power inequities within relationships and within ecclesial structures, so that she could point to patterns of domination and exploitation by observing systems that tended to exclude particular voices with regularity (street children, married women, women religious, incarcerated people); once identified, those are the voices she sought to amplify in her scholarship. Her colleague Mark Douglas shared with us that one of Melissa's gifts was an ability to

---

[32] Browning, *Risky Marriage*, 3.

be both simultaneously moving and a good listener. She maintained this paradox of "motion/still listening" because she practiced it well.

Community Engagement

Melissa's approach to action research sought to transform unjust social structures through action, research, and critical reflection (personal and communal). Hers was not an approach to theology that stayed in the library. She wanted to understand what theology meant in real life and how theologians might foster social change. Melissa's approach to community engagement shaped our activism and research. Melissa worked to support women who are survivors of gender- and sexual-based violence, those living with HIV, single mothers, and many others. Melissa also thrived in creating and strengthening community. In Kenya and Tanzania, she created community-building, long-lasting relationships with women and communities she worked with. Some of Damaris's fondest memories are when Melissa took her to visit Ethiopian women refugees in Kenya who undertake incredible craft works to support themselves and their families. Damaris accompanied Melissa to many such communities which she supported both financially and spiritually. Melissa was deeply moved by pain and injustice and sought to create a just and less painful world through her ministry, research, and humanitarian undertaking.

Melissa's Christian worldview helped her to make sense of the disparities she encountered and the injustice she named, especially structural sins of colonialism, poverty, and sexism. But she could hold together a deep and radical hope for a better world at the same time that she named sin in many forms. This hopeful worldview also shaped her ability to create joy in everyday moments with friends and family. She had a great sense of humor, loved to share wisdom and beauty and bits of inspiration, and genuinely built up her friends who were struggling.

Building Bridges

Rev. Dr. Melissa Browning defied easy categorization: she was an ordained Baptist minister who spoke with a Southern drawl; at the same time she was a fierce feminist scholar who was committed to reading and writing at a very sophisticated level; simultaneously she was an easygoing team leader who loved to travel and bring people together for fun. Her work cannot be captured by describing her denominational affiliation(s), political stances, places of worship, or the schools where she taught. Her intellectual curiosity and openness to new ideas kept her always "searching" in her spirituality. She was especially eager to build bridges among people of different cultures, races, ethnicities, national identities—honoring people's self-descriptions while inviting us beyond identity politics and toward mutual work for transformation. Her "asset" based approach to community work was inclusive, messy, and modest all at the same time. She wanted people to experience a sense of belonging while also stretching themselves to learn about what life was like for people different than themselves. Her passion for travel and language study gave her a sense of how big the world is and how small our theological categories often are. She was not afraid to try new foods, not afraid to embarrass herself when learning a new language, and was always interested in making new friends. Melissa and Wes Browning shared a passion for adventure and for building community across cultures—Wes through documentary film and Melissa through practical theology. They welcomed their daughter Olivia into their world and showed Olivia what it meant to be a citizen of the world. Melissa delighted in her daughter's life and nurtured Olivia's creativity and voice; while Melissa wrote about how Christian marriage traditions could disempower women, her own experience of married love was a powerful witness of trust, fidelity, and mutual self-giving and growth over time.

Concluding Reflections about Our Friend Melissa

Melissa was active on Facebook, sharing her journey of parenthood, teaching, activism, and travel. Throughout her battle with cancer, her Facebook and Post Hope posts were a testament to her bravery, faith, humor, and hope. Her treatments for cancer, and the experience of being immunocompromised during the coronavirus pandemic, forced her to confront suffering in her own life in a way that she had often witnessed in the lives of others. She experienced the "negative contrast" event Schillebeeckx describes in the loss of her voice and in seizures that scared her and her family. At the same time, her desire to live and her thirst for adventure never left her. She continued to plan family vacations from her deathbed, and at her funeral, friends wept while Wes announced that Olivia's new passport had arrived, just as Melissa had wanted.

Melissa died on April 8, 2021, and is now among the ancestors. Words cannot express the loss her friends feel. Her spirit lives on in her writings, her family and friends, and in anything you do to challenge patriarchy, empower vulnerable women and children, learn about a culture different from your own, or dream of a world in which all people have what they need to thrive.

As her friends, we invite you to keep her legacy alive by sharing her work with your students and by living out these commitments to justice that she held so dear.

Preface
Blurring Boundaries

What is Theology? What is Religion? What is Christian ethics? Where and how do they happen? Who creates (or possesses the license to produce) them? What sources are central (and legitimate) to these endeavors? As in 2011 when the first edition of this work was published, these are among the first questions and lectures in many introductory courses. They are ancient ones, explored since the time of Plato at least, that continue to be discussed and contested in contemporary scholarship. While some consider the basic definitions and boundaries around theology and ethics settled, this volume intentionally muddies the waters. In the thirteen years since the original publication, a critical mass of scholars who find ethnography integral to their endeavors has only continued to grow. And the methodological shift has made important ripples in the academy. Indeed, a number of articles and books continue to emerge (including by many of the authors in this and the earlier volume), as part of blurring of boundaries between systematic and practical theology, theology and ethics, and the academic study of religion, religious participation, and prophetic critique.

Specifically, this volume grows out of a number of years of path-forging, ethnographic work done by several Christian theologians and ethicists. Initially, this kind of research was found only at a couple of doctoral programs in religion, but now it is present within the curricula of several seminaries, divinity schools, and departments of religion. A key starting place for the two of us was in 2003, when a group of us held a panel on "Ethnography and Normative Ethics" at the Society of Christian Ethics (SCE), leading to a formal interest group that meets annually at the SCE. In subsequent years, a growing number of scholars have been connecting at various academic meetings to share our respective work, learn from others exploring similar research trajectories, and discuss future possibilities. We regularly participate on panels, give papers, and meet in working groups at national conferences such as the SCE, the American Academy of Religion, the Association for Practical Theology, along with international networks (both informal and formal) such as the Ecclesiology and Ethnography network that began meeting in 2007. A vibrant Facebook group, Ethnographically Driven Theology, regularly shares articles, questions, and mutual support. A 2022 *Wiley Blackwell Companion to Theology and Qualitative Research*[1] explores a wide range of methodological choices and questions. Given these dynamic conversations and the increasing number of qualitative research projects, we again feature in Part II exemplar

---

[1] See *The Wiley Blackwell Companion to Theology and Qualitative Research*, ed. Pete Ward and Knut Tveitereid (Hoboken: John Wiley & Sons, Ltd, 2022).

chapters of scholars doing ethnography as theology and ethics, showcasing research not yet available in 2011.

Yet, apart from featuring specific projects, this book aims to contribute focused reflection on matters of method, attending to how methods and reflection on methods have continued to develop since 2011. In other words, it wishes to not only encourage others to "go and do likewise," but to offer helpful insights into *how* to go about it and how to avoid problematic pitfalls. While it is not a pragmatic "step by step" handbook for designing an ethnographic study, throughout readers will find recurring attention to methodological qualities that we find essential to responsible and nuanced research.

Central Argument and Intention

Within theology and ethics, there is significant variety among scholars working with ethnography in terms of both content and subdisciplines. For our parts, while we both identify with Christian ethics, Scharen identifies particularly with practical theology, liturgical studies, and ecclesiology while Vigen roots herself in Christian social ethics. In the midst of such contrasts, a major theme that connects our scholarly concerns is the notion of moral and theological formation of persons and communities—how who we understand ourselves to be in light of our faith in the divine informs our ethical commitments and responsibilities to others in creation. To explore this path, we have found that conversing with other academics and with texts is only one significant part of a larger research process. In this spirit, we—along with a growing cohort of scholars—resonate with the sensibilities of feminist ethnographer Ruth Behar as she reflects on why many anthropologists choose their particular vocational path:

> For many anthropologists, who enter the profession out of a desire to engage with real people in real (and usually forgotten) places, the literary critic, with "his" reading list of the great books of Western civilization, is a symbolic antithesis.... Even today, we do not totally believe in books and archives; we believe somehow (still!) in the redemptive possibilities of displacement, of travel, even if, as happens lately, our voyages only return us to our own abandoned hometown or our high-school graduating class.[2]

While we do not disdain reading the "great books," we share Behar's sense that engaging people can be just as important to learning, and we would add, to moral and theological formation. Indeed, to echo Behar's phrasing, there can be something redemptive—healing—about being displaced through ethnographic study. This theme of displacement or decentering surfaces throughout the volume. For now, it is sufficient to note that in a similar vein as Behar's contention for anthropology, the overall argument of this book posits that in order to do theology and ethics well,

---

[2] Ruth Behar, "Introduction: Out of Exile," in *Women Writing Culture*, ed. Ruth Behar and Deborah A. Gordon (Berkeley: University of California Press, 1995), 1–32 (10).

scholars need to explore them through visceral ways, within embodied communities, and in particular contexts.

As it makes this case, the book serves three primary purposes. First, at the most fundamental level, we intend for the book to encourage the use of ethnography. The first edition became a standard text for graduate students getting started and supported the work of scholars already working in these areas. The second and third goals may seem more provocative because they urge scholars to think a bit differently about their work. Specifically, we intend the volume to challenge scholars in the social sciences to think through normative commitments they may bring (even if unwittingly) to their work. Third, and perhaps even more unsettling to some, we hope it will inspire scholars in theology to not "use" social science as nontheological knowledge, but explore that work as part of the work of theology proper. Chapter 2 and several chapters in Part II explore this last claim in significant depth.

Basic Assumptions

For the sake of both clarity and transparency, we think it is important to touch upon four primary convictions we bring to this work as co-authors/editors. Together, they shape the theoretical framework within which we operate. They also appear in key places within the exemplary chapters of Part II.

The Interconnection of Theology and Ethics

We understand Christian theology and ethics to be integrally related, yet somewhat distinct disciplines. While there are many areas of overlap (e.g., sources, themes, method), *theology* is often construed as "God-talk"—inquiring into the mysteries of divine being and doing and concentrating on elaborating formal, systematic categories (e.g., sin, salvation, revelation, ontology, Christology, atonement, eschatology)—without making explicit or strong connections to human being, doing, and responsibility. For its part, *ethics*, also termed moral theology, explores human relationships, failures, and obligations in depth—grounded in an understanding that human action and accountability flow from who God is to and for creation. In all, there are both thematic and methodological differences in the formal training of theologians and ethicists along with strong points of connection. This reality is even more complicated in practical theology and other interdisciplinary sites for theological-ethical work. While it is possible to work primarily in either systematic or ethical categories without much reference to the other, we find such formulations increasingly unsatisfying and offer this book as a contribution to a greater integration between these disciplines.

Therefore, while not all theologians may agree, for us, theology and ethics are necessarily bound up with one another. At least, the two ought not be divorced. As mentioned above, inquiry into the nature of God should also help us contemplate who we are—and what we ought to become and do—in light of divine being. This orienting assumption permeates the works and worldviews of both classic Christian thinkers (e.g., Augustine, Aquinas, Luther, Calvin) and many diverse, modern theologians and ethicists.[3] In the way we conceive of our work, it is impossible to do good theology without Christian ethics and *vice versa*. Theology is both doxological and normative in nature. Consequently, with respect to terminology and in order to avoid tedious repetition, we may refer to "theologians" in certain places and "ethicists" in others; however, we have both in mind throughout this volume.

Confronting and Contesting Sites of Privilege

This assumption will take a bit longer to explain because it deals with particularly thorny terrain—owning up to ways certain people and groups benefit from structured inequalities. There are numerous forms of privilege that scholars may embody *vis-à-vis* their ethnographic subjects (educational, religious, cultural, etc.). This possibility is intensified given the fact that many well-intentioned researchers are committed to working with, and learning from, communities who dwell on the margins of a given society. As just one example from Part II, Boopalan and Jongte emphasize that ethnography can center "crucified bodies" in ways that intentionally attend to the intersectional layers of oppression. They, like we, see this commitment as a potential way to foster justice within their/our vocational endeavors. Many scholars, including us, hope that ethnographic work will raise insightful public awareness, engender respect and empathy among people, and perhaps even lead to transformation through what Behar calls "redemptive displacement."

Yet, potent dangers often lurk within the best of intentions. The category of race illustrates the point. Complex issues and potential problems arise whenever a white scholar does research that focuses on members of other racial–ethnic groups, including misunderstanding, misappropriation, and disrespect. As Hoskins notes in Part II, researchers who identify as minoritized may also uncritically employ racialized or colonizing methods that violate the narratives and personhoods of their subjects. Indeed, several of the exemplary chapters thoughtfully wrestle with the dynamics of being either complete outsiders or complicated combinations of insider-outsiders in relation to the communities they engage. In short, it is possible for researchers—whatever the specific kinds of privilege they embody—to do violence in their characterizations and to use whatever they learn for their own advancement and without sufficient accountability to those who teach them with their stories and insights.

As two white scholars, we think it is imperative to emphasize that un-interrogated assumptions based on whiteness, socioeconomic class, and ethnic/national identity found in much of Christian theology (and in public discourse) merit rigorous critical examination. As Black cultural theorist bell hooks, an author whose work has been subjected to book bans in 2022 and 2023,[4] knew all too well, "White scholars can write about black culture or black people without fully interrogating their work to

---

[3] See especially various discussions of theological anthropology and its relation to ethics.
[4] See https://www.nytimes.com/2023/02/01/us/college-board-advanced-placement-african-american-studies.html and https://www.ala.org/advocacy/bbooks (accessed June 20, 2024).

see if it employs white western intellectual traditions to re-inscribe white supremacy, to perpetuate racist domination."[5] Put simply, white (especially affluent and/or well-educated) persons must no longer be the frame of reference for understanding what it means to be human.

In a related vein, to work toward justice in society and right relations among people, Jennifer Harvey, a white Christian ethicist, contends that those in positions of relative privilege (due to race–ethnicity, education, citizenship, socioeconomics, religion, language, etc.) must actively interrogate and subvert these very sites in our advocacy, in larger structural and material relations, and in our scholarship. And in so doing, Harvey maintains, we also (re)form our own moral identities.[6] As Harvey explains in depth, an often unconscious sense of entitlement or superiority (racially, morally, culturally) insidiously malforms the self-identities of white people who grew up in racially discriminatory societies. In this same spirit, Vigen elsewhere explores an "ethic of white listening" in which she articulates important methodological steps that can help hold white scholars accountable to darker-skinned communities.[7] These steps can help produce self-aware and self-critical work that responds meaningfully to the realities and concerns surfaced by these communities. Suffice it to say that ethnographic work is neither simple nor without significant risk. Given this fact, white theologians, ethicists, and researchers especially need to be nuanced in whatever research or dialogue we pursue that involves racial, socioeconomic class, cultural, or religious issues.

In contrast with the 2011 volume, it is important to note that the contributors to this 2024 volume predominantly identify as minoritized in some fundamental way; for example as Black, Brown, Indigenous, people of color, female, members of the Global South, with many working within their own communities of accountability. They embody models of scholars and methods in which the complexities of privilege and intersectional forms of oppression are taken seriously. Specifically, a recurring theme is

---

[5] bell hooks, *Yearning: Race, Gender and Culture Politics* (Boston: South End Press, 1990), 124. She adds that cultural studies (and we would add theology, ethnography, and ethics) can be an intervention, but only if certain conditions exist:

> Cultural studies can serve as an intervention, making a space for forms of intellectual discourse to emerge that have not been traditionally welcomed in the academy. It cannot achieve this end if it remains solely a privileged "chic" domain where, as Cornel West writes ... scholars engage in debates which "highlight notions of difference, marginality, and otherness in such a way that it further marginalizes actual people of difference and otherness." When this happens cultural studies reinscribes patterns of colonial domination, where the "Other" is always made object, appropriated, interpreted, taken over by those in power, by those who dominate. (Ibid., 125)

[6] Jennifer Harvey, *Whiteness and Morality: Pursuing Racial Justice through Reparations and Sovereignty* (New York: Palgrave Macmillan, 2007). See also *Dear White Christians*, 2nd ed. (Grand Rapids: Eerdmans, 2020); *Antiracism as Daily Practice* (New York: St Martin's Press, 2024).

[7] See Aana Marie Vigen, "To Hear and to Be Accountable Across Difference: An Ethic of White Listening," in *Disrupting White Supremacy from Within: White People on What WE Need to Do*, ed. Jennifer Harvey et al. (Cleveland: The Pilgrim Press, 2004); *Women, Ethics, and Inequality in U.S. Healthcare: "To Count Among the Living"* (New York: Palgrave Macmillan, 2006; 2nd ed., 2011); and "Neglected Voices at the Beginning of Life: Prenatal Genetics and Reproductive Justice," in *Catholic Bioethics and Social Justice*, ed. M. Therese Lysaught and Michael McCarthy (Collegeville: Liturgical Press, 2018).

reflexivity—explored in depth in Chapters 1 and 4 and seen in the exemplary chapters in Part II.

Ethnography as Fitting Tool for Embodied Theology

Ethnography is a way to take particularity seriously—to discover truth revealed through embodied habits, relations, practices, narratives, and struggles. And as it is joined with a theological sensibility, our conviction is that each particular life, situation, or community is potentially, albeit only partially, revelatory of transcendent or divine truth. Undeniably, just as when scholars with significant privilege set out to learn from others with less, this assumption is not value- or risk-free. Indeed, it is possible, as critics note in Chapter 3, to reduce theology to anthropology. In other words, it could turn particular experiences into a kind of over-simplified, static, and idealized "stand-in" for a more complex, even infinite, reality. Our point is that while this is a potential pitfall, with methodological care and critical self-awareness, it is not a reason to rule out ethnography as theology.

Certainly, as Chapter 1 highlights, even within the history of secular anthropology, the possibility for creating simplistic and flat characterizations is evident. However, there has been a noticeable and significant evolution in how ethnography is done and in its basic assumptions. As anthropologist James Clifford explains in the Introduction to *Writing Culture*, "Ethnography in the service of anthropology once looked at clearly defined others, defined as primitive, or tribal, or non-Western, or pre-literate, or nonhistorical—the list, if extended, soon becomes incoherent. Now ethnography encounters others in relation to itself, while seeking itself as other."[8] In other words, an uncritical ethnography (or we would add theology) is no longer intellectually viable. It now has to turn the spotlight on itself—its own assumptions, narrative, and depictions—even as it attempts to illuminate a specific context.

To step back a bit, there are two distinct ways to conceive of the role of, and relationship between, ethnography and theology. Until recent decades, the standard approach was the use of social science by theology where the central aim is to craft a "thick description" (Geertz) of what "is". The goal is decidedly not to confirm or prove a given hypothesis; rather, it is to explore and describe as fully as possible a discrete slice of reality—what is seen, heard, witnessed, experienced. And in such complex descriptions of a specific time, person, or place, ethnography can help to keep researchers honest because before we can offer up any theological or normative conclusions about what ought to be, we must ensure that we adequately understand—perceive and appreciate—what is. And much is to be said for this use and goal. Distinctions between description and normative claims are further discussed in Chapters 1 or 4 and are astutely challenged by Nicole Hoskins in her exemplary chapter.

Yet, we (Scharen and Vigen) have been part of making the case for another way to conceive of the relationship between theology and ethnography that brings the two

---

[8] James Clifford, "Introduction: Partial Truths," in *Writing Culture: The Poetics and Politics of Ethnography*, ed. James Clifford and George E. Marcus (Berkeley: University of California Press, 1986), 1–26 (23).

even closer together. Specifically, this distinct view argues that the situation or context of study is already theological, and as such, has its own normative claims. And if this is the case, then the normative and/or theological conclusion cannot come solely from the researcher no matter how well they attend to the ethnographic data. Rather, what is normative is revealed through the partnership between the researcher and their collaborators. Said differently, rather than pairing ethnographic facts to universal theological truth, the ethnographer—through apprenticeship to the situation—aids in the articulation of those embedded theological convictions as primary theology itself. This perspective does not preclude bringing into the conversation other theological or theoretical materials, but the point is that they do not automatically have privilege over the local theological understandings operative in the lives of those studied. We find that this latter understanding of ethnography as embodied theology is a more accurate depiction of what really happens in the field. It is also the one that is growing in prominence, as evidenced by chapters included in this Second Edition.

Ethnography as Related to Discipleship

A basic, relatively uncontested, ethical dimension of social science is found in the accountability researchers have to ethnographic subjects. The fundamental requirements such as informed consent and freedom from coercion in terms of participating in the research reflect this concern. Yet, the responsibilities of researchers go further to include critical self-reflection (reflexivity), transparency, and relevance. The first two qualities are discussed at length in the pages that follow.

In terms of relevance, we refer to what ethnographer James Spradley emphasized in 1979 when he argued that the choice of the research topic ought to be informed by "community-expressed needs."[9] More recently, Natalie Wigg-Stevenson argues that it "is not enough to map the theological terrain; we also have to understand the relationship between the terrain, the map, and our bodies' movements—a relationship we often negotiate intuitively."[10] In other words, it is not only the scholar's research agenda that ought to set the course, but rather the project should be meaningfully related to the pressing issues and challenges faced by a particular community.[11] In short, it matters very much how the research is designed, what themes or issues are focused upon, how the researcher relates to the collaborators, and what is done with the fruits of the research.

Moreover, beyond being responsible to the subjects it explores, there is an additional aspect to the inherent moral character of social science. We contend that it is normative in the sense that in the descriptions it offers, there is often (implicitly if not explicitly) hope for certain outcomes.[12] Hoskins artfully describes the blurring of descriptive and

---

[9] James P. Spradley, *The Ethnographic Interview* (New York: Holt, Rinehart, and Winston, 1979), 14.
[10] Natalie Wigg-Stevenson, *Ethnographic Theology: An Inquiry into the Production of Theological Knowledge* (New York: Palgrave MacMillion, 2014), 11.
[11] Such a framing of research driven by local challenges animates Bent Flyvbjerg's strong call to social scientists in *Making Social Science Matter: Why Social Inquiry Fails and How It Can Succeed Again*, trans. Steven Sampson (New York: Cambridge University Press, 2001).
[12] See Robert N. Bellah, "The Ethical Aims of Social Inquiry," in *The Robert Bellah Reader*, ed. Robert N. Bellah and Steven Tipton (Durham: Duke University Press, 2006), 381–401.

normative dimensions in Part II. Other examples of such action-oriented research include hope for socioeconomic justice; the diminishment of poverty and human misery; improved health; better racial, cultural, and religious understanding across differences.

Consider the work and scholarly convictions of Paul Farmer (1959–2022), both an MD and a PhD in medical anthropology. Throughout his remarkable, thirty-five-year career, Farmer approached healthcare and human suffering with a robust transdisciplinary lens. In a passionate (at times prophetic) voice and with vivid description (coupled with weighty public health, sociological, and epidemiological statistics) Farmer explored the myriad ways "structural violence" wreaks havoc on the lives of impoverished people around the globe.[13] Millions suffer acutely and needlessly from highly preventable and treatable diseases. To illustrate briefly, the World Health Organization (WHO) reports that in 2020, "an estimated 5 million children under the age of 5 years died, mostly from preventable and treatable causes" such as "preterm birth complications, birth asphyxia/trauma, pneumonia, diarrhea and malaria, all of which can be prevented or treated with access to affordable interventions in health and sanitation."[14] Similarly, the WHO estimates that between 2030 and 2050 the rapidly changing climate will cause "approximately 250,000 additional deaths per year, from malnutrition, malaria, diarrhea and heat stress."[15] Again, these health threats are all largely avoidable when sufficient infrastructures are in place and functioning well. Thus, when people succumb to them, Farmer refers to them as "stupid deaths," borrowing from a Haitian Creole expression. In their chapter, Boopalan and Jongte highlight how Farmer's vocation and approach to such healthcare injustices is deeply informed by Latin American liberation theology and the preferential option for the poor. They, along with Grigoni in his chapter, make a strong appeal for Christian theology and ethics to root itself in the realities, voices, and experiences of "crucified bodies." They see ethnography as a key methodological partner in doing so.

Indeed, Farmer went beyond reporting these disturbing facts to ask poignant questions—both of ethics and of methods of inquiry. Specifically, he asks throughout his work how the rest of us—those not cut down by ruthless and unjust health disparities—can let these realities continue without doing more to abate them. Farmer well understood that it is not only a problem of resources but of moral imagination:

> [T]hese numbers have lost their ability to shock or even move us. What are the human values in question when we hear, and fail to react to, the news that each

---

[13] Farmer defines this term in his book *Pathologies of Power* and roots it in Latin American Liberation Theology's discussion of "sinful" social structures. See Paul Farmer, *Pathologies of Power: Health, Human Rights, and the New War on the Poor* (Berkeley: University of CA, 2005), especially chapters 5 and 8. This book also makes his method clear—how he draws upon various kinds of sources and knowledge (biology, public health data, sociology, theology, anthropology, etc.).

[14] The WHO, "Child Mortality (Under 5 Years)," January 2022, https://www.who.int/news-room/fact-sheets/detail/levels-and-trends-in-child-under-5-mortality-in-2020 (accessed June 12, 2023).

[15] https://www.who.int/news-room/fact-sheets/detail/climate-change-and-health (accessed June 13, 2023). The WHO also warns of the financial implications: "The direct damage costs to health (i.e. excluding costs in health-determining sectors such as agriculture and water and sanitation), is estimated to be between USD 2-4 billion/year by 2030." Ibid.

day thousands die of these maladies unattended? Where in the midst of all these numbers, is the human face of suffering? Can the reader discern the human face in these reports? A failure of imagination is one of the greatest failures registered in contemplating the fate of the world's poorest. Can photographs and personal narratives play a role, even as rhetorical tools, in promoting those human values that might lessen the magnitude of these disasters?[16]

What do we do when horrific numbers are not enough to push those with disproportionately ample resources into action? Farmer turned to a strategy that combines pressing statistics with poignant narratives, weaving evocative stories and images throughout the reporting of stark statistics. The resulting synthesis reveals not only the devastating inequalities and callous insults to human rights but also witnesses to the humanity, courage, and resolve found in Haiti, Rwanda, Russian prisons, Peru, and Boston.[17] Throughout his life, Farmer documented the impressive health and healthcare achievements possible when assumptions about what is "cost effective" are rigorously and scientifically challenged.[18]

Undeniably, the insidious demons of objectification and paternalism found, for example, in neocolonialism and "white saviorism," are not automatically circumvented by the use of ethnographic, liberationist, or feminist methods. In her scintillating book *Solidarity and Defiant Spirituality*, Traci C. West powerfully exposes the limits and harms inherent within "well-intended" research modes that lack sufficient reflexivity, vulnerability, and self-awareness.

Even in explicit pursuits of solidarity, scholars with relative power and privilege, as compared with those from and with whom they intend to learn, can nonetheless do real violence in their representation of their subjects. Too often academics—who are always in some ways outsiders once they take on the role of ethnographic researcher (even if they share some aspects of the social locations)—fail to unpack rigorously

---

[16] Paul Farmer, "Never Again? Reflections on Human Values and Human Rights," in *The Tanner Lectures on Human Values*, ed. G. B. Petersen, Vol. 25 (Salt Lake City: University of Utah Press, 2006), 137–88 (144–5), https://tannerlectures.utah.edu/_resources/documents/a-to-z/f/Farmer_2006.pdf (accessed June 12, 2023).

[17] For a wonderful read on Farmer's work in global health, see Tracy Kidder, *Mountains Beyond Mountains: The Quest of Dr. Paul Farmer, a Man who would Cure the World* (New York: Random House, 2004).

[18] For a concise example of both his argument and method, see Paul Farmer, "New Malaise: Bioethics and Human Rights in the Global Era," *Journal of Law, Medicine, and Ethics* 32 (2004): 243–51. To illustrate: Elsewhere, after showing the remarkable transformation in the life and health of a young Haitian man, Joseph, after receiving six months of effective therapy (infected with both AIDS and TB), Farmer remarks on the depth and kind of changed needed—one that moves beyond a "charity" or "pity" mentality:

> The medications that saved Joseph's life are commodities available throughout the global economy to those who can pay for them, and this is no less true in Kenya or any other place. The people who have died without a single dose of effective therapy over the past decade are, almost without exception, people who lived and died in poverty. In order to make sure that poor people dying from AIDS stop dying, it will be necessary to move beyond what Sontag referred to as the "unstable emotions" of compassion and pity, to more stable arrangements for all those afflicted with this and other treatable diseases. Translating compassion, pity, mercy, solidarity, or empathy into policy or rights is a difficult task. (Farmer, "Never Again?," 150)

their own cultural assumptions, values, and lenses they bring to the study. For example, they frame those from whom they hope to learn as two-dimensional tropes, whether "victims," "poor," "oppressed," or "problems to be fixed" who lack full personhood and agency. As West astutely puts it: "Decolonizing goals ought to be reflected in corresponding decolonizing methods—their design, tools of analysis, and execution. The pursuit of activist ideas that promote expansive, daring moral imaginations demands similar means for discovering them."[19] Precisely in pursuit of these goals, this Second Edition features the nuanced reflection and efforts by contributors who model aspects of decolonizing methods.

Indeed, the scholars featured in the pages that follow offer glimpses of the kinds of transformations to which we aspire and for which so many hope. For example, Williams and Grigoni reflect openly about their own social locations as outsiders and how it affects their relationships and research. Hoskins reflects on her identity as both insider and outsider and resists neat compartmentalizations and visions that fail to capture the complexity of what people who live at the center of environmental racism know and experience. Symmonds "studies up" to explore how whiteness infects the anti-trafficking efforts of predominantly white evangelicals.

In sum, we (Vigen and Scharen) continue to concur with Todd Whitmore and others, who argue that ethnographic work can even flow from a commitment rooted in the call of Jesus to "love the neighbor as yourself." In this sense, we can still consider our work as a kind of discipleship.[20] Many—both within and outside of the formal discipline of theology—are dedicated to the notion of pursuing knowledge for the sake of something—well-being, understanding, justice, or as we prefer to put it, "to have life and to have it abundantly" (John 10:10). In these kinds of pursuits, there is a fundamental connection between theology and social science.

Outline of the Book

Part I (Chapters 1-4) is the Prolegomena. Pivotal methodological themes are integrated throughout. Its purpose is to sketch the main contours of the territory—in Chapter 1, defining ethnography and elucidating pivotal moments in its history and then in Chapter 2 describing the turn to ethnography in theology. Next, Chapter 3 takes up debates among the critics of this turn and considers possible responses to them. With these concerns in view, it then makes a case for theological ethnography in Chapter 4.

With this orienting context and the tracing of theoretical and theological issues laid out, Part II (Chapters 5-13) turns to a new generation of exemplars of theological and ethical work engaging in ethnography. These chapters offer concrete embodiments of possibility. We will briefly highlight the focus of each.

---

[19] Traci C. West, *Solidarity and Defiant Spirituality* (New York: New York University Press, 2019), 12.
[20] Todd Whitmore, "Crossing the Road: The Case for Ethnographic Fieldwork in Christian Ethics," *Journal of the Society of Christian Ethics* 27, no. 2 (2007): 273-94.

Professor Elina Hankela and (at the time) graduate researcher Clementine Nishimwe grapple with a crucial yet little interrogated space of research ethics: the relationship between a project lead and their research team. Exemplifying a kind of shared critical reflexivity, this chapter opens up important dynamics related to race, class, institutional position and through it all, power.

Sunder John Boopalan and RC Jongte center their own social identities as part of oppressed groups in India in a form similar to autoethnography to argue for authentically liberative theological ethnography. Calling out the ways superficial solidarities damage efforts at liberative practice and hegemonic powers co-opt liberative movements for their own purposes, Boopalan and Jongte argue for a path that avoids social erasure and systematic oppression through theological ethnography grounded in the epistemological privilege of the crucified bodies of history.

Hee-Kyu Heidi Park traces the precarity of the human body in public space through a case study of a one-person protest against a multinational company in Seoul. Through a thick description of his—and his community's—history and context, including connections to local churches, she offers an eschatological theological imagination that aims to transform the onlooker into a participant in social transformation.

Lailatul Fitriyah engages in multifaith theological ethnography constructed from careful listening to female migrant workers (FMWs) in Singapore, as well as those who advocate for their rights and protection. Through what she calls "border theologies," FMWs create authentic, empowering spiritual conviction as they grapple with experiences of suffering and evil in their daily lives.

Nicole Hoskins draws on an ethnographic study of Chicago's Altgeld Gardens, a historically Black housing project, and Black women environmental activists living there who are fighting land, air, and water pollution. Seeing their "livingness" through a poetic-ethical frame, Hoskins complicates traditional Western ethnographic constructions of narrative linearity and blurs the boundaries between the descriptive and the normative.

Sara Williams investigates what she calls the "Swedish Woman Affair" as a traumatic memory of Western feminist harm among Palestinian Christian women. Focusing her attention on ethnographic reflexivity, she seeks to open possibilities for Western women to inhabit more equitable relationships with non-Western women on the basis of negotiation with complex communities of difference.

Nicole Symmonds engages in an innovative excavation of evangelical whiteness via a careful study of white evangelical Christian engagement in the antisex trafficking movement in Atlanta. Finding moral frames leading this work (purity especially), Symmonds raises questions regarding problematic racialization of trafficking victims and survivors.

Michael Grigoni bought a handgun and joined evangelical Christian handgun owners to explore how they hold together Christian care and protection (their aim) with the inherent violence entailed in the tool used for this care. But soon he was drawn into the vigil ministry of the Religious Coalition for a Nonviolent Durham, and came to see their practices as powerfully disclosing the opposite of Christian handgun owners. For him, the vigil practices enact a poignant way of "being with" those bodies crucified by gun violence.

AnneMarie Mingo's chapter offers a sensitive portrayal of the resiliency of displaced New Orleans residents following Hurricane Katrina's devastation. Specifically, she learns from those who found themselves in her small Pennsylvania town, centered around the life of a local Methodist church. Drawing on her ongoing participation in the life of the church and community, as well as historical research, Mingo shows the limits of an ethics of hospitality and instead sees in their lives an ethic of receptivity that grounds their resilience, "making lemonade out of lemons."

Part III elucidates a few central and pragmatic dimensions of method and offers benedictions—good words—for those who would like to head out and give ethnography a try. We offer some concrete advice, but with humility because of the diverse, dynamic range of work taking place at the intersections of ethnography, theology, and ethics. In Part I, we are in a sense "thinking out loud," but in the context of readers who are, presumably, similarly grasping for something beyond the tidy confines of their disciplines and academic training. Our colleagues writing in Part II share with us the continually evolving construction of this dynamic multidisciplinary space. In all, the existence of the book and its multiple authors is evidence of the strong desire for new integrative spaces in which to carry out meaningful theological and ethical work through ethnographic research.

Concluding Thoughts for Beginning

This book's origins can be described by charting two distinct paths: the direct route and the detours. Above, we briefly summarize the formal road taken through academic circles. Yet, in another sense, this book came about through a longer, winding, serendipitous, and somewhat unpredictable path of friendship. Much scholarship, whether explicitly acknowledged or not, comes out of collaboration (formal and informal) among two or more people.

In our case, we met in graduate school and soon discovered common scholarly commitments amid somewhat differing backgrounds and thematic interests. We each took courses outside of the formal disciplinary boundaries of Christian theology and ethics at the University of California Berkeley (Scharen in Sociology, Anthropology, and Philosophy, and Vigen in Women's Studies, Postcolonial Theory, and Film Studies). During these years, we talked a lot about what we were learning from these diverse disciplines and on a couple of occasions, we got to work together on a specific project. Yet, we did not then imagine that our shared scholarly commitments and differing areas of expertise would lead us both to ethnographic methods. Nevertheless, through numerous geographic moves and stages of vocational development, the conversations (both within and between us) have continued—about how to do our work, what matters to us as scholars, and what we hope to create. These vocational and methodological explorations have progressed amid detours and over bumps, and ultimately, brought us first to developing this volume, and now roughly a decade later, a revised second edition reflective of the vibrant work now happening.

With this second edition, then, while offering useful thematic and methodological contributions that have served readers well thus far, and we trust that will continue, it has also given us the additional opportunity to live out our friendship. In the writing, editing (and numerous conversations that preceded both) not only did this book take shape, but we have been able to realize again how central friendship and collaboration are to the creative process. And we have found this welcome gift to be true in terms of our learning from, and appreciation for, others in various streams of theology and ethics—specifically in this case, for those working with ethnography. So as we prepare to share this work with others, the predominant feeling is gratitude—for the contributors in this volume, for other colleagues who are integral to our scholarly lives, and for the opportunity to offer up these kinds of creative and collaborative endeavors as models for others to consider.

And in this spirit, we have specific thanks for our colleagues who joined us in writing of both editions of this book: Melissa Browning, Peter Gathje, Robert Jones, Emily Reimer-Barry, Jeffery Tribble, Andrea Vicini, Todd Whitmore and now Damaris Parsitau, Elina Hankela, Clementine Nishimwe, Sunder John Booplan, RC Jongte, Hee-Kyu Heidi Park, Lailatul Fitriyah, Nicole Hoskins, Sara Williams, Nicole Symmonds, Michael Grigoni, and AnneMarie Mingo. Aana thanks her home institution, Loyola University Chicago, for its ongoing support and research assistance. She is also grateful for the consistent moral support of numerous Loyola colleagues, especially Susan A. Ross, Robert DiVito, and Jennifer Parks.

The volume would not exist without T&T Clark Bloomsbury Press who said "yes." Sincere thanks to Thomas Kraft on the first edition and Anna Turton on the second edition, who were above all patient, helpful, and gracious. We also greatly appreciate other staff at T&T Clark Bloomsbury Press who have been incredibly efficient and helpful at every stage. We benefited from the adept technical and copy-editing assistance of Alia Norton, a doctoral student at Loyola University. She was consistently available and exceedingly helpful in all her work. Loyola doctoral candidate Nick Mitchell also offered initial editing eyes early on. We continue to appreciate Grant Gholson and Daniel Cosacchi who offered significant research, bibliography, and formatting assistance for the 2011 volume.

For each of us, other conversation partners—some we have met and others we have not—have shaped our sense of these issues and they are scattered throughout the footnotes of this book. In addition, we are grateful to Mary McClintock Fulkerson for her theological leadership, her collegiality, and her early and earnest encouragement of this work. Traci C. West was exceedingly patient with us as our work unfolded, and we are truly humbled by her Foreword to this second volume.

Christian Scharen especially gives thanks for one of his doctoral professors with whom he studied ethnography and alongside whom he carried out ethnographic research projects over a period of four years: Nancy L. Eielsand. Nancy tragically died of cancer in 2009 at the age of forty-four. The incandescence that she lived, I hope, finds continued life in the work represented by this volume. He also thanks his family for all their love and support: Pierrette, Isaiah, Finn, and Owen.

Aana Marie Vigen continues to be grateful for mentors in ethnography and/or Christian ethics from whom she continues to learn, especially Mindy Fullilove, Beverly

Wildung Harrison, Karen Lebacqz, Emilie M. Townes, and Larry L. Rasmussen. She also profoundly thanks her extended family (the Vigens, Hemstads, and Stricklers) who always takes a keen interest in her scholarly adventures and who offer much encouragement. Finally, the completion of this (or any of her) work owes everything to the constant, unconditional love and support of her beloved Alison and to the irrepressible, empathetic, soulful person that is Benjamin Gabriel.

Part I

Prolegomena

1

What Is Ethnography?

What does "research" look like in the twenty-first century? What images come to mind?—A library? A lab? A river bed? A remote village? A microscope? An oncology ward? Many—probably most—academic theologians and Christian ethicists envision a desk and computer—complete with books, electronic databases, web search results, and a cup of coffee. Theologians generally don't do much walking (unless they are pacing) while doing research. Instead, many associate research with an intense—often solitary—communion with texts. So, there is certain truth in the conclusion that theological methods of inquiry, along with those of other disciplines in the humanities (e.g., English, Philosophy, Classical Studies), are rather different from scientific ones.

However, there are at least a couple of problems with the view that theological methods are wholly distinct from those found in the natural and social sciences. First, it is over-simplified. Theologians learn (or have the capacity to learn) as much from natural and social events as much as any other person. We are not a different species after all. Second, it is worth asking why some still assume that certain methods are the sole property of specific disciplines and "off limits" to others in an age where academia consistently praises "interdisciplinarity" as key to scholarly and pedagogical vitality. Third, the *telos* of a given research project, whether theological or scientific in nature, may be as important to explore as any methodological differences between them.

Perhaps what stands out most about Christian theology and ethics is that both are fairly bold in confessing that they are up to more than description; there is often an explicit normative dimension to the work. Christian theology and ethics are not content to describe reality as it is, but also how it ultimately *is* or *ought to* be. As Catholic theologian Clare Watkins underscores, searching out divine revelation is an integral dimension to theological pursuits.[1] Said differently, theology claims to provide a foretaste of ultimate truth yet to come or to be fully experienced.

Some natural and social scientists resonate with this aim in the sense that they intend their work to foster greater understanding, respect, and responsibility among human beings.[2] For example, many ecologists hope that their work will lead to stronger

---

[1] Clare Watkins, *Disclosing Church: An Ecclesiology Learned from Conversations in Practice* (New York: Routledge, 2020).
[2] Robert N. Bellah, "The Ethical Aims of Social Inquiry," in *Social Science as Moral Inquiry*, ed. Norma Haan, Robert N. Bellah, Paul Rabinow, and William Sullivan (New York: Columbia University Press, 1983), 360–81.

responses to the climate crisis; medical researchers studying cancer and dementia hope their work will lead to more effective preventions and cures. In specific terms of qualitative research, more and more anthropologists and sociologists openly acknowledge that the separation of "fact" from "value" is not so tidy as once assumed. British theologian Paul Fiddes makes the case that secular ethnographers inevitably bring normative views and valuations with them that inform their choices in what to study and what they are looking for in their research designs.[3]

Yet, a caution and caveat: as much as I (Vigen) stand behind these observations, I also worry that such insights can be employed to question the validity of scientific findings as in the case of certain Christians disputing evolution. And living through the COVID-19 pandemic makes plain the danger of large groups of people denying the need for, and safety of, vaccines. Per WHO 2023 data, nearly seven million people have died from COVID-19, with over one million deaths alone in the United States.[4] People risk their own and others' well-being when they flatly dismiss scientific truth as biased or "fake." Thus, while it is important and necessary to question the view that science is wholly neutral/value free, it is equally important to defend what it can accurately and uniquely tell us about reality.

Finally, it is important to note that there is a lot of variety within *both* theological and scientific methods. In order to appreciate the complexity and variety, we will briefly describe the difference between quantitative and qualitative research methods. In doing so, we wish to underscore that both are used by scientists and theologians alike.

Contrasting Quantitative and Qualitative Methods

Most natural scientists, along with many social scientists, depend upon the methods of quantitative analysis that are rooted in presumptions of objectivity and large, generalizable findings—resulting in irrefutable, conclusive "hard" evidence. To do so, they utilize techniques such as testing a hypothesis, double-blind trials, control groups, and uniformity in sampling. Findings that hold up across specific regions (large sample sizes), that demonstrate statistical accuracy and validity, and whose methodological purity is above reproach (making sure all but one variable is controlled for) are prized. Quantitative methods are essential to many kinds of important work: clinical drug and medical treatment trials; national polling samples; demographic and census statistics;

---

[3] Paul Fiddes, "Revelation and Normativity," in *The Wiley Blackwell Companion to Theology and Qualitative Research*, ed. Pete Ward and Knut Tveitereid (Hoboken: John Wiley & Sons, Ltd, 2022), 123. Fiddes cites French anthropologist Gerard Lenclud and Swedish sociologist Mats Trondman as two examples: See Gerard Lenclud, "The Factual and the Normative in Ethnography: Do Cultural Differences Derive from Description?," *Anthropology Today* 12, no. 1 (1996): 7–11 and Mats Trondman, "Taking Normative Sense Seriously: Ethnography in the Light of a Utopian Reference," *Ethnography* 18, no. 1 (2017): 10–23.

[4] WHO Covid 19 dashboard—https://covid19.who.int/?adgroupsurvey={adgroupsurvey}&gclid=Cj0KCQjwnrmlBhDHARIsADJ5b_mLfk_cyl1UQDGZ47-iKmz0aZOId4cCTxv1KrV9i_XuDyLHM0JXwUcaAuwqEALw_wcB (accessed July 12, 2023).

economic data; biological and ecological studies of species, climates, habitats, and the corresponding effects human beings have upon each.

In terms of theological pursuits, a method similar to quantitative research is found in the works of scholars who carefully track the number and kinds of usages of specific terms in scripture or other theological writings. Another example of a shared method is that of national polling and public opinion surveys. The *Public Religion Research Institute* (PRRI)[5] founded by Robert P. Jones (author of an exemplar chapter in the 2011 edition) is known for pathbreaking research on culture, public policy, and religion. PRRI is an internationally recognized authority for its surveys of varied American religious and cultural views on a host of pressing topics (e.g., politics, abortion, guns, immigration, climate change, religious liberty, and LGBTQAI+ policies).

In sum, the shared assumption between deductive, interpretative approaches in theology and their counterparts in secular, quantitative methods is that there is an "objective" truth that can be discovered through observation of the phenomena in question. In other words, for those immersed in quantitative studies, "good" scientific or theological inquiry depends on the proper deduction of facts derived from careful reading, reflection, interpretation, and recording of data. Thus, whether the pursuit is theological or scientific in nature, the method is deductive, meaning that general, *a priori* principles are discovered in sources of information (e.g., sacred texts, nature, philosophical writings) that hold true in concrete situations across time and space and thus can be applied in specific contexts and hold universally.[6]

In strong contrast to quantitative protocols and reports, ethnography values a very different kind of data—often that emerges through disciplined attention to a few research sites or participants. Consequently, some researchers who prioritize quantitative data find qualitative methods too narrow and their findings too anecdotal to be of scientific value, dismissively likening it to quaint storytelling. For their part, as Scharen discusses in greater depth in Chapter 3, some theologians (Hauerwas, Milbank) are skeptical of qualitative methods because they think they import secular theologies implicitly under the guise of "neutral" or "objective" social science. Instead, they favor theological inquiry that starts with scripture and other primary theological texts that give a faith community its distinctive identity.

Yet, as we discuss elsewhere,[7] scientists of various kinds use qualitative methods and find substantial value in them. For our part, we contend that both quantitative and qualitative methods have important places in numerous kinds of research. Rather than cast them as necessary competitors that demand an "either/or" allegiance, we see them as complementary methods, but with distinct aims and objectives. Moreover, we question the undervaluing of qualitative methods and find that they merit more respect and serious consideration than they sometimes receive—from scientists and theologians alike.

---

[5] https://www.prri.org/.

[6] The classic move in philosophical ethics is Kant's, although Stephen Toulmin argues for Descartes's turn to the universal as a response to the horrors of subjective religious belief that funded the bloody "wars of religion" in the seventeenth century. See Toulmin, *Cosmopolis: The Hidden Agenda of Modernity* (New York: The Free Press, 1990).

[7] See Vigen, *Women, Ethics, and Inequality* (New York: Palgrave Macmillan, 2006), 84-98.

The Origins and Meanings of Ethnography

A Personal Account

Before succinctly sketching the evolution of ethnography, it is integral to our particular method to locate ourselves in relation to our work. In this brief section, I (Vigen) describe what is at stake for me in using ethnography, how I came to it, and the tensions and challenges that I continue to grapple with in doing this kind of research. Early on in graduate studies, I felt a strong need to connect what I had been reading in coursework with other domains of knowledge. Consequently, I sought out concrete experience in medical ethics by working as a hospital chaplain and serving on a hospital bioethics committee. At times, I found reading theological and ethical texts—along with abstracted medical ethics case studies without sufficient, real-life context—tedious and unsatisfying. I yearned to learn about, and talk through, various theological and medical quandaries with people who did not identify as academics.

Persistent questions interrupted my contemplation of the traditional scholarly sources: "So what? What resonance (if any) might a given theological or ethical claim have for people in the pews and/or those living with a serious illness? Would they agree or disagree with it? What more might they see or know? How might they perceive and articulate the central issues and questions at stake?" Even more urgently, I wondered: "How can I as a scholar connect what I think and write to what others live, especially those too often ignored both in scholarship and in the public square? How might their knowledge correct mine? How is my work in dialogue with them? Is there any way that what I am doing could be relevant to people outside of academic circles?" In my most vulnerable hours, I asked, "Is there any tangible use to getting an advanced degree in theology and Christian ethics?"

Thankfully, a previously untapped part of my scholarly identity came alive as I talked with patients and participated in clinical bioethics case discussions. Here were vital faith questions and ethics in action. Theological musings about life after death, human responsibility, and sin were no longer hypothetical. Each day at the hospital, the rubber hit the road with force and urgency. Similarly, questions about quality care played out in palpable, sometimes tragic, ways along the hospital corridors and in the daily (even routine, seemingly mundane) decisions, conversations, and unspoken actions.

To briefly illustrate one example of my learning, a chaplaincy internship made me acutely aware of the fact that many patients felt ill at ease not only because of their medical condition, but because of a lack of common language, understanding, and respect between them and their care providers. As a part-time intern in California in 1995–6, I was the only non-Latino/a/x staff person who spoke Spanish with any degree of efficacy at the hospital. When I was not on duty, the hospital called an AT&T operator or a family member to translate. On other occasions, a member of the housekeeping or food service staff was called to translate. Such realities question claims and procedures regarding informed consent and patient confidentiality.

Proposition 187, later found unconstitutional, was in effect at this time. While in force, it mandated that undocumented immigrants were to be denied medical care.[8] Consequently, many Latino/a/x patients (regardless of immigration status) felt viewed with suspicion and were uncomfortable in the hospital environment. As a chaplain, it was my responsibility to discuss Advance Directives with all patients for whom there was nothing on file. Since I spoke Spanish, I was asked to do this especially for these patients. I noticed that when I spoke with white patients (who were predominantly upper-middle class or affluent and insured) they were eager to fill out the paperwork, noting sometimes that they did not want to end up on life support without having previously voiced their wishes regarding heroic measures and end-of-life care.

In glaring contrast, when I went over the same information in Spanish, patients would look at me more guardedly and none filled it out while I was there. While no one made this exact comment to me, their expressions and reserve gave me the sense that they thought filling out the paperwork would give hospital staff an excuse to not do everything to save their lives. What was clear is that the level of trust and rapport between many of the Spanish-speaking patients and their providers was not nearly as high as it was between many of the white and English-speaking patients and providers.

In all, working ultimately in two different hospitals and on a bioethics committee contributed significantly to my understanding as it pushed me to interrogate what I thought I knew as an emerging scholar. Furthermore, as I describe elsewhere, working with the Rev. Dr. Annie Ruth Powell and witnessing her struggle with cancer made my own shortcomings and outright failures—as a listener; as a white person; and as a well-intentioned, lay caregiver—all too apparent.[9] Thus, before I knew anything really about the formal discipline of "ethnography" per se, I instinctively knew I needed to incorporate into my ongoing research method some kind of substantial dimension that would enable these kinds of dialogues, self-critical analyses, and interruptions.

What I did not fully understand then is that my desire to engage the wisdom and insights found outside the common domains of academic Christian ethics, and within embodied persons very different from myself in key respects, would not only involve learning through conversation with such people, but also necessitated an even greater *conversion* on my part—a conversion to the other, to learn and labor with others. And implicit in this desire was a budding sense that as a scholar, I needed to do more than simply advance a thesis. Instead, I felt called to seek (or at least strive for) transformation in society, in practices, and importantly, in my own heart and way of being in the world. Yet, I don't think I realized at first how I would be changed by the

---

[8] Even as it is no longer California state law, a similar ethos of Proposition 187 can be glimpsed in current federal policy: "Under rules issued by the Centers for Medicare and Medicaid Services (CMS), individuals with Deferred Action for Childhood Arrivals status are not considered lawfully present for purposes of health coverage eligibility and remain ineligible for coverage options. Medicaid payments for emergency services may be made on behalf of individuals who are otherwise eligible for Medicaid but for their immigration status." Kaiser Family Foundation, Fact Sheet, December 2022 (updated March 2023), "Healthcare and Coverage of Immigrants," online: https://www.kff.org/racial-equity-and-health-policy/fact-sheet/health-coverage-and-care-of-immigrants/ (accessed June 20, 2023).

[9] Vigen, *Women, Ethics, and Inequality*, xviii–xxiii.

research—or how important it was that I be open to such change. I also don't know if I fully comprehended the degree and complexity of self-critical awareness that would be required.

So many years following my ethnographic study with Black and Latina women with breast cancer and with healthcare providers, I still reflect on the experience of learning from these women and I feel disquieted by the fact that this work has benefited me in tangible ways (completion of a PhD, an offer of an academic position, tenure) while they did not benefit in any obvious ways. At least one of the women with cancer has died. One other (perhaps more) faced a recurrence. Perhaps telling their stories was cathartic for them. I hope I succeeded in making them feel heard and respected. I hope they left the interview(s) knowing how much I cherish their stories and insights. Yet, even assuming these positive outcomes, the overall imbalance of benefits remains. They gave me a gift that has changed my life in important ways. And yet I cannot say that my work has had as dramatic, or even tangible, an effect on their lives, let alone on the state of healthcare quality or provider–patient relations.

Such inequality in terms of power and benefit keeps me clear-eyed on what my life's work needs to be about. As a white, presently healthy and well-insured academic, Christian, and US citizen, I have discerned that my vocational calling entails learning from and advocating for those who are disproportionately vulnerable to being ignored, silenced, or harmed by societal inequities and injustice, whether due to race, socioeconomics, illness, immigration status, and so on. And as I listen, I need to reflect critically on my own assumptions, privileges, "good intentions," and awkward missteps lest I misunderstand or misappropriate the sacred gift that is the stories, lives, experiences, and truths of others.

Since first publicly writing about the steps leading me to ethnographic research in 2011, I have continued to traverse and ponder qualitative paths. Specifically, spurred by my own pregnancy experience, I embarked upon a qualitative study exploring reproductive justice, prenatal genetics, and the experiences and perspectives of Black and Brown new moms, genetic counselors, midwives, and physicians. I gave academic papers based on this work and published two chapters.[10]

Yet, despite strong encouragement from scholars of varied racial–ethnic backgrounds, and even as I amassed a healthy volume of individual interviews and medical sociology data, something inside me kept holding myself back from publishing a monograph. Paradoxically, I criticized myself both for not putting a book out there and for undertaking the work as a white scholar. Even as I knew I was learning highly valuable things (especially pertinent in a post-Roe world) I did not feel comfortable being the sole author sharing them. I was not content with the sophistication of my research method. And since I had already achieved the increasingly rare prize of tenure, I had the luxury of knowing that my job security did not depend on publishing

---

[10] See "Neglected Voices at the Beginning of Life: Prenatal Genetics and Reproductive Justice," in *Catholic Bioethics and Social Justice*, ed. M. Therese Lysaught and Michael McCarthy (Collegeville: Liturgical Press, 2018) and "Prenatal Genetic Testing & the Complicated Quest for a Healthy Baby: Christian Ethics in Conversation with Genetic Counselors," in *Suffering in Medicine, Theology and Medical Ethics*, ed. Christof Mandry (Germany: Schoeningh Verlag [scientific imprint Brill International], 2021).

it. In sum, simply having a good idea for a research topic and question, along with the best of intentions, does not inherently mean that any given individual researcher is best positioned on her own to do the work.

My particular history with ethnography is a microcosm of a much larger history within the field. Given that this book intends a resounding call to theologians and Christian ethicists to take ethnography seriously as an important dimension to our work, it is crucial that it is accompanied by a sharp understanding of pitfalls and limits as well. The history of ethnography itself shows how anthropologists, cultural theorists, sociologists, and others have questioned and critiqued ethnography as a way to complexify its assumptions, methods, and practices.

A Condensed History: Three Key Moments in Ethnography's Evolution

In Western Europe and the United States, ethnography emerged as a recognized method of scientific inquiry within the disciplinary home of anthropology in the nineteenth century. Shantelle Weber, an emerging leader among South African practical theologians, underscores that integral aspects of qualitative methods (e.g., storytelling, close attention to specific contextual traditions, values, practices) have earlier and non-Western roots as well.[11] For too long, predominantly white/Western scholars have constructed the history of ethnography as yet another tale of their/our original creation when, in fact, many cultures—both ancient and contemporary—highly value and take concerted efforts to listen to, remember, and pass on knowledge embedded in particular oral and textual traditions.

Keeping in mind this larger picture, in terms of its evolution since the mid-twentieth century in the West, ethnography has become a major subcategory within qualitative research methodology and is used not only in anthropology, but in sociology and across many fields including religious studies and medicine.[12] Given our commitments to self-critical reflection and to white antiracism, it is important to highlight three central moments in its history prior to elaborating our working understanding of the term and method. Specifically, it is imperative for us as white, settler[13] scholars to address the reality that modern anthropology has often been intertwined with colonialism, imperialism, and racial prejudice.

---

[11] Shantelle Weber, "Practical Theology Rooted in and from African: The Tide is Turning," in *The Wiley Blackwell Companion to Theology and Qualitative Research*, ed. Pete Ward and Knut Tveitereid (Hoboken: John Wiley & Sons, Ltd, 2022), 59.

[12] Two powerful examples from medical anthropology are João Biehl, *Vita: Life in a Zone of Social Abandonment* (Berkeley: University of California Press, 2005, updated 2013) and Seth M. Holmes, *Fresh Fruit, Broken Bodies: Migrant Farmworkers in the United States* (Berkeley: University of CA Press, 2013); from religious studies, David Mellott, *I Was and I Am Dust: Penitent Practices as a Way of Knowing* (Collegeville: Liturgical Press, 2009).

[13] We neglected to mark ourselves as settlers in the 2011 volume. Both of us descend from European immigrants (Norwegian, German, Swiss, English) who settled on land in the Midwest and Western United States. Our ancestors reaped the unjust benefits of the violent and forced removal of Indigenous peoples from these lands. Scharen explores his roots and the fraught legacy they have engendered in his forthcoming book, *After Laura Ingalls Wilder: Facing my Family's Pioneer History Amidst the Battle over the Story of America* (forthcoming 2025).

The first moment comes at the turn of the twentieth century. Histories of anthropology commonly identify its modern beginnings with the notable legacies of anthropologists and ethnographers such as Franz Boas, Bronisław Malinowski, and E. E. Evans-Pritchard. In the late nineteenth century, while some careful work was being done in areas related to modern anthropology, there were many more individuals who used their travels, diaries, and anecdotal observations to justify Western colonial projects, cultural and religious imperialism, Christian missionary ventures, and racial discrimination and subjugation. Sensational accounts were published in both scholarly and popular venues telling tales of the "savages," "cannibals," and "primitive man" that reinforced stereotypes and prevalent Western views of the "superiority" and "civility" of Europe and the United States.[14] At the same time, these voyeurs, voyagers, and thrill-seeking adventurers ransacked Indigenous societies and filled Western museums with their art, valuables, tools, symbols, and textiles.

In significant contrast to many of their contemporaries, Boas, Malinowski, and Evans-Pritchard were among the first Western scholars to use sustained, empirical methods of study to explore cultures outside their own. They spent extended periods living among Indigenous people in Africa, the South Pacific, and the Americas—taking detailed field notes, learning Indigenous languages, and building relationships with their informants. They developed contextual theories about cultural symbols, traditions, social patterns, intimate relations, and so on that functioned in particular places through intensive study and observation of various facets of daily living. In the course of this work, they not only attempted to communicate with people in their native languages, they developed complex relationships with members of the communities they observed.

For example, Malinowski (1884–1942) is considered by many as a front-runner in social anthropology whose ethnographic studies of people in New Guinea, Australia, and the Trobriand Islands made influential marks in the discipline. His meticulous ethnographic work, along with that of Franz Boas, is often signaled as a pivotal break both with "armchair" theorists and untrained travelers whose methods they critiqued for their respective overreliance on grand generalizations accompanied by cursory anecdotes as support for them (e.g., Lewis Henry Morgan and Sir James Frazer) and their lack of care, time, and detailed analysis in their research. Malinowski is seen by many anthropologists as contributing critical innovations to fieldwork (e.g., participant observation) and as one of the first anthropologists to give significant attention to studying all aspects of daily living—not ruling any part out as too ordinary or mundane.[15]

---

[14] See for an example from the early years of anthropology: Henry Lewis Morgan, *Ancient Society* (New York: Meridian Books, 1877/1963). He outlines there a social evolutionary classification moving from savage to barbarism to civilization with European society as the prototype of what it is to be civilized.

[15] See Michael W. Young, *Malinowski: Odyssey of an Anthropologist, 1884–1920* (New Haven: Yale University Press, 2004). For central examples of Malinowski's work, see *Argonauts of the Western Pacific* (1922), *Crime and Custom in Savage Society* (1926), *Sex and Repression in Savage Society* (1927), *The Sexual Life of Savages in North-Western Melanesia* (1929).

Boas (1858–1942) is commonly thought of as the founder of both modern and also American anthropology.[16] He was born in Germany and immigrated to the United States in 1887. He started the first US doctoral program in anthropology (Columbia University) and contributed richly to anthropology's theoretical underpinnings. Furthermore, Boas left a legacy of students, many of whom shaped the emerging field for the next decades and became its preeminent scholars in the early and mid-twentieth century (e.g., Ruth Benedict, Zora Neale Hurston, Margaret Mead, among many others).

In particular, Boas is credited with making cultural relativism, empiricism, and rigorous, intensive field study (living with a society being studied for an extended time, learning Indigenous language(s), taking detailed field notes) all standard norms for anthropology. Unlike many of his academic contemporaries, Boas did not see Western civilization as superior to others. Cultural and racial bigotry masquerading as scientific observation were commonplace in anthropology, and Boas sought to keep such bias in check by placing greater authority on doing the research and in making careful, sustained, detailed observations of what was actually found in the field. In doing so, he developed a theoretical and practical method for anthropological research, modeled partially after that used by Darwin and in the natural sciences more generally, but with a sharp critique of theories of social evolution (a.k.a. social Darwinism), for example central in his fellow New Yorker Henry Lewis Morgan. In short, his idea was that rigorous field research and scrupulous methods would test, correct, and necessarily revise any theory or hypothesis found lacking.

In addition to establishing distinctive theoretical and methodological base points for anthropology and educating a leading generation of scholars, Boas blazed public activist trails as well. For example, he is remembered for passionately and publicly confronting racial inequality and "scientific," essentialist arguments related to racial superiority/inferiority. Indeed, he may have been the first white scholar in the United States to publish the view that whites and Blacks were essentially equal.[17] He is also credited with formally training some of the first anthropologists and folklorists of color (e.g., Gilberto Freyre, Manuel Gamio, Williams Jones, Ella Deloria, Zora Neale Hurston). Boaz came under scrutiny himself when he publicly denounced peers who used anthropology as a cover for spying on behalf of the US government.

Yet unchecked biases and presumptions are stubborn and pernicious. Boas is no exception. Indeed, even as he strongly critiqued ethnocentrism, he generally assumed

---

[16] See Norman F. Boas, *Franz Boas 1858–1942: An Illustrated Biography* (Mystic: Seaport Autographs Press, 2004); Douglas Cole, *Franz Boas: The Early Years, 1858–1906* (Seattle: University of Washington Press, 1999); Regna Darnell, *And Along Came Boas: Continuity and Revolution in Americanist Anthropology* (Amsterdam: John Benjamins, 1998); Adam Kuper, *The Invention of Primitive Society: Transformations of an Illusion* (London: Routledge, 1988). For central examples of Boas's own work, see Franz Boas, *The Mind of Primitive Man* (New York: The Macmillan Company, 1911); *Anthropology and Modern Life* (New York: W. W. Norton, 1928); *Race, Language, and Culture* (New York: The Macmillan Company, 1940). See also this collection of his works: George W. Stocking, Jr., (ed.), *A Franz Boas Reader: The Shaping of American Anthropology, 1883–1911* (Chicago: University of Chicago Press, 1974).

[17] Vernon J. Williams, *Rethinking Race* (Lexington: The University Press of Kentucky, 1996); George W. Stocking, Jr., *Race, Culture, and Evolution: Essays in the History of Anthropology* (New York: Free Press, 1968); Thomas Gossett, *Race: The History of an Idea in America* (New York: Oxford University Press, 1963).

the intellectual superiority of whites based on the studies that measured brain/cranial sizes popular in his day. Boas and his legacy are complex and multifaceted.[18]

Thus while giving due credit to what was revolutionary given the larger historical contexts in which they are situated, subsequent anthropologists point out that, even if unacknowledged, Boas, Malinowski, Evans-Pritchard—along with their contemporaries and students—nonetheless used unexamined filters through which they viewed and interpreted the cultures and peoples they observed. They understood cataloging and categorizing the objects, symbols, roles, and activities they studied to be integral to their work. They assumed they were simply "reporting objective facts." In actuality, they created systems of meaning with their interpretations that could never exhaustively describe or "capture" the self-understandings and worldviews of the people they studied. And they too collected a treasure trove of artifacts for display, study, and enjoyment in Western museums.

In summary, a problematic lack of self-criticism accompanied by the gaze of colonialism/colonizer infused much of anthropological scholarship through the early and mid-twentieth century.[19] White and predominantly male scholars created the categories and typologies that "made sense" of others' realities for Western understanding and consumption. Yet, for the most part, they did not fully acknowledge the subjective nature of their interpretations and characterizations.[20]

This provocative insight is part of the fundamental and groundbreaking point of the collective essays in *Writing Culture* (1986) and constitutes a second key historical moment. Of particular note, collectively this text emphasizes and critically analyzes the process of writing integral to ethnographic study. James Clifford contends that the above forerunners took the process of writing about culture for granted—as the transparent recording of observed, objective facts. In contrast, Clifford underscores that the contributors to *Writing Culture* begin:

---

[18] See Audra Simpson, "Why White People Love Franz Boas; or The Grammar of Indigenous Dispossession," in *Indigenous Visions: Rediscovering the World of Franz Boas*, ed. Ned Blackhawk and Isaiah Lorado Wilner (New Haven: Yale University Press, 2018), 166–81; Rosemary Lévy Zumwalt, *Franz Boas: Shaping Anthropology and Fostering Social Justice* (Lincoln: University of Nebraska Press, 2022); Williams, *Rethinking Race: Franz Boas and His Contemporaries* (Lexington: University of Kentucky Press, 1996).

[19] See, for example, Talal Asad (ed.), *Anthropology & the Colonial Encounter* (Atlantic Highlands: Humanities Press, 1973); Frederik Barth, Andre Gingrich, Robert Parkin, and Sydel Silverman, *One Discipline, Four Ways: British, German, French, and American Anthropology* (Chicago: University of Chicago Press, 2005); Stocking, Jr., *Race, Culture and Evolution* (Chicago: University of Chicago Press, 1968)

[20] To be fair, the writings of Boas along with later, detailed studies of his work and life reveal that he thought of the Indigenous people he studied as his teachers and that he had some awareness of the contextual, contingent, subjective nature of his findings and descriptions. Yet, Boas and his contemporaries never followed these insights as far as they might have. See Herbert Lewis, "Boas, Darwin, Science and Anthropology," *Current Anthropology* 42, no. 3 (2001): 381–406; Matti Bunzl, "Boas, Foucault, and the 'Native Anthropologist,'" *American Anthropologist* 106, no. 3 (2004): 435–42. James Clifford comments that the 1967 publication of Malinowski's Mailu and Trobriand diaries "publically upset the applecart" that took objectivity for granted: "Henceforth an implicit mark of interrogation was placed beside any overly confident and consistent ethnographic voice. What desires and confusions was it smoothing over? How was its 'objectivity' textually constructed." "Introduction," *Writing Culture*, 14.

not with participant-observation or with cultural texts (suitable for interpretation), but with writing, the making of texts. . . . The fact that [writing] has not until recently been portrayed or seriously discussed reflects the persistence of an ideology claiming transparency of representation and immediacy of experience. Writing reduced to method: keeping good field notes, making accurate maps, "writing up" results.[21]

Starting especially in the 1960s, scholars in fields such as cultural studies, critical theory, history, anthropology (e.g., Barthes, Bourdieu, Clifford, Foucault, Geertz, Marcus, Rabinow, Said) critically interrogate the view that writing is a mere tool in the objective task of creating accurate description. Clifford makes the contrast with earlier anthropology plain:

> [The contributors to *Writing Culture*] see culture as composed of seriously contested codes and representations: they assume that the poetic and the political are inseparable, that science is in, not above, historical and linguistic processes. They assume that academic and literary genres interpenetrate and that the writing of cultural descriptions is properly experimental and ethical. Their focus on text making and rhetoric serves to highlight the constructed, artificial nature of cultural accounts. It undermines overly transparent modes of authority, and it draws attention to the historical predicament of ethnography, *the fact that it is always caught up in the invention, not the representation, of cultures*. (Emphasis ours)[22]

Thus, a hallmark of both ethnographic and critical theory beginning in the 1970s is the radical explorations of the historical and social processes involved in the construction of knowledge.

> Anthropology no longer speaks with automatic authority for others defined as unable to speak for themselves ("primitive," "pre-literate," "without history"). . . . Cultures do not hold still for their portraits. Attempts to make them do so always involve simplification and exclusion, selection of a temporal focus, the construction of a particular self-other relationship, and the imposition or negotiation of a power relationship.[23]

The curtain concealing the wizard is pulled back. Omniscient vantage points were discovered to be limited in their scope after all. If subjective, partial visions in a given ethnography try to mask themselves as objective and/or complete, they are quickly exposed in scholarly exchanges.

In all, *Writing Culture* made a significant intervention in the assumptions and practices of ethnography. It prompted a series of vigorous discussions and debates

---

[21] James Clifford, "Introduction," in *Writing Culture: The Poetics and Politics of Ethnography*, ed. George Marcus and James Clifford (Berkeley: University of California Press, 1986), 2.
[22] Ibid., 2.
[23] Ibid., 10.

related to race, gender, privilege, and class. Indeed, it was quickly followed by a third key development—both critical and creative.

Two years after its publication, feminist theorist Deborah Gordon[24] published the first feminist response to *Writing Culture*, and bell hooks contributed a substantive and provocative critique in 1990.[25] Ruth Behar and Deborah Gordon subsequently published a thought-provoking collection of essays entitled *Women Writing Culture* (1995) partly as a response to its shortcomings and blind spots. All call attention to the lack of serious engagement with feminism (even as this is weakly justified in the introduction) and with white privilege.

Behar begins her rigorous critique by first acknowledging the weighty significance of *Writing Culture*. She credits its publication with demolishing the realist tradition and setting off a wave of debates that forever changed American anthropology: "[N]ever before had the power of anthropological rhetoric been subjected to such keen and sophisticated textual analysis, extinguishing any remaining sparks of the presumption that ethnographies were transparent mirrors of culture."[26] This self-awareness is a major contribution and one that we carry forward as fundamental to efforts to represent others faithfully within the domains of theology and Christian ethics.

However, as Behar and others explore in greater depth, it is both ironic and disappointing that Clifford and Marcus failed to acknowledge both the contributions of feminism to anthropology and the way *Writing Culture* reinscribes authority and inequalities along the very gender and racial lines that it seeks to undermine. *Writing Culture* gives only a cursory reference to Margaret Mead, a prolific scholar, considered by many the most famous anthropologist of the twentieth century. And just as—if not more—troubling, it completely ignores the rich contributions to the history and practice of modern anthropology made by women such as Ruth Benedict, Zora Neale Hurston, and others along with male anthropologists of color such as Gilberto Freyre and Williams Jones. Thus, even as it acknowledges that social thought and culture are constructions, it continues a long history of building it in male, mostly white and/or European, terms. Behar sternly challenges the erasure of women and patriarchal canons:[27]

---

[24] See Deborah A. Gordon, "Writing Culture, Writing Feminism: The Poetics and Politics of Experimental Ethnography," *Inscriptions* 3/4 (1988): 7–24. See also Frances Mascia-Lees, et al., "The Postmodernist Turn in Anthropology: Cautions from a Feminist Perspective," *Signs* 15 (1989): 7–33.

[25] hooks, *Yearning* (Boston: South End Press, 1990), 123–33.

[26] Ruth Behar, "Introduction," in *Women Writing Culture*, ed. Ruth Behar and Deborah A. Gordon (Berkeley: University of California Press, 1995), 4. Behar continues:

> At the same time, the "new ethnography" was also expected to reflect a more profound self-consciousness of the working of power and partialness of all truth, both in the text and in the world. The "new ethnography" would not resolve the profoundly troubling issues of inequality in a world fueled by global capitalism, but at least it would seek to decolonize the power relations inherent in the representation of the Other.

[27] See also the searing challenge to the traditional anthropological canon by Kamala Visweswaran, "Defining Feminist Ethnography," in *Turning Points in Qualitative Research: Tying Knots in a Handkerchief*, ed. Yvonna S. Lincoln and Norman K. Denzin (Walnut Creek: AltaMira Press, 2003), 73–94.

Why is it that the legacy of what counts as social theory is traced back only to Lewis Henry Morgan, Karl Marx, Emilie Durkheim, Max Weber, Michel Foucault, and Pierre Bourdieu? ... Why is the culture concept in anthropology only traced through Sir Edward Tylor, Franz Boas, Bronislaw Malinowski, Claude Levi-Strauss, and Clifford Geertz? Could the writing of culture not be traced ... through Elise Clew Parsons, Ruth Benedict, Margaret Mead, Ella Deloria, Zora Neale Hurston, Ruth Landes, and Barbara Myerhoff to Alice Walker?[28]

The irony is that had Clifford and other contributors explored this history, they would have found that lighter and darker-skinned women along with a few men had begun to question and resist realist assumptions back in the era of Boas, Malinowski, and Evans-Pritchard. Moreover, these early scholars had long experimented with creative blendings of genres (e.g., personal diaries, fictional novels, poetry, ethnographic field notes, autobiography) long before it became *en vogue* within mainstream academic anthropology to question the rigid divisions among them.

Another level of serious critique shifted attention away from words as representation to zero in on the power of image. Specifically, both Gordon and bell hooks take Clifford and Marcus to task for their choice of cover image that makes a white male ethnographer (one of the contributors to the book working in the field) the center with a darker-skinned man off to the side, possibly observing the ethnographer in the act of writing. In addition, the cover text literally writes over the image of a darker-skinned woman and small child relegated—nearly obscured—to the edge of the frame. hooks pointedly asks: "Why does this cover doubly annihilate the value of the brown female gaze, first by the choice of picture where the dark woman is in the shadows, and secondly by a demarcating line?"[29] For Gordon and hooks, the cover image visualizes blind spots found in the written text, meaning the relative absence of perspectives of darker-skinned people and the general lack of robust engagement with feminist insights and contributions.[30] hooks laments:

> Despite the new and different directions charted in this collection, it was disappointing that black people were still being "talked about," that we remain an absent presence without voice. . . . [The editors] give no attention . . . to anthropologists/ethnographers in the United States who are black. . . . [This collection] in no way challenges the assumption that the image/identity of the ethnographer is white and male.[31]

---

[28] Behar, "Introduction," 12. See also Ibid., 17–20.
[29] hooks, *Yearning*, 127.
[30] Only one woman (white) contributed to the volume, and she did not draw upon feminist analyses. Two darker-skinned men contributed to it. Deborah Gordon, bell hooks, and Ruth Behar all note, and then roundly criticize, Clifford's weak acknowledgment of the lack of engagement with feminism in his introduction. However, hooks goes on to explain how disconcerting it is that the editors think to offer an explanation for a lack of feminist contributions, but do not even think to comment on the lack of scholarship and contributions by Black anthropologists and other dark-skinned scholars. See hooks, *Yearning*, 126–7. To be fair to the editors and contributors of *Writing Culture*, much of their subsequent work shows they took the critiques seriously and continued to reflect on them.
[31] hooks, *Yearning*, 126.

In short, hooks and Gordon, while acknowledging that the contributors problematize ethnographic authority, expose colonialization, and call attention to the textual form of ethnography and its inherently constructed and subjective nature, they identify important limits. Even as it makes a vital contribution to scholarship, taken as a whole, *Writing Culture* nonetheless reflects and reinforces common engendered and racial presumptions embedded within Western academic notions of authority, authorship, and scholarship.

Such problems endure. In a wonderfully provocative 2014 chapter, Japanese American practical theologian Courtney T. Goto calls out white academics for being given the microphone to speak of central issues in the field while scholars of color and others from minoritized positionalities are relegated to speaking and writing primarily on the subject areas related to this marginalization. Goto asks us collectively as scholars to question and critique the "division of labor that implies and reinforces an assumption that those with power and privilege in the field speak about what is privileged (often without realizing that the field itself and they are in fact privileged), while those who are historically marginalized address what is often treated as marginal."[32]

To summarize, critical theories—found in some white feminism and especially in scholarship by theorists of color (e.g., Collins, Conquergood, hooks, LaDuke, Pui-Lan, Trinh, Spivak, T. West)—not only deconstruct others' efforts who fail to take gender, race, and colonialism seriously, they break new ground from which all scholars stand to benefit. The foundational essays collected in *Women Writing Culture* and in *Turning Points in Qualitative Research* exemplify the rich and renewing theoretical and practical insights that are needed to keep ethnography (and theology and ethics) relevant and accountable. In particular, they concretize what self-critical awareness and collaboration mean for ethnography. Such contributions are discussed below following a brief explanation of how we employ the term ethnography in this 2024 volume.

A Renewed Working Definition of Ethnography

Countless works in anthropology and sociology, along with increasing numbers of works in Christian theology and ethics, unpack in various ways the root definition of ethnography as writing culture: *ethno* (culture) and *graphy* (writing). Rather than compare and contrast them, we wish to share the sense of the term that has come to inform our work. In doing so, we want to underscore two things: first, the active, necessarily imperfect and yet potentially revelatory process of meaning-making; and second, ethnography as a process with distinct and disciplined aspects that together contribute to its particular character.

To begin, it is helpful to conceive of ethnography less as a tool, product, thing, or even research strategy and more as a dynamic process of meaning-making that

---

[32] Courtney T. Goto, "Writing in Compliance with the Racialized 'Zoo' of Practical Theology," in *Conundrums in Practical Theology*, ed. Joyce Ann Mercer and Bonnie Miller-McLemore (Leiden: Brill, 2017), 111.

is inherently intertwined with power dynamics. Clifford contends: "Ethnography is actively situated between powerful systems of meaning. It poses its questions at the boundaries of civilizations, cultures, classes, races, and genders. Ethnography decodes and recodes, telling the grounds of collective order and diversity, inclusion and exclusion. It describes innovation and structuration, and is itself part of these processes."[33] Ethnography does not stand wholly outside that which it explores—it itself and its narrative is also part of the inquiry. Thus, it and the ethnographer need to interrogate themselves as much as they seek to learn from the people with whom a study is undertaken. Indeed, there is an inescapable dimension of vulnerability in qualitative research—often most acutely born by the people being studied. Yet, if it is done well, the researcher is vulnerable as well.

Before elaborating further our understanding of ethnography, we (Vigen and Scharen) first need to complexify our prior discussion of representation. In the 2011 edition, the predominant focus was exploring how those in relative privilege (racially, religiously, culturally, socioeconomically) could learn from and, as we put it then, "give voice" to those who are too often silenced. This emphasis aligns with what Boopalan and Jongte call for in Chapter 6 in terms of ethnography rooting itself in the lives, experiences, needs, and wounds of "crucified bodies." Yet, to this, we want to add that, as others have made clear, researchers do not actually "give voice" to others. Informants and collaborators—whoever they are—already have their own agency. Rather, we/they learn from others, share their voices, and amplify them as best we can—especially in more dominant circles who have not yet heard or understood the wisdom they embody and speak.

Furthermore, it is not sufficient to imagine or suggest that researchers are complete outsiders to the contexts/people they/we seek to engage. Some turn the focus onto communities/families with whom they closely relate to or identify with in important ways. AnneMarie Mingo's chapter in Part II is an example. For her part, Nicole Symmonds, also in this volume, shares some of what she learns—about herself and her informants by "studying up." This kind of study entails research not with peoples who are marginalized with respect to a predominant culture, but rather, with those who have significant power via race, class, religious, political identifications.

Moreover, the 2011 volume did not sufficiently interrogate assumptions related to "outsider" versus "insider" status. In all kinds of complicated ways, researchers embody some of both facets, to varying degrees. There are advantagess and limits no matter how much or how little qualitative scholars personally identify with the subjects and the contexts they study. Scholars who are primarily outsiders may well misunderstand, misinterpret, and mistranslate what they see, hear, and observe. On the other hand, those who share strong affinities with the context/people may take too much assumed knowledge and familiarity for granted and miss being surprised and corrected by what is actually said, done, felt, witnessed. As Hoskins underscores in Part II, even when studying a people and neighborhood one grew up in, as soon as you become a researcher, you are always at least a bit on the outside, necessarily so, and it is important to respect the distance. Grigoni found himself relating to and identifying with in complex ways both to gun owners and to those keeping vigil for the victims of gun violence.

---

[33] Clifford, "Introduction," 2–3.

With these nuances in mind, we understand ethnography as a process of attentive study of, and learning from, people—their words, practices, traditions, experiences, memories, insights—in particular times and places in order to understand how they make meaning (cultural, religious, moral) and what they can teach us about reality, truth, beauty, moral responsibility, the divine. The aim is to understand what God, human relationships, and the world look like from their perspective—to take them seriously as a source of wisdom and to decenter our assumptions and evaluations. By decentering, we mean that while it is impossible (and not desirable) to cast off completely our own views and values as researchers and as people of faith, it *is* both possible and helpful to put them off to the side in order to focus on the stories, perspectives, and lived realities of others—who may or may not share the lenses we bring or the positionalities we embody.

Said differently, and in contrast to quantitative research, ethnography utilizes primarily an inductive method, which means rather than apply a broad principle to a concrete situation, it seeks to discover what valuable insight is found within specific locations—discovered in communal and individual stories, cultures, practices, and experiences. Ethnographic methods provide a path *by which* truth emerges, rather than a way to apply truth. The researcher assumes the posture of a learner who wants to be taught rather than that of an expert who possesses the crucial theory for analyzing what is going on or what is "really real."

To be sure, it is exceedingly difficult to put one's assumptions and lenses aside and be truly open to rethinking and questioning what we think we know—to be genuinely surprised by what we learn. Sociologist Gerardo Martí underscores how easy it is to mix together our own (imposed) theologies as scholars/of faith and frameworks while claiming they were "found" in the contextual site and cautions against unwittingly imposing one's own filters and theology onto a specific context.[34] As he puts it, "Showing up to observe and taking notes is not enough"[35] to safeguard against these tendencies. Martí urges theologians and ethicists to cultivate specific sociological habits and sensitivities to avoid the temptation to heavy-handedly construct frameworks, meanings, and close gaps with our own "preheld schemas." In her chapter, Hoskins illustrates this point exactly by interrogating the preponderance of characterizations by outsiders with respect to those living in environmentally unjust contexts with language that casts them as "suffering victims," a numerical death toll in a tragic play.

Tools and Values

It is true that when some use the term "ethnography" they have a specific method in mind—long-term (a year or more) immersion in a place/community/culture and

---

[34] See the conversation on this point between Todd Whitmore and Gerardo Martí: Marti, "Ethnography as a Tool for Genuine Surprise: Found Theologies Versus Imposed Theologies," in *The Wiley Blackwell Companion to Theology and Qualitative Research*, ed. Pete Ward and Knut Tveitereid (Hoboken: John Wiley & Sons, Ltd, 2022); T. Whitmore, "Bringing the Mess That is Life into Theology: The Representational Task of Ethnography," *Ecclesial Practices* 8, no. 2 (2021): 142–64.

[35] Martí, "Ethnography as a Tool for Genuine Surprise," 472.

extensive data collection through various means. For our part, we use "ethnography" as a shorthand for a range of qualitative research methods. Since the 2011 publication, the variety of kinds of ethnographic studies and methods continues to grow within theology, ethics, and religious studies.

Ethnographers across disciplines continue to draw upon multiple research tools in their work (e.g., participant observation, focus groups, individual interviews, participatory action research, autoethnography, visual ethnography, varied kinds of collaborative research, extended immersion within a particular culture or community). We will not attempt to outline all of the possible qualitative strategies to utilize; others have described these in detail, and we commend them to interested readers as logistical and strategic guides (see Part III: Method). Having said that, at the most basic level, we urge all considering ethnographic projects to do a thorough literature review of research methods so that one has a clear sense of the resources, collaborators, and particular tools that will be most helpful and needed. And it goes without saying that Institutional Review Board approval will almost always be needed so the time to work through the exams, protocols, and approval process must also be figured into the equation.

Here we wish to highlight central features of ethnographic methods that are integral to responsible research. These qualities are glimpsed in four adjectives: humble, reflexive, collaborative, and audacious. What follows is a succinct discussion of what is most important to us in understanding and incorporating ethnography—its value and key qualities that ought to characterize any ethnographic research endeavor.

Humility amid Sustained, Attentive and Careful Observation

The first, and perhaps most fundamental, ingredient necessary for successful and enlightening ethnographic research is a genuine spirit of openness to what others know and live. A posture of humility and friendly curiosity are crucial character traits of a skilled and responsible ethnographer. Ethnographic researchers must not come into the work assuming they are the experts; rather, they need an ardent desire to learn and to be taught by others who often possess very different kinds of knowledge and expertise. As in 2011, Part II features exemplars who embody this commitment.

Undeniably, such a posture can be challenging to assume for academics and professionals who are understandably invested in their identities as "scholar, Ph.D., MD, leading authority, Reverend." Indeed, we spend significant years and financial resources precisely on becoming experts! Similarly, many pursue our professions because we enjoy and have discernible gifts for teaching others. So, it makes sense if the idea of relinquishing this status of teacher and expert—or at least loosening our grasp of it (after working so hard to achieve it)—chafes a bit. And as Hankela and Nishimwe model in Chapter 5, there is absolutely a constructive place for more experienced scholars to mentor those newer to the work and profession.

To be clear, we do not wish to suggest that a scholar or professional renounces or erases what one knows or has endeavored to master through study and training. Central pieces of this learning become part of who we are, and it would be both impossible and foolish to attempt to divorce ourselves from it. Ethnographic work involves both subjective and objective dimensions and also inductive and deductive modes of inquiry. This observation means that researchers cannot become (nor need to be) completely "blank slates." We may well bring some (relatively limited) assumptions, understandings, and particular commitments to the ethnographic field. The critical question is whether we are both honest and transparent about them *and also* genuinely willing to test them—open them to being altered and even disproved by what we learn through the research. In other words, we need to identify in a self-conscious way the subjective posture we bring with us to the field.[36] And we need to test our subjective convictions and responses by what we learn—especially that which catches us off guard. In short, new breakthroughs in understanding can happen when we put to the side "what we think we know" in order to discover what we do not. Being open to surprises and complications enriches both our knowledge base as researchers and subsequently any analyses or prescriptions we may offer up for public consideration.

Scholarly humility is also needed in terms of the scope of what we claim to know or describe. Even with intensive and prolonged ethnographic research, we never arrive at full or complete understandings of a particular situation or the lives of others. Clifford remarks on the liberation possible once we acknowledge our limits in knowing or discovering the truth:

> In cultural studies at least, we can no longer know the whole truth, or even claim to approach it. The rigorous partiality I have been stressing here may be a source of pessimism for some readers. But is there not a liberation, too, in recognizing that no one can write about others any longer as if they were discrete objects or texts? And may not the vision of a complex, problematic, partial ethnography lead, not to its abandonment, but to more subtle, concrete ways of writing and reading, to new conceptions of culture as interactive and historical?[37]

While Clifford is speaking in terms of cultural theory and anthropology, we see a connection to theology. For us, all theology represents human (and thus inherently finite) attempts to know the infinite. Moreover, human beings, albeit imperfectly, are incarnate images of God (*imago dei*). Consequently, just as we cannot ever claim to know completely the transcendent God, we cannot ever claim final or complete knowledge of one another.

As Knut Tveitereid puts it, "qualitative research is at its best when it investigates moving targets, and lived theology is in many ways a moving target–negotiated, expressed, ambivalent, inspired, and practiced."[38] Theologians and ethicists doing qualitative work are *decidedly not* studying preserved specimens under a microscope

---

[36] Clifford remarks: "Since Malinowski's time, the 'method' of participant-observation has enacted a delicate balance of subjectivity and objectivity. The ethnographer's personal experiences, especially those of participation and empathy, are recognized as central to the research process, but they are firmly restrained by the impersonal standards of observation and 'objective' distance." Clifford, "Introduction," 13.

[37] Ibid., 25.

[38] Knut Tveitereid, "Lived Theology and Theology in the Lived," in *The Wiley Blackwell Companion to Theology and Qualitative Research*, ed. Pete Ward and Knut Tveitereid (Hoboken: John Wiley & Sons, Ltd, 2022), 69.

or mounted on a wall. Instead, the aim is to learn from and with living, breathing, dynamic people, actions, beliefs, places, and moral questions. We can discover real and relevant truth—about God, creation, human beings—through ethnographic study. And in many cases this truth is transformative. But it is never perfect or all-encompassing. Thus, even as we will hopefully gain significant insight through ethnographic study, we never come to "own," "possess," or "master" the subjects or material. Rather, it is more apt to say that we continually deepen our awareness and awe of all that we do not know *and also* of our profound indebtedness to those who teach and collaborate with us.

Reflexivity: Self-Critical Awareness and Accountability

Intimately related to the virtues of humility and sincerity in learning from the lives and wisdom of others is the courageous willingness to being changed by what one sees, hears, learns, and observes. Reflexivity means that the researcher is willing to look honestly at one's self—location, filters, biases. And it is needed at *every* stage of the research and writing process. Critical self-reflection involves taking a hard look at one's own assumptions. It means genuinely being open to surprise. Simply put, ethnographers must be profoundly committed to learning from research collaborators and informants. Doing so may very well mean altering one's research (questions, focus, etc.) to take into account what one is learning and to candidly report data— especially when it does not line up with what one expected to find. This self-critical and reflexive process continues well beyond the point of the research project itself, even after any publication. Formative works by Fulkerson, Spradley, Swinton, Vigen, Ward, Whitmore, among others, all underscore this point.

Since 2011, several leading scholars, for example, Dreyer, Green, González-Justiniano, Goto, Hunter-Bowman, Kaufman, T. West, and Wigg-Stevenson, have all contributed significantly to discussions and understanding of reflexivity. For example, Tone Stangeland Kaufman details the many layers of reflexivity needed (relational, epistemological, sociological) in order to attend as comprehensively as possible to our "default modes" as researchers and to make any implicit theological/moral norms we bring to the work explicit.[39] Another way of thinking about this is to intentionally attend to what one considers "intuitive" and to seek out the "counterintuitive." And here emotions and bodily responses can lead researchers to important insights if they take the time to attend to them.[40]

Through working directly with Colombians for nearly ten years on peace efforts, white US Christian ethicist Janna Hunter-Bowman has learned that a researcher's

---

[39] Tone Stangeland Kaufman, "Practicing Reflexivity: Becoming Aware of One's Default Mode and Developing an Epistemic Advantage," in *The Wiley Blackwell Companion to Theology and Qualitative Research*, ed. Pete Ward and Knut Tveitereid (Hoboken: John Wiley & Sons, Ltd, 2022), 114–15.

[40] Traci C. West, *Solidarity and Defiant Spirituality: Africana Lessons on Religion, Racism, and Ending Gender Violence* (New York: New York University Press, 2019), 20 and Natalie Wigg-Stevenson on the affective in her book *Transgressive Devotion: Theology as Performance Art* (London: SCM Press, 2021).

"positionality affects all aspects from the research process"[41]—including our bodies, emotions, affects, and commitments. Yet, she also warns researchers of attending to self-reflexivity in individualistic, even insular and lonely ways. She asks: "Are there exercises of self-reflexivity that do not turn our eye from corporate ways of knowing and living?"[42] In response to her own question, she points to the use of decolonial participant research models found in Latin America and elsewhere that focus on intentional accompanying people—living and working in collaboration for an extended period of time and bearing witness to how participants claim and exert their agency and identity even in contexts of great duress.

Of particular note, Black feminist Christian ethicist Traci C. West, who offers the incisive Foreword to this volume, takes great care in her own work to ponder how intersectional, interreligious, and intercultural layers of power and assumptions inform relationships and knowledge claims. Specifically, over the course of seven years and engaging with 180 individuals, including dozens of activist leaders in three very different contexts (Brazil, Ghana, South Africa), West learned about distinct forms of gender violence and antiviolence activism. Her expansive, cutting-edge transnational research shows how such aggression is shaped in complicated and diverse ways by particular cultural, racial, and religious dynamics. She intentionally does not ask the exact same questions in each place/interview. Nor is she seeking a universalized understanding of gender violence or of religion. She understands that religion is often a root cause of gender violence and yet she, in dialogue with others, searches out examples and ways it may be part of remediation and healing.

What stands out especially in West's method is her ability, as a Black Christian from the United States to elucidate colonial, white supremacist and Christian logics that so profoundly shape the US context and to construct intentionally a decolonial method in response. As West explains,

> the transnational nature of [my focus] involves resistance to the racialized and heteropatriarchal Christian values that American colonialism and chattel slavery helped to shape. But it also necessitates resistance to those values reproduced in newer, current forms of global neocolonialism and human trafficking, which continue to contribute to and uphold gender-based violence.[43]

In doing so, West is deeply aware of her own parochialisms given her specific positionality.

To practice this kind of self-awareness, West deftly pivots among elements of critique, self-reflexivity, and a focus on concrete actions/practices as she incorporates a variety of research methods (storytelling, Black feminist autoethnography,

---

[41] Janna L. Hunter-Bowman, "Representation and Intersectionality," in *The Wiley Blackwell Companion to Theology and Qualitative Research*, ed. Pete Ward and Knut Tveitereid (Hoboken: John Wiley & Sons, Ltd, 2022), 143. See also her book: *Witnessing Peace: Becoming Agents under Duress in Colombia* (New York: Routledge, 2022)
[42] Hunter-Bowman, "Representation and Intersectionality," 145.
[43] West, *Solidarity and Defiant Spirituality*, 13.

performative activist ethnography) in order to learn what leaders in these places might teach the United States about what to do in response to *our* enduring, systemic gender-based violence problem. Similarly, Goto asks researchers from relatively privileged positionalities (racially, culturally, socioeconomically) to reflect substantively on their *own* cultures and contexts. Context is not something to be "found" in the ethnographic site of study.[44] It comes with all the baggage the researchers innately bring with us/them.

Unfortunately, it remains all too possible for careless ethnographic work to become "pornographic" in that it serves only to objectify and profit from the act of sensationalistically narrating and exposing isolated parts of others' lives and personhoods. When this happens, it does textual, symbolic, epistemological, and quite tangible (financial, social, psychological) violence to the persons/communities it narrates. Such simplistic creations utterly fail to do justice to people's lives and perspectives. They are often found in forms of pseudo-journalism—problematic amalgamations of news and entertainment found in many popular media. For example, exposé programs and reality shows claim to show the "true" lives of people—unsolved mysteries, crimes, and sordid events. In actuality, they often (re)produce dangerous stereotypes and amount to little more than a circus show of gawking at the misfortunes, imperfections, and struggles of others. Meanwhile and notably off-camera, producers and directors rake in the profits from these shows that are fairly cheap to produce since they don't have to pay trained actors.

One final cautionary note: as emphasized above, vulnerability is an integral part of qualitative work. However, care must be taken so that it does not devolve into (re)centering one's own experiences, hurts, needs. When that happens, it can quickly become self-serving or even narcissistic. Traci West, drawing on Ruth Behar, emphasizes that the need for vulnerability on the part of the researcher is not a free pass for "anything personal goes."[45] Too often, those in power (in terms of race, gender, etc.) shift attention away from the people and acute issues at hand in order to expound upon themselves, which serves to re-center the researcher—turning them into the focus, even "hero" or "victim" of a romanticized tale. Elsewhere, Scharen shares his questions on how to avoid re-centering whiteness as one attempts anticolonial study.[46]

In summary, when ethnographic research lacks rigorous and sustained self-critical analysis it fails on at least two key levels: First, it does not create a complexified and multidimensional picture of "what is going on" and instead uses the ethnographic data simply to confirm its own assumptions (tautology). Thus, the quality and depth of the research suffers. For example, theologian Mary McClintock Fulkerson acknowledges that initially she did not grasp the intricacy of the dynamics at a congregation, Good Samaritan, because her "frame for thinking about what mattered was too

---

[44] Courtney T. Goto, *Taking on Practical Theology: The Idolization of Context and the Hope of Community* (Leiden: Brill, 2018).
[45] West, *Solidarity and Defiant Spirituality*, 18.
[46] Christian Scharen, "Fieldwork in White Theology," in *The Wiley Blackwell Companion to Theology and Qualitative Research*, ed. Pete Ward and Knut Tveitereid (Hoboken: John Wiley & Sons, Ltd, 2022).

intellectualistic to capture what seemed important to the community."[47] Her theoretical framing concealed more than it revealed.[48]

Second, it fails to hold the scholar accountable because it does not demand that the researcher locate themselves in the work or reflect on missteps, assumptions, surprises that foster new awareness and perspective. Moreover, without reflexivity, often there is no feedback loop in which the researcher wrestles with the person's or community's subsequent response to the work. Indeed, whenever possible, offering up what we write to those who have been so instrumental in the writing is imperative for the credibility and substance of the work itself. Doing so is crucial because scholars can make or advance careers on the basis of what others live. For example, anthropologist Paul Rabinow calls for critical explorations into the academic contexts ("how careers and made and destroyed") in which texts and truth claims are written and published.[49]

Even more pointedly, practical theologian Rachelle Green reflects on her deep desire to create a theology program informed by incarcerated women that is thoroughly informed and shaped by the "needs, hopes, and concerns of those living and surviving in prison." She continues: "I wanted to know what good theological education was in prison and what greater good it could become"—not good in terms of prison, not in terms of chaplaincy, not for seminaries—rather "good for people surviving incarceration."[50] Green worries that too often without such sustained commitments to deep listening and inclusive practices, academics will simply continue to create educational programs that serve needs other than those for whom the programs are actually intended, ending up, as she borrows from Paulo Freire, "teaching to the desert."[51]

In sum, researchers and scholars—by definition privileged—need to be upfront about the inequalities and sites of privilege that are present in any room where formal academic(s) come together with research subject(s). Moreover, we need to reflect deeply on how the scholarship is disseminated, shared, used—who reads it, what kinds of effects it has, and how the benefits might be shared beyond the scope of an

---

[47] Mary McClintock Fulkerson, *Places of Redemption: Theology for a Worldly Church* (New York: Oxford University Press, 2007), 10.

[48] The same thing happened with Renato Rosaldo and his effort to understand Ignot head-hunting. See "Grief and a Headhunter's Rage: On the Cultural Force of Emotions," in *Text Play, and Story: The Construction and Reconstruction of Self and Society* (Long Grove: Waveland Press, 1988), 178–95.

[49] Paul Rabinow writes: "My wager is that looking at the conditions under which people are hired, given tenure, published, awarded grants, and feted would repay the effort. . . . How are careers made now? How are careers destroyed now? . . . Whatever else we know, we certainly know that the material conditions under which the textual movement has flourished must include the university, its micropolitics, its trends. We know that this level of power relations exists, affects us, influences our themes, forms, contents, audiences. We owe these issues attention—if only to establish their relative weight." Paul Rabinow, "Representations are Social Facts: Modernity and Post-Modernity in Anthropology," in Marcus and Clifford, *Writing Culture*, 253–4.

[50] Rachelle Green, "Ethnography as Critical Pedagogy: Prisons, Pedagogy, and Theological Education," in *The Wiley Blackwell Companion to Theology and Qualitative Research*, ed. Pete Ward and Knut Tveitereid (Hoboken: John Wiley & Sons, Ltd, 2022), 38–9.

[51] Green, "Ethnography as Critical Pedagogy," 40–1.

individual's career/tenure record. Because we are the ones to present and publish others' accounts and gain materially from them, robust and multidimensional accountability is absolutely essential.

Collaborative: Pushing the Notion of Authorship

At its best, ethnographic work embodies a conversation among numerous and varied voices. Rather than simply presenting an individual's scholarly reflection or observations, it reflects an engaged dialogue with others.[52] In other words, it is participatory on a fundamental level. Ethnographic subjects *are not* objects of study, but rather collaborators—experts in their own right who have valuable knowledge that the ethnographer needs.[53]

This recognition points out the degree of respect and consideration owed to ethnographic subjects. They are not resources to be mined and then abandoned. Nor are they unreflective works of art to be interpreted and revealed by the scholarly gaze. Instead, they are, in a real sense, coauthors. Anthropologist Kamala Visweswaran comments on the significance of such a move in the way scholarship is conceived: "[W]hen the 'other' drops out of anthropology, becomes subject, participant, and sole author, not 'object' then . . . we will have established a 'hermeneutics of vulnerability' and an 'anthropology which calls itself into question.'"[54] Realizing intellectual and hermeneutic vulnerability exemplifies the kind of genuine reflexivity we value so highly.

Moreover, when this happens—when those who speak to ethnographers are no longer considered simply resources to be explored (or worse exploited)—then, as Clifford notes, all kinds of new questions emerge. "Once 'informants' begin to be considered as co-authors, and the ethnographer as scribe and archivist as well as interpreting observer, we can ask new, critical questions of all ethnographies."[55] For example, what might it mean for ethnographers not to narrate or represent others, but instead create a space for collaborators and informants to speak in their own voices—represent themselves? Visweswaran rightly notes: "If we have learned anything about anthropology's encounter with colonialism, the question is not really whether

---

[52] Clifford explains:

> Dialogical modes . . . need not lead to hyper self-consciousness or self-absorption. . . . [D]ialogical processes proliferate in any complexly represented discursive space. . . . Many voices clamor for expression. Polyvocality was restrained and orchestrated in traditional ethnographies by giving to one voice a pervasive authorial function and to others the role of sources, "informants," to be quoted or paraphrased. Once dialogism and polyphony are recognized as modes of textual production, monophonic authority is questioned, revealed to be characteristic of a science that has claimed to *represent* cultures. (Clifford, "Introduction," 15, emphasis in the original)

[53] Scharen discusses these issues in "Interviewing Interpreted as Spiritual Exercise and Social Protest," *Ecclesial Practices* 4, no. 2 (December 2017): 218–36.
[54] Visweswaran, "Defining Feminist Ethnography," 89.
[55] Clifford, "Introduction," 17.

anthropologists can represent people better, but whether we can be accountable to people's own struggles for self-representation and self-determination."[56]

As Green laments, "Too much research about incarcerated people has been performed for and not with the incarcerated."[57] As a partial way to correct this tendency, her team invited a wide range of knowledge mediums to the work—stories, semi-structured interviews, focus groups, and also drawings, music, homework, space for silence, classroom conversations—as the researchers sought to learn who God is and what the good life looks and feels like in prison and for these incarcerated women enrolled in the program. "Without an ongoing ethnographic commitment to understanding students' hopes for living and without proper knowledge of the systems that constrain life, theological education in prison risks becoming a teaching model that reinscribes systems of power and domination at its worst or becomes irrelevant, at its best."[58] Hoskins in Part II asks researchers and writers to consider carefully how they frame their subjects. Regardless of how good the intentions may be, they can still do violence to their subjects with two-dimensional characterizations.

When the scholar divests a bit from being the "author" and "expert," those from whom they learn are more likely to be rightly regarded as full human subjects, rather than as research objects. And when this happens, they do not merely inform the researcher about specific facts of their lives; instead, they can become witnesses to truth on a much more profound level. Similarly, ethnographers are not simply passive observers, they take on a witnessing role as well. Interestingly, as Gordon highlights the distinctive connotations of identifying ethnographers as "participant witnesses" rather than "participant observers," she invokes explicit theological language:

> Carrying a host of conflicting associations, including informant, litigant, function of the Holy Ghost, and spectator, a witness is less an observer than a teller—that is, one who translates what s/he sees and hears for an audience. . . . As an informant, the witness purposely informs or tells, with all of the potential for betrayal implied. Yet witnessing in the context of the Americas also brings to mind the long-standing indigenous tradition of personal testimony, with the witness calling up a broken humanity to redeem it. Characteristically, American traditions of African American preachers, Latin American human-rights activists, and the advocates for the poor continually reinvent stories of redemption through suffering to challenge social injustice. . . . In participant witnessing, the lines between ethnographer and informant blur as each hears the other in a way that encourages self-representation.[59]

Gordon's comments highlight two important things: First, ethnographic witnessing on the part of both the ethnographer and collaborator/informant can take on a normative quality in the sense that witnessing to human struggles can implicitly or explicitly

---

[56] Visweswaran, "Defining Feminist Ethnography," 89.
[57] Green, "Ethnography as Critical Pedagogy," 43.
[58] Ibid., 46.
[59] Deborah A. Gordon, "Border Work: Feminist Ethnography and the Dissemination of Literacy," in *Women Writing Culture*, ed. Ruth Behar and Deborah A. Gordon (Berkeley: University of California Press, 1995), 383.

carry an imperative to transform suffering into healing and well-being. Second, this kind of collaboration means that all involved attend to one another—hear one another into a fuller sense of being—and all participate in the resulting representation. The ethnographer is not the sole (or even primary) authority.

Gordon takes the notion of collaborative writing to a concrete level as she discusses specific projects that directly link academic with other community needs and goals. She lifts up the example of El Barrio, "a community-based program of action research initiated by the Center for Puerto Rican Studies at Hunter College" which operated from 1985 to 1989 in New York City.[60] This program combined an ethnographic, oral history project with empowering Latina women through literacy education.

The work of El Barrio testifies to the ways in which power and identity can shift through dialogue, joint writing, collaborative education, and the teaching of one another throughout. And even when joint writing is not desired or possible, research subjects and collaborators can offer vital insights and corrections through critiques of what the academic writes. Through this kind of partnering, while the power dynamics and inequalities between researchers and collaborators may be stark and tangible, they can also be dynamic (not static).

We perhaps did not highlight sufficiently the varied kinds of collaborative research in the 2011 edition. Related models with specific, distinct emphases include ethnography as: Participatory Action Research and Community Action (Browning, Dreyer, Fals Borda, Hall,[61] Hunter-Bowman, Swinton), Action Research (Idestrom), Theological Action Research (Cameron, Watkins), Community Organizing (Crowser), and Critical Pedagogy (Green). Henk de Roest published a helpful work on detailing kinds of collaborative research in practical theology and summarizes eight strong rationales for this kind of work.[62] Together, these models push qualitative research to do more than consult people/communities from and with whom they hope to learn. Instead, the research questions and actions are decided upon together. The collaborators are active in designing, doing, and reflecting on the work. They own it as much as any formal researcher.

It is this quality that I (Vigen) found lacking in my work on reproductive justice and reproductive genetics. As a white scholar with job security, I ultimately decided that anything I might have to offer on this topic needs to be cultivated through more robust collaboration and co-authorship with others, especially women and professionals of color. And in such a method, I don't have an inherent right to claim primary authorship of any work that is produced from it.

To be sure, this degree of collaborative work is challenging in an academic culture that demands efficiency and that prizes solo-authored works. Those with job and financial security in their disciplines can and need to do more to work in genuinely

---

[60] Ibid., 377.
[61] See, for example, O. Fals-Borda, "The Application of Participatory Action-Research in Latin America," *International Sociology* 2, no. 4 (1987): 329–47; Budd Hall, "In from the Cold? Reflections on Participatory Research from 1970–2005," *Convergence* 38 (2005): 5–24; Henk de Roest, "Collaborative Research," in *The Wiley Blackwell Companion to Theology and Qualitative Research*, ed. Pete Ward and Knut Tveitereid (Hoboken: John Wiley & Sons, Ltd, 2022), 437
[62] de Roest, "Collaborative Research," 438–9; Henk de Roest, *Collaborative Practical Theology: Engaging Practitioners in Research on Christian Practices* (Leiden/Boston: Brill, 2019).

collaborative ways than we often have. We have less to lose and we owe it to those from and with whom we learn. For those who do not have job security, in the form of tenure or otherwise, it is a tall order. Still, we invite readers to think creatively and boldly in designing their research approach.

In all, authentic collaboration means that ethnographers are accountable to those from whom they learn and that they ought—whenever possible—to show them what they write, or discuss their writing and conclusions with them, and so on. There ought to be some kind of feedback loop so that informants and collaborators know what becomes of their stories—what is written, discussed, produced. They may not like or agree with the researcher's narrative, but they should at least have some kind of opportunity to know what it is and to respond to it. Indeed, being an attentive and empathetic listener does not mean the researcher has to endorse the views of those with whom they learn. Rather, they need to represent the views and people as fully and honestly as possible. The researcher may or may not amend what they create. Regardless, they/we have a responsibility to be aware of it and to acknowledge areas of (dis)agreement.

Audacity: Efforts at Pragmatic Solidarity

Undeniably, there is a potent danger—and an visible track record—of academics (especially white, Western) aiding colonialist and/or patronizing forces as they naively attempt to "save" or "liberate" people whose intellect, religious and cultural commitments, and agency they underestimate (or disrespect). The methodological steps related to humility, reflexivity, and collaboration might help to avoid such problematic outcomes and processes. Assiduously attending to these safeguards, theologians and ethnographers might then find a measure of appropriate audacity. Illuminative ethnography often requires that the researcher be bold enough to claim that the work reveals truth—albeit partial—but nonetheless real and significant.

Even more, this kind of revelation is not only mystical, theoretical or abstract; it is embodied in tangible practices and iinterventions in the way things are. Speaking truth involves pragmatic solidarity with those who suffer or are too often rendered invisible by the power structures of the world. Carrying forward commitments to liberationist methods, Boopalan and Jongte argue in their chapter that sustained attention to "crucified bodies" remains essential in the twenty-first century. For her part, Fitriyah shows how listening to Indonesian migrant workers nuances how liberation, survival, faith in the divine, and thriving are experienced and understood by these women. Research that hopes to be both relevant and to speak truth must consider the priorities and needs of the communities with which it hopes to work. And it must do so without falling into the traps of voyeurism, saviorism, and simplistic characterizations.

Behar comments that the kind of dynamic, illuminative work such as that in El Barrio shows how "collaborative texts can be created when ethnographic research takes place within community agendas. Sharing privilege, sharing literacy, sharing information—which in our world is power—is one way for feminist relationships in postcolonial conditions of inequality to bridge the gaps between women in the academy and women in ethnic communities."[63] This kind of endeavor exemplifies what we mean by pragmatic solidarity.[64] A genuinely humble, reflexive, and collaborative ethnographic process means that research agendas ought to be integrally linked to community-expressed needs.

To illustrate, Gordon puts the success and significance of El Barrio in these terms:

> The centerpiece of the El Barrio project, one critical in any discussion of feminist ethnography, is research that attempts to redistribute educational privilege. That redistribution is centered in teaching critical rather than function literacy.... Life histories were collected by teaching women participants to write in a way that changed their sense of self and led to collective empowerment. For example, as women reinterpreted their lives through the life-history process, they become more willing to resist welfare workers.[65]

While it is not always so, qualitative research, especially when it takes concerted efforts to be reflective, anticolonial, and intersectional, can be transformative. As Traci West puts it so well: "We desperately need daring moral imaginations to ignite more culturally nuanced understandings and reject self-congratulatory satisfaction with our inadequate remedies."[66] At the least, such work can be a vehicle for positive change.[67] With careful methodological attention and accompanied by appropriate humility, ethnographic study can contribute to the material, psychological, spiritual, and social flourishing of individuals and communities.

To be sure, it may not realize such goals (and at worst, it could obstruct them). Yet, the point is that a scholar's research agenda ought to connect with, perhaps prioritize, the "on the ground" needs and challenges a particular community faces. This commitment is poignantly expressed in the vibrant life and fierce work of Melissa D. Browning[68] and in the varied contributions in Part II.

---

[63] Behar, "Introduction," 21.
[64] Gordon explains why pragmatic solidarity is of such great importance:

> [O]riginal ways of conceiving experimental ethnography may be lost if feminist ethnography simply means more academic books rather than material dispersion of authorship. Feminist experimentalism with ethnography will be impoverished without sustained reflection on how to mix sociological, political-economic, and historical analysis as well as policy recommendations such that women historically excluded from higher education gain from its material resources. (Gordon, "Conclusion: Culture Writing Women: Inscribing Feminist Anthropology," in *Women Writing Culture*, ed. Ruth Behar and Deborah A. Gordon (Berkeley: University of California Press, 1995), 432)

[65] Gordon, "Border Work," 378.
[66] West, *Solidarity and Defiant Spirituality*, 4.
[67] The tradition of "action research" is but one specific means toward this end. See, for example, the cutting-edge work on display in Helen Cameron, et al., *Talking About God In Practice: Theological Action Research and Practical Theology* (London: SCM Press, 2010).
[68] See Melissa D. Browning's ethnographic research focusing upon women and HIV/AIDS in sub-Saharan Africa in anthologies and journal issues (2011 and 2012).

Conclusion

Pragmatically, these four qualities translate into significant time and effort spent listening, looking, and taking detailed notes—without coming to conclusions prematurely. The initial stages, that can last several months or longer, involve writing down and reflecting on as much as possible—before knowing fully what will evolve into central insights or pivotal turning points. Thus, the ability to ask good—evocative—questions is essential. Sometimes ethnographers grope for questions—stumble around to find the right phrasing that gets at the matter, speak to the person's experience, and cultivate a sense of rapport and shared understanding. Yet, we are convinced that this awkwardness is necessary because it can be a way for researchers to embody imperfection and to find keys to understanding what they previously did not. When others witness the researcher being a human being, rather than an expert—complete with flaws and humor—they are often more likely to trust the person and share more of what they have come to know.

Indeed close, attuned observation and the meticulous recording of data are the bread and butter of both quantitative and qualitative methods. The difference in ethnographic/qualitative methods is that the researcher does not stand as far apart from the research subject or assume the same kind of objectivity. Rather, the ethnographer owns their assumptions, biases, hopes, and concerns as part of the process. This quality is discussed above in terms of reflexivity.

It takes significant patience and discipline to get past the surface of things in ethnographic research. Ethnographers who are in too much of a hurry often frustrate their own efforts—people don't like to be pressured into self-revelation, and they have little reason to trust those who seem only interested in "getting the goods" and moving on. Moreover, there is often significant uncertainty over what "the goods" are. It takes significant time (often a year or more) to learn what the actual issues, questions, and themes are. Seeking to explicate this dimension of the "untimeliness" of ethnography, Paul Rabinow contrasts journalism, investigating and writing on a publishing deadline, with the open-ended practice of ethnographic research.[69]

Being in a hurry often means that the researcher only wants confirmation of what they think they know—of the themes and issues already chosen as foundational. Proceeding in such a way leads to a tautological circle where one's assumptions substitute for the evidence needed to support them. The aim of ethnography is not merely to confirm or prove false one's hypothesis or theoretical claim. Rather, it is to learn from the scene itself—to let the questions and knowledge bubble up from the situation—to get a deep reading of what is there—on its own terms.

Of course, at the outset, the research will likely need some kind of map. We do not recommend that anyone begin research with no sense of likely central questions and issues. What we wish to underscore is that the map probably needs to be written in pencil rather than indelible ink. It demands flexibility because ethnographers cannot fully predict where the research will take them.

---

[69] Paul Rabinow and George E. Marcus, et al., *Designs for an Anthropology of the Contemporary* (Durham: Duke University Press, 2008).

Finally, if it was true in 2011, it is even more so in this second volume: to do ethnographic work well requires apprenticeship. We are so grateful that in Part II Hankela and Nishimwe share so openly with us all their experience of mentoring and apprenticeship. And we are glad more graduate programs offer classes and mentors in qualitative methods than they did when we published the first edition. Yet, we invite more transdisciplinary collaboration and even more programmatic development so that students of theology and ethics who wish to embark upon a qualitative study can find the support, mentorship, classes, and intellectual community needed to do so.

This is our sense of the history, purpose, significance, and key features of ethnography as a research method as it has continued to evolve since 2011. In Chapter 4, we make a particular case for why and how ethnography can be at home within theology and ethics. But before we make that case, we need to trace two other histories. Chapter 2 charts the turn to ethnography in Christian theology up to the present, and then Chapter 3 engages, and responds to, some criticisms of such a move to depend upon social science theory and methods.

2

The Ethnographic Turn in Theology and Ethics

In response to a variety of critical intellectual currents, scholars in Christian theology and ethics are increasingly taking up the tools of ethnography as a means to ask fundamental theological and moral questions and to make more compelling and credible claims. Privileging particularity, rather than the more traditional effort to achieve universal or at least generalizable norms in making claims regarding the Christian life, echoes the most fundamental insight of the Christian tradition—that God is known most fully in Jesus of Nazareth. Echoing this "scandal of particularity" at the heart of the Christian tradition, theologians and ethicists involved in ethnographic research draw on the particular to seek out answers to core questions of their discipline: who is God and how do we become the people we are, how to conceptualize moral agency in relation to God and the world, and how to flesh out the content of conceptual categories such as justice that help direct us in our daily decisions and guiding institutions.

This perspective does not deny the possibility or credibility of larger moral claims that can cross contexts. Yet, it does argue that in order to make anything like generalized claims of what ought to be, Christian theologians and ethicists ought to start with the particular as integral to their methods of inquiry. In other words, before such scholars can state what is normative, they need to cultivate a "thick description" (Geertz) of what is real to and within concrete congregations and communities. Parallel circumstances in social theology and social science forced a new attention to particularity. Movements such as post-colonialism and postmodernism have expanded the breadth of acceptable sources for doing Christian theology and ethics and the desire to be accountable to those beyond the academy, especially the church—in terms of describing faithful discipleship—and those on the margins—in terms of listening to their voices rather than simply speaking about them or on their behalf.

Numerous avenues might be pursued that begin to show how scholars are responding to the shift to particularity, especially to those on the margins. Of course, the scholars whose work is featured in Part II of this volume represent one avenue. However, they primarily show their work in action rather than telling about the reasons and routes they followed in coming to such an ethnographic approach to theological and ethical research and writing. In this chapter, we point to a few trajectories that bear within them some of the reasons and persons relevant to the "turn" to ethnography in theology.

Trajectories

Mary McClintock Fulkerson, a professor emerita of theology at Duke University Divinity School, whose gracious foreword opened the first edition of this book, exemplifies this turn to ethnography in her own professional evolution. Her first major book, *Changing the Subject*, drew on critical social theory to elaborate a critique of feminist theology's "universalist" claims regarding women's experience. Arguing that the "female subject" is multiply constructed and plural, embodying complex and competing discourses, she seeks to "change the subject" so that such multiple subject positions are the basis for further theoretical work on difference and identity.[1]

Fulkerson's initial work in feminist theology and social and cultural theory led to her participation in a conference at the University of Chicago in 1997 seeking to more explicitly articulate the ways theologians were turning from philosophy or the history of ideas to culture as a primary conversation partner for their work. Fulkerson brought her ideas of complexity and hybridity to the study of the culture of a local congregation, Good Samaritan, where she had spent "two years of interviewing and observing participants."[2] Here, drawing on sociologist Pierre Bourdieu, she emphasizes the creative habituation of values of inclusion at the heart of the church's interracial identity. Yet rather than agree on some simple movement from belief and ritual to the formation of habits, she argues for a more open and contested notion of a "repertoire" available for the persons and community as they act out their life together.

By the time of Fulkerson's book-length analysis of this congregation, published in 2007 as *Places of Redemption*, she explicitly describes her fieldwork as ethnography, and begins the book recalling her ethnography class in which she gained the fieldwork practices by which she sought to "bring something fresh to theological reflection on ordinary Christian community."[3] She aims not for an "objective" analysis of the community (having, along with the postmodern anthropology she had read, given up on such an idea). Rather, she tried to do research and writing "adequate to the full-bodied reality that is Good Samaritan, one capable of displaying its ambiguity, its implication in the banal and opaque realities of ordinary existence, even as it allows for testimony to God's redemptive reality."[4]

While we can make some sense of this turn to ethnography in the trajectory of Fulkerson's public career, we can show with even more particularity how this turn took shape in our own lives drawing for the moment on the genre of autobiography. We describe how one of us (Scharen) became disaffected with theology and "crossed over" to be doubly trained—in social science as well as theology; how by doing so he hoped to correct the too idealized pictures theology consistently drew of church and

---

[1] Mary McClintock Fulkerson, *Changing the Subject: Women's Discourses and Feminist Theology* (Minneapolis: Fortress Press, 1994).
[2] Mary McClintock Fulkerson, "'We Don't See Color Here': A Case Study in Ecclesial-Cultural Invention," in *Converging on Culture: Theologians in Dialogue with Cultural Analysis and Criticism*, ed. Delwin Brown, Sheila Greeve Davaney, and Kathryn Tanner (New York: Oxford University Press, 2001), 140–57.
[3] Mary McClintock Fulkerson, *Places of Redemption: Theology for a Worldly Church* (New York: Oxford University Press, 2007)., 3.
[4] Fulkerson, *Places of Redemption*, 7.

the Christian life; and under the tutelage of mentors in sociology and anthropology, began a series of comparative ethnographic studies of worship and social ethics in urban congregations that took theology with great seriousness. These studies were eventually written up in a stuttering theological voice, a voice struggling to unite the conflictual pair he had grappled with from the start: theology and ethnography.[5] While his early work did not fully accomplish the hoped-for integration of the two, it did lead to developing a theological counterpart to the enormously fruitful proposal for, and embodiment of, an ethnographic approach called "carnal sociology" in the work of Pierre Bourdieu developed further in important ways by his student, Loïc Wacquant.

Positing that Bourdieu is right that "we learn by body" Scharen pursued studies that position the worshipper and, in a broader sense, the congregation as a whole not merely as objects to be understood, as perhaps a part of the burgeoning sociology or theology *of* the body, but also *from* the body, requiring submitting himself to the painful apprenticeship in context that allows forging the corporal and mental dispositions that make up the competent worshipper within the crucible of congregational life. A bodily submission, then, to the rigors of apprenticeship *in situ* becomes both the object and means of inquiry, opening, as Merleau-Ponty shows, access to sensory-motor, mental and social aptitudes—a corporal intelligence that tacitly guides "natives" to a particular "familiar universe."[6] It is, as Wacquant argues, a "mutual molding and immediate 'inhabiting' of being and world, carnal entanglement with a mesh of forces pregnant with silent summons and invisible interdictions that elude the scholastic distinction between subject and object as they work simultaneously from within, through the socialization of cognition and affect, and from without by closing and opening viable paths for action."[7] Such a "carnal sociology" transfigured into a "carnal theology" illumines dynamics at the heart of Christian faith, which one might gesture toward in a preliminary way through categories such as God's "in-dwelling," or perhaps better, "in-carnation."

On Crossing Hearst Avenue

Drawing on the genre of autobiography interspersed with elements of theory, theology, and reports from ethnographic fieldwork, we begin here with a brief version of how I (Scharen) came to the academic study of theology and social science. Prior to arriving in Berkeley, California, for master's studies in theology, I had been actively engaged for five years in ministries serving people without adequate shelter and living in under-resourced urban areas. This work began as part of a religious intensification during undergraduate studies, one that through a powerful experience of the college chapel life initiated me to a way of living the Eucharist as deeply intertwined with

---

[5] Christian Scharen, "Lois, Liturgy, and Ethics," *The Annual of the Society of Christian Ethics* 20 (2000): 275–305; Scharen, *Public Worship and Public Work: Character and Commitment in Local Congregational Life* (Collegeville: The Liturgical Press, 2004).

[6] M. Merleau-Ponty, *Phenomenology of Perception* (New York: Routledge, 1947/1962).

[7] Loïc Wacquant, "Carnal Connections: On Embodiment, Apprenticeship, and Membership," *Qualitative Sociology* 28, no. 4 (Winter 2005): 466.

questions of worldly justice. However, it took on full weight in a year spent as part of the Lutheran Volunteer Corps (LVC) sharing life and ministry with a Franciscan-based ministry with people experiencing homelessness near Philadelphia. In the late 1980s, the housing crisis had burgeoned under the weight of Reagan-era policies of deinstitutionalization of the mentally ill along with the scourge of crack cocaine that ravaged lives and spiked US incarceration rates. Nightly vigilance was required to keep the crack dealers off of the front steps.

During the year working in LVC, I was learning skills of liturgical leadership at a local Lutheran parish located in the city but as distant from the realities of my work in the homeless shelter as might be imagined. The intricacies of chant tones and properly assisting the lavabo after the offering, for example, seemed ridiculous at the time—examples of ritual for its own sake deeply disconnected from the context and its broken, plaintive cries. In part in an effort to cope with the screaming disjuncture of my daily existence, I began keeping a notebook of observations, reactions, and suppositions related to the daily occurrences, the coming and going of the men, the activity in the neighborhood, and my oscillation between the Lutheran congregation and the Franciscan house that served as home for two brothers and up to fourteen men. The liturgy of dignity eating hearty meals together around a dining room table, cooked and presided over by Fr. Hilary, seemed a much more profound embodiment of eucharistic hospitality than the stilted distribution of wafers and a small glass of overly sweet wine on Sunday mornings.

The initial move into seminary education then sought to interpret and understand the disjuncture between these various ritual experiences, some seeming to be springs of a way of understanding and action deeply connected to the cries of suffering and injustice in the world, and others seemingly asleep with dreams of individual peace and eternal reward. My sense then was that the world was on fire, that God was implicated deeply in the suffering, and the story of Jesus' body and blood "for us" meant our incorporation into the shape of that suffering love, working in solidarity with those most broken and in need as indeed God already was doing.

The influence of liberation and feminist theologies was also important, playing a role for those who desired to break out beyond the confines of cloistered classroom education to engage the streets, neighborhoods, and lives of the Bay area. However, as I progressed in my theological studies, simultaneously investing myself in a local congregation as an apprentice to a mentoring pastor, I found myself quite without tools for understanding the distinctiveness of what I was experiencing, or how to speak of the yawning gap between the thrilling intersection of vibrant communal worship and work for justice and the frankly boring recital of dry biblical, historical, and theological data seemingly hovering above history. This abstract theological material felt as if it was required for professional hazing; that is, required as much for its inscription of distinction—a class marker painfully achieved for those ascending to the pulpit and altar—as for any practical use in ministry.[8]

So I crossed over Hearst Avenue to study social science at UC Berkeley. One key intersection was with Robert Bellah. Trained at Harvard under Talcott Parsons

---

[8] Pierre Bourdieu, *Language and Symbolic Power* (Stanford: Stanford University Press, 1991), 123.

during the late 1940s and early 1950s, Bellah had by 1970 established himself as one of the leading sociologists of religion in the United States. His important collection of essays, *Beyond Belief*, was a sociological watershed on many fronts including classic arguments about civil religion in America and about religious evolution, the topic of his last major book.[9] *Beyond Belief* especially impressed me for its eloquent description of the "religious implications of social science" and Bellah's hoped-for "integration" or "open interchange" between the two leading to a much more powerful understanding of ourselves and the realities in which we live.[10] In the trajectory of his work, from early books on the role of religion in Japan's modernization to his major study of individualism in American culture, *Habits of the Heart*, the religious element of social science has mostly been evidenced in a powerful normative agenda funded by faith.[11] The appendix to *Habits*, titled "social science as public philosophy," argues that for social science to be good in a technical sense it must also be good in a moral sense, that is, seek to do good.

The other very significant early encounter in the social sciences was with anthropologist Paul Rabinow. Rabinow is widely known for his early works introducing Michel Foucault to a broader English-speaking audience (and hosting Foucault as a visiting scholar at UC Berkeley in the early 1980s).[12] Yet within anthropology, Rabinow has participated in nothing less than a refashioning of the field, pioneering new forms of the ethnographic practices that are more or less constitutive of anthropology. Classically trained in anthropology at the University of Chicago under Clifford Geertz, Rabinow did the requisite field studies abroad in rural Morocco but by the early 1980s had joined in a dramatic challenge to the practice of ethnography captured in the jointly authored classic *Writing Culture*.[13] We put this watershed volume in perspective relative to the developments in anthropology in Chapter 1.

Rabinow's seminal work at the intersection of philosophy and social science depends upon critiques of modern epistemology (Wittgenstein, Heidegger) and offers an alternative, through Foucault and Pierre Bourdieu, that claims the place of knowledge is embedded in forms of life, or to put it simply, in practice; as Rabinow puts the point: "thought is nothing more and nothing less than a historically locatable set of practices."[14] Claiming anthropology needed to turn its gaze upon the West, Rabinow developed lines of research into the anthropology of reason but also the anthropology

---

[9] Robert N. Bellah, *Religion in Human Evolution: From the Paleolithic to the Axial Age* (Cambridge, MA: Harvard University Press, 2011).

[10] Robert N. Bellah, *Beyond Belief: Essays in Post-Traditional Religion* (New York: Harper, 1970), 244.

[11] Robert N. Bellah, *Tokogowa Religion: The Cultural Roots of Modern Japan* (New York: The Free Press, 1957); Robert N. Bellah, et al., *Habits of the Heart: Individualism and Commitment in American Life* (Berkeley: University of California Press, 1985).

[12] Paul Rabinow and Hubert L. Dreyfus, with Michel Foucault, *Michel Foucault: Beyond Structuralism and Hermeneutics* (Chicago: University of Chicago Press, 1983); Paul Rabinow (ed.), *The Foucault Reader* (New York: Vintage, 1984).

[13] See Paul Rabinow, "Representations are Social Facts: Modernity and Post-Modernity in Anthropology," in *Writing Culture: The Poetics and Politics of Ethnography*, ed. George Marcus and James Clifford (Berkeley: University of California Press, 1986).

[14] Ibid., 239.

of the contemporary leading to entirely novel ethnographic studies, for example, of biotechnology laboratories both in the United States and in France.[15]

Rabinow shares Bellah's deep commitment to social science as practical ethics, yet his work is not theological. Despite little help making the connections to the life of faith and the practices of congregations, I entered doctoral studies at Emory University in Atlanta with a substantial repertoire of perspectives for studying congregations. In my research in Atlanta, guided by Steven Tipton (himself a student of Bellah) and Nancy Eiesland, another sociologist of religion, I focused on the logic of lived theological identity and the embodied shape of moral commitment. I focused on worship or liturgy as the nexus where such interplay between theological identity and moral commitment could be found. However, as Martin Stringer has pointed out in his similarly placed ethnographic studies of congregational worship in Manchester and Birmingham (England), very little literature existed in the late 1980s and early 1990s at the intersection of theology, worship, and ethnography.[16]

Much of the relevant literature was just emerging during the 1990s. Of use were both virtue ethics approaches that argued worship formed Christian character, on the one hand, and practical theology and congregational studies that argued ritual had a formative power shaping congregational identity, on the other. In this vein, the work of theologian Stanley Hauerwas was pivotal. Yet his allergic reaction to social science generally and ethnography in particular made his self-described "naive" observations of congregational life both embarrassingly self-serving and descriptively weak (see Chapter 3 for this critique). On the congregational studies side, the work of Nancy Ammerman has been pivotal, yet as with most work in congregational studies, her work has remained solidly within its domain as a subdiscipline of sociology of religion and thus had little engagement with theology.[17] Within practical theology, Don Browning's labors to introduce a "descriptive theological" moment to the overall task of theology moved beyond most congregational studies literature in seeking to bring to explicit focus implicit normative claims present in particular situations.[18]

For those seeking to integrate ethnography and theology, it was a gift to be entering graduate school at a time when practical theology was going through something of a revival. This was in part noted in the case of Don Browning, drawing on congregational studies and ethnographic fieldwork as a key way to approach such study. The intersection of practical philosophy, theology, and ethnography clearly rode the wave of the "turn to culture" so prominent across the disciplines in the 1980s and 1990s, a trajectory masterfully unfolded in Kathryn Tanner's book *Theories of Culture*.[19] There she offers a sharp critique of George Lindbeck, Stanley Hauerwas, and others whose appropriation of the "turn to culture" resulted in a relatively holistic notion of culture

---

[15] Paul Rabinow, *French DNA: Trouble in Purgatory* (Chicago: University of Chicago Press, 2002); Rabinow, *Making PCR: A Story of Biotechnology* (Chicago: University of Chicago Press, 1997).
[16] Martin D. Stringer, *On The Perception of Worship: The Ethnography of Worship in Four Christian Congregations in Manchester* (Birmingham: The University of Birmingham Press, 1999).
[17] Nancy Ammerman, *Congregation and Community* (New Brunswick: Rutgers University Press, 1997); Penny Becker, *Congregations in Conflict: Cultural Models of Local Religious Life* (New York: Cambridge University Press, 1999).
[18] Don Browning, *A Fundamental Practical Theology* (Minneapolis: Fortress Press, 1996).
[19] Kathryn Tanner, *Theories of Culture: An Agenda for Theology* (Minneapolis: Fortress Press, 1997).

formed through worship and existing as a counter-community and story against the dominant culture and story of modern liberal democratic society. Her critique pointed to the need to understand congregations as particularly shaped *by the world* in order to see how their formative power worked *over against the world*.[20] Help in articulating such a complex understanding also emerged from sociological and liturgical writings on ritual, including the fruitful approach to ritual practice in the work of Pierre Bourdieu.[21] With these conversation partners, I was able to move from studying, as I put it then, "the Church" to studying "churches," or as theologian Nicholas Healy puts it, from "idealized" to "concrete" ecclesiology.[22]

Over the course of a few months I visited multiple downtown churches in Atlanta, walked the streets, and learned some of the history of the center city. I settled on three churches that had been founded along with the city itself 150 years prior, and represented the oldest Catholic, white Protestant, and African American Protestant congregations: The Shrine of the Immaculate Conception, Central Presbyterian, and Big Bethel African Methodist Episcopal. By way of procedure, briefly, I planned to spend a season of the year that made internal sense to each, fully immersing myself in the life of the congregation, including all ordinary worship, education, and social activities but also staff meetings. I interviewed clergy and staff, older members who served as volunteer or informal congregational historians, and a wide variety of members. I read archives, anniversary booklets, and whatever else of the congregation's life and ministry I could find to deepen my sensibilities. Most important, however, was simply becoming a churchgoer as fully and as enthusiastically as I could in each place, feeling what it was to be there.

Looking for a "Eucharistic Self"

Plunging into fieldwork in these urban congregations required qualitative sociology and ethnography in particular as a means for understanding rather than explaining the church's public life, seeking immersion in "primary" or "lived" theology observed, heard, seen close at hand, and portrayed by articulation of its practical logic—the wisdom embedded or embodied in practice. David Ford's writing played an important role, especially what he called "a worshipping self" or perhaps more particularly "a eucharistic self."[23] In the book *Self and Salvation*, Ford posed a basic question "about the formation of the self through the Eucharist. What happens to the self shaped through that worship?"[24] Drawing on Timothy Jenkins's creative deployment of Bourdieu for ethnographic study of local congregations and communities, Ford outlined four aspects

---

[20] This is one of the key arguments in Scharen, Public Worship and Public Work.
[21] Catherine Bell, *Ritual Theory, Ritual Practice* (New York: Oxford University Press, 1992); Pierre Bourdieu, *Outline of a Theory of Practice* (New York: Cambridge University Press, 1977).
[22] Nicholas M. Healy, *Church, World and the Christian Life: Practical-Prophetic Ecclesiology* (New York: Cambridge University Press, 2000), 150.
[23] David F. Ford, *Self and Salvation: Being Transformed* (New York: Cambridge University Press, 1999), 137.
[24] Ibid., 138.

of such inquiry into actual practice.²⁵ These aspects of ethnographic investigation guided me as I sought means in each congregation to participate, pay attention to, listen for, and begin to understand those characteristics of social, religious, and cultural competency through which God was animating their worship and work in the world.

Such practical modes of knowing are gotten at, Ford begins, through first clearly stating that these are "nonverbal and habitual." He points to the absolutely basic fact that Christian identity is constituted in and through worship, through a practice, and not through many other things, from law and ethics to an alternative worldview or set of doctrines. Here he introduces Bourdieu's concept of *habitus*, briefly summarizing it as "the durably installed generative principle of regulated improvisations."²⁶ The ritual of the Eucharist, Ford suggests, is in its many variations "a condensation of the Christian habitus." Yet it is not the words nor the confessed theological understandings but rather the "patterns" of "how and why these particular" are "rooted in distant or recent history" and so on.²⁷ Second, and implicit in the first, Ford argues, such embodied knowledge comes by "the apprenticeship undergone by all actors."²⁸ Noting the "synoptic illusion" that allows supposing a map to be what people follow in traversing the paths of their daily lives, Ford describes the parallel for the Eucharist that requires apprenticeships in practical mastery rather than overviews based on ritual texts or doctrine. Rather, the Eucharist incorporates participants, and distinctively, particularly, in ways not easily articulated in scholastic terms favored by the theologian.

Third, the nature of apprenticeships is intensified by the multiple apprenticeships within each life that overlay each other creating complexities of many sorts, all coexisting within what Bourdieu calls the "socially informed body" with all its senses.²⁹ A final ethnographic point follows in that this complex embodied mastery is not easily given representation in language and in doing so its best path for offering a similarly rich conception of human and divine action comes through being itself diverse. Eucharistic language, Ford argues, includes many genres: "praise, lament, confession, exclamation, narrative, proclamation, petition" as well as "the oral and the written," but both are performed and "resist discursive overview in a somewhat similar way to good drama."³⁰ This kind of diverse "telling" of what is learned through ethnographic research is explicitly what Wacquant achieves in his account of learning boxing in South Chicago. In Wacquant's book *Body and Soul*, he draws upon "sociological analysis, ethnographic description and literary evocation."³¹

Finally, in a theological mode, Ford highlights the way the logic of trinitarian "creativity and abundance" giving way in Christ to a radical singularity in the incarnation offers a way to understand Christian faith as true to itself only in "becoming freshly embodied in different contexts." Life "in Christ," Ford argues, is a matter of

---

25 Timothy Jenkins, "Fieldwork and the Perception of Everyday Life," *Man, New Series* 29, no. 2 (1994): 433–55; Timothy Jenkins, *Religion in English Everyday Life: An Ethnographic Approach. Methodology and History in Anthropology*, Vol. 5 (Oxford: Berghahn Books, 1999).
26 Bourdieu, *Outline of a Theory of Practice*, 78.
27 Ford, *Self and Salvation*, 140–1.
28 Ibid., 141; see also Jenkins, *Religion in English Everyday Life*, 444.
29 Bourdieu, *Outline of a Theory of Practice*, 124.
30 Ford, *Self and Salvation*, 144.
31 Loïc Wacquant, *Body and Soul: Notebooks of an Apprentice Boxer* (New York: Oxford, 2004), 7.

what Bourdieu calls "necessary improvisation" showing "the distinctive and different realizations of the eventfulness of God" and "enact in ways beyond any overview the truth of the doxology: 'Heaven and earth are full of your glory.'" Especially here, Ford can press on the fact that the habituation of a "eucharistic self" is not primarily about forming a self for its own sake but to be "responsive to Jesus Christ and other people, and coping with their responses in turn."[32]

Ironically, his turn in the chapter disappointingly is to biblical interpretation rather than attending closely to formation in particular communities and communion rituals. Despite Ford's own choice to avoid the difficult process of submitting himself to ethnographic research in order to have exemplary portrayals of actual apprenticeships, he "longs to find a full anthropological study of Eucharistic practice along the lines suggested by Jenkins and Bourdieu above. That, if it were theologically informed, could be a most helpful accompaniment." He means by "theologically" that the practice be oriented to Jesus Christ and to others.

In order to show with more fullness here the fruit of the ethnographic turn, and how that trajectory sketched above led to ethnographic "fieldwork," we can highlight briefly an experience in one of Scharen's case congregations: Big Bethel AME. Immediately, however, Ford's language of a "eucharistic self" begs the question of such a life "in Christ" becoming "freshly embodied in different contexts" some of which—as in this case—such language is not even used. But the distinctiveness of their particular practices and the apprenticeships enacted display this diversity in no uncertain terms. It is important to first introduce the context of Atlanta, in the southern state of Georgia, before moving to a particular gathering of the congregation as an example of "eucharistic practice." This narrative description is excerpted from his longer study of these congregations published in the volume *Public Worship and Public Work*.[33]

Context

By far the most imposing building along this stretch of Auburn Avenue in Atlanta, Georgia, Big Bethel's gray granite spire rises high above the modest two-story brick buildings housing businesses and church offices on the rest of the block. As telling for the church's membership, however, one block to the east cars zoom by on the "Downtown Connector," a merger of two interstate highways that curl through downtown Atlanta. The freeway both hastened the out-migration from the neighborhood forty years ago and now provides the ease of access important for helping members drive in to the church from such suburban Atlanta communities as Smyrna and Marietta, fifteen miles to the northeast; Riverdale, twenty miles south; and Stone Mountain, a similar distance straight east. Walking up to the church Sunday morning, signs of such suburban success are present as Mercedes and Lexus automobiles pull up to park alongside the many more moderate sedans and sport utility vehicles.

---

[32] Ford, *Self and Salvation*, 165.
[33] Scharen, *Public Worship and Public Work*, 111ff.

As I noted after my first visit in September 1999, the congregation on a Sunday morning is predominantly African American and composed of all ages. While the congregation is weighted slightly toward middle-aged to elderly, there is a significant group of younger adults (thirties and forties) and many children. As a rule, dress is very formal with men in suits and women in dresses. A few women had large flowing and pastel-colored hats. While the church has long been home to a fair share of educated professional members, its older members still remember days of working as domestics and in other low-end service jobs. Each younger generation, however, grows in the diversity of its work affiliation; the largely public-sector and self-employed work of the civil rights generation (baby boomers) has given way to much more private-sector employment in the post-civil rights generation (Generation X, or the "busters"). Rev. James Davis, the pastor at that time, had especially tried to draw this youngest group into leadership, "planting the seeds now for Big Bethel's future." One evening, he told his Steward Board that "when we have young professionals working at major corporations and IBM trusts them, when Broadcast companies trust them, then the Church has to trust them."

The impressionistic description of the church thus far helps bring to the fore why, when asked for one word to describe the church, members often said, "diverse." In the face of changing demographics in its membership, one of the biggest challenges Big Bethel faces is being more than a historic elite church on Auburn Avenue. On the one hand, its historical status does give it a unique visibility in the city. Often referred to as "the old landmark," its cache of historical importance for the African American church in Atlanta is only rivaled by Ebenezer Baptist Church, the home church of Rev. Martin Luther King Jr., located just two blocks to the east. As the first Black church in Atlanta and the mother church of African Methodism in the region, Big Bethel certainly deserves its designation as a "historical landmark." Its landmark status and many distinguished members make its historical importance central. During the Fall of 1995, while worshipping across town so that Bethel could undergo a $1.6 million interior renovation, Rev. Davis said, "This is a tried and proven facility. We're committed to restoring it because it has a place in history." Featured prominently on its website, its mission statement, the church's 150th anniversary brochure, and on the sidebar of the thank-you letter sent out to visitors, Bethel's historical consciousness embodies the spirit of the AME church as an institution that knows the "stony road" it has trod.

On the other hand, however, the fact that the membership lives nearly everywhere in the city *but* in the surrounding neighborhood means the church has had to foster an identity that draws its metropolitan membership downtown. As one member, a middle-aged banker who lives in southwest Atlanta, put it:

> We're an urban church and it's difficult to get people to drive all the way in here from the suburbs. They have to drive by nice big churches with easy, flat parking lots, where people can just stroll out to their cars talking on Sunday morning. It's a challenge to keep professional people coming all the way down here—there has to be a draw, there has to be excitement.

While members gave many responses to the question about what they like at Big Bethel, the "red thread" stitched through all the responses boils down to spirituality.

Mr. Clark, a middle-aged man and trustee at the church, remarked that at his previous church, "I was drying up." At Bethel, however, he had found a spiritual leader who would inspire and nurture him. "That's what I get here, and it goes back to Rev. Davis." Another noted: "Before Rev. Davis, this was not a tithing church, and not a Word-based church it *should* be. Before Rev. Davis, bible study was only on Wednesday night, and wasn't well attended." Typical of many members, the renewed spiritual depth in the life of the congregation is credited to Rev. Davis's dedication, energy, and vision.

Love Feast as Communion

Come along on one particular morning a few months into my time at Big Bethel. I took the subway downtown and walked the few blocks to Big Bethel through the early morning chill. As I hurried down Butler Street, I could see the looming steeple of the church bearing the famous neon blue "Jesus Saves" sign. I was headed to a "Love Feast," a traditional Methodist ritual that John Wesley learned from Moravians on his boat trip across the Atlantic some two centuries before. Big Bethel holds the "Love Feast Prayer Service" at 7:30 a.m. on the first Saturday before the first Sunday of the month, the Sunday when they celebrate Holy Communion. I walked through the side doors of the imposing granite building and down into the fellowship hall where chairs were set up in two rows of five with a middle aisle, six rows deep for a total of sixty chairs. I found a chair near the rear and waited, noting that in front a table was set up, draped in white linen cloth covering trays.

People steadily streamed in and when the prayer service began, there were nearly forty people, giving the space a cozy, well-filled feel. For the most part, people wore sweat suits, casual clothing such as jeans and sweaters, and only a few people wore dress clothes. The service was coordinated by the Married Couples' Ministry and consisted of an Opening Hymn (Blessed Assurance), Invocation prayer ("Dear heavenly father, we just thank you that you allowed us to gather in your house once again"), a scripture reading, and then alternating prayers and hymns. Jacques, the energetic minister of music, was there to play the old upright piano in the corner. Each section of prayers had three parts, each prayed by a member in his or her own style, from the heart, and regarding a given topic. For instance, the various sections focused prayer on spiritual maturity and Christian discipleship, on national and local government, schools and school officials and teachers, and on the hungry and homeless everywhere. While some prayers were quiet meditations guiding us in our "supplication before the Lord," others built a crescendo plea, boldly approaching "the throne of grace."

As this pattern of prayer and hymn-singing (we always sang two verses of hymns, never more) continued, more people streamed in and before long, the place was packed with nearly hundred people, including at least ten children of varying ages. As the prayers concluded, Rev. Davis moved to the front of the room and offered some words of greeting and asked how many had not been to a Love Feast before, and I joined about ten people who raised their hands. To this, he and other regulars said, "Praise God!" He noted that it is important for members to keep reaching out, to keep getting to know others. As if to make his point, he asked, "Alright, somebody raise their hand if they know every person in the room." No one did. Then he asked, "Somebody raise their hand if you see three people you don't know." Nearly the whole room raised their hands. He took a moment to have each person find three people they didn't know and introduce themselves—it was an upbeat and friendly break of about five minutes with people milling around, talking, and hugging.

We moved into a large circle and Rev. Davis asked Rev. Streator to explain what would happen next. While Revs. Davis and Wood-Powe stepped around the circle with silver communion trays, handing each person a clear plastic communion cup filled with water, Rev. Streator described the "symbolism of the water." Because of the water's transparency and purity, one is encouraged to let go of grudges that prohibit interpersonal transparency. And if one bears a grudge, before going to the altar for communion the next day during Sunday morning service, you should go to them and make amends. He stated that "the purity of the water symbolized that 'transparency of love' that should mark the community." As if drinking the promise of purity, the others and I tipped back our glasses in unison. Then, each person was given a piece of white bread, about a third of a slice lengthwise. I thought we would then eat it in unison as we drank the water. Actually, however, no one eats the bread. Each person gets a piece of everyone else's bread. This happens in the following way, and it is, according to Rev. Streator, "intended to build fellowship, to be a symbol of oneness."

Starting with Rev. Davis, the process began; he gave a piece of bread to the person to his left, and they took a piece of his bread, and they hugged and exchanged God's blessing by saying, "God loves you and so do I." Each subsequent person peeled off and followed Davis, forming a second inner circle moving around the outer circle until everyone had exchanged bread and greetings in a similar way with every other person in the room. I noticed in the process that people stuffed the tidbits of bread they received from others into their little communion cups and I followed suit. The greetings were sometimes strong hugs, and others offered tentative pats on the shoulder, but always faces met, eyes glancing into one another, and smiles. At the end, as if in a collective "*eucharista*" for the communion we had just shared, all the cups of bread were placed upon the altar table and we sang a stirring rendition of the old Gospel hymn, "Amazing Grace." Before closing, Rev. Davis introduced Mother Theodora, who stood hunched over her cane near the altar. He reported that she is one of the oldest members and, he said, "she has adopted Love Feast and comes every time, even today when she doesn't feel well." People applauded and Rev. Davis commented that this might have been the most successful Love Feast yet.

Woven in and through the process of the bread and greetings, I chatted with Ms. Green, a member since 1948, and a stewardess, the ministry group that hosts the "Love Feast." She noted that this ritual was new for Big Bethel, even though it had deep roots in Methodism generally. In a later interview, she credited this to Rev. Davis being "a deeply spiritual man, and a visionary." Indeed, the "Love Feast" and Rev. Davis's enthusiasm for it go to the root of this old church, and account in large part for its current revival. Such a circle ritual has deep roots in the slave "ring shouts" related to me by another old member, Mrs. King.[34] And out of the solace of such song, prayer, and

---

[34] Ring Shout was a dance-like form of Christian worship done by African American slaves, mostly before the Civil War. It involves moving in a counterclockwise circle, singing, clapping, stomping,

common spirit, gatherings in this fellowship hall have given birth to schools, financial institutions, local civil rights actions, and many programs of social uplift for members and beyond.

Yet, the storied history of the first Black church in the city could not alone keep the church vibrant and engaged today. A downtown church whose membership left the neighborhood decades ago faces a peculiar problem of attracting membership and building community. The Love Feast symbolically connects to the purity and unity represented in Holy Communion to be solemnly enacted the next morning. But here as Rev. Davis well knew our very bodies enacted communion, facing each other "in Christ" and "as Christ." As he noted at the minister's meeting held directly after the Love Feast, "we need to work on fellowship, for commitments to do don't *start* with doing—they start with family. We need to put all our commitments down, take time to become brothers and sisters, and then together go and do." The Love Feast is also, however, about doing. Fellowship serves the agenda of "kingdom building." As Rev. Davis often says in his charge to the neophyte Christians who answer the "Invitation to Discipleship" after the sermon on Sunday morning, "Salvation is not a feeling, its faith; now believe and live like a saved person ought." The church that proclaims "Jesus Saves," through programs that reach all over the city and beyond, finds its taproot in becoming a fellowship of disciples, gathered to feast on love given in abundance in order to become love given for others.

Theology *from* the Body

In this research I was not actually after the eucharistic self, or worshipping self, but the congregation as "particular case of the possible" in relation to the world, a variety of distinct lives, a living tradition, and so on, all of which gives way to a complexity of multiple formations.[35] I was able to gain proximity to these congregational worlds and the worshipping selves they produce through a kind of ethnographic apprenticeship, through placing myself in the "vortex of action in order to acquire, through practice, in real time, the dispositions of the [worshipper] with the aim of elucidating the magnetism proper to the [doxological] cosmos."[36] I have come to see in retrospect, through the ethnographic writing of Loïc Wacquant on the world of boxing,[37] what he was doing in his research that went beyond typical "participant observation." It was less "observation" and more a throwing oneself into the life of the congregation as far as was possible, seeking as full a "participant" role as possible.

and beating on the floor rhythmically with a stick or broom. See Art Rosenbaum, *Shout Because You're Free: The African American Ring Shout Tradition in Coastal Georgia* (Athens: The University of Georgia Press, 1995).

[35] Gaston Bachelard, *Le Nouvel Espirit Scientifque* (Paris: PUF, 1949), 58; see also Pierre Bourdieu and Loïc J. D. Wacquant, *An Invitation to Reflexive Sociology* (Chicago: University of Chicago Press, 1992), 75.

[36] Loïc Wacquant, "Habitus as Topic and Tool: Reflections on becoming a Prizefighter," in *Ethnographies Revisited: Constructing Theory in the Field*, ed. William Shaffir, Antony Puddephatt, and Steven Kleinknecht (New York: Routledge, 2009).

[37] Wacquant, *Body and Soul*.

Many fieldworkers in practical theology speak of their research position as "participant observation." But further specification might help us to be very clear about what ethnographers are doing and how it is that the body does or does not play a significant role as a source of data in the research process. For example, James Stevens notes in his book on charismatic churches in England that his 1987–91 tenure as curate at St. John the Evangelist in Welling, Kent, allowed him to experience elements of a Vineyard charismatic culture that had been set in motion some years prior to his coming to the parish. This pastoral experience there, he says, accounted for the "initial stage" of research, giving him "an in-depth example of" his research topic and preparing him for the main period of research 1993–5. At this latter stage, he writes, "I was simply re-entering the research field in which I had already, unintentionally, completed three and a half years of ethnography."[38] While of course being a priest in a charismatic congregation ought to give one some aid in subsequent research on charismatic congregations, it is dangerously confusing to retroactively describe a pastoral tenure as "ethnographic" research. Unfortunately, this confusion continues all too often. Natalie Wigg-Stevenson's work stands out as an excellent example of what should happen to avoid this confusion. That is, a clear introduction of one's self to the church as a researcher who is also in the role of congregational leader (in her case, teaching an adult study class on theology).[39]

When Stevens does describe his research role properly, he offers four positions within the range of options for participant observation:

a. The "complete participant"—sustained participation, observation concealed
b. The "participant-as-observer"—sustained participation, observation acknowledged
c. The "observer-as-participant"—contact is brief, formal, observation acknowledged
d. The "complete observer"—eavesdropping, little contact with informants' views

His study of churches was brief, and hosts regarded him as one who had come to "look at" their worship, so his work fits closest to the "observer-as-participant" model. He reports "following what was expected of congregational participation in its various forms: standing, sitting, kneeling, singing, greeting, and receiving the sacrament." How was his participation different? He writes, "Whilst others were worshipping, and 'letting themselves go' in singing and acts of devotion, I was working, maintaining an analytical frame of mind that was anathema to the situational ethos."[40]

Wacquant offers another possibility, one that makes sense of my attempt to learn "from the body" and seems near to what Mary McClintock Fulkerson engaged in as well during her two and a half years at Good Samaritan. This is to "push the logic of participant observation to the point where it becomes inverted and turns into observant

---

[38] James H. S. Stevens, *Worship in the Spirit: Charismatic Worship in the Church of England, Studies in Evangelical History and Thought* (Carlisle and Waynesboro: Paternoster Press, 2002), 39–40.
[39] Natalie Wigg-Stevenson, *Ethnographic Theology: An Inquiry into the Production of Theological Knowledge* (New York: Palgrave Macmillan, 2014).
[40] Stevens, *Worship in the Spirit*, 42.

participation." The typical warning, and one Bourdieu gave to Wacquant during his immersion at Chicago's Woodlawn Boxing Club, is "don't go native." Wacquant's position, in turn, is to "say 'go native' but 'go native armed,' that is, equipped with your theoretical and methodological tools, the full store of problematics inherited from your discipline, with your capacity for reflexivity and analysis."[41] The idea, to revise Stevens's description, is to indeed enter into the worshipping, to "let oneself go" in the singing and acts of devotion and exactly in and through those experiences attend to the ways the apprenticeship "enables us to pry into practice in the making and to realize that the ordinary knowledge that makes us competent actors is an incarnate, sensuous, situated 'knowing-how-to' that operates beneath the controls of discursive awareness and propositional reasoning."[42]

The point is, as Wacquant puts it, that meaning-making in such bodily worlds as the boxing gym and the worshipping congregation "is not a mental affair liable to an intellectualist reading, as the hermeneutic tradition, trapped in the scriptural metaphor of social action as text, would have us believe."[43] A carnal sociology, and, we want to suggest, a carnal theology, that:

> seeks to situate itself not outside or above practice but at its "point of production" requires that we immerse ourselves as deeply and as durably as possible into the cosmos under examination; that we submit ourselves to its specific temporality and contingencies; that we acquire the embodied dispositions it demands and nurtures, so that we may grasp it via the prethetic understanding that defines the native relation to the world—not as one world among many but as "home."[44]

As we noted earlier, early on in my training and career I was critical of theology in its scholastic forms because of its relative lack of connection to lived experience in particular communities and persons. But in and through the careful attending ethnographic practice required, I slowly gained a sense that this was constitutive of a way of doing theology that both allowed me to merge theology and social science (what Nick Healy is after in commending "ecclesiological ethnography"[45]), and to articulate the substance of such theology as an emerging form of formal or secondary theology but much more immediately responsible to the practical contexts of life and faith from which it spoke.

A full accounting of what ethnography as theology looks like—in my own work, let alone in the work of the many who have taken up this mode of theology and ethics—is the task of this whole volume, and beyond it, the work of those who share its aims and practices. However, perhaps we might briefly conclude by returning to David Ford's concluding frame for "a Eucharistic self" in which he hopes for "a full anthropological study of Eucharistic practice, theologically informed." To do such would, he argues, embody an approach that takes with utter seriousness the "radical singularity of the

---

[41] Wacquant, "Habitus as Topic and Tool," 7.
[42] Wacquant, "Carnal Connections," 466.
[43] Ibid.
[44] Ibid.
[45] Healy, *Church, World and the Christian Life*, 174.

incarnation" as a theological support for claiming the Christian faith as true to itself "only in becoming freshly embodied in different contexts."[46]

Presumably, the "love feast" at Big Bethel AME offers such a "fresh embodiment" of the church. In my apprenticeship among them, however, I not only learned that the rite of the Eucharist is not celebrated—or even known in those terms—but that the ritual of the Love Feast enacted the day prior to communion carries their practice of Holy Communion in the sense that communion is enacted through the Love Feast in the laborious process of sharing oneself with another, one by one, as thread stitches cloth, offering and receiving greetings, prayer, confession, reconciliation, singing, cups of water, broken bread, and thanksgiving.

Conclusion

We have come a ways toward making sense of the shape and character of the "turn to ethnography" in this chapter, partly through more tentative general reflections and through the risk of telling a particular tale of formation in scholarly disciplines. While each person's trajectory has its distinctive elements, there are cultural and intellectual currents that have prevailed over the last few decades or so that have helped bring ethnography to the fore. In summary, we wish to simply state those more clearly. First of all, it is necessary to situate the rise of ethnography as a means for doing theology and ethics within the larger rise of the study of culture as a major grounding discourse for theology. Second, it is a way for theology to have broader relevance within the academy (it is tied to the social sciences and broadly practiced—in the humanities and professional schools as well as social science). Yet that very relevance is also clearly compelling to the practical interests of ordinary people and the organizations and communities they inhabit.

Ethnography is also an effective tool for doing certain kinds of work, and it bears noting how it does this. Historically, as we describe in the first chapter, ethnography has tended to be a way to understand a people, community, or culture "other" than one's own. While this has often meant some exotic locale, it can mean a nearby locale with which one is not familiar (as in Fulkerson's Good Samaritan or Scharen's Big Bethel). On the other hand, the work of Paul Rabinow among others has shown how ethnography might be used to offer an "untimely" and therefore rich and suggestive view of a familiar site.[47] Rabinow has done this with science laboratories both in the United States and in France. In Part II, AnneMarie Mingo does this through dwelling with a congregation where refugees from Hurricane Katrina in New Orleans make a surprising home through, as she notes, developing an ethics of receptivity.

Finally, ethnography—in part because of its "untimeliness"—can offer a way to test out the truth of particular claims, something for example that Scharen has done with theological ethicists claiming some simplistic unidirectional formation of the

---

[46] Ford, *Self and Salvation*, 144.
[47] Paul Rabinow, George E. Marcus, James D. Faubion, and Tobias Rees. *Designs for an Anthropology of the Contemporary* (Durham: Duke University Press, 2008), 59ff.

self through ritual participation. From the perspective of one's office, the idea that "worship forms Christians" has an attractive self-evidence that serves certain claims about the distinctiveness of Christian identity and witness (as Kathryn Tanner pointed out above). Ethnography, however, takes time to show the complexity of how such formation happens, when and how it works, and the various ways such a view is complicated by the formative power of participation in other institutions humans inhabit. We pick up this last point in the next chapter as a weak spot in some of the critiques of the use of ethnography and social science generally in theology and ethics. To that discussion we now turn.

3

Critiques of the Use of Social Science in Theology and Ethics

Thus far, we've outlined an understanding of ethnography and described some of the terrain involved in the turn to ethnography in theology and ethics. It is clear by this point that we believe ethnography ought to be a means of doing theology. We've explained what we mean by ethnography as "writing culture" and that we assume it includes some level of direct, qualitative observation/participation *in situ* using a combination of practical disciplined methods of attending as well as theoretical frames and insights. Yet even as ethnography has risen in visibility among theologians and ethicists, its use—as part of a whole range of social science methods and theories—has been and remains controversial.

In order to describe and evaluate this critique, the following chapter takes stock of debates set in motion by John Milbank's influential 1990 book, *Theology and Social Theory*, echoed in the theologian Stanley Hauerwas and then picked up by anthropologist Joel Robbins. While attempting to take their critiques seriously, it is clear that each in their own ways can be shown to imply, or explicitly say that, ethnography provides the most robust response to the sorts of work they themselves call for in working to understand the church and the daily lives of Christians in the world. Robbins—and others engaging his work—takes this further, questioning how theology substantively informs anthropology, which goes beyond the scope of our aim here.

The chapter proceeds by way of questioning Milbank and then Hauerwas regarding their critiques of the use of social science in theology. While developing independent arguments, they have learned from one another and considerable connection exists between their respective positions. We answer these critiques by first examining Robin Gill's argument for and use of social science in theological ethics but find his dependence on broad social survey method limited. Second, we engage theologians like Nicholas Adams and Charles Elliot who argue for the use of ethnography in theology. We then bring this proposal into conversation with the more recent conversations between anthropology and theology, also starting with Milbank. This conversation fruitfully affirms that our argument for ethnography is not merely as a method borrowed from the social sciences, but rather a properly theological and theoretical way of understanding—and even participating in—human and divine action in the world.

Questioning Milbank

John Milbank's *Theology and Social Theory* dazzles most scholars with its immense learning and broad-ranging discussions in contemporary social theory.[1] He soundly trounces theological dependence on social science, describing this phenomenon of modern theology with the strong and memorable term "policing the sublime."[2] He means by this that through generating its own theory of society, sociology ensures that "religion is kept, conceptually, at the margins—both denied influence, and yet acclaimed for its transcendent purity."[3] The standpoint from which social science positions and describes the phenomena of religion, Milbank argues, is not objective. It is, rather, a "positivist theology" that continually rediscovers the "religious" as one aspect of society.[4] Although his book is long, and beyond adequate summary here, as Fergus Kerr has put it, its argument is "simplicity itself": there is no need, as has become commonplace, to bring social theory and theology together, for social theory is already theology, and theology already a social theory.[5] Milbank shows that, like theology, modern social theory tends to colonize and compartmentalize religion, effectively turning it into spirituality.

Kerr, whose summary of Milbank's complicated book received the approval of the author himself, recommends a reading strategy that begins with the last chapter. Here, under the title "The Other City: Theology as Social Science," Milbank's Augustinian intentions become obvious. In particular, he wants to argue for theology itself as a social science, an aid and guide for the "inhabitants of the *alterna civitas*, on a pilgrimage through this temporary world." When theologians depend on a particular analysis of social scientists, in doing so, they import functional explanations of events and actions that effectively bracket the agency of God (in Milbank's classical framing, "efficient" rather than "final" causes).[6] As Milbank puts it, theology has:

> frequently sought to borrow from elsewhere a fundamental account of society or history, and then to see what theological insights will cohere with it. But it has been shown that no such fundamental account, in the sense of something neutral, rational and universal, is really available. It is theology itself that will have to provide its own account of the final causes at work in human history, on the basis of its own particular and historically specific faith.[7]

---

[1] John Milbank, *Theology and Social Theory: Beyond Secular Reason* (Cambridge: Blackwell, 1990); by way of response, see the various review articles and Milbank's response in the special issue of *New Blackfriars* 73 (June 1992).
[2] See Milbank, *Theology and Social Theory*, 101ff.
[3] Ibid., 109.
[4] Ibid., 140.
[5] Fergus Kerr, "Simplicity Itself: Milbank's Thesis," *New Blackfriars* 73 (1992): 306–10.
[6] Michael J. Baxter, C.S.C. shows how this point is lost on some who critique Milbank's basic thesis in "Whose Theology? Which Sociology? A Response to John Coleman," in *Theology and the Social Sciences*, ed. Michael H. Barnes (Maryknoll: Orbis, 2001), 34–42.
[7] Milbank, *Theology and Social Theory*, 380.

Why? Because Christian social theory derives from and has as its task the explication of a Christian mode of action, a Christian practice, and thus such a theory of this "other city" must also be ecclesiology. In this sense, then, ecclesiology is also "sociology." But, Milbank contends, "this possibility only becomes available if ecclesiology is rigorously concerned with the actual genesis of real historical churches, not simply with the imagination of an ecclesial ideal."[8]

Rowan Williams picks up Milbank's claim that a "Christian sociology" must "articulate Christian difference" as a description of society grounded in its own distinct society, the church. Williams suggests that Milbank is "fusing historical narrative with 'essentialist,' diagrammatic accounts of ideological options," positioning the church against (especially) the Roman sacralization of dominion and the Jewish commitment to law as the defining good.[9] Williams, in other words, worries that Milbank's desire to have a Christian meta-narrative defining of the present church's difference obscures in his telling the ways in which this difference was achieved through crisis and conflict. Thus, on Williams's judgment, "the risk Milbank's exposition runs is, paradoxically, of slipping into a picture of history as the battlefield of ideal types."[10]

While oblique, in his response Milbank seems to accept Williams's critique. While he first notes that the place where he finds the church most clearly is not a "place" at all, nor an identity achieved through crisis and conflict. Rather, the church is a gift "given, superabundantly, in the breaking of the bread by the risen Lord, which assembles the harmony of the peoples then and at every subsequent Eucharist."[11] Yet, argues Milbank, despite no intention to make his "formal" descriptions exhaustive, he also sees an important role for "judicious narratives of ecclesial happenings which would alone indicate the shape of the Church that we desire." And the need for this, he sees, is sharpened by the tension between his formal and ideal descriptions of the church and his own "rather minimal attempts at 'judicious narrative.'"[12]

Among the challenges emerging from substantial engagement with Milbank's work is how one might learn from and incorporate aspects of sociology into the work of theology so as to achieve more robust examples of wise stories of Christian life and community. Our arguments in this volume propose, in response, that ethnography can be drawn upon as a fairly "theory-free" practice of sociology able to incorporate the full range of the theological imagination in taking stock of the world's life. Yet our extension of Milbank in this way seems rather of the sort one would call not throwing out the baby with the bathwater. Generations of social science researchers have learned practices of research—including ethnography and its attendant methods—that ought to aid the work of theologians attending to the world. Similar mild critique and amendment emerge from dialogue with another theologian tempted to throw out the social science baby with the bathwater, Stanley Hauerwas.

---

[8] Ibid., 380.
[9] Rowan Williams, "Saving Time: Thoughts on Practice, Patience, and Vision," *New Blackfriars* 73 (1992): 319–26.
[10] Ibid., 321.
[11] John Milbank, "Enclaves, or Where is the Church?" *New Blackfriars* 73 (June 1992): 341–52.
[12] Ibid., 343.

Questioning Hauerwas

Hauerwas's understanding of the church offers another angle for critically examining the use of social science by theologians and ethicists—and as part of that discipline, the practice of ethnography. Hauerwas is known for a strong claim that the church's first task is to live the truth of its identity in God through Christ, thus helping the world to know it is the world.[13] His hope and vision for the church is that it be a countersociety, a community living the story of Jesus. Such a community is "God's gesture on behalf of the world to create a space and time in which we might have a foretaste of the Kingdom."[14] The world can, in a sense, see how it really ought to be through its encounter with how the church really is.

Moreover, for Hauerwas, if the church has as its first task to make the world the world by being its contrast, the church has as its essence a social and political task.[15] Worship and the things that constitute it such as prayer, preaching, baptism, and the Eucharist fold Christians into God's life as Christ's body. By one's participation in the body of Christ, one's life includes baptism and Eucharist, but also "immersion in the daily practices of the Christian church: prayer, worship, admonition, feeding the hungry, caring for the sick, etc." Hauerwas concludes, "By these we are transformed over time to participate in God's life. So we become full members in a city ordered to peace."[16] This participation in the body is a political reality produced and maintained through sacraments as political rituals. Sacraments, writes Hauerwas, "are not just 'religious things' that Christian people do. They are the essential rituals of our politics."[17] Therefore, the "liturgy is not a motive for social action, it is not a cause to effect. Liturgy *is* social action."[18] The church in Hauerwas's vision is an alternative public, a society constituted by its own distinct practices, goods, and modes of life.[19]

In defending his view of liturgy *as* social action against the charge that such churches are idealized, and as such, not actually able to engage in meaningful ways in public life, Hauerwas takes on the task of attempting a careful description and interpretation of the significance of an administrative board meeting at his church at that time, Broadway United Methodist, in Notre Dame, Indiana. In so doing, he avoids speaking only about an ideal church. But rather than work from what he understands to be an "objective" sociological perspective, he argues that his "telling of the story" is normative in intent; it serves "not just as an example but as an argument for how Christian ethics ought to be done."[20] Such a telling is informed by, and attempts to

---

[13] Stanley Hauerwas, *Christian Existence Today: Essays on Church, World, and Living in Between* (Durham: The Labyrinth Press, 1988), 102.
[14] Ibid., 106.
[15] Stanley Hauerwas, *In Good Company: The Church as Polis* (Notre Dame: University of Notre Dame Press, 1995), 249, n. 12.
[16] Stanley Hauerwas and Charles Pinches, *Christians Among the Virtues: Theological Conversations with Ancient and Modern Ethics* (Notre Dame: University of Notre Dame Press, 1997), 69.
[17] Stanley Hauerwas, *The Peaceable Kingdom: A Primer in Christian Ethics* (Notre Dame: University of Notre Dame Press, 1983), 108.
[18] Hauerwas, *Christian Existence Today*, 107. A nearly identical phrase is found in *The Peaceable Kingdom*, 108.
[19] Hauerwas, *In Good Company*, 6–8.
[20] Hauerwas, *Christian Existence Today*, 113.

test, his constructive theological and ethical positions. At stake was whether in fact his understanding that liturgy *is* social action could escape the charge that it is merely an ideal, and an ideal that counsels withdrawal from the world rather than engagement in it.[21]

Through the example of his congregation, Hauerwas aims both to show that actual churches do act the way he thinks the church "should" and that the critiques miss the sort of "responsibility for the world" Hauerwas's view of liturgy *as* social action implies. Hauerwas describes a board meeting where two issues—repairing the leaking roof and moving to weekly Eucharist—took center stage in discussions. Given the impoverished neighborhood surrounding the church, Hauerwas interprets the commitment of large sums of money for roof repair as a theological-ethical stance to be a witness of God's presence in and for that neighborhood. Weekly Eucharist, Hauerwas argues, subsequently led the congregation to propose not a soup kitchen for the needy, but rather an after-church lunch shared among the members and all who wanted to come from the neighborhood. Again, this action held powerful symbolic and actual power for Hauerwas in that it embodied the church's calling to be a witness to the kingdom come near in Jesus Christ, and a concrete symbol to the neighborhood that all was not lost. While their first concern was not city politics, Hauerwas notes, their commitment to be a presence in the neighborhood included concern "about what was happening in the politics of the city."[22]

Hauerwas's empirical analysis of the church permitted him to develop a theological ethic that helps people "appreciate the significance of their worship." In Broadway, he:

> saw a congregation formed and disciplined by the liturgy that made possible an extraordinary social witness. That congregation's life belies distinctions between theology and liturgy, ethics and liturgy. The meal they prepare every Sunday for the neighborhood is not the way they express their social ethical commitments in distinction from their liturgical life. Rather, the meal they prepare and liturgical life are for them parts of a single story. The theological task is first and foremost to help us and them understand why that is the case.[23]

Hauerwas wants his description to take up the ordinary experiences of the congregation, but told with their significance. Thus, his theological task begins with the admission that:

> We have not paid enough attention to how difficult it is to understand the common things we do as Christians: pray, baptize, eat meals, rejoice at the birth of a child, grieve at illness and death, re-roof church buildings, and so on. If we cannot describe theologically the significance of these activities, we will distort what we do by having to resort to descriptions and explanations all too readily provided by our culture.[24]

---

[21] See Whitmore, "Crossing the Road," 273–94.
[22] Ibid., 122.
[23] Ibid., 125.
[24] Ibid., 123–4.

What our culture provides us, he says, are social scientific accounts of the life of congregations. He does not mean to "deny the value of sociological, psychological, and general social-scientific accounts of the life of congregations." Yet, he continues, "the issue is the uncritical use of the social-scientific paradigms which often, if applied rigorously and consistently, methodologically preclude the theological claims necessary for the church's intelligibility."[25] Harkening back to Milbank's claims that social scientific paradigms limit themselves to efficient causes, Hauerwas means the church must draw on final causes, especially THE final cause, God, in order to make any proper sense of itself. In short, Hauerwas fears that in the translation of theological claims to publicly intelligible claims, the church implicitly takes for itself the role of national handmaiden, blessing and supporting the secular civil order.

Yet, we claim that Hauerwas's rejection of social science limits his work in two ways. First, Hauerwas defeats his own aim of grounded theological work because he does not go far enough, carefully enough, in his attending to congregational life. For example, Hauerwas emphasizes the importance of the liturgical practices of congregations generally, as well as how important eucharistic practices were at Broadway, but does not offer any description of those practices. He asserts that such practices were done and meditates on their theological meaning at length. This approach seems at best to minimally fulfill his own call to understand everyday practices of congregations, practices that are at once theological, liturgical, and ethical, but maybe also utilitarian and self-serving, shallow, or even explicitly unjust in one way or another.[26] Our advocacy of a critical, yet empathetic ethnographic inquiry does not repeat the external and causal critiques, nor the "spiritualization" of the church that worries Hauerwas, but instead calls for critical work that can understand and articulate the many practices located in various spheres of social life formative of church members, including but clearly beyond the church.

Second, it follows that Hauerwas's polemically driven theological framework, "liturgy as ethics," does not include a view of culture nuanced enough to capture the significance of cultural pluralism forming contemporary Christians and their congregations. Whereas Hauerwas's rhetoric draws a simple church-world distinction necessary for discussing a Christian culture and its practices contrasted to the world and its practices, actual modern people, including Hauerwas, have commitments to work, family, citizenship, and leisure, in addition to religion. All of these are legitimate commitments for contemporary Christians, commitments Kathryn Tanner frames much more adequately in terms of the problem of complexity in identity formation. This problem cannot be ignored, as Hauerwas does, because American society, like all societies that have passed through the painful process of modernization, is constituted by differentiated yet interrelated and interconnected spheres of activity, each with potentially significant tensions with theological commitments. While critical use of

---

[25] Ibid., 130n.
[26] Susan A. Ross develops these issues in relation to the question of women religious who are required to have a priest, who is always a man and thereby an outsider to their community, come to preside at celebrations that include the Eucharist. See her "Like a Fish without a Bicycle?" *America* 181/17 (November 17, 1999): 10–13; "Liturgy and Ethics: Feminist Perspectives," *Annual of the Society of Christian Ethics* 20 (2000): 263–74.

social science is not the only way to understand such complicated interconnections in the Christian moral life, it is one viable and sophisticated way to accomplish such a view. While the next three sections begin to pay down on this claim about the potential role of social science, and especially ethnography, the whole volume intends this as well.

Answering Milbank and Hauerwas: Robin Gill

In a powerfully argued book titled *Churchgoing and Christian Ethics*, Robin Gill critiques Milbank along the lines indicated by Rowan Williams. Gill places Milbank within the broad revival of virtue ethics begun by Alisdair MacIntyre and Stanley Hauerwas that sees theology's task not as deducing from ideas a set of actions to follow, but reflection upon a Christian mode of action, a Christian practice that forms an alternative society. Gill takes a first appreciative step with such theologians, for he fundamentally works out of a virtue ethics model as well. Yet, as Gill maps out the arguments of Milbank and Hauerwas, he balks at what he perceives as their strong rhetorical position that the church is the sole repository of Christian virtues and that the church exists as a strong contrast society over against the world. The problem is, Gill notes, that Milbank and Hauerwas speak mainly of an idealized church, but especially Hauerwas, by his investment in a character ethics approach, depends on the actual church for schooling Christians who will be the citizens of this alternative society constituted by a "given" eucharistic peace.[27]

The difficulty in such an argument, depending on an idealized understanding of the church, Gill argues, is that actual church people look rather a lot like everybody else! He makes the argument that Hauerwas's and Milbank's claims of Christian culture and practices forming a distinctive alternative social life are quite testable. Along the way, he dismisses sociologists who consider churchgoing as an epiphenomenon, instead arguing for a "cultural theory" which posits that churchgoing and especially communal worship shape and reinforce Christian beliefs and behavior. Thus, he argues that a decline in churchgoing should precede declines in Christian belief and behavior, while active churchgoing should evidence increases in Christian belief and behavior.

The center of Gill's argument, Chapters 4–7, consists of detailed statistical analyses of the annual British Household Panel Survey that includes questions about churchgoing as well as a variety of beliefs and behaviors. Gill's original analysis of this survey data focuses on three general areas—indicators of Christian beliefs (faith), indicators of seeing life as worthwhile (hope), and indicators of altruism (love). He concludes that churchgoing is strongly correlated with certain values and virtues, beliefs and behaviors, not unique to churchgoers but more distinctive of them than of non-churchgoers.

Gill then asks the obvious question: How does churchgoing have such an influence? If, as Gill argues, a cultural theory of churchgoing states that people learn these beliefs and virtues in church, how is this so? By way of an answer, Gill engages in a long

---

[27] Robin Gill, *Churchgoing and Christian Ethics*, New Studies in Christian Ethics 15 (New York: Cambridge University Press, 1999), 13–30.

discussion of various worship practices central to traditional Protestant (Presbyterian, Anglican) and Roman Catholic churches. These, he argues, are the constitutive practices of "the distinctive culture of churchgoing and act as crucial carriers of Christian identity."[28] He goes to great lengths to show that they together contain the values his survey analysis found more strongly present in churchgoing people. He concludes:

> Significant traces of faith, hope, and love have been detected amongst those most exposed to the culture of churchgoing. The staple ingredients of this culture—hymns, sermons, intercessions, public confessions and, above all, readings of Scripture and celebrations of the Eucharist—all act as carriers of this distinctive culture. Together they continue to shape lives—however imperfectly—of faithful worshipers.[29]

In this conclusion, Gill makes clear resonance with a character ethics approach—by going to church and engaging its practices, one's habits and thus character are formed.

It is ironic, however, that in trying to escape claims for an idealized church, Gill ends up with another sort of idealized church—his churchgoers don't go to any actual church but are generic Christians who go to generic churches. Depending on survey data, Gill individualizes the question of churchgoing and then makes a pseudo-communal claim about churchgoing itself, aside from the character of the particular local church. Because his measures of Christian belief and behavior are so general (faith, hope, love), this fact does not matter as much as it could. Still, the fact that he brushes over denominational, cultural, racial, and other differences within and among churches limits the real resonance his churchgoers can have for the reader, and limits the clarity his analysis has regarding exactly how parishes have such formative effects.

Such preference for a generic-real church may be understandable given his dependence on survey data yet it feeds a second problem that Gill shares generally with those working in the Aristotelian tradition of virtue ethics: his conclusions still depend on a "simple" cultural view of church and world as distinct.[30] Theologically speaking, such a distinction can be attractive. But without a means to directly account for cultural pluralism and the complicated, bifurcated social-structural worlds shaped by and shaping Christian people and their communities, one may miss the ways real communities of faith are Christian in ways that tightly interrelate with what I refer to as their congregational "communal identity." Without this more complex understanding of culture and community, it is difficult to account for the identity "given" through eucharistic participation, never "generic" but always particularly incarnate within the life of this or that Christian community.

---

[28] Ibid., 226.
[29] Ibid., 229.
[30] And they have good Augustinian and Pauline reasons for doing so (to a point). But too strong a version of this division opens one to the charges Adian Nichols puts to Milbank ("hermeticism") and James Gustafson puts to Hauerwas ("sectarian"). See Aidan Nichols, "Non Tali Auxilio: John Milbank's Suasion to Orthodoxy," *New Blackfriars* 73 (June 1992): 326–32; James Gustafson, "The Sectarian Temptation: Reflections on Theology, the Church, and the University," *Catholic Theological Society of America Proceedings* 40 (1985): 83–94.

Answering Milbank and Hauerwas: Adams and Elliott

To be fair, Robin Gill knows that more is required; his deep and substantial work in sociology has taught him exactly the limitations of survey research. Thus, he writes "there is indeed something very crude about reducing beliefs and moral attitudes to such collectable and measurable forms."[31] In the words of Steven Tipton, the problem with survey research is that "opinions are like noses, in short, or at length, if you will: everyone has one and everybody's is a little different. All you can do is count them up in polls and check for the sociological equivalent of family resemblances."[32] Seeing this problem, Gill concludes his book calling for "more qualitative research to be done on local congregations and parishes."[33]

This is not an unproblematic call, however, especially given how Hauerwas has cautioned against the hidden agendas disguised within apparently neutral description. According to Hauerwas, here giving a disclaimer before attempting his own description of his church in North Carolina, "'description' is, of course, anything but innocent. The methodological assumptions that often shape the 'sociology' governing such descriptions reproduce the kind of 'spiritualization' of the church for which I am trying to provide an alternative."[34] In lieu of whatever he thinks a sociological description might be, Hauerwas offers his own "naive" description, an odd adjective for an approach equally freighted with assumptions as any sociological approach would bring.[35]

Milbank, by way of a corrective of his own work, calls for "supplementation by judicious narratives of ecclesial happenings." In other words, prudence in the use of description; I take it, he intends something like what Nicholas Adams and Charles Elliott have recently called for in their programmatic article "Ethnography is Dogmatics."[36] By merging Barth's dictum that ethics is dogmatics and Michel Foucault's understanding that ethics is ethnography, they propose an approach recommending "that theologians take ethnographic description at least as seriously as dogmatics: indeed, the latter (if it concerns 'the real') is, and should be, the slave of the former."[37] Hardly objective or neutral observers, they simply argue a full metaphysically shaped eye is all anyone has to look with, and for a theologian, theism simply implies a God-shaped eye.

Therefore, Adams and Elliott provocatively suggest ethnography as dogmatics ought to be descriptive and eschatological; that is, it ought to teach Christians how to see the world as it is, and in the light of how it shall be. While strongly suggesting that theologians learn from social anthropology and sociology about the skills of ethnography, they do not reduce theology to social anthropology. Adams's and Elliott's ethnographic work in Northern India portrays "powerless people" who nevertheless find "the capacity to change radically" the circumstances of their lives.

---

[31] Gill, *Churchgoing and Christian Ethics*, 43.
[32] Steven Tipton, "A Response: Moral Languages and the Good Society," *Soundings* 69 (1986): 165–80.
[33] Ibid., 262.
[34] Stanley Hauerwas, *Sanctify Them in Truth* (Nashville: Abingdon, 1998), 160.
[35] Ibid.
[36] Nicholas Adams and Charles Elliott, "Ethnography is Dogmatics: Making Description Central to Systematic Theology," *Scottish Journal of Theology* 53 (Autumn 2000): 339–64.
[37] Ibid., 363.

In one case, a forest-dwelling community faced massive deforestation by aggressive logging companies. Another details the conflict between the World Bank and local communities over the construction of a huge dam. The resistances offered in each case are described in great detail and are summarized as "miracles," examples of the eschatological exaltation promised for the humble and meek. In arguing thus, they break the disciplinary divide, calling for theologians to be better students of the real exactly as they see it: both now and not yet. Such a call offers another approach to the dilemma of narrative theology and its too ideal portrayal of the church.

Answering Milbank and Hauerwas: Robbins et al.

It turns out Milbank's broadside against theological "borrowing" of social science analyses not only drew the attention of theologians but of social scientists as well. Perhaps the most influential of these is the anthropologist Joel Robbins whose 2006 article "Anthropology and Theology: An Awkward Relationship?" galvanized a conversation both within anthropology and in conversation with theologians.[38] Noting that Christianity has become a growing area of research interest for anthropology, Robbins asks what relationship anthropology should have to theology. He points out two existing ways and posits a third possible direction, one that to him seems promising. The first two, the critical examination of theology's role in the formation of the disciple of anthropology (here, see key work by Talal Asad[39]), and a view of theology as another sort of data about particular Christian culture (here, see Susan Harding[40] among others), engage theology in ways that do not challenge or change anthropology. His third direction suggests an openness of anthropologists admitting that theology has a more adequate purchase on understanding the world in some way or another—and through the encounter, anthropology is substantively changed.

In pursuing this possibility, Robbins turns to Milbank. His reasons for doing so are in part the theological impact *Theology and Social Theory* made in its own field, and in part because of its unusually significant engagement with and critiques of social science. Robbins hones in on Milbank's core critique of social theory—that its fundamental ontology is "an ontology of violence, 'a reading of the world which assumes the priority of force and tells how this force is best managed and confined by counter-force.'"[41] Milbank doesn't seek to counter social theory's ontology of violence and instead simply provides an alternative, the authentic Christian social ontology marked by the peace of Christ, and the reconciliation afforded through him.

Robbins laments that in previous generations, social science and anthropology specifically had depicted otherness as potentially desirable, as possible directions of change for Western societies. Yet this view came to be seen as at best naive, and at

---

[38] Joel Robbins, "Anthropology and Theology: An Awkward Relationship?" *Anthropological Quarterly* 79, no. 2 (Spring 2006): 285–94.
[39] Talal Asad, *Formations of the Secular: Christianity, Islam, Modernity* (Stanford: Stanford University Press, 2003).
[40] Susan Harding, *The Book of Jerry Falwell: Fundamentalist Language and Politics* (Princeton: Princeton University Press, 2001).
[41] Ibid., 289.

worst, oppressive, following the liberation movements of the 1960s and 1970s. Yet, Robbins says, theological capacity to theorize otherness as desirable and possible is something indicates "to us something we have lost . . . not of course our failure to theorize on the basis of a belief in God, but for our inability to anymore show the world how to find hope for real change without him [sic]."[42]

Robbins continues to find these questions animating, and more than a decade after the initial article, published a book on the topic: *Theology and the Anthropology of Christian Life*. Drawn from a series of lectures Robbins gave, the book has the character of a series of proofs that indeed, theology can provide anthropology with theoretical materials that reorient anthropological theory when taken seriously. As Lutherans, it was particularly intriguing to see Lutheran theological notions of the divine gift of grace and human passivity in relation to the gift as sources for rethinking classical anthropological approaches to gift giving. This sort of more substantive, theoretical mutual transformation between disciplines seems to be his goal, rather than remaining on the methodological level in which theologians (like us) borrow ethnography as a way to do theology, and anthropologists borrow theology as another sort of ethnographic data.

While of course all the contours of his argument are beyond the scope of this discussion, his particular take on Milbank's critique of social theory—and ethnography as a fundamental approach for generating it—is helpful to our overall purposes in this book. In a revealing moment late in the book, Robbins appreciatively cites Bruce Kapferer's aphorism that "anthropology is secularism's doubt." This has a double meaning, on the one hand acknowledging Milbank's point regarding the secular identity of social science as constitutive; yet on the other hand, by virtue of "its insistence that fieldworkers engage in 'the willing suspension of belief' in order to enter as far as possible into the lifeworlds of those they study, anthropology constantly exposes secular thought to ways of understanding the world that are not its own."[43] Though the diverse examples of anthropology Robbins cites are very often by its depictions of lives lived "otherwise," they still rarely even try to escape the secularism social theory assumes.

Yet Robbins's engagement with Lutheran theologian Ingolf Dalferth leads him to the insight that "discussions about secularity unfold in terms of a secular/religious binary that itself is wholly situated within secular thought."[44] As a theologian, Dalferth argues, his interest is not in a this-worldly division between sacred and secular, but rather in a division between realms: God's and the world, a division necessitated by the division between creator and creation. In their work in contexts of social oppression in Northern India, Adams and Elliot as theologians argue for ethnography within this second sort of division, naming it as seeing the world as it is, and as it shall be—that is, descriptively and eschatologically. Our argument with Milbank has to do in part with the disciplined attention required to see the world as it is, and to learn from the social sciences ways of understanding that derive theory or, in our case, theology, inductively.

---

[42] Ibid., 293.
[43] Ibid., 163.
[44] Ibid., 161.

Anthropology, as Sara Williams points out in her critique of Robbins's writing, has long had an engaged or activist agenda that if not theological was most certainly normative, moving beyond the "is" to the "ought."[45] Rather than merely positing a dialogue between generic anthropology and generic theology, the question is which and whose versions of the discipline one attends to. She raises classical examples like Franz Boaz, a German immigrant who we note in Chapter 1 engaged in critiques of racism and fascism, working with W. E. B. DuBois and mentoring BIPOC women studying anthropology at a time when that was quite unusual—Zora Neale Hurston and Ella Deloria being important examples. And while theologians have most often found dialogue with philosophy their mainstay, Williams points out, for example, that Christian social ethics—Protestant social gospel or Catholic social encyclicals—has long focused on grounded analysis so that its "ought" was deeply shaped by disciplined understandings of the "is."

In a related vein, in Chapter 9, Nicole Hoskins contributes to this methodological conversation by interrogating the assumption in predominant modes of Christian ethics that also assumes a separation between description of what is and the normative claim of what ought to be. As she unpacks the meaning of "rants" among Black environmental justice activists, she sees that the lines are blurred between the descriptive and normative. And to try to separate them out would do injustice to the meaning of them. Ethnography (or qualitative social science more broadly), although dominated by the domains of anthropology and sociology today, in fact has been and should be available to theologians *as* theologians. What, after all, was Tertullian up to in his classic critique of the Roman games in *Spectacles*?[46] It was ethnography *as* ecclesiology, in the sense that he intended it for use in baptismal catechesis. Such descriptive work shows the world as it is and as it should be. The work of those contributing to this volume offers examples to and a challenge for theological work that would speak of the "real" church, and not simply a formal or ideal one.

"Judicious narratives," it seems to us, are prudent or wise exactly here: that they show us who we are just now as *this or that part* of the one, holy, catholic, and apostolic church, or of the wider world, so that we know what we must do to be faithful to the particular identities we claim. In such work, ethnography is the rightsized tool to build a complex enough understanding of culture and community to account for the sorts of hybrid identities and complex communities actually lived out today. In the following chapter, we seek to more carefully articulate theological justifications for the disciplined practice of ethnographic inquiry.

---

[45] Sara Williams, "From Disciplinary Transactions to Political Practice: Moving Past Theology and Anthropology 'in General'," *Political Theology*, May 12, 2022.

[46] Tertullian, *De Spectaculis*, trans. T. R. Glover, Loeb Classical Library 250 (Cambridge, MA: Harvard University Press, 1931).

4

Theological Justifications for Turning to Ethnography

Do You Belong Here?

Feeling, sensing, or hearing that one "doesn't belong" is generally a jarring experience. Untold numbers of people—especially queer, Black, Brown, female, trans, unhoused, religious/cultural minorities—who do not "fit" the predominant expectations prescribed by a majority have felt the fear and sting in their bodies from being marked as "other." As both US history and the present testify, it is not a far leap from denying belonging to concerted efforts to extinguish the existence of a particular people or other. One only has to remember the forced removal of the Cherokee, Choctaw, Chickasaw, Creek, Lakota, and Seminole from their homelands in the 1800s[1] or recognize the dozens of legislative efforts striving to curtail basic respect and care for the preferred gender identities of non-binary and trans people (from bathroom use to recognition of pronouns to access to healthcare).[2] For example, as of 2024, 25 states have passed laws banning gender-affirming healthcare for trans minors.[3]

Though less overtly violent, the question of belonging or not nonetheless creeps into various kinds of vocational and academic contexts as well. In 1987, Gloria Anzaldúa, Chicana scholar, poet, and feminist, published a rich, landmark exploration of the multilayered (geographical, spiritual, cultural, linguistic, sexual, racial) borderlands she experienced as a lesbian woman of color who grew up on the Texas-US Southwest/Mexican border. In evocative language, Anzaldúa explores how she (along with thousands of Mexicans and Mexican Americans) manage to create a home and identity that straddles numerous boundaries simultaneously. From our distinct, respective social locations, we resonate with her sense that one's home (culturally, academically, religiously, etc.) is not found on one side of the border or the other. Rather, it is found at the creative, albeit uncomfortable, place of the intersection itself—where differing disciplines, ways of knowing, and being come together—in Anzaldúa's words, on a "thin edge of barbed wire."[4]

---

[1] Claudio Saunt, *Unworthy Republic: The Dispossession of Native Americans and the Road to Indian Territory* (New York: W. W. Norton & Company, 2020).
[2] https://www.aclu.org/legislative-attacks-on-lgbtq-rights-2023 (accessed January 10, 2024).
[3] https://www.npr.org/2024/05/22/1252987492/there-are-now-25-states-with-bans-on-trans-health-care-for-minors (accessed May 22, 2024).
[4] Gloria Anzaldúa, *Borderlands La Frontera: A New Mestiza* (San Francisco: Aunt Lute Books, 1987), 13. Earlier in the Preface, she elaborates:

Anzaldúa's life story speaks to the personal costs of questioning culturally fortified boundaries and chipping away at them. Living and working on such a sharp, toothy edge is uncomfortable and inherently involves multiple risks. One's professional identity can be called into question—by others and by one's own self-doubts. It is possible to be overwhelmed by the complexity of the work and to get stuck indefinitely. Sometimes researchers are not emotionally or intellectually prepared for what they hear and have no way of knowing how to respond. Then, even when the work is complete, writing in unconventional ways or with new methods does not necessarily lead to academic milestones such as a PhD, a first job, or promotion and tenure.

In terms of carrying out ethnographic research, and as Scharen reveals in Chapter 2, it is a risk to go where "one does not belong"—and does not know exactly what to do, what to ask, or even how to "be" in the space. And as Chapter 1 discusses, since 2011, there has been a significant and much-needed grappling with the reality that researchers embody complicated combinations of "insiders" and "outsiders." Even for those who share much of the positionality with whom they study, the decision to do qualitative research creates an important, unavoidable measure of distance.

Thus, anyone who has done ethnographic work knows of the awkwardness felt in one's bones when it is painfully apparent how much the researcher "sticks out"—in terms of the various, often simultaneous differences or privileges a researcher may embody (e.g., race, education, gender, socioeconomic status, nationality, religion). On top of these tenuous power imbalances, ethnographers often stumble as they grope to learn about the distinct contexts and lives of others, perhaps especially when they share little/none of the positionalities of those from and with whom they aspire to learn.

In fact, as argued in Chapter 1, it may well be that the missteps are needed in order for nuanced learning to happen. For example, in *Transgressive Devotion*, Natalie Wigg-Stevenson insightfully describes how researchers may miss important learning opportunities by charging ahead with agendas and failing to pay attention to the affective—the emotions, tensions, questions—happening in the moment and within those present, including the body of the researcher.[5] Wigg-Stevenson argues that there are crucial things to learn when theology is done as performative art, which blurs the lines between official theology, practiced theology, orthodoxy, and heterodoxy. But we cannot learn about these nuanced ways of lived theology if we do not reflect on the disjunctures between heads and hearts, the affective dynamics within us and in the field.

In short, without taking the time to reflect honestly about such awkward disconnects, researchers may not even realize that they did not know the most important questions to ask or how even how to be at the outset. Indeed, making gaffes, fumbling, looking silly—even embarrassing one's self—can lead to crucial epiphanies for researchers in

> The actual physical borderland that I'm dealing with in this book is the Texas-US Southwest/Mexican border. The psychological borderlands, the sexual borderlands, and the spiritual borderlands are not particular to the Southwest. In fact, the Borderlands are physically present whenever two or more cultures edge each other, where people of different races occupy the same territory, where under, lower, middle, and upper classes touch, where the space between two individuals shrinks with intimacy.

[5] Natalie Wigg-Stevenson, *Transgressive Devotion: Theology as Performance Art* (London: SCM Press, 2021).

that previously subconscious assumptions come to the surface for critical reflection at work. In fact, such instances often teach, or at least remind, academics what it means to be human.

Yet, for as uncomfortable as it can be to feel out of place, the dangers associated with this work extend into the far more serious concerns of invading the lives of others. It can be all too easy to take what we hear/learn for selfish gain; to manipulate the stories and insights so that they fit into the researcher's predetermined frames; to violate the privacy and the integrity of others by treating what they offer for research as something cheap rather than as sacred. In short, ethnographers are often asked—*should* be asked—and need to ask themselves if they belong where they are. Do they have a good enough reason to impose upon the lives of others for a time in order to learn from and with them? Rigorous interrogation coming from various quarters—while vexing and frustrating at times—can be integral to the overall quality of the work. Responding to questions—both friendly and less so[6] in nature—constitutes an ongoing part of the research process.

As Chapter 3 makes clear, not all welcome this attempt to create more of a home at the crossroads of theology, ethics, and ethnography. The use of the social sciences in the doing of theology and ethics has been met with strong resistance by some prominent theological minds. In a sense, they ask: "Why seek theological insights through illegitimate theological sources, ones that at best bracket faith and at worst deny it?" In a similar vein, social scientists raise their own critical questions. "What do theologians and Christian ethicists know about qualitative research? What right do they have to venture into this terrain given their lack of formal training?" As theologians and Christian ethicists cross disciplinary boundaries, a valid concern is that they will run "fast and loose" with the methods of ethnography and, minimally, do shoddy work, and of even greater concern, put others at risk or expose them to discomfort, pain, or risk.

For example, one significant concern rightly raised by social scientists revolves around what one "does with the data." Sociologists and anthropologists who use ethnography emphasize the central tasks of in-depth, accurate observation and reporting of life, people, and events. The aim is decidedly *not* to over-interpret or issue claims of "ultimate meaning" or what "ought to be" based upon what is seen, heard, understood, and so on. So asking the kinds of questions that theologians and ethicists might tend to ask such as, "what does this practice indicate about atonement" or "how is this liturgical move reflective of a particular ecclesiology?" or "what normative implications flow out of what is observed in an ethnographic study of climate refugees?" may strike a sociologist or anthropologist as precisely the *wrong* questions to pose. This complex disciplinary disconnect may be one reason why theologians and theological ethicists sometimes face prolonged and arduous Institutional Review Board processes. It takes time to explain the goals and rationale and to translate terms and methods across distinct disciplines.

---

[6] Vigen encountered this lesson during an intensive Institutional Review Board (IRB) process. See Aana Marie Vigen, *Women, Ethics, and Inequality in U.S. Healthcare: "To Count Among the Living"* (New York: Palgrave Macmillan, 2006), 102–9.

In sum, this endeavor—ethnography as theology and ethics—continues to encounter resistance from two different academic borders/sides: from theological ones that want to safeguard the purity and preeminence of traditional theological sources and methods from the "muddiness" of secular, experiential modes of inquiry; and from social scientific ones that take issue with an ethnographic project done by disciplinary "outsiders" and/or that would have the audacity to make theological or normative claims out of such research. In light of these concerns, two important questions surface for theologians: 1. *Why* attempt ethnography? and 2. *How* ought a Christian theologian or ethicist go about it responsibly? Here we respond to the first query; the latter question is the subject of the concluding chapter in Part III.

Considering How Ethnography Is Properly Theological: Source, Substance, Self-Critique

Embodied Knowing

Epistemology is a big word that denotes the realm of ideas and theories that explore how we as human beings know what we claim to know. It asks not *what* is true, but rather, *how* do we know truth? How do we arrive at it? Traditionally, theologians are formally trained to draw especially upon the disciplines of religious doctrine, biblical studies, and theological and ecclesial history in their quests for truth. In Christian ethics, the four commonly cited sources of moral knowledge are scripture, reason, tradition, and experience. While we affirm the centrality of each of these sources, this volume represents a sustained case for giving more attention and weight to the realm of human experience. And ethnography is an invaluable tool in revealing its profound and complex wisdom.

Notions around what constitutes an adequate method in the doing of formal theology and ethics have been earnestly discussed and hotly debated by Christian scholars, institutions, clergy, and laypersons for centuries. In particular, a focal point of contention has been differing takes on the role and category of human experience. While most theologians and ethicists acknowledge it as valid source, it is still often viewed with suspicion and/or dismissed as overly subjective, personal, and emotional. In a nutshell, the persistent fear is relativism—in belief and in ethics. The argument can be summarized this way: if experience is given too much weight in the analysis, claims to transcendent or universally normative truth will degenerate into biased, or at least problematically limited, visions based on one's own preferences and encounters. Experience cannot be given too much authority in efforts to know the divine or the good because it is not rooted in an objective or transcendent ground—it is too vulnerable to individual dispositions, filters, interpretations, and blind spots. Consequently, taking experience as a central source will lead to "anything goes" in theology and ethics, meaning that there will be lack of objective criteria by which to measure more or less adequate descriptions of God, God's relation to humanity, or of human responsibility in the world in light of this relationship.

In contrast to such views, the authors in this volume understand that experience is a multidimensional source and is accessed through varied disciplines and mediums (not only anthropology, sociology, or personal narrative).[7] Indeed, a rich understanding of human experience is cultivated through the critical use and interpretation of multiple and mutually corrective sources, among them: sociology, natural sciences, anthropology, literature, storytelling, the arts, history, sacred scriptures, autobiography, ethnography, ecclesial doctrines, and theological accounts. When described in this manner, many Christian scholars are more amenable to the category because they see that experience includes a range of disciplines and sources that put an individual experience into a larger context. It is not simply "my experience," but rather the experiences of individuals, communities—in history, over time, and as discovered through the careful study of texts, artifacts, embodied practices, living traditions, and so on. Thus, by the term "experience" we do not have in mind a simplistic "my personal experience tells me" kind of thinking. Rather, our understanding of the category triangulates experience *with* experience—integrating ethnographic, sociological, economic, cultural, theological, biblical, and so on sources of knowledge along the way.

Professing to have a repository for sacred traditions, doctrines, texts, ritual, or other practices is not sufficient to keep theology "relevant and real" in a particular context. These sources of theological and moral wisdom and identity must be accompanied with an interpretive competence that resonates within a given community. Sacred scriptures and faith claims must somehow be visible and active within embodied contexts or else they cease to "live."[8] The process of moral and spiritual formation is complex and ongoing. Does the practice still mediate identity? How is a given community interpreting texts, rituals, practices, doctrines—which ones are they actively engaging and which are sidelined? How are they using these resources? How are they (re)interpreting these sources and thus how does the interpretative process shape them—read and constitute the sources themselves?

While so much concern around "identity" (religious, denominational, etc.) centers around the question, "Is the community holding fast?" (aka interpreting and using the sacred deposits of the tradition faithfully), Mary McClintock Fulkerson asks a very different question. She asks not *if* a community is being faithful, but "*how* is it faithful?" What holds meaning for community members as they express that meaning in many different ways (verbal and nonverbal; textual and visual; in their bodies, emotions, and actions)? Pivotal community practices and rituals involve not only Bible studies or formal worship, but also the full range of activities and projects engaged by members of a faith community (prayer, soup kitchens, walking labyrinths, secondhand stores, dinner churches, shelters, unhoused youth accompaniment, public policy advocacy, etc.).

---

[7] For elaboration on this point, see Aana Marie Vigen, "Conclusion: Descriptive and Normative Ways of Understanding Human Nature," in *God Science Sex Gender: An Interdisciplinary Approach to Christian Ethics*, ed. Aana Marie Vigen and Patricia Beattie Jung (Urbana: University of Illinois Press, 2010), 241–58.

[8] See, for example, Paul Fiddes, *Seeing the World and Knowing God: Hebrew Wisdom and Christian Doctrine in a Late-Modern Context* (Oxford: Oxford University Press, 2013); Fiddes, *Participating in God: A Pastoral Doctrine of the Trinity* (London: Darton, Longman and Todd, 2000).

Indeed, rational knowing is often overvalued over other kinds of understanding. Qualitative research can help scholars expand our appreciation of the diverse ways of knowing that move beyond a predominant cultural bias that favors Western logic and rationality to the detriment of others. To illustrate, in her ethnographic study, Lorraine V. Cuddeback-Gedeon centers the agency and ways of knowing of people with intellectual disabilities so as to not impose her framing and interpretations of their insights and experiences.[9]

Moreover, giving the category of experience priority can create a lively space for interaction and reflection among *all* of the sources—traditions, sacred scriptures, doctrines, the sciences, and so on. It can inspire and support transdisciplinary conversation and reflection. Appreciating the complexity and rigor of experience helps us see the ways human beings are both shaped by all of these sources and then in turn shape them and reinterpret them. Such awareness can lend to the vitality of faith traditions and communities—rather than working to dismantle them—because it can both reveal inadequacies in academic theological and ethical reflection *and also* suggest ways for nuancing them that are both rigorous and grounded. In short, giving more weight to experience shows respect *both* for the traditions and scriptures we inherit *and* for the lives and events we create and encounter.

Moreover, we make a further claim, shared by several womanist and feminist theologians and ethicists, that experience is not simply a source for theology and ethics. Rather, it is the *primary lens* through which human beings access any and all scientific, moral, or theological knowledge.[10] This argument is more controversial than making the case that experience is discovered in a variety of sources and disciplines. Here, experience functions as a "type of truth claim;" in itself, it contains moral knowledge.[11] As Scharen contends elsewhere:

> While many disagreements over the proper balance of [reason, scripture, tradition, and experience] exist in the scholarly literature, I wish to point out that experience is never simply just one among the four sources. Rather, it infuses all the others, as a sort of founding source or means of knowing. So, for example, Holy Scripture records people's experience and reception of God and God's revelation in Jesus Christ; the church's traditions represent the collective experiences of God's pilgrim people over time; and it is now common to assume scholarly work to be influenced by the experiences of the scholar her—or himself. In addition, our experiences

---

[9] Lorraine Cuddeback-Gedeon, *The Work of Inclusion: An Ethnography of Grace, Sin, and Intellectual Disabilities* (London: T&T Clark Bloomsbury, 2022).

[10] See M. Shawn Copeland, *Enfleshing Freedom: Body, Race, and Being* (Minneapolis, MN: Fortress Press, 2009); Margaret Farley, *Just Love: A Framework for Christian Sexual Ethics* (New York: Continuum, 2006); Carter Heyward, *Touching Our Strength: The Erotic as Power and the Love of God* (San Francisco: Harper & Row, 1989); Emilie Townes, *Womanist Ethics and the Cultural Production of Evil* (New York: Palgrave Macmillan, 2006); Traci C. West, *Disruptive Christian Ethics: When Racism and Women's Lives Matter* (Louisville: Westminster John Knox Press, 2006).

[11] See Susan L. Secker, "Human Experience and Women's Experience," in *Dialogue about Catholic Sexual Teaching: Readings in Moral Theology, vol. 8*, ed. Charles E. Curran and Richard A. McCormick (Mahwah: Paulist Press, 1993), 577–99.

deeply influence how we interpret the data drawn from sources: how and what we draw from Scripture, tradition, and the secular disciplines.[12]

In other words, experience is not simply a category among others; it is the interpretative vehicle. We mediate all moral and theological knowledge through our flesh—inclusive of bones, hearts, emotions, conscience, and embodied minds. Certainly for some Christians, this view threatens a sense of the transcendent divine presence in creation (that is uniquely revealed in scripture and tradition). To this concern, we respond that such an understanding is instead a way to take God's incarnation in the world seriously.

Fulkerson's landmark work is instructive with respect to the depth and breadth of the category of experience. *Places of Redemption* explores a complex matrix of multifaceted materials[13] in an attempt to get at the richness of experience within a particular congregation. Her model shows the density of experience and how, in order to do justice to it, an ethnographer must take into account an expansive range of material—visceral ways of knowing, daily practices, desires, varied kinds of power, liturgies, and complex ways that cripture or doctrine is incorporated and interpreted. All of these dimensions help develop a multivalent description of the situation, of the life of a community.

In pursuing this rich account, Fulkerson takes seriously postmodernist deconstructions of presumed neutrality and objectivity. There is no completely impartial "view from nowhere." All claims to truth—including those made by theology—are situated within particular convictions and stances. As part of a larger and thoughtful discussion of the significance and meaning of "place," which she redefines as "a structure of lived, corporate and *bodied* experience," Fulkerson remarks: "When understood as *bodied ingression into the world*, place is truly fundamental in generating knowledge. . . . The world *takes shape* through our bodies."[14] All human knowing is embodied knowing. Subsequent works by Cuddeback-Gedeon, T. West, Wigg-Stevenson, and Whitmore further testify to this truth.[15]

Consequently, rather than fearing subjectivity in theology and ethics, we find that acknowledging its presence is the most honest and authentic theological and ethical response. All truth claims—even as they grasp and reach toward the transcendent—come from specific positions, perspectives, and bodies. Even as they may very well

---

[12] Christian Scharen, "Experiencing the Body: Sexuality and Conflict in American Lutheranism," in *Sexuality and the Sacred*, 2nd ed., ed. Marvin Ellison and Kelly Brown Douglas (Louisville: Westminster John Knox, 2010), 39.

[13] Fulkerson attends to a wide spectrum of elements such as hidden inheritances, habituated bodies with desires, local and political powers, rituals, behaviors, kinship relations, and all kinds of beliefs that are present at various levels. See Mary McClintock Fulkerson, *Places of Redemption* (Oxford: Oxford University Press, 2007), 11-12.

[14] Emphasis hers. See Fulkerson, *Places of Redemption*, 25; 24-31 offer an in-depth discussion of place.

[15] See Traci C. West, *Solidarity and Defiant Spirituality: Africana Lessons on Religion, Racism, and Ending Gender Violence* (New York: New York University Press, 2019); Natalie Wigg-Stevenson, *Ethnographic Theology: An Inquiry into the Production of Theological Knowledge* (New York: Palgrave Macmillan, 2014) and *Transgressive Devotion: Theology as Performance Art*; Todd Whitmore, *Imitating Christ in Magwi: An Anthropological Theology* (London: T&T Clark, 2019); Cuddeback-Gedeon, *The Work of Inclusion*.

reveal some of the truth, none is exhaustive—they are always partial in scope. Thus, they continually merit reexamination and critical reflection to see both what they reveal and also what they miss or conceal.

If this insight is off-putting, historical perspective can be helpful. Throughout human history, a particular truth is discovered in light of prior limits of human thought and then becomes overemphasized in its own time and thus needs to be corrected with an opposite polarity in the next. For example, consider the revolutionary notion of human autonomy that came out of the Enlightenment and owes much to thinkers such as Hume, Locke, Kant, and Jefferson. The notion that all individuals (at least white, male, landowners)—regardless of social stature or economic standing—were ordained with equality and had equal rights was absolutely revolutionary in the context of feudalism. Yet, many theologians and ethicists (among others) have argued that in the late twentieth and early twenty-first centuries of US society, autonomy and negative rights have been overvalued to the detriment of positive rights and the common good. In light of this predominant cultural view, they conclude that a refocusing of priorities and conceptions of the human person and the good is desperately needed—for both human and larger ecological survival and well-being.[16]

"Recognisably Real" Theology and Ethics

Several scholars included in this volume (Boopalan and Jongte, Grigoni, Hankela and Nishimwe, Hoskins, Mingo) showcase the integral role that human experience plays in the cultivation of adequate claims to theological and moral knowledge. Extending the significance of experience even further, numerous theologians make the case that ethnography is a way to access *both* human experience *and* knowledge of the divine. Thus, it can be more than a mere tool in the doing of theology; it in itself can be an *expression* of theology.

Speaking specifically with practical theology and ecclesiology in mind, Clare Watkins explains: "The turn to qualitative methods is, itself, a response to a fundamental theology of revelation. This practical turn is not, then, only pragmatic; it has something to do with our doctrine of the Trinity, our understanding of divine revelations, and, above all, our belief in the Holy Spirit and the difference such belief makes."[17] Of course, there are often striking differences between practiced faith and doctrine-based faith. Qualitative methods help us explore the kinds of ethical and faith convictions that are lived out in a concrete place/community, which may or may not align with the formal theology/ethics espoused by the denomination/tradition/community. In short, both divine being and human being are knowable and can be revealed in powerful ways. But

---

[16] See Lisa Sowle Cahill, *Theological Bioethics: Participation, Justice and Change* (Washington, DC: Georgetown, 2005); Allen Verhey, *Reading the Bible in the Strange World of Medicine* (Grand Rapids: W.B. Eerdmans, 2003); Larry L. Rasmussen, *Earth-Honoring Faith: Religious Ethics in a New Key* (New York: Oxford University Press, 2013); and Rasmussen, *The Planet You Inherit: Letters to My Grandchildren When Uncertainty's a Sure Thing* (Minneapolis: Broadleaf Books, 2022).

[17] Clare Watkins, "Qualitative Research in Theology: A Spiritual Turn?" in *The Wiley Blackwell Companion to Theology and Qualitative Research*, ed. Pete Ward and Knut Tveitereid (Hoboken: John Wiley & Sons, Ltd, 2022), 17. See also Watkins, *Disclosing Church: Generating Ecclesiology through Conversations in Practice*. (London: Routledge, 2020).

as soon as we claim to command a mastery, we have turned our understanding of this truth of the other (human or divine) into a static, reified idol.

As Chapter 3 discusses, John Milbank and others view such a claim with suspicion. Yet, Milbank accepts the critique of his own work in *Theology and Social Theory* that his elaboration of the church is too idealized. We suggest in Chapter 3 that ethnography can offer the most robust corrective to the problematic of too formal an ecclesiology. It can, therefore, offer just the sort of "judicious narratives" called for by Milbank that can make such ecclesiology more "recognisably real." In other words, ethnography can help us create theology that is relevant—that attends meaningfully to living and historically rooted traditions; the Gospel; and to contemporary human encounters, practices, and needs. In a similar vein, Fulkerson argues that theological reflection "does not begin with a full-blown doctrine of God or of the church. Such a method misses that strange, often unremarked thing that *compels* a theological response—how it is that theological reasoning is provoked at all."[18] Theology does not emerge from a vacuum; concrete dilemmas inspire its creation. Or as practical theologian Yara González-Justiniano reminds us, "all theology is contextual."[19] It is only a question of whether that fact is acknowledged or not.

Elaborating upon the insights of Charles Winquist and Walter Lowe, Fulkerson poignantly describes theology as a "response to a wound," meaning that it arises in direct response to our most intimate and urgent needs, hurts, crises, and questions:

> Wounds generate new thinking. Disjunctions birth invention—from a disjuncture in logic, where reasons is compelled to find new connections in thought, to brokenness in existence, where creativity is compelled to search for possibilities of reconciliation. Like a wound, theological thinking is generated by a sometimes inchoate sense that something *must* be addressed.[20]

In its most primary sense and purpose, theology is not a system of thought; nor is it a static or perfect elaboration of divine being and doing. Instead, it is a visceral and sensual response to hurts and harms. It strives to respond to the disconnect between the love and right relationship human beings sense is possible—even taste in some of their experiences—and yet is not completely fulfilled in them. At its best, theology and ethics represent intentional and nuanced efforts to make sense of suffering *and* to do something (e.g., prophetic, pastoral, constructive, hope-filled) about it—to create "places of redemption."

As support for this provocative claim, Fulkerson cites the example of Karl Barth's theology of the Word responding to the wound of "idolatries of the German Church" and James Cone's Black theology calling white theology to account for its false claims

---

[18] Fulkerson, *Places of Redemption*, 13. Emphasis in the original. She cites Walter Lowe, *Theology and Difference: The Wound of Reason* (Bloomington: University Press, 1993), 9–10.
[19] Yara González-Justiniano and Christopher P. Ney, "Contextual Theology," in *The Wiley Blackwell Companion to Theology and Qualitative Research*, ed. Pete Ward and Knut Tveitereid (Hoboken: John Wiley & Sons, Ltd, 2022), 185.
[20] Fulkerson, *Places of Redemption*, 13–14. Emphasis in the original.

to universality and for its "deeply entrenched racism."[21] Dietrich Bonhoeffer's theology also comes to mind, but so does the theology of earlier theologians as well. Certainly Augustine's and Martin Luther's theological visions were rooted in the concrete and practical questions and crises of their days—whether in the particular political and doctrinal controversies and violence of Hippo in fifth-century North Africa or in those of sixteenth-century Saxony.

So too it is with theological and ethical endeavors in the twenty-first century. For theology to remain vibrant, it must resonate and meaningfully address the wounds of embodied, dynamic communities of faith. And to do this, it cannot simply be applied to situations; it must, at least in part, take flesh within them. Ethnography can be an illuminating way to take seriously God's incarnation in the world. Fulkerson hopes that such theological responses will create a space for "appearing," meaning that those previously lost to ignorance, apathy, and, as she puts it, "obliviousness" will be finally seen, heard, and attended to.[22]

In this way, ethnography can serve as an intervention that calls into question antagonistic "Church or theology vs. world" kinds of thinking. Instead of a sectarian understanding of faithfulness as setting one's self or religious community apart from the world, exploring "worldly theology" through the use of ethnography invites scholars and others to see how intertwined faith, theology, church, culture, and larger societies are. Acknowledging how utterly enmeshed these domains are does not rule out the need for critique among them. Indeed, at times, faith communities can be prophetic in their calling of governments, common practices, and predominant values into question. For their part, democratic institutions, the natural and social sciences, and secular humanism can all, in their distinctive voices and methods, starkly reveal the limits of particular theological perspectives. To say that these ways of knowing and being are mixed up with one another does rule out mutual correction and critique.

Rather, it means that no one domain ever truly exists in a "pure" or isolated state. While we profess a guiding, normative role for scripture in Christian theology and ethics, we also acknowledge its enactment is interpretative and therefore contested. Cultures, the sciences, historical events, theology, and ethics are all in a dynamic spiral—informing, revising, reinforcing, critiquing, and responding to one another. Rather than seeing theology or the church as set apart from secular society, we follow Jesus' teaching that Christians and Christian communities are called—created by God to be—persons and entities that are "in the world, but not wholly of it" (e.g., the Gospel of John, Chapters 17–18).

With specific regard to the task of ethics, we contend that Christian ethicists have an obligation to test what we claim normatively against what others live. For ethics to offer constructive insights and norms for shaping social relations and values, it must demonstrate that it has first taken the complexity of reality and lived experience into account. Moral claims lack force if they jump too quickly into prescription without

---

[21] Ibid., 14; n. 22.
[22] Ibid., 18–22.

taking a full enough view of the complexity of the issues at stake. Key sources of information and moral knowledge are not only those found online and in texts but also in embodied lives of people and communities.[23] The turn to ethnography in Christian theology and ethics, then, makes the bold claim that what nonacademics think, live, know, practice, do, and experience matters in a *fundamental* (not merely illustrative) way. Poignant examples of such nonacademic contributions to moral knowledge can be found in many disciplines.[24] Furthermore, we contend that this kind of wisdom matters not only as a source of moral knowledge *but also* as part of theology proper.

For example, in Vigen's work in medical ethics, the central conviction that runs throughout is this: if ethicists want to understand what justice and right relationship mean in healthcare contexts, we need to explore the needs and experiences of those who are most often marginalized by structural health and healthcare inequities. At its best, theology offers the insight that to understand what it means to be human, one has to think concretely, relationally, and contextually.

Roman Catholic womanist theologian M. Shawn Copeland argues that the only viable conception of what it means to be human is the one that takes seriously as its frame of reference the concrete bodies of the most despised, namely, "the exploited, despised, poor woman of color."[25] Theological and ethical definitions of what it means to be human only approach adequacy if they include explicit, substantive respect for these actual persons. What it means to love the neighbor as one's self only becomes real in the particular—discovered inductively. The poetic command to "love one another as one's self" needs to be enfleshed—surrounded—by the knowledge that comes out of concrete relationships, especially with those who are in some way vulnerable—those who have to fight to live, to be seen, heard, understood, and to be loved as an end in herself.

Ethnography is one possible means by which to make the above theological and moral commitment concrete. To illustrate: publicizing the principles,[26] goals, and mission of a hospital on every wall by the elevators does not ensure that they are lived out in the practices, sensibilities, cultures, and bodies of healthcare providers. Qualitative research may help to expose problems in perception—e.g. how care providers' perceptions of patients can be impaired by socioeconomic and racial assumptions and

---

[23] For a fuller argument on this point, see Vigen, "Conclusion," 245–55.
[24] For example, see texts in medical anthropology, sociology, illness narratives, and medical ethics: David Moller, *Dancing with Broken Bones* (Oxford: Oxford University Press, 2004); Arthur Kleinman, *Illness Narratives*; Margaret E. Mohrmann, *Attending Children: A Doctor's Education* (Washington, DC: Georgetown University Press, 2005); Arthur Frank, *The Wounded Storyteller: Body, Illness, and Ethics* (Chicago: University of Chicago Press, 1995); Joao Biehl, *Will to Live: AIDS Therapies and the Politics of Survival* (Princeton: Princeton University Press, 2007); Marian Burchardt, "Illness Narratives as Theory and Method," in *SAGE Research Methods Foundations*, ed. P. Atkinson, S. Delamont, A. Cernat, J. W. Sakshaug, and R. A. Williams (New York: Sage Publications, 2019). See also *Subjectivity* edited by Joao Biehl, Byron Good, and Arthur Kleinman.
[25] M. Shawn Copeland, "The New Anthropological Subject at the Heart of the Mystical Body of Christ," *CTSA PROCEEDINGS* 53 (1998): 30 and *Enfleshing Freedom*.
[26] Tom L. Beauchamp and James F. Childress, *The Principles of Biomedical Ethics*, 8th ed. (New York: Oxford University Press, 2019).

the consequences these assumptions have on patient well-being.[27] Indeed, numerous studies show how provider bias and misunderstanding have disproportionately negative, at times lethal, outcomes for minoritized patients, including spending less time with them, missing diagnostic clues, failures in building trust and rapport.[28]

In their respective chapters in Part II, Grigoni and Symmonds show how textured understandings of those with relative privilege undercut simplified generalizations and caricatures. Grigoni spent significant time listening to predominately white Christian gun owners in addition to attending vigils for those killed by gun violence. For her part, Symmonds took care to participate in and engage with white Christians who are invested in anti sex trafficking ministries with predominant Black and Brown women. Studying people with whom we share identifiers or locations of social power, or in Symmonds's case "studying up," is vital work, especially in polarized contexts such as the United States in 2024. We earnestly hope that this kind of qualitative engagement can foster more nuanced understanding of why disparate people think and care about what they do and open up additional possibilities for reflection among them, rather than shut off potential dialogue and connection.

Critical Self-Reflection: The Imperative of Reflexivity

As Williams lifts up in Chapter 10, responsible ethnographic scholarship must be profoundly self-aware. She shows that it often takes time to understand how the researcher is "read" by those from whom she hopes to learn. In her case, over time, she understood why her initial questions on gender led her to be somewhat regarded with hesitation as a Western outsider. Indeed, qualitative study must reflect back upon itself—examining the scholar's preconceptions and assumptions that they bring to the study and how they may be received by participants. As discussed in Chapter 1, various postmodern and postcolonial critiques have soundly trounced any *naiveté* that would purport that ethnographers simply "report" facets of reality. To be credible observers, researchers must acknowledge the filters through which they view that which they study.

A self-aware stance helps to guard against creating a purportedly perfected system of thought. In other words, it protects against the idolatry of one's own theological and ethical creations. Nuanced reflection owns its limits. No theology fully conveys divine being and action. Our understandings of revelation are never final or complete. At best, we glimpse transcendent truth in partial, yet illuminating fragments.

For its part, ethnography ought not attempt to tidy the messy contradictions it may find or create a false sense of unity, homogeneity, synthesis. Instead, it is necessarily open to finding disconnects, ruptures, and paradox—indeed, it expects them.

---

[27] See Vigen, *Women, Ethics, Inequality* for an in-depth discussion of these and related themes and Vigen, "Neglected Voices at the Beginning of Life: Prenatal Genetics and Reproductive Justice," in *Catholic Bioethics and Social Justice* (Collegeville: Liturgical Press, 2019).

[28] See, for example, Linda Villarosa, *Under the Skin: The Hidden Toll of Racism on American Lives and on the Health of our Nation* (New York: Doubleday, 2022); Liz Hamel, Lunna Lopes, et al., *KFF/The Undefeated Survey on Race and Health* (October 13, 2020), https://www.kff.org/report-section/kff-the-undefeated-survey-on-race-and-health-main-findings/.

Fitriyah's chapter in Part II exemplifies this point well. The female migrant workers she interviewed shared their complicated understandings of God active in their lives. For example, she shows how their embodied theologies understand God as both all-powerful and as limited.

Put simply, ethnographers, theologians, and ethicists alike do not need to be "all-seeing" or "all-knowing" in order to offer up relevant and illuminating insights about what is true or relevant. Instead, they can offer up as valid the partial—but no less true or significant—perceptions they gain through situating themselves in particular contexts, listening thoughtfully to others, and reflecting upon their own lives, emotional responses, and even (or especially) internal biases.

Thus, researchers have to be gutsy enough to check our own assumptions and to be open to being surprised, wrong, and changed by what we learn in the ethnographic field. Such a posture is not only essential for methodological credibility, it is also a way to model intellectual and spiritual humility. In a word: transparency. Scholars need to confront the subjective stances they bring to the work and open them to critical examination— in their analysis and by inviting critique from others.

In an effort to practice self-disclosure, some ethnographic models combine ethnography with autobiography. There can be dangers in doing this—the work can amount to little more than glorified "navel-gazing." Yet, if it is done with care and a degree of restraint, it can help reveal the (mal)formations and transformations within the person who writes the narrative, instead of training a spotlight on others while remaining hidden. In other words, it is one possible way to enact intellectual honesty and authenticity.[29]

Fulkerson models this kind of humility in acknowledging the discomfort she felt on her first visit to a congregation very unlike those to which she was accustomed. Her candor is instructive:

> While I am expecting a mixed-race group, I am surprised at my own response to all the dark skin in the room. A black woman approaches me. Extending her hand with a bulletin, she introduces herself and welcomes me warmly. I find myself aware of the paleness of my skin as I respond, trying to hide any signs that I am not used to worshiping with more than a few token black people. The overeager sound of my voice tells me I am probably failing. A good three-fourths of the people gathering to worship are black, or rather ebony, dark tan, bronze, and shades of color for which I have no names.
>
> Next I notice a thin white man sitting twisted in a wheelchair parked next to a short man who looks like he has Down syndrome. As I approach the man in the wheelchair my body feels suddenly awkward and unnatural. . . . My height feels

---

[29] See, for example, works that tell one's own story of professional moral and spiritual formation: Mohrmann, *Attending Children*; Frank, *The Wounded Storyteller*; Arthur Kleinman, *The Illness Narratives: Suffering, Healing, and the Human Condition* (New York: Basic Books, 1988); and Jerome Groopman, *How Doctors Think* (Boston: Houghton Mifflin, 2007). Though none of these is categorized as formal ethnography per se, they offer up models for theologians and ethicists to think about how they might be more transparent in their scholarship. Vigen and Scharen's work also attempts to model critical self-reflection combined with some personal storytelling, but neither fits within categories of autobiography or personal narrative.

excessive and ungainly. I tower over this pale man strapped in his wheelchair. Do I kneel down? Bend down to be face level to him? Speaking to him from above feels patronizing. Or is it the crouching down that would be patronizing? My hand moves to touch his shoulder, as if to communicate, "I care about you, despite your mildly frightening, contorted body and guttural gurgling sounds." But I withdraw my hand quickly, wondering if this, too, would be a sign of condescension. What was it like to be unable to command a safe space with your presence, to be vulnerable to the groping of other peoples' hands?[30]

It takes more than a little courage to show the places where we do not "shine" as stellar individuals or communities—to be honest about how we often grope and fumble in our relationships. And for those whose identities are tied up with notions of "expertise, intellect, scholarship" and professional titles, it can be especially threatening to admit how little we really know and how awkward we can feel around people dissimilar to our accustomed ways of being. It can feel a bit like we are naked—the robes, lab coats, and professional garb stripped away (or at least cast in a chair). Some may fear a loss of authority or credibility. Others may feel unsure of who they are without the security of the professional cloaks.

Undeniably, it can be disquieting and risky to reveal our own humanity in the research. Yet, finding the wherewithal to do so is vital—not only for the quality of the work, but for the intellectual and moral formation of the scholar. Critical self-reflexivity provides not only a way to check for preconceptions and blinders, it helps teach us to be human—imperfect, embodied, a member of a larger community that calls us to accountability, to relationship. And in this reckoning, there is not only embarrassing revelation of our shortcomings as people, there can also be grace, forgiveness, reconciliation, compassion, and even perhaps, approximations of justice. It is for these reasons that we have tried to reflect consciously and conscientiously on our identities and sites of privilege as white, Western, Christian, educated, employed persons. And in order to do so, we have had to relate stories where our actions fall short of the ideals to which we aspire.[31] Doing so helps us not only be better scholars, but to learn to be more human—both worthy of love and fallible.

Moreover, it is not just our story at play here. Individual stories can reveal larger social, political, economic, cultural, and racial dynamics that are too often hidden or silenced. For example, as Fulkerson reflects on her particular visceral experience described above, she makes connections to larger societal dynamics:

> My feeling of strangeness in response to the unaccustomed "blackness" of the place and the presence of people with disabilities at that first visit suggests that my conscious commitments to inclusiveness were not completely correlated with my habituated sense of the normal.... This tacit sense that surprised me when I became self-conscious of my whiteness and my able-bodiedness suggests forms of occlusion

---

[30] Fulkerson, *Places of Redemption*, 4–5.
[31] Vigen, *Women, Ethics, and Inequality in U.S. Healthcare*, xviii–xxiii; Scharen, "Experiencing the Body."

operating in my own internalized sense of the world. Evidence of a broader social "unaccustomedness" to black and disabled bodies, this discomfort has significance far beyond my own sense of dis-ease. It is an unaccustomedness and obliviousness with widespread parallels, not only at Good Samaritan, but in the larger society as well. It is an obliviousness that comes with dominance, and it foreshadows fracture in the smooth veneer of welcome and Christly inclusivity in the church as well.[32]

Fulkerson's story shows that there was a disconnect between her intellectual assent to inclusiveness and her habituated, embodied sense of what is considered by many in society as "normal." The problem is that it can be far too easy for certain groups (based on race, socioeconomics, and physical/mental abilities) to not truly see others—in Fulkerson's terms to remain oblivious to them. Obliviousness is not only a personal character flaw; it is also operative at social and structural levels as well—most clearly seen when one considers education, neighborhood demographics, health indicators, and so on. Indeed, Fulkerson goes on to discuss related scholarship and statistics that exposes the many layers of segregation in the US population—how seemingly invisible yet palpable lines divide differing racial, socioeconomic, and (dis)abled communities from one another.[33]

As an intervention to interrupt social obliviousness, Fulkerson, drawing on the work of Kimberley Curtis, focuses on ways to cultivate a "shared space of appearance." Profound changes in consciousness are needed—changes in rational thought, but also accompanied by changes in hearts and concrete practices as well. Those changes which primarily receive lip service or even those codified (e.g., through legislation) are not complete if they do not permeate the daily rituals of a society. Change must be registered at embodied levels for it to take full root in mind-sets and habitual ways of being.

Fulkerson draws on Bourdieau's elaboration of *habitus* and MacIntyre on practices to get at the dynamic combination of understanding and action that is needed for conversions in worldviews and in the ways a person or community lives its life:

> Just as books about boxing are not enough to make a good boxer, a *habitus* of justice is not adequately defined by knowledge of principles (or stories) of love, or of what

---

[32] Fulkerson, *Places of Redemption*, 15.
[33] Fulkerson cites relevant scholarship on the persistence of racial segregation and inequality in various arenas of US life (religion, schools, neighborhoods, etc.), see, for example, The Civil Rights Project at Harvard University Report, "Race in American Public Schools: Rapidly Resegregating School Districts" (2002); Michael Emerson and Christian Smith, *Divided by Faith: Evangelical Religion and the Problem of Race in America* (New York: Oxford University Press, 2000). For data on racial–ethnic disparities in health and healthcare, see the Commonwealth Fund Report: *Racial and Ethnic Disparities in U.S. Health Care: A Chartbook* (2008) and The Kaiser Family Foundation Report, "Key Facts: Race, Ethnicity and Medical Care, 2007 Update." For additional incisive social and philosophical analysis, see Iris Marion Young, *Justice and the Politics of Difference* (Princeton: Princeton University Press, 1990); Glenn C. Loury, *The Anatomy of Racial Inequality* (Cambridge, MA: Harvard University Press, 2002); Ellis Cose, *Color-Blind: Seeing Beyond Race in a Race-Obsessed World* (New York: Harper Perennial, 1997). For analysis of disabilities, stigma, and inequality, see Nancy Eiesland, *The Disabled God* (Nashville: Abingdon Press, 1994); Rosemary Garland-Thomson, *Extraordinary Bodies* (New York: Columbia University Press, 2017); Rebecca Spurrier, *The Disabled Church* (New York: Fordham University Press, 2019).

the church or even Jesus have said in the past. Any such *habitus* requires a feel for and grasp of the "items, events, and power" of an environment and how they "gather," to use the earlier language of a situation; *situational competence* is fundamental to the successful continuity of a practice.[34]

On its own, intellectual assent or professed commitment will not suffice—too often that means people say what they think they are supposed to say and keep their actual beliefs, feelings, and concerns beneath the surface. All dimensions of human being and doing need to be integrated through words, deeds, embodied senses, thoughtful reflection, prayer, and various rituals of daily existence.

Furthermore, people (especially those of us who benefit from one or more sites of privilege in society) have to face our fears and sites of dis-ease—working through the anxiety and discomfort so that our visceral reactions and daily practices are more consistent with our stated beliefs. We concur with Fulkerson that such transformation is not only important for political and social life, but bears on the spiritual dimensions of our existence in a fundamental way:

> What is needed to counter the diminishment and harm associated with obliviousness is a *place to appear*, a place to be seen, to be recognized and to recognize the other. Being seen and heard by others, being acknowledged by others—these are said to be essential to the political life; my point is that they are also essential to a community of faith as an honoring of the shared image of God.[35]

Park's description in Chapter 7 of the public protest of K on a downtown Seoul CCTV pole and the Christian community's recognition of his claims created, despite the (literal) precarity of his position, a space for him and for his claims for justice to appear. Ethnography is one way to work toward such appearances and to give flesh and bone to the theological concept of *imago dei* (image of God).

To be even more explicit theologically, ethnography can be radically related to both divine creation and incarnation. By paying strong attention to what exists—in creation, in a community, in embodied practices, it offers a method for heeding Luther's call to "honor God's handiwork." Similarly, and as poignantly expressed by Todd Whitmore,[36] theo-critical ethnography can provide a way to take up Christian discipleship. In immersing itself in the depths and complexities of suffering in the world, ethnographic methods can become a way both to witness to—and express solidarity with—those who are hurting and in need. In this sense, ethnography can be a way to testify.

---

[34] Fulkerson, *Places of Redemption*, 46. See also her earlier discussion of Bourdieau and MacIntyre on p. 35 and pp. 38–9. She continues this point on p. 47: "The point here, however, is that the wisdom suggested by the *habitus* requires a shift away from a rule- or content-driven model for normative thinking about traditioning. The kind of 'knowledge' at stake here combines flexibility with identity in a way best described as improvisational."
[35] Fulkerson, *Places of Redemption*, 21.
[36] Whitmore, "Crossing the Road," 273–94. Here, he draws on William C. Spohn, *Go and Do Likewise: Jesus and Ethics* (2007), Chapters 2–3. And see Whitmore, *Imitating Christ in Magwi*.

Moreover, as several contributors to Part II make plain, when qualitative researchers focus their study on communities with whom they share important aspects of identity (Grigoni, Hoskins, Mingo, Park), while not simply "insiders," they nonetheless may be able to see and interpret the realities with greater dimensionality than those who are more outsiders to the particular context. And as both Grigoni and Symmonds demonstrate in their projects, it can be illuminative when researchers aim to understand the worldviews of those with significant social or economic capital. Without defaulting to two-dimensional stereotypes, such work can unpack the ways of thinking, active faith, and underlying concerns of those with a large measure of power and resources to pursue their goals. Finally, several of the chapters in Part II also model the complex ways in which researchers are simultaneously, awkwardly "insiders" and "outsiders"—having more, and also at times less, power in relation to their subjects. Hankela and Nishimwe go a step further to show the power dynamics—including both potential opportunities and pitfalls—within the research team itself. Thus, each chapter, in its own way, contributes to an ever-more sophisticated understanding of reflexivity and power dynamics inherent in qualitative study.

Conclusion

In one sense, these three contributions of ethnographic methods offer a somewhat novel, and perhaps unnerving, way of thinking about the task of Christian theology and ethics. Indeed, Fulkerson's description may unsettle some: "Theological reflection is not a linear form of reflection that starts with a correct doctrine (or a 'worldly' insight) and then proceeds to analyze a situation; rather it is a situational, ongoing, never-finished dialectical process where past and present ever converge in new ways."[37] Yet, what Fulkerson describes is what faith communities have been doing for centuries—these dynamic processes did not begin with postmodernity. Indeed, they are as ancient as the faith traditions themselves—for they are part of the perennial quest to make meaning, discover truth, and remain relevant amid complexity and thorny challenges.

Speaking specifically as ethicists and with Part II in view, we would take Fulkerson's insight even a step further: the ethical questions of our day demand that we simultaneously leverage the very best information from all possible sources and also profoundly appreciate the complex degrees of interpretation unavoidably happening. Christian ethicists don't have the luxury of turning our noses up at sociology or anthropology any more than we can ignore economics, politics, or the natural sciences when addressing financial inequalities, wartime conflict, or the rapidly-changing climate.

Put even more bluntly, if we want to produce work that speaks meaningfully to realities such as health pandemics, end-of-life care, sexual ethics, economic ethics, bioethics, ecological ethics, democracy and capitalism, poverty, or the prison industrial complex, we have to work with all of the pertinent data. And doing so may very likely

---

[37] Fulkerson, *Places of Redemption*, 234.

mean talking with people or observing groups at work who deal daily with these issues in their own lives. Otherwise, why should anyone—in academia, public policy, or the larger society—listen to what we have to say? The burden of demonstrating credibility and relevance is on our shoulders. With this set of methodological and theological commitments and rationale clearly in view, we now turn to see examples of theological ethnography in the making.

Part II

Exemplars

A Conversation between the Researcher and the Research Assistant on Ethnographic Praxis

Elina Hankela and Clementine Nishimwe

Introduction

A few years ago scholarly discussion of the positioning of research assistants (RAs) was described as "limited but recently growing,"[1] yet questions related to hiring and working with RAs were and still are often left out of methodology handbooks[2] and researcher training.[3] This lack of engagement with questions related to the involvement of RAs is also reflected in Sarah Turner's claim that RAs as "key partner[s] in the research process ha[ve] been rendered invisible and effectively silenced" even in the context of the reflexive turn, which has made the researcher visible in much social scientific writing.[4] In light of these observations, it is clear that thinking about the roles, relationships, and power relations within a research team is an ethical imperative for theologian-ethnographers who wish to advance ways of doing ethnographic theology. Furthermore, since RAs inevitably impact both the research process and the data that are collected,[5] critical reflection on this partnership is also linked to the quality and trustworthiness of research findings.[6]

While the role of RAs is not relevant to all ethnographic projects, there are numerous fields which frequently require them, such as when Western researchers

---

[1] Nausheen H. Anwar and Sarwat Viqar, "Research Assistants, Reflexivity and the Politics of Fieldwork in Urban Pakistan," *Area* 49, no. 1 (2017): 114; Sara Stevano and Kevin Deane, "The Role of Research Assistants in Qualitative and Cross-Cultural Social Science Research," in *Handbook of Research Methods in Health Social Sciences*, ed. Pranee Liamputtong (Singapore: Springer, 2017), 1–16.
[2] Kevin Deane and Sara Stevano, "Towards a Political Economy of the Use of Research Assistants: Reflections from Fieldwork in Tanzania and Mozambique," *Qualitative Research* 16, no. 2 (2016): 214.
[3] Sarah Carter Narendorf et al., "Managing and Mentoring: Experiences of Assistant Professors in Working with Research Assistants," *Social Work Research* 40, no. 1 (2016): 19–30.
[4] Sarah Turner, "Research Note: The Silenced Assistant. Reflections of Invisible Interpreters and Research Assistants," *Asia Pacific Viewpoint* 51, no. 2 (2010): 206.
[5] Deane and Stevano, "Towards a Political Economy of the Use of Research Assistants."
[6] Martina Angela Caretta, "Situated Knowledge in Cross-Cultural, Cross-Language Research: A Collaborative Reflexive Analysis of Researcher, Assistant and Participant Subjectivities," *Qualitative Research* 15, no. 4 (2015): 489–505.

work in the Global South—an important angle in our reflections in this chapter as Elina (researcher) is a white Finnish scholar, albeit living in South Africa, and Clementine (RA on the project discussed) is a Black Rwandan, recently awarded her PhD. Methodological thinking related to the involvement of RAs in this context provides opportunities for challenging West-centered norms of knowledge production that are deeply embedded in present-day academia[7] in general, as well as how African Christianities are represented, in particular.

We join this conversation from the perspective of our lived experiences as a researcher and an RA in a research project related to xenophobia and Pentecostal theology in South Africa, which ran from 2018 to 2020.[8] We comprised one of two case study teams in this project—part of the African Theological Advance (ATA) initiative run by the Nagel Institute of Calvin University (USA)—which involved multiple studies across Africa that explored "a fresh understanding of how Christianity engages contemporary African realities."[9] In common with the whole initiative, our project celebrated grounded, locally circulating theologies that we accessed using ethnographic methodologies.

While thinking critically of the involvement of RAs could be useful for any project that involves assistants, this is particularly relevant in the context of ethnographic theology where both researcher and RA are deeply embedded in weaving the data together and making sense of it. When writing this chapter, we drew on our field notes and our recollections in an autoethnographic manner, meaning that how we thought and felt about our journey during fieldwork and how we now remember and perceive it became the basis of analysis.

In this kind of writing, who we are is an important analytical tool, thus we want to briefly introduce ourselves. Clementine is a migrant woman from Rwanda, a wife and a mother of two daughters, who has lived in South Africa since 2007. She was raised Catholic but now worships as an Anglican. While she has since graduated, at the time of this research project, she was a doctoral student at the University of Johannesburg (UJ), supervised by Elina, who migrated to South Africa from Finland, living here first from 2009 to 2010 and then since 2013. She too is a wife, and since 2021 also a mother. Brought up by missionary parents in her native Finland, as well as Ethiopia, the UK, and Namibia, Elina grew up Lutheran but has spent a lot of time with Methodists in South Africa. She was made a permanent member of the academic staff of the Department of Religion Studies at UJ during the fieldwork period.

---

[7] Kim Ozano and Rose Khatri, "Reflexivity, Positionality and Power in Cross-Cultural Participatory Action Research with Research Assistants in Rural Cambodia," *Educational Action Research* 26, no. 2 (2018): 199–200.

[8] The research project was part of the African Theological Advance (ATA) initiative (2018–20) of the Nagel Institute for the Study of World Christianity (Calvin University, Grand Rapids, MI). It was led by Prof. Ignatius Swart under the working title "Xenophobia and the Re-imagination of Evangelization amongst Migrant Dominated Churches in South Africa." The research project received a grant from the Nagel Institute for the Study of World Christianity, which was funded for the ATA initiative by the Templeton Religion Trust, Nassau, Bahamas.

[9] "African Theological Advance," Nagel Institute Website, https://nagelinstitute.org/project/african-theological-advance/ (accessed April 12, 2023).

The claim that RAs are silenced, referred to above, is multilayered and approached by scholars from various angles, explicitly or implicitly. In our reading of existing literature on RAs, three sets of questions emerged as particularly pertinent and relevant to our journey, and we have organized the chapter according to these themes: hierarchy and power relations in the researcher–RA research team,[10] RAs in cross-cultural research teams,[11] and the recognition or lack thereof of the contribution of RAs.[12] We analyze our own story in light of each theme in order to single out their important methodological and ethical issues.

We have chosen the image of "two wings" from the Circle of Concerned African Women Theologians (henceforth, the Circle) as a theoretical tool to assist in thinking about what could and indeed ought to be the positioning of RAs when doing ethnographic theology. The Circle was born in a context of brokenness, with the intention of healing the theological conversation on the continent by including women's voices. Taking the metaphor of two wings seriously today in ethnographic theology means mending other kinds of broken wings and considering the relationships between other pairs of wings, such as the researcher and the RA.

Two-Winged Theology as a Theoretical Lens

Just as a bird cannot fly on one wing only, neither can theology. This image was used to articulate the need for African women to participate in the theological task in Africa in the 1980s,[13] and it is amid this need that the Circle was birthed. Mercy Amba Oduyoye, who often employs the image of two wings, speaks of the importance of growing the second wing in order to "[fill] in the blanks that men have started, [correct] images that we women did not think were accurate."[14] Likewise, writing about Oduyoye's use of the notion of two-winged theology, Mombo maintains that the Circle was established to

---

[10] Ozano and Khatri, "Reflexivity, Positionality and Power in Cross-Cultural Participatory Action Research with Research Assistants in Rural Cambodia"; Deane and Stevano, "Towards a Political Economy of the Use of Research Assistants"; Suzanne Zerger, Caitlin Anne Newberry, and Naveed Ahmed, "Research Assistants Caught in Limbo: Considering Their Role in Quantitative, Longitudinal Research with Vulnerable Populations," *Journal of Health Care for the Poor and Underserved* 26, no. 4 (2015): 1391–400.

[11] Ozano and Khatri, "Reflexivity, Positionality and Power in Cross-Cultural Participatory Action Research with Research Assistants in Rural Cambodia"; Anwar and Viqar, "Research Assistants, Reflexivity and the Politics of Fieldwork in Urban Pakistan"; Daniela Lazoroska, "Hot Topics, Gringo Parties, and the Dependent Independence of Friendship in the Field," *Etnofoor* 31, no. 1 (2019): 63–78; Deane and Stevano, "Towards a Political Economy of the Use of Research Assistants"; Caretta, "Situated Knowledge in Cross-Cultural, Cross-Language Research"; Turner, "Research Note: The Silenced Assistant. Reflections of Invisible Interpreters and Research Assistants."

[12] Jane Hobson, Gar Jones, and Elizabeth Deane, "The Research Assistant: Silenced Partner in Australia's Knowledge Production?," *Journal of Higher Education Policy and Management* 27, no. 3 (2005): 357–66.

[13] Oluwatomisin Oredein, "Interview with Mercy Amba Oduyoye: Mercy Amba Oduyoye in Her Own Words," *Journal of Feminist Studies in Religion* 32, no. 2 (2016): 160–1.

[14] Ibid., 161; Nyambura J. Njoroge, "A New Way of Facilitating Leadership: Lessons from African Women Theologians," *Missiology: An International Review* 33, no. 1 (2005): 34–5.

make women part of the story—of the church and of Africa.[15] The name Circle in and of itself also constitutes an invitation for people to see each other and talk together.[16] While the emergence of African Women's Theology is thus part of the broader critique of the liberation theologies of the time, which largely ignored the voices and experiences of women, the Circle was, meanwhile, also critical of Western feminists for not taking race and class seriously in their analyses.[17] Thus, the Circle highlighted, and continues to highlight, the particular experiences of African women, the power of positionality, and the need for intersectional analysis—be it in understanding experience, knowledge, or bias.

At its heart, the analogy of two wings underscores the value of every story: "If you pass on without leaving a story, then it's as if you never existed."[18] For every story to be audible, the Circle calls for solidarity, not competition. This is reinforced in other images with a similar emphasis, such as communal theology.[19] Doing communal theology together has been framed as a form of mentorship[20] and the analogy of "lift[ing] as we climb" emphasizes the responsibility of academic women to "extend our hand down and lift up those younger than ourselves."[21] These additional expressions are reminders of the importance of one wing supporting the other, perhaps even more clearly than the image of two wings. At their core lies the need to join hands, rather than cutting wings, or people, off. In this space, differences in gender, race, nationality, or other social factors are a blessing and not a curse,[22] suggesting that the aim is not to produce clones but to empower people to join the conversation.

In our use of the image of two wings, we are aware of our different starting points: our key concern is not one of introducing a missing "wing" as such; rather, we use the image of wings and the theology born in the Circle—which saw itself as the long-lost missing wing—to assist us in thinking about the relationships in a researcher–RA research team, and team dynamics in academia more broadly. As is clear from the above, the choice of interlocutors in the Circle, on the one hand, centers on those who are on the margins, while, on the other, has the ultimate goal of including everyone as part of the storytelling and collaboration.

---

[15] Mercy Amba Oduyoye, "The Search for a Two-Winged Theology: Women's Participation in the Development of Theology in Africa-The Inaugural Address," in *Talitha Qumi! Proceedings of the Convocation of African Women Theologians 1989*, ed. M. A. Oduyoye and M. Kanyoro (Ibadan: Daystar Press, 1990), 27–48; Esther Mombo, "Doing Theology from the Perspective of the Circle of Concerned African Women Theologians," *Journal of Anglican Studies* 1, no. 1 (2003): 91.
[16] Oredein, "Interview with Mercy Amba Oduyoye," 161.
[17] Mombo, "Doing Theology from the Perspective of the Circle of Concerned African Women Theologians," 93.
[18] Oredein, "Interview with Mercy Amba Oduyoye," 162.
[19] Njoroge, "A New Way of Facilitating Leadership: Lessons from African Women Theologians"; Musimbi Kanyoro, "Engendered Communal Theology: African Women's Contribution to Theology in the Twenty-First Century," *Feminist Theology* 9, no. 27 (2001): 36–56.
[20] Njoroge, "A New Way of Facilitating Leadership: Lessons from African Women Theologians," 31.
[21] Beverley Haddad, "The South African Women's Theological Project: Practices of Solidarity and Degrees of Separation in the Context of the HIV Epidemic," *Religion & Theology* 20, no. 1–2 (2013): 15. Haddad notes that the phrase is attributed to African American scholar, Mary Church Terrell.
[22] Mercy Amba Oduyoye, *Introducing African Women's Theology* (Sheffield: Sheffield Academic Press, 2001), 77.

Transforming Hierarchy in Co-conducting Research

Not unlike RA–researcher relationships in general, we embodied the roles of a case study leader and RA, a dynamic in which control and, consequently, power and ownership are not shared equally, as the story from the field we tell below demonstrates.[23] As we reflect on this particular story and our experiences in the field more broadly, we focus on the potential of hierarchy to inform ways of working together positively, pointing out that the hierarchical relationship—which could undermine the RA—can actually assist in making space for everyone in the Circle. In our analysis, however, what hierarchy is and how it affects those involved are treated as open-ended and fluid. To draw on Karen Barad, "[r]esearching phenomena [here, hierarchy], then, is a methodological practice of continuously questioning the effects of the way we research, on the knowledges we produce. This unfolds itself as an ethico-onto-epistemology of knowing in being."[24] When looking at hierarchy through the autoethnographic lens of this chapter, we are pushed to reimagine hierarchy as a possible force for good due to the opportunities that, in our experience, it offers the RA. While hierarchy, unsurprisingly, is not often explicitly discussed as a positive tool by the Circle, the fact that the Circle is geared toward uplifting fellow women—by empowering them through theological education,[25] for instance—not only acknowledges that hierarchies exist but also implies what we have come to appreciate through our own experiences. As indicated by our following description of a Sunday afternoon in May 2019, hierarchies can be a force for the common good if coupled with mentoring and dialogue.

That Sunday, we met with the leading pastor and a few members of the leadership of one of our case study churches after the church service, an important step toward getting permission to conduct fieldwork in the church. It was a positive meeting with well-informed questions from those present, and in many ways this kind of thoroughness inspired confidence in us that our presence at the church was indeed welcome. The group of people in the room clearly knew what research entailed and what they were signing up for. We learned that many of them were or had been involved with academia as students or lecturers. Yet, on the following day, Elina started thinking about what had transpired in terms of her and Clementine's presence in that space. Not knowing in advance how the meeting would be arranged, when asked to introduce our project, Elina took it on herself, as the case study leader, to do so. As she reflected on this at home, she wrote in our joint field notes:

> In hindsight, from the perspective of the ethics and politics of co-research, I think I should—at least could—have [asked] Clementine to introduce the project to the people in the room, and then just add[ed] at the end what else I still thought was useful. This would have turned the hierarchy

---

[23] Stevano and Deane, "The Role of Research Assistants in Qualitative and Cross-Cultural Social Science Research"; Deane and Stevano, "Towards a Political Economy of the Use of Research Assistants."
[24] Karen Michelle Barad, *Meeting the Universe Halfway: Quantum Physics and the Entanglement of Matter and Meaning* (Durham: Duke University Press, 2007), 381.
[25] Njoroge, "A New Way of Facilitating Leadership: Lessons from African Women Theologians," 41.

upside down and shown them my trust in her. It would also have been a learning opportunity for her. On the other hand, it might have been unfair to Clementine: Would I not have pushed the responsibility that I have onto her shoulders? Would I not have asked her to take on a sensitive task without prior notice? Not sure what would have been "right," but I think these are questions we should think about—if we want to contribute to an empowering relationship with so-called "research assistants."[26]

After reading this reflection, Clementine added the following in our Google document:

> I think that many factors can explain this situation and I guess that is what research is all about—our experiences should indeed reveal some of these things. . . . It is so interesting how I always expect Elina to speak, even on my behalf as well. I thought about it but I discovered that I was not so sure about how far I can go to give more information, especially when she was there. I always thought that she will deal with all matters relating to our access to the church.[27]

The two-winged approach stems from a context wherein a previously ignored party, woman, was being imagined as an equal partner in doing African theology. In light of Elina's dilemma above, for us it became important to consider what exactly equality means in this particular relationship, one that is characterized by difference in relation to prior knowledge, professional experience, and responsibility for outputs: here Elina was the more experienced person—or mentor—as the supervisor and case study leader, and Clementine the less experienced mentee as the PhD student and RA.[28] We are guided by Njoroge's prophetic voice, which we take to apply not only to women but to African academia as well: "Let us lend supportive hands to one another and help one another to arise. For Africa will not arise unless its womenfolk, the mothers and bearers of life, arise."[29] As argued below, we came to understand equality in an RA–researcher team based on our journey as being first and foremost about making and maintaining space for the RA and "lifting as we climb,"[30] in such a way that the hierarchy is not wiped away but rather used as a transforming tool.

First, the RA context became a teaching and learning space, an extension of an already existing mentorship relationship and something that informed the parameters of equality in our team. As we reflected on our small research team, Clementine spoke of the choice the stronger wing has: either to fly away or choose to take the time and put the effort into offering support to the weaker wing in order to prepare them to *become* an equal cocreator of knowledge. As a case study leader, it was Elina's task to guide Clementine in the work and as a mentor it was her task to advise and create space for growth. Thinking of this goal, we believe that there is no single answer to the dilemma

---

[26] Field notes, May 2019.
[27] Ibid.
[28] Dana L. Haggard et al., "Who Is a Mentor? A Review of Evolving Definitions and Implications for Research," *Journal of Management* 37, no. 1 (2011): 289–90.
[29] Njoroge, "A New Way of Facilitating Leadership: Lessons from African Women Theologians," 451.
[30] Haddad, "The South African Women's Theological Project," 15.

above when it comes to how, exactly, we ought to have behaved before or after the meeting. On the one hand, as Clementine listened to Elina introduce the project to the church leadership that Sunday morning, she found Elina's way of speaking about our expectations at the church new and exciting to her and, as such, it was a learning space even though she was largely an observer. What is obvious, however, is the importance of taking time to think about the question together, if growth is the aim, and in particular to consider what our alternative choices could have meant. This also applies to other instances where Elina, for instance, had to step in and address a shortcoming in Clementine's work. It would have been easier to say nothing, especially in instances when it was not possible to redo what was done but, in the name of mentoring, not speaking of "the done damage" would have meant leaving the mentee behind.

Related to this, our journey highlights the need to recognize the privilege of the researcher—not only skills-wise but more broadly in the academic system—so that the power that the researcher holds in the hierarchical system can become transformative in nature and benefit the RA.[31] Blurring the fundamental hierarchy between RAs and researchers could also blur the opportunities for sharing the privilege with the RA, for providing the RA with room to grow. Emphasizing Elina's responsibility to use her privilege to benefit Clementine instead of highlighting Clementine's need to claim space could perhaps be partly a relational issue, but we believe it is, more importantly, molded by the hierarchical power relations in academia. Elina, in actual fact, does have the power to involve Clementine. Claiming otherwise would seem dishonest. Thus, the traditional conceptualization of mentorship as a hierarchical relationship between the more and less experienced fits the RA–researcher relationship due to the way in which it is located in a hierarchical academic structure. However, importantly, this kind of a mentorship relationship can be harnessed to benefit the RA if the goals and commitment are shared.[32] Many scholars have had academic mentors who have assisted them in going places, literally and metaphorically, and what we learned is that the RA–researcher relationship provides a good platform for this. Research projects often have funds and opportunities linked to them in a way that provides opportunities for mentoring that are not available in the academic everyday. In our context, this meant, for instance, Clementine being invited to participate in a workshop organized for researchers working on different projects across Africa under the umbrella of the ATA.

Second, it is obvious that Clementine also brought assets and strengths to the project and there was a need to acknowledge this actively: she excelled at finding willing interviewees and, as a French speaker, navigated our French-speaking case study church with ease, just to mention a couple of examples. Thinking with two wings, or in a circle shape, it becomes clear that even the "most uneducated among us" can teach,[33] and PhD candidates are hardly that. The fact that the RA is not as far on

---

[31] Mercy Amba Oduyoye, "Transforming Power: Paradigms from the Novels of Buchi Emacheta," in *Talitha Cum! Theologies of African Women*, ed. Musa W. Dube and Nyambura Njoroge (Pietermaritzburg: Cluster Publications, 2001), 223–5.
[32] Haggard et al., "Who Is a Mentor?" 289–90.
[33] K. Kiboko, "Sharing Power: An Autobiographical View," in *Talitha Cum! Theologies of African Women*, ed. Musa W. Dube and Nyambura Njoroge (Pietermaritzburg: Cluster Publications, 2001), 219.

the academic journey does not mean that they have nothing to contribute; quite the contrary, as at times this means they can also think outside the box to solve a situation. But as the story above shows, if we do not actively make space for the RA, it is easy to proceed by way of the easiest route, even if it leaves the RA to simply tag along. It takes a conscious effort from both parties to consider the best ways of creating opportunities for the RA to use their existing strengths or their situated knowledge,[34] or to practice techniques of which they have little experience.

Additionally, we believe that a two-winged approach to fieldwork—and to reflecting on incidents in the field, such as the one narrated above—necessitates open dialogue about all aspects of a research project or event in the field. Looking at our field note exchange suggests that we should have invested more time than we managed to do in speaking about our roles in the field—at least if RA–researcher collaboration is imagined as a space of empowerment, and not simply one of data collection. On the other hand, the field notes in themselves in this one instance became a tool for dialogue, and we could have routinely used them in this manner. Writing things down is a powerful tool, one that we hardly implemented, that could be used alongside talking in the car or the department corridor, which happened a lot over the months.

Making use of the hierarchical relationship in a way that promotes the academic growth of the RA, as we have spoken about it thus far, largely aims to help the RA become what academia expects. But should there be a balance between embracing academic ways of being and challenging those that are rooted in Western frameworks, and what should it look like? Are we numbing RAs and our students into accepting the status quo given that training in the existing ways of academia takes such a long time? When they master the code, are they then still willing and able to challenge the system in the spirit of the decolonial, antiracist, antisexist struggle, and the inclusive God of the Bible?

Race as a Transformative Lens in the Ethnographic Research Team

We both actively think about the impact of our positionality and social location, including racial location, on our work and lives. But in relation to the story we share in this section, we did not connect the dots between our experience, race, and best practice when we first discussed the issue at the time of conducting the fieldwork. Here we want to examine the story in light of the understanding that our racial location may mean that the two of us should actually do fieldwork differently, with all the implications that has for researcher–RA teamwork. Resonating with the idea of a positive hierarchy, here too our lived experiences push us to acknowledge that what we regard as good research practice is entangled with who we are and how we have been trained to think—and hence there is space for being and knowing differently.[35] If we celebrate

---

[34] Ozano and Khatri, "Reflexivity, Positionality and Power in Cross-Cultural Participatory Action Research with Research Assistants in Rural Cambodia."
[35] Barad, *Meeting the Universe Halfway*, 381.

difference together and take seriously the impact of positionality on voice, experience, and bias, as called for by our theological lens of two wings, it would be awkward to aim at finding a uniform, one-size-fits-all manner of doing research.

In the context of a research team consisting of members that the world sees differently due to racial and cultural background, and who thus possess different situated knowledge, it has been asked: Whose report of what is going on is more truthful, and who should be deciding how the emerging knowledge is constructed?[36] From this perspective, involving RAs from racial[37] or epistemic[38] locations other than those of the researchers is argued to be beneficial for the research itself. While the question is also valid from a liberationist perspective, for us the question in this chapter is more about how we ought to approach the truth from our multiple positionalities around the circle in order to do ethnographic theology communally in the web of relationships of which the research team consists.

Clementine, who was at the time still a doctoral candidate, found the informality with which some of the research participants treated her uncomfortable. After meeting with Sandra for an interview at her home, Clementine wrote this:

> When I arrived Sandra had visitors. . . . She asked if they can do this interview together. She also asked her visitor to read the information letter we give to interviewees. They subsequently spoke in their mother tongue. . . . They were talking about what if she said something and pastors will hear it. Then Sandra came to me and asked what could be the consequences if she said things that pastors would not like to hear. I assured her that her participation is confidential and that her name will not be linked to her story in any way. Both asked to read the questions before we could do the interview. They said that they do not see anything wrong. As she cooked her fat cakes, [we started the interview]. She was often interrupted by her children and her visitors. . . . She refused to sign the consent form because she saw a sentence that was addressing the leadership but she said she will do the interview.[39]

While Clementine agreed in theory that the way Sandra behaved is the way every interviewee should behave, what made her uncomfortable was the fact that she had hoped that Sandra would have made time specifically for the interview instead of having visitors with her. On top of this, Sandra comfortably invited her visitors to discuss the consent form without even consulting Clementine about it and continued with her chores while they conversed. In Clementine's mind, her priority was to collect data, get as much detail as she could out of the conversation, and also perhaps keep Sandra closer to the recorder, making it easier to transcribe the interview. Sandra's

---

[36] Turner, "Research Note: The Silenced Assistant. Reflections of Invisible Interpreters and Research Assistants," 217.
[37] Ozano and Khatri, "Reflexivity, Positionality and Power in Cross-Cultural Participatory Action Research with Research Assistants in Rural Cambodia."
[38] Anwar and Viqar, "Research Assistants, Reflexivity and the Politics of Fieldwork in Urban Pakistan," 120.
[39] Field notes, March 2019.

relaxed behavior around her seemed to complicate her work. This was not the only situation of this type that Clementine encountered in the field. On a separate occasion, she found herself pounding *sombe* (cassava leaves) at the home of another interviewee, Pauline. Finally, after the pounding, Pauline had to leave, and the interview had to be postponed.[40] Clementine felt she had not been taken seriously as a researcher and even doubted whether it was professional of her to have helped Pauline pound the *sombe*.

Elina saw these kinds of encounters as positive opportunities and also spoke to Clementine of this kind of informality as a strength in fieldwork. Oduyoye explains that Circle theology "is crafted in the midst of ongoing life in Africa,"[41] and it seems clear that Clementine's positionality allowed her easy access to moments in Sandra and Pauline's lives. While Clementine wanted to feel like a professional researcher, Elina highlighted being as authentic as possible. For Elina, the preference for informality is also a personality issue; generally speaking, she is energized by relationships in the field that go beyond her formal role as a researcher. This was also true in this project, during which Elina, for instance, got to know a woman in her thirties, a wife and a mother, with whom she chatted on and off on WhatsApp since they met and Elina interviewed her—mainly about family, kids. She is no longer just a research participant but a fellow woman, living and hoping and making it work in this world. But here, more importantly, the appreciation of informality also has a bearing on her positionality: it is in the informal spaces of human connection that Elina's own doubts about whether she, a white researcher, should be conducting research in a Black community become less pronounced.

What went unnoticed during our fieldwork were possible links between our racial locations and our feelings: indeed, Elina could have been more supportive of Clementine's experiencing uneasiness and discomfort. Yes, Elina herself would have loved to spend time pounding cassava leaves! But as a white academic with a permanent academic post, it is not just her personality that frames this experience. While we did talk about these feelings related to informality, this would have provided an opportunity for a much deeper discussion about race and its impact on fieldwork and academic life.

The above examples aim to illustrate the manner in which our racial locations had a concrete impact on what we felt and did. If such dynamics are made visible and a part of the methodological process, the Black RA's presence in the project can challenge academic ways of being from the place of Blackness. Her perspective then also "represent[s] [a] valuable and alternative epistemic [location] from which to rethink the privilege accorded to western-trained researchers,"[42] and, indeed, here may assist us to approach and imagine field methods in multiple ways. This is, then, a serious call for open-minded introspection and dialogue, between colleagues, with the aim of making space for academic ways of being that are sensitive to how the world sees race—in a manner that truly makes space for variety in how we are and how we practice our craft. Both wings augment this process, but—following decolonial and liberationist logic—

---

[40] Field notes, February 2019.
[41] Oduyoye, *Introducing African Women's Theology*, 23.
[42] Anwar and Viqar, "Research Assistants, Reflexivity and the Politics of Fieldwork in Urban Pakistan," 120; Caretta, "Situated Knowledge in Cross-Cultural, Cross-Language Research."

the voice of the less privileged in the system should be prioritized due to its otherwise having less space than the voice that represents Western academic norms. But again, mentorship is needed here, too, when speaking of young, emerging scholars, so that celebrating difference is not used as a shortcut that compromises excellence, whatever excellence may look like.

In order for the RA–researcher relationship to have this impact, it matters whom we hire as RAs. If we aim at reversing the history of racism that informs the foundation of much of what we do in academia, and if we want to include voices from the margins of the academic power matrix in the circle, opting for a Black RA is a form of exercising transformative power. Moreover, this approach means that the RA–researcher team is a mentoring relationship that perhaps primarily aims at reaching beyond and affecting change in the academic world outside the research project itself. In our context, this mentorship took place across the color line; involving a Black RA also meant that the project provided space for further educating the white researcher to see and deal with less obvious issues related to race in academia. From our experiential knowledge, however, we cannot speak of whether, or how, race should also inform the constitution of ideal mentorship teams, and we also leave the discussion of race relations between team members for another time.

Coauthoring as Mentoring and Sharing Power with the RA

The issue of copublishing is an important ethical question for us in a context where publications are used as a measure of one's academic worth. Reading scholarly writing on RAs, we found work that scrutinizes the RA–researcher relationship in a reflexive, insightful manner, yet the RAs in question were not active participants in this reflection. For example, Lazoroska, Ozano, and Khatri discuss cross-cultural RA relationships in an in-depth manner but ultimately only as researchers: the RAs are central to both articles but do not participate in the writing.[43] Turner and Caretta are also the sole authors of their articles on RAs but here the voices of the RAs are also audible in their own right, Turner's article being based on in-depth interviews with local RAs working with Western doctoral students in Vietnam and China, and Caretta drawing on RAs' reflexive diary entries discussing their role in situated knowledge production.[44] In this context, and in neoliberal academia where publications are often used to decide who counts in the system and who does not, we found value in writing about research assistance together.

Writing together is a much broader question than simply asking who can and should write about research assistance as such. Hobson, Jones, and Deane's question about the lack of RA recognition when it comes to the knowledge that RAs have been

---

[43] Lazoroska, "Hot Topics, Gringo Parties, and the Dependent Independence of Friendship in the Field"; Ozano and Khatri, "Reflexivity, Positionality and Power in Cross-Cultural Participatory Action Research with Research Assistants in Rural Cambodia."
[44] Turner, "Research Note: The Silenced Assistant. Reflections of Invisible Interpreters and Research Assistants"; Caretta, "Situated Knowledge in Cross-Cultural, Cross-Language Research."

part of producing does not seem to be outdated almost two decades later.[45] Exposing the nature of the academic game, they note that the list of authors of an academic article may include names of "those who have provided facilities or the need to 'keep them sweet' for potential future benefit as collaborators, reviewers, or referees [a practice which is] to be condemned," while even a solid contribution of RAs "may end up being only a 'thank you' in a preface or acknowledgements."[46] In this final section of the chapter, we focus on this question, fully aware that any answer or solution is fluid and situated.

According to Kanyoro, African women's theology as "engendered communal theology" is committed to changing an oppressive system.[47] In the context of our discussion, the change we are considering is not about the content of ethnographic theology produced in a coauthored paper but the way in which it is produced. For Elina, it was important to consider how Clementine would benefit from the project if she budgeted time and energy for it, other than getting further experience in fieldwork. Coauthoring seemed the natural answer to the question, as Clementine was interested in an academic career. As we now work on this chapter, a research article that the two of us coauthored together with the leader of the project has been published. Copublishing with an RA, we suggest, goes against the logic of the academic game. In South Africa, where we are based, a university gets a subsidy from the Department of Higher Education for every article published, and at our institution, a portion of this money is directed to the author's research cost center. Additionally, the number of publications per annum could contribute toward a bonus at the end of the year and toward a line manager concluding that the academic has or has not done their job satisfactorily. When as academic coauthors, only a percentage of the article is in their name, and this affects both scenarios described above. In reverse, the RA gets to be seen by the system as a productive person and thus someone that might, for instance, be considered when future hires are underway. Making the route of including RAs in publishing more normal than it is currently would be part of transforming a system that benefits those who already have the most, making it more inclusive, even if still working within the system instead of struggling to abolish it.

Although involving Clementine in the writing process was important to Elina, Clementine had mixed feelings at first. She felt it was a privilege to have the opportunity to learn from how the other two plan and write a joint paper; however, she also began to wonder if she would actually earn her place as coauthor. This has been her ongoing worry in academia in general, and she did not want her name to be added just because a Black RA needed to be acknowledged. Once the work started, the worries dissipated; her involvement in the process made her feel at ease knowing that she had indeed contributed to the paper. She felt confident about the argument we made, something that was also reflected in her presenting the paper with the project leader in a conference to which the latter invited her.

---

[45] Hobson, Jones, and Deane, "The Research Assistant."
[46] Ibid., 362.
[47] Kanyoro, "Engendered Communal Theology," 46.

The coauthoring process was a learning curve for both of us as, on the one hand, Elina often wondered if she, as the lead author of the article, gave Clementine enough space. In a joint discussion of an issue on Zoom, for instance, she wondered if she should have more actively invited Clementine to weigh in, whereas, Clementine, on the other hand, experienced the process as being forced to step out of her comfort zone. On a Friday afternoon just before the submission of the coauthored article, Elina called Clementine and we had a lengthy phone conversation on the use of the word "migrant" and whether it should be complemented with "African" or "international" or nothing at all. Clementine had been using this word for a while in her own work and felt pretty comfortable with it—until this conversation. The first time Elina called Clementine to discuss this kind of detail, Clementine could not help wondering why a certain word or a sentence could not simply be overlooked. Furthermore, English is not Clementine's first language and she wondered why someone would want to discuss a particular word with her—granted that that "someone" also speaks English as a second language. Yet she began to notice that these discussions changed the way she reads and writes and also drew her closer to the project. Having to discuss ideas related to the article, over and over again, and do several rounds of work with the data that we coded and analyzed together, made Clementine feel that she did have something to say about the data—beyond handing interviews over to the transcriber and moving on.

As a mentoring tool, copublishing is an invitation for the RA to join the circle of researchers, and a mechanism to allow the RA truly to become part of the academic story, to become a wing in her own right. One of the achievements of the Circle has been to enable women to speak for themselves; rather than someone else writing about African women, it became African women writing about themselves. Copublishing provides RAs with this opportunity as they get to co-tell the story in their own names and become visible in academia. Clementine had seen two other articles being written from the same data by the time we started the coauthoring process, but their stories were told by those authoring the papers. Being the one to write about our story made her feel like she had truly achieved something of the professionalism for which she yearned.

Conclusion

The field of ethnographic theology has become established over the decade since the publication of the original version of this book. Perhaps it is this coming of age that opens up space to think critically about our practice and search for more life-affirming research ways of being and doing. In this chapter, we are challenged by the Circle, which was born to mend brokenness and help nurture the second wing of African theology into being. Listening to the Circle calls us to look critically at what is happening today in our research practice; as the chapter has shown, we believe that theologian-ethnographers now need to be more intentional about reflecting on the methodological and research ethics of relationships in research teams, particularly when involving RAs. To this end, the chapter has highlighted three such ethical issues related to hierarchy, race, and publishing, respectively. Each theme is underpinned by an understanding that things can be portrayed, known, and done differently.

First, we argued that hierarchy should be embraced and actively used as a positive tool by researcher–RA teams. What is then required is that open dialogue related to power relations between the "stronger" and "weaker" wings in academia and in the research team becomes routine in any team doing ethnographic theology. Such dialogue is important for what transpires in the field. It is also important for the researcher to be equipped to make and maintain space for the RA. From this methodological tool stems the following ethical imperative for research: the researcher, who is more privileged in the academic power matrix, ought to "lift as they climb" by using their privilege actively for the good of the researcher's community and, in particular, the RA. Ethnographic theology is, then, the home of an active community that, on the one hand, does theology together, and, on the other, nurtures growth.

Second, when it comes to thinking of race in the context of mixed-race research teams, we suggested that researchers and RAs actively consider how their different racial locations make the field a different space, and that different members of the team may need to do research differently. The Circle was always clear about doing theology their way, not aiming to mimic male theologians. We suspect that, to a degree, Black and white people involved in research already behave differently in the field, which after all is just an extension of the rest of the world. Yet we believe that thinking and writing about it openly as a team can become a tool for becoming sensitized to the use of ethnographic methods in doing theology. As home to an active community, the nature of ethnographic theology remains open-ended and genuinely challenged by its members. As we argued above, as much as the community nurtures growth, what counts as growth is not fixed.

The ethical imperative relating to the second theme is for researchers to think carefully about whom they hire, particularly in relation to the racial background of RAs. This will inevitably have an impact on how, and from what place, the presence and input of the RA challenge research conventions. Perhaps more importantly still, it has an impact on the academic future of ethnographic theology.

Third, in relation to publishing, the insight from the first two sections is brought to bear on practice in a specific context. On the one hand, copublishing becomes a space for an active community to exercise mentoring and nurture growth; on the other, bringing RAs into the writing process as authors allows ethnographic theology to speak with multiple voices. Incorporating the voice of the RA makes for a more nuanced picture of the phenomenon or argument at issue, meaning that the whole team has had an impact on it. Furthermore, the RA's perspective can challenge what becomes published theology.

6

Ethnography and Crucified Bodies

A Liberationist-Incarnational Approach[1]

Sunder John Boopalan and RC Jongte

Introduction

As global scholars of religion from distinct—namely, Dalit and Indigenous—social locations in the Indian context, we approach the task of this chapter by describing two problems surrounding movements for liberation. The first of these two problems is the hegemonic manner in which dominance co-opts liberative movements. Co-option happens not only in ways that dispose us into explicitly violent ways but also in little subtle ways, undermining ethical impetuses. The power of co-option lies in such subtlety, and we are not aware of it until it has already happened and stolen parts of our ethical impulses. In addition, we use the particular phrase "hegemonic dominant co-option" in the chapter to refer not only to hegemony as a phenomenon, but also how in specific geographical contexts, locally dominant groups co-opt histories and cultures of minoritized groups including the liberatory language and practices of such oppressed groups. Examples offered below will make this problem clearer.

Superficial pursuit of solidarity is the second problem. In describing these problems, the chapter argues for a liberationist-incarnational approach that focuses on crucified bodies. What we are calling for here relates to the methodological commitment in liberation theologies that is captured by the axiom "preferential option for the poor." The chapter's self-reflective focus on crucified bodies draws from this axiom. Crucial to this argument is that crucified bodies have an enduring epistemological privilege that draws inspiration from the incarnation.

In focusing on bodies, we cautiously look to ethnographic work as an ally. We begin by describing our social locations in first-person narrative to make the case for an ethically critical attention to social location that ought to inform ethnographic work. Here we caution readers against the danger of pursuing superficial solidarities. If anti-discriminatory work is to have ethical integrity, then sustained, self-reflective, and self-

---

[1] We are grateful to the editor of *Bangalore Theological Forum* for giving us permission to adapt our coauthored essay, "Renewing Dalit-Indigenous Theological Dialogue," *Bangalore Theological Forum* 53, no. 1 (2021): 166–86 where we first explored some of the ideas we elaborate here.

critical descriptions of social locations and embodied dispositions are necessary. We think here of ethnography as a deep excavation of societal realities that goes beyond conventional (and often majoritarian) understandings. It is in this connection that we propose an ethnography of crucified bodies (following Ignacio Ellacuría's formulation of "crucified people"[2]) by lifting up a liberationist-incarnational approach.

Social Location 1 of 2: Boopalan

Identities matter less as ontological states and more as opportunities to think about personal, societal, and structural matters in the pursuit of liberation. I describe my self-identity with respect to such a goal. I am the child of a Pariah (Dalit) father and a dominant caste (Naidu) mother who got married under the auspices of a church that emphasized the commonality of being Christian over any other marker of difference. That was a quiet revolution. I didn't appreciate this fully until my adulthood. Intercaste relationships are some of the most antagonistic and potentially violent-laden encounters in India. Dalit filmmaker Nagraj Manjule's film, *Sairat*, makes this point well, capturing both the reality of Dalit resistance and ensuing dominant caste rage against those who move out of place. In my book, *Memory, Grief, and Agency*, I compare Indian and US contexts of casteism and racism to argue that structural wrongs today are better understood as socially conditioned practices of domination affected by discriminatory logics of the past enacted against people who move out of place.[3] Wrongs against Dalits are both disturbing and common in India. Despite banning the practice of "untouchability" as a crime in 1950, caste-based dominance continues to plague modern India. This ranges from lynching, "honor-killings" in which the dominant caste relatives of an intercaste couple murder their own in order to protect the so-called sanctity of caste, daily humiliations of Dalit students by dominant caste teachers and administrators, and refusal of local police officers to appropriately register caste-based crimes, to a number of other overt and covert discriminatory actions. The chapter invites readers to better learn of this horrific reality. Such murdered persons provoke our imagination for a kinder world.

If I knew as a child what I now know about casteism, it might have led to a few possibilities much earlier in my young adult life. I might have been embarrassed that I was a mixed-caste child who did not belong to any one neatly classified caste-based group. Or, I might have been proud that my parents—from two historically antagonistic castes—transgressed the violent logic of caste and celebrated the holiness of their Christian witness. Or, I could have understood how structural violence operated through caste and consequently pursued anti-discriminatory work and collective liberation. If I had undertaken an ethnographic study—that is, an excavation of deep societal realities that might not be apparent on first view—of crucified bodies, I might

---

[2] Ignacio Ellacuría, "The Crucified People," in *Mysterium Liberationis: Fundamental Concepts of Liberation Theology*, ed. Ignacio Ellacuría and Jon Sobrino (Maryknoll: Orbis Books, 1993), 580–603.
[3] Sunder John Boopalan, *Memory, Grief, and Agency: A Political Theological Account of Wrongs and Rites* (New York: Palgrave Macmillan, 2017).

have been conscientized much earlier. I would have seen crucified bodies for what they are—that is, bodies *crucified* by cruelty and structural injustice, and not as those who suffered by accident or abstract contingency.

I did not actively pursue a deep engagement with societal realities until I was finishing up my undergraduate education and entered graduate theological education. This is counterintuitive at first. After all, I grew up in a church that was intentionally multilingual and multiethnic in its membership. It was a church in which members from different castes sat together, ate together, and intermarried. Such practices continue to be taboo elsewhere in India, often with lethal consequences. While Hindutva (a nationalist and xenophobic interpretation of Hinduism) imaginations justify and rationalize violence[4] against minoritized communities that assert their self-identities against a majoritarian nation-state, the church I grew up in embodied a unity in diversity. In a deeply embodied way, I knew in my bones, therefore, the lie of the Hindutva narrative of India as a glorious, harmonious, and unified identity, which was destroyed by Muslim and Christian invading alien forces. We'll have more to say about these contradictions later in the chapter. Let me return to my story.

Despite the broader social reality of caste-based discrimination and violence, instances of caste-based cruelty were mentioned only in passing at home. As I have written elsewhere,

> We hardly discussed the horrific wrongs faced by Dalits every day in India. We did not make a connection between our Dalit identity and the struggles that people faced because of their hierarchically assigned identities. In retrospect, I believe that we were conditioned to be ethically enclosed and individualist when it came to structural wrongs. All the wrongs we knew and discussed had an individual case-to-case character. We did not seek a critical analysis of social structure, power, and systems of domination.[5]

Consequently, while we eschewed caste-based discrimination, "we never discussed conditions and processes by which people were discriminated against in the first place. The *what*, the *how*, and the *why* of structural injustice were so minimal as to have no impact on my sense of identity."[6] My social location and self-identity as "Dalit" matter in this connection.

A question that is often asked to Dalits is why Dalits want to claim a term that seems to have a negative meaning. Dalit is not an ontological state of being. "Dalit" is, first, a political marker of identity. "Dalit" has Marathi, Sanskrit, and Hebrew linguistic roots and means "oppressed," "crushed," "broken." It highlights how Dalits continue to suffer caste-based discrimination and simultaneously celebrates the survival and

---

[4] Christophe Jaffrelot, *Modi's India* (Princeton: Princeton University Press, 2022); Richard Fox Young and Sunder John Boopalan, "Studied Silences? Diasporic Nationalism, 'Kshatriya Intellectuals' and the Hindu American Critique of Dalit Christianity's Indianness," in *Constructing Indian Christianities: Culture, Conversion and Caste*, ed. Chad M. Bauman and Richard Fox Young (New York: Routledge, 2014), 215–38.
[5] Boopalan, *Memory, Grief, and Agency*, 10.
[6] Ibid.

resilience of Dalit communities that have been wronged for centuries. Second, "Dalit" is a positive marker of identity. It is an ecumenical and inclusive force for solidarity among various distinct Dalit communities across language and region in India. Third, by centering people who continue to experience the violence of structural injustice and oppression, the term "Dalit" functions to perpetually dispose theology and ethics toward marginality and sites of oppression, resisting co-option by dominant logics and forces. In this light, intersectional dialogue with persons from other historically marginalized social locations is paramount. In the pursuit of collective liberation, our histories and hopes are bound up with each other. Thus, antidiscrimination efforts are best undertaken intersectionally, in conversation with other historically marginalized communities both within and outside particular geographical contexts.

Social Location 2 of 2: Jongte

To further a sense of the intersectional and contextually thick description that we believe aids the work of liberation, I will give an account of my social location by way of telling the story of the region I come from in India. Owing to its geographical distance from the so-called mainland and its perceived ethnocultural otherness in the dominant "Indian" imagination, it remains a region that is relatively unknown. Or, to be more precise, it is a region that is invisibilized. This region is collectively referred to as Northeast India, a frontier region sharing extended international boundaries with Bangladesh, China, Myanmar, and Nepal. Describing my social location in terms of a biography of peoples and of a region, rather than a personal biography, highlights the collective and specific experience of marginalization and oppression of the region under India and "mainland" Indians.

The fact that the region is referred to by some as the "Mongolian fringe"[7] *vis-à-vis* "mainland" India highlights how it occupies a remote and peripheral place in the consciousness of the majority of Indians. This is true for both the general "Indian" populace (who see themselves as the real representation of India) and the Indian State. Inhabited mainly by various Indigenous groups, the hill people of the Northeast have East Asian features and their own Indigenous cultures that mark them off as "other" to Indians in the "mainland," resulting in their exclusion and marginalization. Besides, unlike other parts of India, Christianity is the dominant religion in a number of states in the region and has become a powerful marker of identity against Hindu India.

I belong to the Mizo ethnic community. Mizos (meaning "hill people") have a strong sense of ethno-national consciousness and historically did not consider themselves as Indians, or geographically as a part of India. It was only through the British annexation that the region was tacked on to British India. So, it was a "historical accident" occasioned by the colonial search for "administrative convenience" that the region was incorporated into India.[8] Like some other Indigenous groups of the region,

---

[7] Sanjib Baruah, "The Mongolian Fringe," *Himal Southasian* 26, no. 1 (2013): 82–6.
[8] Robert Reid, cited in Arkotong Longkumer, "The Power of Persuasion: Hindutva, Christianity, and the Discourse of Religion and Culture in Northeast India," *Religion* 47, no. 2 (2017): 207.

the Mizos under the Mizo National Army (later renamed to Mizo National Front) rose in revolt and fought for independence for twenty years beginning in the 1960s. The primary reason for the uprising was fear of assimilation or *"chim ral"* (a Mizo term that literally means "to be submerged to extinction")[9] of their distinct ethnic identity and religion (Christianity) by dominant Hindu India. This continues to be an enduring apprehension.

The immediate cause for the uprising was the neglect and indifference of the Indian government toward the plight of the Mizo people who were ravaged by famine in the late 1950s and early 1960s. India responded to the rebellion with heavy-handed violence that was very much felt and perceived as imperial violence subjected against the Indigenous Mizo people. Unsurprisingly, there is a glaring power difference between a small Indigenous group fighting to retain its identity and an imposing nation-state with its centralized armed forces ready to "pacify" what they perceived as a threat. Acts of horrific violence enacted by the Indian nation-state remain etched in the memory of the Mizo people to this day.

One of the horrors was the forcible relocation of clusters of independent local villages into grouping centers which were aimed at flushing out militants. For Mizos who were and are intrinsically connected to local land and environment, this forced relocation—many a time permanent—was an indescribable loss and blow to their sense of identity and was experienced as being completely uprooted. Other acts of horrific violence perpetrated by the Indian nation-state include rape of Mizo women by Indian military personnel along with the harassment, torture, and imprisonment of Mizo men on mere grounds of suspicion of being clandestinely linked to or aiding the underground Mizo army. What cannot be overstated is also the general atmosphere of visceral fear among the Mizo people that even banal and ordinary acts might anger the Indian army under whose constant watch they had to live and survive.

The two-decades long conflict ended with the signing of a peace accord between the Mizo National Front and the Government of India in 1986, and Mizoram became a full-fledged state under the Indian union. Secession movements are still present among Indigenous groups like the Nagas but on a much smaller scale compared to the intense period of armed resistance that followed India's independence from British rule.

With this brief historical background, I want to transition to the contemporary scenario of the relationship between the Indigenous people of Northeast India and "mainland" India. In this regard, I register two grievances: exclusion and deformed inclusion. First, on exclusion, Indigenous people from the Northeast continually experience discrimination and marginalization in other parts of India because they look physically different, as I have stated earlier. To "mainland" Indians, Northeasterners with such physical features do not belong to India or simply "can't be Indian." However, interestingly, these exclusionary politics and practices are never named by the Indian government or its officials as instances of racism. Most "mainland" Indians see racism "as a phenomenon that exists in other countries [and] see themselves as victims,"[10]

---

[9] Joy L. K. Pachuau, *Being Mizo: Identity and Belonging in Northeast India* (New Delhi: Oxford University Press, 2014), 15.

[10] Jilangamba Yengkhom, cited in Dolly Kikon, "Dirty Food: Racism and Casteism in India," *Ethnic and Racial Studies* 45, no. 2 (2022): 279.

making the implicit argument that "racism" is not a category that can be applied for analyzing Indian social hierarchy.

This is ironic because it is precisely on account of casteism combined with racism that Northeasterners are very often harassed, mocked, vilified, denied housing, and even killed in Indian cities.[11] Derogatory slurs like "chinky" ("chinky" negatively refers to the shape of one's eyes) are commonly used to refer to Northeasterners and are also often derisively labeled as "Chinese," "Japanese," and other East Asian nationalities. The intended message is clear: Northeasterners are "other" and do not belong in the dominant imagination of "India" or "Indian." I myself am no stranger to such experiences of racist abuse. Joy Pachuau insightfully applies Edward Said's notion of orientalism to the Indian context to observe processes of othering within the Indian context. According to Pachuau, if *Orientalism* was "an epistemology that was essentially created to dominate the other," then "similar forms of representations and assertions of cultural hegemony are exhibited in India's own engagement with its Northeastern margins. In other words, 'Orientalist'-type constructions persist within India itself, despite its own subjection to them in the colonial period."[12]

The second grievance I want to raise might sound rather different from the first when taken at face value, maybe even contradictory, but no less malicious. If anything, it is even more sinister and connected to the topic of co-option this chapter explores. I am referring to the Hindu nationalists' attempt to "include" Northeast India and its people under Hindutva's idea of India—an "inclusion" that is sought to be achieved through forced assimilation and co-option of Indigenous histories and cultures; hence, making it a deformed inclusion. Such "inclusions" are attempted through reconstruction of Hindu mythologies that try to secure historical, geographical, and mythological connection between Northeast India and other parts of "mainland" India. Given the religious, ethnic, and cultural othering that Northeasterners continue to face in "mainland" India, such so-called inclusions are nothing but co-options of Indigenous people and their histories.

These threats have become more prominent with the rise and mainstreaming of Hindu nationalism as a consequence of the comprehensive 2014 electoral victories of the Bharatiya Janata Party, which is the political wing of the Rashtriya Swayamsevak Sangh, India's right-wing Hindu nationalist organization. Recall from previous paragraphs that the fear of being assimilated, understood as the loss and death of ethno-religious identity by Indigenous people in the Northeast, is one of the primary reasons for Indigenous peoples' animosity toward India.

To conclude this section on social location, I want to make it clear that in the foregoing discussion of ethnic identity and national belonging, my interest does not lie in ontologizing Indigenous identities *as such*, but rather in embracing and asserting such identities in service of liberation of the oppressed, that is, deploying them to name and unmask oppression and strive for liberation.

---

[11] Dolly Kikon's aforementioned essay, "Dirty Food: Racism and Casteism in India," makes this point particularly well.
[12] Pachuau, *Being Mizo*, 35.

Hegemonic Dominant Co-options of Liberative Movements

While we critically interrogate co-option in the Indian context and value our own intersectional Dalit–Indigenous dialogue, we are simultaneously interested in the global implications of such a dialogue. As theologians invested in global antidiscrimination work, we find it important to form bonds of solidarity in North American contexts with communities that are similarly historically marginalized by racism and other forms of dominance. Nevertheless, these pursuits are not straightforward. A few examples might help convey why.

In her book, *Caste*, Isabel Wilkerson recounts an encounter with a security agent at an airport. Wilkerson is returning from India with a bronze bust of B. R. Ambedkar. Noticing the confusion and curiosity of the security agent, Wilkerson responds by noting that Ambedkar is "the Martin Luther King of India." It helps to cite the broader context here and then offer commentary:

> "So who is this?" he asked. The name Ambedkar alone would not have registered; I had learned of him myself only the year before, and there was no time to explain the parallel caste system. So I blurted out what seemed to make the most sense. "Oh," I said, "this is the Martin Luther King of India." "Pretty cool," he said, satisfied now, and seeming a little proud. He then wrapped Ambedkar back up as if he were King himself and set him back gently into the suitcase.[13]

The encounter between Wilkerson and the security guard is significant not only because interlocutors in North American contexts often do not know Ambedkar's name but also because such lack of awareness is caused by the iconic presence of other Indian figures like Gandhi. Ambedkar was the chairman of the Constituent Assembly that drafted India's constitution. He was Gandhi's most prominent ideological opponent. Ambedkar believed firmly that India's caste system was rooted in dominant Hindu religious texts and culture and thus made good on his 1935 declaration "I was born a Hindu but I will not die a Hindu." On October 14, 1956, Ambedkar, along with four hundred thousand Dalits, converted from Hinduism to Buddhism. This is one of the largest religious conversions in modern history. Given this significance, is it not curious that Gandhi has overshadowed Ambedkar?

This example allows us to see how the "if-one-remembers-Gandhi-then-every thing-is-all-right" approach is hegemonic, socially conditioning people's imaginations "to remember and forget, to keep some things in one's frame of thinking and to keep others out."[14] Because all this "often happens without overt ill will or explicitly stated intention,"[15] it is cause for serious concern in a global climate in which email tags and memes meant to evoke positive thoughts often have Gandhi's words and pictures. The ubiquity of Gandhi is not totally undeserved. We find it important, for instance,

---

[13] Isabel Wilkerson, *Caste: The Origins of Our Discontents* (New York: Random House, 2020), 32.
[14] Boopalan, *Memory, Grief, and Agency*, 22–3.
[15] Ibid., 23.

to reflect on the fact that Gandhi was assassinated by a Hindu supremacist[16] who continues to be variously celebrated by Hindu nationalist political parties in twenty-first-century India.[17] However, given Gandhi's problematic and morally ambivalent positions on caste and race,[18] such ubiquity does become part of hegemonic dominant co-options of liberative figures and movements.

Going back to the encounter between Wilkerson and the airport security worker, we ask, what might have needed to happen differently so Wilkerson and her interlocutor learned of Ambedkar earlier than they did? Would an ethnography attuned to sites of produced suffering have led to an earlier and more meaningful comparison between King and Ambedkar? That would have been, to use the words of the security person, a "pretty cool" phenomenon, because it would have allowed for organic points of connection between marginalized communities so we can learn each other's histories and undertake acts of solidarity with integrity.

We offer another example from the Indian context to show how recognition through misrecognition is another mode of hegemonic co-option. Indigenous communities—alternatively called "tribals" (a term we reject) or *adivasis* (meaning "first peoples" or "original inhabitants")—in India are reclaiming their identities and ancestral lands that often put them into direct conflict with the nation-state that uses sedition laws inherited from British colonialism to suppress Indigenous self-determination. Ironies abound in this realm. The Indian government voted in favor of the UN Declaration on the Rights of Indigenous Peoples (UNDRIP) with an innovative albeit oppressive condition. India argued that all Indians residing in India after 1947 (the year India gained independence from the British) are "Indigenous," thus erasing the claim of first peoples or original inhabitants. It is not surprising, therefore, that India charged ten thousand Indigenous people of sedition in the state of Jharkhand for creating a "law and order problem"[19] for asserting their rights. This is just one of several available examples.

In other parts of India, misrecognition of Indigenous claims has religious nationalist entanglements that evidence hegemonic dominant co-options of liberative movements. The Indian nation-state's effort to "integrate" such majority-Indigenous states could thus be seen as an effort to de-indigenize (by way of problematically claiming all Indians are Indigenous) and de-Christianize (by way of problematically claiming that Hinduism is the most representative inclusive label available to all Indians). For co-opting nationalist forces, "Indian," "Indigenous," and "Hindu" become interchangeable synonyms. This posture, as Longkumer argues, is "aided by the Indian

---

[16] Dhirendra K. Jha, *Gandhi's Assassin: The Making of Nathuram Godse and His Idea of India* (New Delhi: Penguin, 2022).

[17] "BJP MP Pragya Thakur refers to Nathuram Godse as a 'Patriot', yet again," *The Hindu*, https://www.thehindu.com/news/national/other-states/bjp-mp-pragya-thakur-refers-to-godse-as-patriot/article33568997.ece (accessed February 1, 2022).

[18] Ashwin Desai and Goolem Vahed, *The South African Gandhi: Stretcher-Bearer of Empire* (Stanford: Stanford University Press, 2015).

[19] Supriya Sharma, "10,000 People Charged with Sedition in One Jharkhand District: What Does Democracy Mean Here?" *Scroll*, https://scroll.in/article/944116/10000-people-charged-with-sedition-in-one-jharkhand-district-what-does-democracy-mean-here (accessed February 1, 2022).

state's classification of STs [Scheduled Tribes, which is the official government term for India's Indigenous people] as Hindus, unless explicitly stated otherwise."[20] What seems like a unifying nationalist argument thus becomes part of a co-opting strategy to hegemonically include particular identities by erasing their claims of sovereignty.

What, then, does one do when "dominance, not marginality, [has entered] the discourse of indigeneity?"[21] The mention of non-Indian Indigenous persons visiting India under the auspices of Hindutva ideologues and organizations thus caught our attention in Longkumer's book. Because we are interested in global antidiscrimination efforts, these problems are especially important to name. What is sinister in this connection is that Indigenous articulations in North American contexts are employed in such co-option. Longkumer's Hindutva informant tells Longkumer that the Lakota people's saying *mitakuye oyasin* ("we all are related") is equivalent to the saying *vasudeva kutumbakam* ("the whole universe is one") in the Hindu tradition. The informant is part of a Hindutva-adjacent organization Research Institute of World's Ancient Traditions Cultures and Heritage in Arunachal Pradesh where they invite Indigenous scholars from other parts of the world to come and study there. International scholars, including global Indigenous actors, are fed with a Hindutva-inflected version of indigeneity. What is deeply sinister about this strategy is that it leads to a situation in which solidarity between two marginalized groups across the globe is thwarted and a superficial solidarity is hegemonically crafted. In this way, locally dominant players who otherwise subscribe to a majoritarian and oppressive worldview problematically end up falsely positioning themselves as the real representatives of indigeneity in India.

Longkumer's remarks on these developments are astute. He notes,

> Hindutva activists are not necessarily shouting to be heard when it comes to the UNDRIP [United Nations Declaration on the Rights of Indigenous Peoples] or to be recognized as Indigenous peoples. But what they are doing is aligning, or positioning, themselves with Indigenous religions precisely to allow them to make certain worlds possible that might easily slip under the radar, in spaces that people might least suspect.[22]

Much work is to be done locally and globally to avoid being co-opted into nationalist and other imaginations that seek to assimilate Dalits and Indigenous people by erasing the question of our struggles. Our hope is that this chapter sparks conversations that lift up, as the terms "Dalit" and "Indigenous" do, sites of marginality and oppression as the grounding center for theological thinking and action. Before we dive further into this area to propose an ethnography of crucified bodies, we would like to caution readers against superficial pursuits of solidarity.

---

[20] Arkotong Longkumer, *The Greater India Experiment: Hindutva and the Northeast* (Stanford: Stanford University Press, 2021), 102.
[21] Ibid., 123.
[22] Ibid., 122.

Superficial Pursuits of Solidarity

Movements for freedom have always inspired other oppressed communities. A well-known example is how the Black Panther Party inspired the Dalit Panther Party in India. Such cross-pollination is cause for celebration. Superficial solidarities, however, need to be named and resisted, especially when one takes a global antidiscrimination approach.

Take, for instance, the various global protests in 2020 after the death of George Floyd. While Black movements for justice have galvanized movements globally, they had a particular catalyzing force after the murder of George Floyd. Notable Indian celebrities went on Twitter, tweeting with #BlackLivesMatter hashtags. Some discomforting questions arise that evidence superficial solidarities. Some of these tweets came from Indian celebrities who endorsed fairness skin creams in India. These creams—"Fair and Lovely" is an infamous example—are essentially bleaching products that damage human skin. "How can one say black lives matter when simultaneously endorsing skin creams that promote anti-blackness?"[23] If solidarity with those on the margins was really what the celebrities were after, why do instances of caste-based violence—an everyday occurrence in India—not gain as much traction among media-savvy Indians? Could that have something to do with their dominant caste social locations? Perhaps it has to do with the fact that one simply cannot, in good conscience, condemn caste-based violence while holding on to caste-based identities that are the basis upon which such violence occurs. Picking and choosing while evading what's immediate is a superficial pursuit.

Solidarity goes wrong when we align ourselves with those we perceive to have more subaltern power. When one moves to Canada from the United States, one comes across a different formulation of BIPOC. Some in Canada use the term IBPOC. Notice how in such iterations, "Indigenous" supplants "Black" as the first word? Is it because Indigenous people have more social capital in the Canadian context? Is it the case, relatedly, that Black people have more social capital in the US context? What does solidarity mean for us collectively in these cases? If we are in India, should one jump onto the POCBI bandwagon? We do not intend to trivialize contextual histories and realities. What we are noting, instead, are the ways in which dominant groups assign differential value to marginalized groups based on who they perceive to have more subaltern power. How does one resist such superficial pursuits? The Dalit–Indigenous dialogue of this chapter is methodologically relevant in this regard.

We find describing other Indian contradictions in the pursuit of superficial solidarities important because discrimination goes beyond colorism in India. As we highlighted earlier, Brown "mainland" Indian people (having physical features like Boopalan, one of the two authors of this chapter) are often not simply anti-Black, but simultaneously anti-Asian, that is, anti-Asian against those Indigenous Indians who visibly look "East Asian" in India. When "mainland" Indians meet such Indigenous people in India, they often ask them, "Where are you from?" "Are you *really* from India?" Hate crimes and sexual assaults against those who "don't look Indian" are reported

---

[23] Sunder John Boopalan, "Transnational Solidarities," *Conrad Grebel Review* 39, no. 1 (2021): 15.

regularly. Dolly Kikon's commentary is instructive here: "Racism against migrants from Northeast India goes beyond the existing conversations about colourism/dark-skinned discrimination."[24] We want to be clear here. Colorism and discrimination based on dominant caste-based logic against dark-skinned people in India is a long-standing epidemic that predates colonialism. The question we are raising is, why are everyday experiences of racism against Indigenous people from Northeastern states in India "not framed as incidents of racism and racialization"[25] in the dominant Indian imaginary? This question is important to raise to mark our protest against aforementioned pursuits of solidarity that evade the kind of ethnographic task the real work of solidarity entails.

The Asian and Asian American Working Group's preparatory document for the 2022 Annual Meeting of the Society of Christian Ethics made an insightful observation in its preparation for the session, "Between the Los Angeles Riots (1992) and the Atlanta Shootings (2021): Anti-Asian Racism and Anti-racist Christian Ethics." It observed, "Anti-racist work requires an intersectional analysis and intentional, sustained efforts to build up interracial solidarity." The examples we offer enable us to make explicit such intersectional analyses in order to meaningfully pursue solidarity with integrity. Readers might discern that these examples have much to do with the privileging of ethnographic work that we believe can assist in the work of solidarity.

We believe that ethnographic work may assist theologians to undertake "the risk of learning about a narrative that isn't immediately your own—a different genealogy."[26] Learning about a narrative that is not immediately one's own requires a deep recognition of bodies and the mechanisms of their crucifixion. For instance, Brown-skinned Indians in North America are often identified as "people of color." This can be a good thing if one lives into the anti-discriminatory intention behind the term. However, the term can be problem if it hides the mechanisms of crucifixion that particular racialized bodies are subjected to. Going back to some of the earlier commentary regarding caste-based discrimination in India, how does one approach the fact that both dominant caste persons and caste-oppressed persons are Brown and thus identified as "people of color?" This reality presents a problem to white-identifying persons in North American contexts who might want to express solidarity but find it convenient to begin with the "Brown" person they already know. The authors of this chapter have met many a white person who feels fulfilled in their anti-discriminatory efforts for befriending a Brown person but do not know what to do when they encounter conflicting "Brown" narratives about crucified people—like, for instance, a Brown person who sincerely but mistakenly (constituting a hermeneutical violence) notes that "caste-based discrimination is a thing of the past." It is easier to buy into the worldviews of dominant Brown persons but more difficult and necessary to navigate the complexity that privileges crucified people.

When there are conflicting positions, one needs to epistemologically privilege crucified bodies. To be clear, we are not making a case here for what's been called

---

[24] Kikon, "Dirty Food," 279.
[25] Ibid.
[26] SueJeanne Koh, "Excavation, Interrogation, and Incommensurability: Navigating Theological Landscapes as an Asian American, Feminist Scholar," in *Christianity Next* (Women and Biblical Traditions, Winter 2020), 60.

"oppression Olympics"[27]—that is, oppressed people competing with one another for more power. Such a problem arises when intersectional analyses fail. What we are more concerned with is how locally dominant players in various parts of the world, when they or their ideas move transnationally, hide their dominance under the guise of "person of color." An example might help. In India, there are dominant voices that seek to portray India in a pan-Indian framework that minimizes India's rich—and often antagonistic—identities. Such problematic logics are present in the Hindutva imagination of India. As Sathianathan Clarke rightly observes, Hindutva could be seen as a comprehensive political and cultural ideological concept that seeks to fuse by co-opting distinct particularities and differences into a hegemonically conceived homogenous unity and identity.[28]

One of the voices that propose such a pan-Indian framework, Sai Deepak, presents a seemingly postcolonial idea by noting that "India" existed even before the creation of the modern nation-state called India in 1947. What Deepak is arguing for is an ancient India that transcends modern categories. One of the key arguments that this kind of thinking—one that is broadly represented and promoted by majoritarian Hindu nationalists today—makes is that "caste" is a colonial invention. While this might seem like a fresh postcolonial take, it is, from the perspective of those on the margins of power in India, very much part of the hegemonic co-option of liberative impulses that otherwise point fingers at casteist religious and social practices in modern India.

Caste-based discrimination predates colonialism. Despite this reality, many North American commentators are often drawn to problematic Hindutva-inflected postcolonial arguments that evade casteism. Taking such arguments at face value does disservice to liberative impulses. While there are numerous examples of this problem that fall "under the radar," as it were, the reason we mention this is to emphasize how even leading Brown decolonial scholars fall prey to such arguments. Walter Mignolo's endorsement of Sai Deepak's book,[29] despite Mignolo's subsequent withdrawal of the endorsement, shows the limits and dangers of an uncritical approach to global solidarity. The fact that decolonial theory can be problematically deployed by hegemonic forces and the processes by which leading decolonial theorists can fall prey to them is cause for concern. In light of such problems and dangers, we find it crucial to name the problem of hegemonic co-options and superficial pursuits of solidarity and lift up, instead, the need for a sustained and deep engagement with crucified bodies.

---

[27] Ange-Marie Hancock, *Solidarity Politics for Millennials: A Guide to Ending the Oppression Olympics* (New York: Palgrave Macmillan, 2011).

[28] See Sathianathan Clarke, "Hindutva, Religious and Ethnocultural Minorities, and Indian-Christian Theology," *The Harvard Theological Review* 95, no. 2 (April 1, 2002): 197–226; G. Aloysius, "Trajectory of Hindutva," *Economic and Political Weekly* 29, no. 24 (1994): 1450–2; G. Aloysius, *Nationalism without a Nation in India* (Delhi: Oxford University Press, 1997); K. N. Panikar, "Culture and Communalism," *Social Scientist* 21, no. 3/4 (1993): 24–31, https://doi.org/10.2307/3517629.

[29] We are grateful to Iskander Abbasi for drawing this to our attention. The book in question is Sai Deepak's work, *India, that is Bharat*, published by Bloomsbury Press. Bloomsbury has since removed Mignolo's endorsement from its web-based promotion of the book, but the first edition copies still contain the endorsement.

Ethnography of Crucified Bodies

In light of the foregoing discussion that underscores the two problems, this section highlights how crucified bodies are the real "test" of liberative theological impulses. In doing so, we want to cast theologies of liberation, taking Latin American liberation theology—which has impacted Dalit and Indigenous liberation theologies in India—in particular as an example of ethnographic theology that attends to the historical crucifixions of the poor. We draw here on a central axiom in liberation theologies, namely the "preferential option for the poor." Epistemologically privileging crucified bodies is necessary to resist superficial pursuits of solidarity and hegemonic dominant co-options of liberative movements. We draw inspiration from the Spanish-Salvadoran Jesuit priest and theologian, Ignacio Ellacuría, who was assassinated in 1989 for his opposition to the repressive El Salvadoran government. Ellacuría formulated a powerful theological and social category to designate the poor and oppressed masses of Latin America, calling them the "crucified people."[30]

The suffering of crucified people is not because of some inevitable or unidentifiable cause. In Latin America and elsewhere, they are victims of systemic evils and injustice. In other words, there is an intentionality in operation that ought to be identified. As Ellacuría notes, their crucifixion is the product of unjust human actions in history and therefore "must be regarded as sin."[31] Crucified people are, therefore, those "who die before their time"[32] due to such institutionalized violence. Theologies of liberation are thus less interested in responding to the challenge posed by the so-called non-believer and more interested in the challenge posed by "non-persons,"[33] the crucified people. As such, questions about the existence of poor and oppressed human persons are more urgent than questions about God's existence.[34] It is this kind of ethnographically driven theological impulse that allows Jon Sobrino, for instance, to note that the problem is not first about the death of God but the death of the poor.[35]

As a people's theology that arises from the experiences of those who live on the "underside of history," the birthplace of liberation theologies are sites of crucifixion, then and now. This is why theological reflection is always understood as a second step in liberationist theological enterprises, the first step being commitment to crucified people. So, liberation theologies emerge on the theological scene as a fruit of commitment to and solidarity with crucified bodies. It is a "theology of

---

[30] Ellacuría, "The Crucified People," 580–603. See also Francisco Pelaez-Diaz, "Central American Migration as the Way of the Cross: Ignacio Ellacuría's Notion of the 'Crucified Peoples' for Theological Reframing of the Migrant Experience," in *Migration and Public Discourse in World Christianity*, ed. Afe Adogame, Raimundo Barreto, and Wanderly Pereira da Rosa (Minneapolis: Fortress Press, 2019), 229–46.

[31] Ellacuría, "The Crucified People," 590.

[32] Gutierrez, *The Power of the Poor in History*, trans. Robert R. Barr (Eugene: Wipf & Stock, 2004), 77.

[33] Gustavo Gutierrez, *A Theology of Liberation: History, Politics, and Salvation*, trans. Caridad Inda and John Eagleson, 15th Anniversary ed. (Maryknoll: Orbis Books, 1988), xxix.

[34] Devin Singh, "Liberation Theology," in *The Oxford Handbook of the Epistemology of Theology*, ed. William J. Abraham and Frederick D. Aquino (New York: Oxford University Press, 2017), 553.

[35] Jon Sobrino, *The True Church and the Poor* (Maryknoll: Orbis, 1984), 30.

accompaniment"[36] that is possible only by being in the company of crucified people. It is in these senses that liberation theologies can be characterized as an ethnography of the oppressed. Here, the *ethnos* constitute the locus of reflection, denunciation, and annunciation. In this way, the oppressed bring a normative content and direction to theology and, relatedly, to ethnography as well. We use the term ethnography in a less technical manner, trying to capture the fact that liberation theology is a theology that emerges from the collective everyday life of the poor that encompasses their pain, suffering, struggles, joy, and aspirations. Theologians and others have engaged positively with ethnography undertaking both thick descriptions and other creative methodological pathways.[37]

A possible worry for a theologian could be that an ethnographic approach to theology could mean surrendering of theology's particular character. Such a worry is unnecessary. If theology is to be truly incarnational it has to make bodies, crucified bodies in particular, its focus. This implies that theology has to be in some sense ethnographic. Put differently, what is theological about ethnography is its attention to bodies; again, not just any bodies, but bodies that are crushed under the weight of the world's injustice. This is where methodological considerations attain fundamental significance. Francisco Moreno calls this the "ethical dimension of methodology" because, he argues, "the very choice of methodology carries moral implications."[38] This is to say that theological-ethical methodologies, including ethnographic research as theological method, are not neutral or value free but have ethical consequences.

The primacy of method can also be seen in Juan Luis Segundo's characterization of the liberatory character of a theology. "The one and only thing that can maintain the liberative character of any theology," according to Segundo, "is not its content but its methodology."[39] Therefore, a crucial question is whether the use of a particular methodology unmasks or obscures systems of domination, and whether it engenders liberation or maintains the oppressive status quo. In this regard, ours is an attempt to cast theological ethnography in the service of the liberation of the oppressed. It is only when theological and ethnographic research attentively focuses on crucified bodies, alternative liberatory knowledge can be produced. When ethnography accords primacy to crucified bodies, it becomes distinctly theological by embracing a preferential option for crucified bodies. Such a focus on crucified bodies allows theology and ethnography to have a symbiotic relationship.

Only an epistemological privileging of crucified bodies can help resist co-option, on the one hand, and evasion, on the other. Differently phrased, what we propose here

---

[36] Jennie Weiss Block and Michael Griffin, "Introduction," in Paul Farmer, "Reimagining Accompaniment: A Doctor's Tribute to Gustavo Gutierrez," in *In the Company of the Poor: A Conversation between Dr. Paul Farmer and Fr. Gustavo Gutierrez* ed. Michael Griffin and Jennie Weiss Block (Maryknoll: Orbis Books, 2013), 5–6.
[37] See the *Journal of World Christianity* 2020 special issue, "The Ethnographic Method in World Christianity: A Conversation among Emerging and Seasoned Scholars."
[38] Francisco Moreno, *Moral Theology from the Poor* (Quezon City: Claretian Publications, 1988), 32.
[39] Juan Luis Segundo, *The Liberation of Theology*, trans. John Drury (Eugene: Wipf and Stock, 1976), 40.

is an approach to ethnography which begins "at the scene of a wound."[40] Theologians can thus befriend ethnographic work by beginning at the scene of the wound and allowing crucified bodies to guide their ethical compass[41] as has been done in theologies of liberation. Just like theology, ethnography is not innately liberatory. It is the commitment to crucified bodies that makes ethnography and theology have a meaningful two-way conversation.

For theologians, the incarnational core of Christianity might serve as a gravitational force that pulls theologians into material encounters with the world. It was that incarnational core that drew the first generation of liberation theologians to the everyday materiality that they encountered among the people—songs, stories, and quotidian realities. Christianity's incarnational core is better seen as a methodological embrace of "real, finite bodies" and "the wisdom of body-words and their transformative power."[42] Incarnation matters insofar as it allows theologians to epistemologically privilege crucified bodies and the normative force such a privileging brings about. As James Cone rightly notes, "God did not become a universal human being but an *oppressed* Jew."[43] Incarnation, in this sense, already pays attention to crucified bodies. Importantly, in this connection, Jesus' incarnation as an oppressed Jew has liberation as its telos. This is the reason why we emphasize the both–and dimension of incarnation *and* liberation we hold as coterminus in the subtitle of the chapter, namely, "a liberationist-incarnational approach."

In the liberationist-incarnational approach we lift up, we are not simply highlighting the epistemological privileging of "Christian" crucified bodies. As Andrew Prevot rightly observes, "a decolonial shift can happen within Christian theology only if Christian theologians reinterpret the mystical body of Christ anthropologically and without reserve—that is, as a doctrine that raises up and celebrates human flesh as such, regardless of communal belonging or sacramental status."[44] This necessitates an epistemological privileging of crucified people anywhere and everywhere. Such attention to crucified bodies "here" and "there," as it were, by engaging in active dialogue

---

[40] Mary McClintock Fulkerson, cited in Timothy K. Snyder, "Theological Ethnography: Embodied" in *The Other Journal: An Intersection of Theology and Culture* (2014), https://theotherjournal.com/2014/05/27/theological-ethnography-embodied/. See also Mary McClintock Fulkerson, *Places of Redemption: Theology for a Worldly Church* (New York: Oxford University Press, 2007).

[41] An example of an anthropological fieldwork focusing on crucified bodies is the case of Paul Farmer, a medical anthropologist who works among the poor in Haiti. Farmer was inspired by the liberationist axiom of preferential option for the poor which he learned through befriending Gustavo Gutierrez. Farmer was rightly convinced that diseases themselves "made a radical preferential option for the poor." Therefore, Farmer was not satisfied with mere treatment of individual patients and made efforts to remedy the structural aspects of Haiti's health system. The mission statement of Partners in Health, which Farmer helped found, explicitly mentions that their mission is to "provide a preferential option for the poor in health care." See Paul Farmer, "Reimagining Accompaniment: A Doctor's Tribute to Gustavo Gutierrez," in *In the Company of the Poor*, 22–3.

[42] Mayra Rivera Rivera, "Thinking Bodies: The Spirit of a Latina Incarnational Imagination," in *Decolonizing Epistemologies: Latina/o Theology and Philosophy*, ed. Ada Maria Isasi-Diaz and Eduardo Mendieta (Fordham: Fordham University Press, 2011), 221.

[43] James Cone, *A Black Theology of Liberation*, 40th Anniversary ed. (Marknoll: Orbis, 2010), 91. Emphasis ours.

[44] Andrew Prevot, "Mystical Bodies of Christ: Human, Crucified, and Beloved," in *Beyond the Doctrine of Man: Decolonial Visions of the Human*, ed. Joseph Drexler-Dreis and Kristien Justaert (New York: Fordham University Press, 2020), 141.

with local and global commentators on crucified bodies, is the only safeguard against hegemonic dominant co-options of liberative movements, deformed inclusions, and superficial solidarities.

Importantly, however, this epistemological privilege is not something that dominant persons endow on crucified people. In other words, crucified people are not simply the object of ethnographic research or anthropological data collection. They evangelize the ethnographer theologian, the church, and the rich countries of the Global North. This is an undeserved gift that crucified people offer to the world to unmask the sins of the oppressor and bring to light the injustice responsible for their crucifixions. The knowledge produced in the encounter with crucified people is no longer simply theoretical and confined to the cognitive sphere; it is a knowledge that is embodied, material, and transformative, inviting us to imagine and work toward a just and kinder world by interrogating complicities, resisting co-options, and eschewing superficial solidarities.

7

A Trauma-Ridden Body Lifted High

Eschatological Imagination in a Public Square[1]

Hee-Kyu Heidi Park

Introduction

How does theology form in the public square?[2] This chapter seeks to answer this question by addressing how the human body can exist in a public space politically and, as a corollary, theologically. Observing the antigovernment mass movement in public places like Tahrir Square of Egypt, Gezi Park in Turkey, and the Occupy movement in the United States, Judith Butler analyzes the phenomenon of public gatherings of bodies in her *Notes Toward Performative Theory of Assembly*. When a diverse group of people gathers in one place, the commonality they form has a characteristic different from the unified political that will presumably be achieved through the principle of representation in a democracy. Butler explores this characteristic through the lens of body politics. In our inescapably neoliberal world, this process of body politics creates a commonality that Butler describes as follows:

> Neoliberal rationality demands self-sufficiency as a moral ideal at the same time that neoliberal forms of power work to destroy that very possibility at an economic level, establishing every member of the population as potentially or actually precarious, even using the ever-present threat of precarity to justify its heightened regulation of public space and its deregulation of market expansion.[3]

Under this paradigm of neoliberalism, bodies gathered in public spaces communicate this precarity in nonverbal ways. According to Butler, precarity denotes the "condition

---

[1] An earlier version of this research was published in the *International Journal of Public Theology* 15 (2021): 575–93. We are grateful for the permission to include it here.
[2] This work was supported by the Ministry of Education of the Republic of Korea and the National Research Foundation of Korea (NRF-2020S1A5A8046265).
[3] Judith Butler, *Notes Toward a Performative Theory of Assembly* (Cambridge, MA: Harvard University Press, 2015), 14.

of living beings [who can be] expunged at will or by accident."[4] "Social and political institutions are designed in part to minimize conditions of precarity,"[5] but they can also act in a way that increases the precarity of certain "individuals who are at risk of not being qualified as subjects of recognition."[6] The effort to decipher the grammar of bodies' nonverbal communication and protestation of precarity can indeed generate ethical questions that let us understand the function of bodies' performances on public streets.

After Butler wrote *Notes*, numerous public demonstrations happened across the globe. Their number includes the Arab Spring and movements like Black Lives Matter in the United States and the Candlelight Movement in South Korea, which ousted the corrupted former president Park Geun-hye.

We are also witnessing public gatherings and movements that are arguably different from these in their public and political characteristics. Such examples include the far-right white supremacist movement in the United States that persisted during the Trump era and the Taegeugki[7] Army movement of conservative Christians demanding the release of former president Park in South Korea. Nonetheless, we should note that throughout history, those gathered in public places have demanded changes based on their bodies' precarity, regardless of their political tendency.

In August 2019, South Korea witnessed a dramatic competition between two large groups over bodily precarity. The scrutiny of the newly appointed minister of justice sharply divided the whole country into two camps with very different understandings of what constitutes justice. As pictures of the masses that filled the vast public spaces of both Gwanghwamun Square[8] and the traffic-controlled, two-kilometer-long multilane streets in Sŏchodong[9] filled the internet, online communities began to boil with arguments about how many people/bodies had gathered in each public place. The political messages of the Butlerian precarity of the body do not depend on the numbers of the bodies, which is the decision-making factor in the principle of representation, but on the vulnerability of the body exposed in the public place. Then, the obsession with the numbers of individual bodies on the street falls short in truly understanding the intent of the messages conveyed by the protesters. If the protests and messages of precarity are not affected by the number of participants, we should then be able to analyze the precarity of a single body in the public square and understand its complexity.

Rather than focus on mass movements, this chapter aims to examine a case that demonstrates one person's body's precarity in the public square and to decipher its messages. In a rather intimate manner, a public spectacle unfolded that demonstrates the action taken by a community of faith in the midst of the politics and economics

---

[4] Judith Butler, "Performativity, Precarity and Sexual Politics," AIBR. *Revista de Antopologia Iberoamericanan* 3 (2009): ii
[5] Ibid.
[6] Ibid., i.
[7] This particular political group chose Taekeukki, the national flag of South Korea, as their political symbol, using it profusely in their demonstration.
[8] Located in front of the main royal palace and surrounded by main government buildings, it is a vast square surrounded by major roads often used for public gatherings.
[9] Where the Supreme Court and the Supreme Public Prosecutor's Office are located.

of the neoliberal order. The case in point has been unfolding in the southern part of Seoul since June 2019. Whereas the large-scale demonstrations of the Taegeukgi Army occupied Seoul's political center, K, a laid-off employee of a multinational conglomerate company, Company X, mounted a protest against the violence he believed that the company had committed against him, his family, and his community.[10] The public space of his choice was on the small platform of a CCTV traffic camera pole that stands over the busy crossroad of the Gangnam subway station area.

His one-person protest, which he faithfully maintained in various forms since 1999, had not gained much public attention prior to August 2019. It did so when a coalition of Christian organizations and churches began to hold public prayer meetings and cultural festivals in solidarity with K, now sixty years of age. In due course, the protest at the top of an 82-foot tower in the busiest intersection in Seoul made its way into the *New York Times*.[11]

At the heart of K's protest lies the question of what is justice. Among many directions pursuable to explore K's complex relationship with Company X, this chapter focuses on how his quest for justice is expressed through the unique message that the precarity of the lone body on the CCTV pole communicates. It is clear that something specific was communicated to the Christian community gathered under the pole which prompted a communal imagination that motivated them to act. The task is one of deciphering what was communicated and unearthing the layers beneath this message.

In order to fulfill that aim, I collected data through participant observation in the public prayer meetings and interviews with the Christian coalition leader.[12] I also analyzed mass media and social network coverage of the protest. The process through which the Christian coalition formed and contributed to the public awareness of K's experience provides insights into his protests' deeper meanings. Through recourse to William Cavanaugh's *Torture and Eucharist*, it becomes possible to interpret the communal, eschatological imagination that generated from the precarity of bodies gathered at the scene and examine its implication and limitation.

Approaching the Scene of the Body Lifted High

The following is how K's case was initially brought to my attention. I had been in discussion with another colleague with the intent of forming a discourse on theology in the public square, focusing on the political movements in South Korea, when I first attended Hyangrin Presbyterian Church. The church announcements included news

---

[10] The issues surrounding K and company X are not completely resolved. For the protection of parties involved, I have substituted their names in this chapter and all references with pseudonyms.

[11] Choe Sang-Hun, "'My Last Stand'. In South Korea, A Protester's Lone Fight Against Samsung," *The New York Times*, April 19, 2020, https://www.nytimes.com/2020/04/19/world/asia/samsung-tower-protest.html; "South Korean Ends Yearlong Tower Protest After Samsung Apologizes," *The New York Times*, May 29, 2020, https://www.nytimes.com/2020/05/29/world/asia/south-korea-protest-tower-samsung.html.

[12] The research was approved by Ewha Womans University IRB. Approval number: ewha-202006-0016-01.

regarding K's protest and an invitation to participate in the public worship service to support him on the street near the Gangnam subway station. That week's worship was going to be led by the Hyangrin community so I attended the meeting on August 28, 2019.

The worship service was small and intimate. It did not attract the attention of any mass media nor that of the public. The CCTV tower stood in the middle of the busiest crossroad in the Gangnam area of Seoul. Several banners adorned both the tower and sidewalk, stating, "There is a person on the top of this tower!" "Reinstate K!" and, "Apologize for destroying human life and dignity! Listen to the voice of K!" but neither the banner nor the gathering seemed to bother the passersby, whose eyes were mostly fixed on their smartphones. At the time, I wondered what was being communicated through the protest; what was the grammar of the communication?

The storyline begins with K's election as a labor negotiation committee member. At that point he had already been employed for about eight years during which time he had endured discrimination and harassment. In this role K organized labor unions in order to advocate for workers' rights. The difficulty lay with the established company policy of no labor unions being allowed, a policy put in place by the company's founder. K claims that he was persecuted severely by means of kidnapping, torture in imprisonment, sudden ambush attacks, and sexual violence against his wife. His father disappeared after a visit by people sent from Company X. K was eventually dismissed without proper documentation. He had been protesting on his own, without support and protection, against Company X since 1999. The chronology of the events with some detail can be found in the press release by the National Human Rights Commission of Korea issued in support of him on July 10, 2019.[13]

---

[13] The following is the chronology from the report (http://laborhealth.or.kr/2019/wp-content/uploads/2019/09/20190909_060241.pdf):
1959. 7. 10. Born
1982. 12. 2. Employed by Company X Aerospace-engineering, Inc.
1984. 2. 1. Transferred to Company X Watch, Inc.
1990. 6. Elected as a member of Labor Negotiation Committee
1990. 8. Chair of the Committee to Organize Company X Labor Union in the Kyeongnam area.
1990. 11. The general manager invited him to visit a technology development site of an affiliated company, which was an abduction to a Taegu hotel. He was imprisoned for seven days, being threatened to give up organizing the labor union. When K did not budge, they moved him to another hotel in Jeonranamdo to persuade and threaten him further, while another team visited K's parents to force them to persuade him. As a result, K's father left a will and disappeared. His whereabouts are still unknown.
1991. 2-3. Communicated the need to organize the labor union to the company's employees and requested an explanation from the management for the mistreatment and irregularity.
1991. 3.28 K fired on the grounds of sexual misconduct, which was fabricated by the company. The alleged victim of the misconduct later confessed that she was coerced to make the accusation and left a notarized document. Later, in 1993, when K sued Company X for the ungrounded dismissal, K's attorney, Moon Jae-in, the current president of South Korea, failed to submit this notarized document, which led to K's loss in the legal case. K eventually appealed to the higher court proper.
1992. 5. 18. A police officer, possibly bribed by Company X, abducted K's wife and sexually harassed her.
1994. Fifteen days before the final decision trial for his appeal at the supreme court to confirm his ungrounded dismissal, Company X's executive officers approached him to persuade him to give up the appeal in return for reinstating his employment at Company X after one year of employment in

K's previous protests had many hiccups in gaining public empathy. Kim Hiheon, the head pastor of Hyang Rin Church, explained that K was shunned during the Candlelight Movement of 2016 that demanded former president Park Geun-hye's impeachment. Moon Jae-in, the twelfth president of South Korea, played a significant role in the movement. K held a sign that criticized Moon for his failure to turn in the notarized document that could have saved him from the ongoing hardship that came after he was not exonerated from the sexual harassment accusation that Company X fabricated to strong-arm K to give up forming the labor union.

K was thus an ambiguous oddity in the movement. When, in February 2018, he posted on the online petition board of Chŏngwadae[14] a petition titled, "Please stop the ugly atrocities of labor-union-less Company X Chaebŏl,"[15] the petition received only eight clicks of supporting recommendations from others.[16] Moon Jae-in's government made it a rule that any petition that received more than two hundred thousand clicks of recommendations would ensure direct action from government officials. This petition was the last activity of his twenty-year effort to gain attention on the ground. Following its failure to gain traction, K climbed the CCTV tower on June 10, 2019. The timing of his ascent marked what would have been one month before his official retirement date had he been reinstated. The traffic's noise often buried his voice, but his hunger strike began to gain attention. There were traces of support from several civil and religious groups, but Hyangrin Church maintained a daily supportive presence beneath the tower.

Kim Hiheon recalls feeling like he was "hit by a mace" when he read about K on an online news media site called OhmyNews. That was around day fifty of K's hunger strike. He had regarded K as one among many who had experienced injustice, but the

---

an affiliated company. K signed the agreement on reinstatement in January 1994 and submitted a letter to give up his appeal to the court in March 1994.

1994–5. Assigned to Company X Construction, Inc. branch in Smolensky District in Russia. There he was coerced to sign a Memorandum of Abandonment of Labor Unions. When he refused, his limbs were tied up for 5 hours, during which those sent destroyed his briefcase and took the letter of reinstatement. They reported K to the Korean Embassy in Russia as a North Korean spy, which led to his interrogation by the national security officers. K was released as innocent.

1997. Still waiting to be reinstated

1998. Company X Watch, Inc. was selected to be expelled from the Company X Group.

1999. 5. 13. Began a hunger strike. On the sixteenth day of the strike, Company X accused him of obstruction of business and stipulation of official secrets of the company. He served 1 1/2 years of prison time and three years of probation.

1999. 11. 13. Began hunger strike at the National Council of Churches in Korea, requesting reinstatement. The strike lasted for forty-eight days.

2000. 2. 3. Incarcerated the second time on defamation charges.

2000–2001. Deputy manager of the restructuring headquarters of Company X Group accused K of blackmail for compensation when Company X had not reinstated him. The lawsuit was getting processed.

2016–17: Protests in front of Company X headquarter and Gwanghwamun.

2019. 6. 10. Began protest on the CCTV tower in Gangnam Station.

[14] The official residence of the president of South Korea.

[15] Chaebŏl is the term for the wealthiest few who usually own conglomerate companies in South Korea.

[16] "Munocho X Chaebŏlŭi Ch'uakhan Manhaengŭl Makachuseyo (Please stop the ugly atrocities of labor union-less X Chaebŏl)." Chŏngwadae Kukminchŏngwŏn Kesipan (Online petition board of Chŏngwadae). https://www1.president.go.kr/petitions/152236.

stories he learned through the news article were heart piercing. There were members of his church who had encountered K's stories, and a small group of people emerged feeling as if they had been called upon to respond to the situation. They organized a small prayer meeting to decide on a course of action while supporting K for two weeks. The group felt that the book of Job seemed appropriate to meditate on so they gathered beneath the tower and began to read it chapter by chapter. They tried to discern whether they could walk with God while participating in both Job and K's desperate struggle to trust God's saving action. K's hunger strike had been going on for more than two months at that point. It had not yet led to a response from Company X. Those beneath the tower were becoming more anxious about the critical limit that K's human body was reaching.

After K decided to begin accepting food, his situation required more support on the ground to provide for his bodily needs. The Hyangrin community, composed of four churches (the Hyangrin Church, Dŭlggot Hyangrin Church, Gangnam Hyangrin Church, and Sŏmdol Hyangrin Church), thereupon began to co-organize daily worship services starting on August 4, 2019. The worship services had a full liturgy prepared by the church community in charge. The liturgy included a phone call to K and shouts of slogans, sometimes followed by a marching protest around the main building of Company X with banners and flags. This spirit of cooperation eventually inspired another group of churches wanting to stand in solidarity. On September 10, 2019, these churches organized the "Strategic Committee of Protestant Churches to Resolve the Issues relating to K, the dismissed X-Employee" and continued their activities until early March 2020. K, himself a Christian and a deacon in his home church and whose disappeared father was an elder, had a deep appreciation for the worship services on the street. He declared that:

> [w]hen I climbed this tower, I gave X and myself one month. After the month, I was going to end my life. However, witnessing the Hyangrin community's steadfast commitment to the prayer services, I decided to live. In the power of the Holy Spirit, I will pay back this debt to our society. I thank the Hyangrin community for the new life I received.

The committee extended its network to support K in many directions, hoping to eventually negotiate with Company X.[17] Through the network, labor activists, political parties, and many other churches were reached to raise awareness and strategize the action plan to move Company X to respond.

Contrary to K's initial expectation that he would quickly gain some sort of response from Company X, his protest extended for almost another year. Many things happened during that time. For example, Company X was involved in a lawsuit for bribing the former president Park and her associate Choi Soon-Sil. In response, the court

---

[17] Ŭnhye Lee, "Kokongnongsŏng 57il Kssi: Hyanrin kongdongch'e Yebe Dŏkbune Maŭm Dachapa . . . Kkŭtkkachi Ssauketta. ([K] on High-Altitude Protest day 57 says, 'I made up my mind to live and fight thanks to Hyangrin community worship services')," *Nyusŭaenchoi*, May 2019, http://m.newsnjoy.or.kr/news/articleView.html?idxno=224684&fbclid=IwAR3GJE9Q0i4MqgdpRs448M7YEefed97REOgpCyoFHqRS6mDbcHmIYdM07cA.

organized a Surveillance Committee for Company X's Law Abidance in order to guide the leadership of X into corrective behaviors. In 2020, the COVID-19 pandemic broke out, and the gatherings under the tower needed to stop for a while. Storms, winter, and all kinds of environmental challenges came to pass. Eventually, when the political pressure on Company X heightened, Company X yielded to the pressure to negotiate, and the Christian coalition carried it out with Company X leadership. However, when the letter of agreement was presented to K, he refused to sign it due to his dissatisfaction with the amount of compensation from Company X. When the negotiation fell apart, another group needed to be organized to carry out the renegotiation. The negotiation concluded on May 30, 2020, marking the 355th day of his high-altitude protest.

Deciphering the Grammar of the Scene

I wish now to consider the basic visual communication happening in the scene of K's protest. When understood as a picture, his protest stands within the "long pedigree" of the "iconography of suffering."[18] It possesses a particular coherence with "torment, a canonical subject in art" as its centerpiece or the "spectacle [to be] watched (or ignored) by other people" as described by Susan Sontag in her *Regarding the Pain of Others*.[19] In response to my questions to do with "what message or resonance do people get by looking at K on the tower?," Sontag notes that such scenes of suffering indicate that the torment "cannot be stopped—and the mingling of inattentive with attentive onlookers underscores this."[20] For the scene to convey a message that brings about changes, there needs to be more than a simple display, but the question that arises from that is: What constitutes "more"?

As a living scene, K's protest establishes both a sense of distance and closeness for the onlookers. It creates such a dynamic with a subtle difference from the pictures with which Sontag is engaging. The CCTV pole is distant enough from passersby for them to ignore and close enough for them to be annoyed by its ugliness—as indeed some citizens complained about in videos captured online. In terms of distance, Sontag notes that people have difficulty absorbing nearby suffering. They can experience faraway suffering as a "voyeuristic lure—the possible satisfaction of knowing, 'This is not happening to me, I'm not ill, I'm not dying, I'm not trapped.'"[21] The ambivalent distance of the pole, neither too near nor too far, creates an interesting dynamic. What is it that connects K to those underneath the tower distanced by five busy traffic lanes and a 25-meter-high pole?

Those first impressions lead into a consideration of his precarity mediated through his breathing and metabolizing body. The tormented body displays the trauma of his twenty years of protest. Trauma fragments the self, as was born out by the fragmented language in his government petition that only eight people understood and resonated

---

[18] Susan Sontag, *Regarding the Pain of Others* (New York: Picador, 2004), 40.
[19] Ibid., 41.
[20] Ibid., 42.
[21] Ibid., 99.

with. Heinz Kohut has argued that such fragmentation generates the sense of a defective self, sometimes even to the point of disintegration: the self thus needs to be reorganized.[22] Fueled by torturous pain, the process of disintegration that fragments the language pushes the self into a seemingly null state, rendering it invisible. In *Torture and Eucharist*, William Cavanaugh states:

> [i]t is the difficulty of expressing pain, its occult nature buried deep in the body of the sufferer, that lends pain to misdescription and manipulation for political purposes. Verbal signs which lift the reality of pain out of the body and into the world of communication are crucial to pain's alleviation. But at the same time the language of pain is so unstable that it can be used not to display pain but to disguise it, to bury it further into invisibility.[23]

His invisible pain was indescribable but became comprehensible as reported in an article in the South Korean online newspaper OhmyNews.[24] The work of Cavanaugh invites a deeper consideration of the dynamics of torture: What is lost in the violence done? Cavanaugh is of the opinion that torture is a "perverse liturgy" that takes the body of the victim as its "ritual site." It enacts a "drama which both makes real the power of the state and constitutes an act of worship of that mysterious power,"[25] with the victim playing the role of the enemy. This role is played out by answering the urgently shouted questions "hurled in a frenzy of threats and blows."[26] It does so while the torture dissolves the ego by disabling its ability to perform processes necessary for its own self-preservation.[27] Elaine Scarry has noted how "[t]he feigned urgency of the questions has the effect" of turning the "moral reality of torture upside down."[28] It can do that "by making the seeking of important answers seem like the motive for the torture, the torturer seems able to justify his brutality."[29] The moment the victim yields to the pressure of pain and urgency, the self-destructive process is enabled. The victim's voice is now "the voice of corruption" or that of filth. In this process, Cavanaugh argues,

> torture humiliates the victim, exploits his human weakness through the mechanism of pain, until he does take on the role of filth, confessing his lowliness and betraying the cause, his comrades, his family, and his friends. Such filth assumes an important role in the mythos of the regime.[30]

---

[22] Heinz Kohut, *How Does Analysis Cure?*, ed. Arnold Goldberg with the collaboration of Paul Stephansky (Chicago: Chicago University Press, 1984), 70.
[23] William Cavanaugh, *Torture and Eucharist* (Oxford: Blackwell, 1998), 35.
[24] Daehi Jŏng, "X sibŏk madahako kokkikkŭnŭn Namcha 'Kŭkakmudohan ilŭl Kyŏkŏtta. (The man who stop eating after refusing 100 million won from [Company X], 'I experienced extreme atrocity')," *OhmyNews*, July 9, 2019, http://m.ohmynews.com/NWS_Web/Mobile/at_pg.aspx?CNTN_CD=A0002552302.
[25] Cavanaugh, *Torture and Eucharist*, 30.
[26] Ibid., 29.
[27] Ibid., 40.
[28] Elaine Scarry, *The Body in Pain: The Making and Unmaking of the World* (Oxford: Oxford University Press, 1985), 35.
[29] Cavanaugh, *Torture and Eucharist*, 29.
[30] Ibid., 31.

The very identity of the torture victim is thereby contaminated and erased. Even the evidence of torture is eventually erased by releasing the victim after the body heals, thus ending the secretive liturgy, or what Cavanaugh calls, the anti-liturgy of torture.[31] As a traumatized victim, K's experience is a process of recovering the identity he lost when Company X's state-like power[32] attempted to strip off his humanity. His self became fragmented as he was isolated from the community to which he once belonged.[33] He now moves in the liminal space between the visible and the invisible once he emerged out of the hidden acts of being kidnapped and tortured. When he finally became visible again, his father had disappeared into thin air, leaving only a will behind.

Now, the display of his suffering on the CCTV tower accomplishes just the opposite of what his past trauma had done; his body is visible now. With his newfound visibility, the fragments of his self began to be glued back together.[34]

For K, this protest was his final act. K put all of his ego-strength on this very last attempt at getting his voice heard by climbing up the tower. His friend, L, who had been fighting along with him as he had also been dismissed from Company X due to a labor union organizing efforts, fiercely tried to dissuade K from executing this high-altitude protest, but this did not stop K's determination. When L was out of town, K packed up water, tissues, a sleeping bag, and batteries for his electronics and climbed the tower by himself. He entered a hunger strike with the hope of getting an answer from Company X in a few weeks, but with no response from Company X, the hunger strike turned into a suicidal protest. He declared "if I jump, I jump, but I will never go down. I am even ready for the winter."

When his written and spoken language failed to make him visible, his suicidal protest on the CCTV tower tapped into comprehensible language, as this embodied

---

[31] Ibid., 30.
[32] Cavanaugh's exploration of torture assumes state power. While Company X is a private company, political scientist Cho Hyŏn-yŏn examines how this particular company has extended its power to the public sphere gaining the position of "Company X Republic," a term that circulated widely among general population. The detailed process in which this company gains its singularly impactful position within Korean society can be found in Cho's article, "Minjuhwa, Segyehwa ihu Kyŏngjejŏk Dokjŏmkwa Chaebŏlŭi Sajŏk Ihaeŭi Jŏngch'ijŏk Kwanch'ŏl Kwajŏng Yŏnku (Examination of Chaebŏls' Economic Monopoly and The Expansion of Their Political Impact)," in *Hankuk Minjuhwawa Sahwejŏk Bulpyŏngdŭngŭi Donghak (Democratization of Korea and the Dynamics of Socio-economic Inequalities)*, ed. Cho Hiyŏn, Kim Dongch'un, and Oh Yusŏk (Seoul: Hanul Academy, 2009), 119–57. If we follow Carl Schmitt's adage in Political Theology, "Sovereign is he who decides on the exception," this company had exercised such decision power especially in the area of economics, according to Cho.
[33] We can say that K's self is fragmented in the Kohutian sense. Kohut argues that "if the child's self has been seriously fragmented and weakened by the lack of empathic responses from the self-object, then the formulations of drive psychology, while not adequately encompassing the crucial psychological oscillations between the cohesive and the fragmented self, may be well suited to explain the new state in experience-distant terms" (*The Restoration of the Self*, 77). Interestingly, K has developed a strong self-object experience of Company X, which he described as the "bad mother bird" in his poem, Ingansae (Human Bird). This poem was published in several news outlets, including at http://www.hanion.co.kr/news/articleView.html?idxno=9826.
[34] Self-cohesion is a state that the fragmented self aims to achieve through self-object experiences in self psychology.

action was part of Korean society's "contentious repertoire"[35]—that is, "the limited set of actions a population uses when engaging in protest activities."[36] The action is now understood even by bystanders. The combination of a high-altitude protest, which can be traced back to Kang Juryŏng in Pyŏngyang during the Japanese occupation of Korea in 1931,[37] and a suicide protest strikes a chord in the history of labor protests in South Korea.

Such a suicidal protest is a tactic of persuasion with obviously high cost. In the context of South Korea, this form of protest, as one of the repertoires of contention, had already formed for itself a powerful narrative. Both the popular presentation and scholarly representation of a suicide protest reckon it to be a "selfless, heroic act against injustice." It is often described as forced or "indirect murder [by] the state," which has the effect of inspiring "movement activism among half-hearted activists and apathy bystanders."[38] For the protest to be effective, the rhetoric of negative assumptions abounding with regard to state power is not sufficient in and of itself. The efficacy of persuasion depends on how well the news and its narrative can spread and resonate with others.

In K's case, an open and well-developed media played an important role. Suicide protest's narrative crystallized around the symbolism of martyrdom, which is traceable back to the legendary narrative of Jeon Tae-il. His suicide protest by self-immolation awakened theologians to Minjung theology and stimulated a Minjung movement activism.[39] K's tower top protest was thus a part of a Korean repertoire of contention: the precarity of his self was displayed not through a fragmented verbal or written language but through what his body was able to convey on the pole.

For K, the body conveyed more than the given martyr narrative. The precarity of his body became the vessel of communication that floated around social media in the form of pictures and description. It had been his hunger strike that first gathered people under the tower. When Hyangrin Church members gathered under the tower, their focus was to persuade him to eat. When I attended one of the prayer meetings that happened right after he broke his fast, part of the liturgy included a phone call to K. The leader put a microphone on the phone so that he could be heard. In that conversation, I heard something that has never been articulated in public media, namely, the real reason that allowed him to break the hunger strike.

K's initial motivation for the hunger strike revealed another layer of precarity: he needed to survive on the CCTV tower without a bathroom. He decided to have no bodily intake so that he would not have any output. Eating without coming down

[35] Sun-Chul Kim, "The Trajectory of Protest Suicide in South Korea, 1970–2015," *Journal of Contemporary Asia* (2019): 3; Charles Tilly, *Popular Contention in Great Britain, 1758–1834* (London: Paradigm Publisher, 1995), 41.
[36] Ibid., 3.
[37] Kyujin Choi, "Dasi Dolaon Ch'ekongnyeowa Kuldduknamŭi Side (The Return of the Age of Ch'ekongnyeo and Kuldduknam)," *Ŭiryowa Sahwe (Medicine and Society)* 2 (2015): 131–5.
[38] Kim, "The Trajectory of Protest Suicide in South Korea, 1970–2015," 2, Citing Hyojoung Kim (2008, 573).
[39] See Myeong Soo Kim, "Yesu-humanismkwa Naŭi Sinhakŭi Kil (Jesus Humanism and My Theological Path)," *Journal of the Christian Literature Society of Korea* 739 (2020): 129. And Kwangsun Suh, "A Political History of Korean Christianity in Case of South Korea in the Early 1970s," *Sinhakkwa Kyohwe (Theology and the Church)* 5 (Summer, 2016): 270–3.

from the tower meant that someone had to help him take his excrements down to the ground, a process that exposed the precarity of his body at its most secretive and vulnerable level. It was the organization of a group of people who were willing to send food up by tying it to a rope and then receiving his excrement coming down on the rope. They erected a tent near the tower, where a small group of people stayed in solidarity with K, helping him deal with his bodily needs. The pain he endured in the tiny space where his 180-centimeter body had to huddle to sleep, along with his refusal to receive medical care, was broadcast through various media. This particular aspect of his precarity did not make it outside of the intimate communication between the prayer meeting members and K, however.

The management of this precarious predicament was at the very center of the solidarity of the community that formed around K. Furthermore, it should be noted that they performed their solidarity by displaying their own precarity on the street in the public space. Thus, this community that stood in solidarity with him by connecting through their own precarity ultimately contributed to K gaining coherence in his story and identity.

Theological Processes

Through the coherence achieved on the tower, what theological message was being communicated in public? Borrowing the language of one of the liturgies used in the prayer meeting, "how may the will of heaven be done on the tower?" Kwon Myŏnga, observing Choi Kimin, who was leading an intense labor struggle (2009–18) at Ssangyong Automobiles, Inc., noted that:

> [t]he common thread observable in these labor struggles is that they all started with concerns for material and monetary issues, but they ultimately turned into a matter of spirituality. . . . As the struggle prolongs, the site of the struggle transports to another universe that cannot be contained in the question of materiality. When their struggle is about human dignity, which had depended on the least material necessity that was denied, it transformed into a symbolic struggle. Such symbolic struggle is not necessarily a fight for an important mandate instead of other material benefits. Rather, this symbolic struggle is a matter of spirituality; thus, it is a spiritual struggle. (My translation)[40]

When the twenty-some years of protests were crystallized on top of the CCTV pole, K's protest became symbolic as well as bodily. The way he lived out this symbolism, though, defied the expectation of the spectators. Kim Hiheon, in his interview, observed that:

---

[40] Myŏnga Kwon, "Sagŏn Ihuŭi Inganhak: Honŭi T'uchaenge Dehayŏ (Anthropology after Events: Regarding Spiritual Struggles," in *P'aengmokhangesŏ Pulŏonŭn Param*, ed. Inmunhakhyŏpdongchohap (Seoul: Hyŏnsilmunhwa, 2015).

[w]hen one runs toward death, shouldn't there be a solemn tune in the background? He has none of that. He does not ask for sympathy. Protesters doing hunger strikes usually show signs of distress and agony to enlist an emotional response and solidarity from the onlookers. He does not ask for that.

Instead, what he does is a simple display of his experience. As Kim Hiheon explained, K's body seems to say, "This is what you have done to me, Company X. I've lived like this, and I'm simply continuing that life." That observation agrees with Kohut's argument that physical illness increases narcissism because it creates a preoccupation with one's body, which is naturally required to maintain the cohesion of the self when pain fragments it.[41] In a tormented body, such preoccupation turns into sharper focus. Cavanaugh observes that "the immediacy of the pain shrinks the world down to the contours of the body itself; the enormity of the agony is the sufferer's only reality. Pain is often called 'blinding' because it eliminates all but itself from the field of vision."[42] Prior to this protest, K's main requirement in life had been to focus on the pain on his body, thus limiting his life's scope to his eventual protest against the perpetrator. Now that he is on this highly lifted platform, has the scope of his vision expanded? Does he see more?

The answer to the question of his vision lies in what had not been visible to him as well as the society that received him back after the torture. Cavanaugh notes how "modern torture . . . is, therefore, not simply a contest over the visible, physical body; it is better understood as a contest over the social imagination, in which bodies are the battleground."[43] The drama in torture and suffering follows a script that subtly dynamizes both visibility and invisibility. When society imagines the real and the unreal, the possible and the impossible according to this script, such social imagination can imprison the body. If that is the case, how are K's actions then to be interpreted? When his tortured, disciplined body did not become a docile body but became instead a body that climbs the pole for the purpose of display, what kind of social imagination forms?

This social imagination is precisely what should be analyzed to understand this high-altitude protest's theological dynamics. Judith Butler notes that once the body's precarity is in the public space, it has a social dimension. "I am, as a body, not only for myself, not even primarily for myself, but I find myself, if I find myself at all, constituted and dispossessed by the perspective of others."[44] When this social, tormented body is lifted high, we are given the opportunity to look up and cast our imagination. The banners on the streets around K stated that "[t]here is a person on top of the steel tower." When Moses lifted the bronze serpent on a pole, a simple gaze at the snake healed the poisonous snake bites in Numbers 21. Could this simple act of casting people's gaze upwards start a process that brings about changes in a community?

---

[41] Heinz Kohut, *The Analysis of the Self* (Chicago: University of Chicago Press, 1971), 215.
[42] Cavanaugh, *Torture and Eucharist*, 37.
[43] Ibid., 57.
[44] Butler, *Notes Toward a Performative Theory of Assembly*, 76.

The bronze serpent and K's lifted body remind other precarious bodies lifted high, namely those of martyrs, whose narratives K's suicidal body tapped on. To understand what martyrdom accomplishes, Cavanaugh noted how:

> [m]artyrdom is a bridge between heaven and earth not because the martyrs are soon to travel one way to her eternal reward, but because heaven has been brought to earth in the form of one who, in imitating Jesus the Christ, has cheated earthly death of its sting. A martyr is one who lives imaginatively as if death does not exist.[45]

His willingness to die on the tower, demonstrated through his actual dwelling on the limited, 25-meter-high tower space, created a liminal space of eschaton of a time and space that is both here and not yet here. In this space, he cheats death, not through the act of either surviving or dying, but by imagination. Thus, in this space, the social imagination turns into an eschatological one:

> The eschatological imagination sees that, although they presume to kill us, Christ has vanquished the powers of death once and for all. The eschatological imagination of martyrdom is not a vertical ascension to another place and time, a distant heaven; the movement instead brings a foretaste of heavenly space-time to earth.[46]

We can then understand the script of visibility and invisibility based upon a perpetrator's effort to kill this eschatological imagination by preventing the martyr from becoming visible. In fact, such imagination has historically resonated strongly in people, often resulting in cults of martyrs. Cavanaugh notes that cults that emerged around martyrs "overturned the well-established barriers between the living and the dead and appalled the sensibilities' of the rulers."[47] The cult of their bodies, especially, "posed a threat to the Empire's cult of power" as they created the liminal space where the dead were brought back to the living, and criminals who refused the rule of the imperial power were brought back to honor. "Their deaths, therefore, involved more than a triumph over physical pain; they were vibrant also with the memory of a dialogue with and a triumph over unjust power."[48] The cult formed around the eschatological imagination gathers to witness such triumph over injustice. Can our society form such a cult through the precarity of a body lifted high on a pole in the middle of a street in Seoul?

In examining K's protest, there is a clear sign of the possibility of a transformative cult. As the seasons turned, the tiny group that gathered for the prayer meeting grew in numbers. The Christian coalition organized a sustained stream of groups of support; more people were transformed from mere onlookers into participants. When COVID-19 struck, the campaign progressively turned to social and mass media, including the *New York Times* and the BBC. The ambivalence began to form into citizenship that spoke against violence toward a fellow citizen.

[45] Cavanaugh, *Torture and Eucharist*, 65.
[46] Ibid.
[47] Ibid., 67.
[48] Ibid., 68.

In the interview at an earlier stage of the protest, I asked Kim Hiheon to imagine what a just response from Company X would look like. He responded that:

> [i]f I were the CEO of the Company X, I would write a drama that can touch hearts, saying the Capital was blind to small things and we are sorry for that. Make it as beautiful as it can be. Just response would be a deep deliberation on ways not to repeat the injustice. That is the core demand of this struggle. This struggle can be meaningful when we can prevent others from agonizing over similar suffering. Imagining from such a line of thinking, the company could create foundations that deal with issues like Vietnam war victims or sex trafficking to signify that they may have oppressed laborers in the past, but now they are turning into a company that tackles global problems. Maybe they can create a co-op for laborers and support them in finding ways to create a common good. If I were Company X, I would do something like this.

The answer to whether a society can form an effective coalition from one man's suffering is "Maybe." It is, nevertheless, a maybe that possesses its own complexity. The coalition that centered around the social imagination of the eschatological hope disintegrated when K's self began to demonstrate its fragility. Toward the end of my research, I learned the details of the conflicts behind the negotiation process with Company X. The very human process in which personal and communal needs, as well as various political wills, collided. K's demand now focused more on personal gains, thus losing sight of the communal cause that formed the community's solidarity around him. This forced each individual to choose whether to stay loyal to him, trusting that he would carry out the group's hope for justice, or to find another way to achieve the group's goal. The community involved found itself left with the burden[49] of maintaining the public perception of the protest scene, thus preserving the theological communication.[50]

Avery Kolers recognizes how solidarity needs to endure: it needs to do so in the face of "some counterfactual disagreement within the group over ends and means."[51] It must negotiate its way into keeping the cause that the members of the group had decided to stand with deferentially, putting aside their individual judgment in favor of

---

[49] L, who had been protesting against Company X along with K in the tent on the ground under the tower, left the protest when K formed a different negotiating body to substitute the Christian coalition to talk to Company X, when Company X was forced to generate socially responsible actions when its CEO was going through trials. In this process, rather than working with the supporting groups, K is said to have made many decisions on his own, including picking the leader of the new negotiating body and choosing the support person who would replace the role of L. Some reported behaviors bordered on abuse of power, which I refrain from describing here. What I want to note here is that when a traumatized person gains cohesion through grandiosity mirrored by communal support, such grandiosity can also easily turn into difficult power dynamics that can hurt the community.

[50] Here, psychological processes within the self of K and within the group collided. From the perspective of K's psychology of self, when the protest turned from the agonistic stage to the negotiating stage, K's traumatized self, which maintained cohesion by tapping into the historic martyr narrative, sustained by the communal support, fragmented again, and his grandiose self was reinforced. K's grandiosity hurt the solidarity of the group that had rallied in support of him.

[51] Avery Kolers, "Dynamics of Solidarity," *The Journal of Political Philosophy* 20, no. 4 (2012): 365.

the group's.⁵² Solidarity works by way of commitment to the cause rather than loyalty to either the group or a particular person. Note that the eschatological social imagination functions as the subconscious theological groundwork that underscores the cause of achieving justice from Company X. Unfortunately, it was loyalty that the grandiose self of K demanded when he deserted the common cause in the negotiating process, resulting in the fragmentation of the group.

Conclusion

What the precarity of K's body accomplished in the high-altitude protest was indeed significant as it brought about cohesion between his own self and his community. K's personal journey was a process of putting together the fragments of his self in order to gain cohesion and traction toward his goal. This required magnificent energy. To employ Freudian language, it was the process of moving "the libidinal cathexis of individual body parts" scattered in fragments in the case of a traumatized person "to a cathexis of an (albeit at first grandiose, exhibitionistic, and unrealistic) cohesive self" as Kohut puts it.⁵³ Spirituality, when mingled in this process, provides a powerful catalyst that intensifies the beneficial aspects of narcissism, providing the necessary energy for the self to achieve cohesion.⁵⁴ In addition, his precarity also gathered the community around him to form a communal spirituality of social imagination. A complex fluctuation of connection and disconnection ensued, however, when K's personal need and the communal commitment of the group that gathered in solidarity with him began to conflict with one another. At the moments of conflict, specters from different periods of Korea's rapid economic and political development came to haunt the scene, complexifying the party dynamics. The eschatological imagination described in this chapter, therefore, also became more complex as the conflict introduced more and more challenges.

As I noted earlier, the question I raised with my colleague that led me to K's case was how theologies form in the public square. In my search for a current public theology in action, the large-scale demonstrations of the Taegeugki army were the most obvious example despite its fundamentalist theological stance. Just like K's case, the Taegeugki army, whose message also warrants a meticulous analysis, involved public worship services on the street and proclamation of theological messages to the public. In both cases of public theological engagement, what struck me was the gap between the proclaimed message and the public perception of the messages conveyed by the bodily presence in the public space. In the era of online media overflow, such perception seems to depend on the scene it creates, rather than on the verbal messages proclaimed in that space. As we have examined, even such a scene complexly transects

---

⁵² Ibid., 367.
⁵³ Kohut, *The Analysis of the Self*, 215.
⁵⁴ I have explored the danger of the spirituality mixed with narcissistic grandiosity in a biblical exegesis, "Divine Jealousy, Human Zeal: Self-Psychology and the Kenotic Spirituality of קִנְאָה in Numbers 25," in *Landscapes of Korean and Korean American Biblical Interpretation*, ed. John Ahn (Atlanta: SBL Press, 2019), 38–48.

with the personalities and histories of persons involved as well as the preexisting social narratives and communal dynamics. This chapter shows that the theological messages of the bodies that compose the public theological protests create impacts in terms of the psychological and communal processes that create theological messages of the precarity of the traumatized bodies.

8

Theodicies at the Border

Grasping with Evil in the Lives of Indonesian Female Migrant Workers in Singapore

Lailatul Fitriyah

The Lord is my shepherd; I shall not want.
He maketh me to lie down in green pastures: he leadeth me beside the still waters.
He restoreth my soul: he leadeth me in the paths of righteousness for his name's sake.
Yea, though I walk through the valley of the shadow of death, I will fear no evil: for thou art with me; thy rod and thy staff they comfort me.
Thou preparest a table before me in the presence of mine enemies: thou anointest my head with oil; my cup runneth over.
Surely goodness and mercy shall follow me all the days of my life: and I will dwell in the house of the Lord for ever.

(Psalm 23:2-6)

This chapter is a part of a larger book project on the construction of anti-patriarchal and anticapitalist Christian and Islamic theologies from the lives of Indonesian female migrant workers (hereafter FMWs) in Singapore. From two sets of fieldwork that were conducted in the Summer of 2018 and the Spring of 2020 in Singapore and Indonesia, I offer the notion of "border theologies" to elucidate the particular forms and characteristics of Christian and Islamic theologies as interpreted from the perspectives of the FMWs. During these periods of fieldwork, I interviewed forty dialogue partners, thirty of whom were Indonesian Christian and Muslim FMWs. Ten were stakeholders who were involved in the advocacy for, and protection of, the rights of the FMWs in Singapore and Indonesia. In the summer of 2018, the research was undertaken by participant observation and nonstructured interviews in Singapore and Indonesia in which I met and spoke with twenty FMWs and closely observed their daily activities. However, in the Spring of 2020, due to the worldwide COVID-19 pandemic, I pivoted to WhatsApp-based interviews with ten Indonesian FMWs who work in Singapore. The pandemic situation made it impossible for me to go to Singapore due to their national lockdown, and I was obliged to change my research method at that time.

The term "border theologies" refers to the Christian and Islamic theologies that are elaborated, believed, and practiced by Indonesian FMWs in Singapore. As contextual theologies, border theologies reflect the abusive and exploitative settings in which the FMWs work and live, as well as their struggles against the patriarchal, capitalist system that oppresses them. There are three components that make up border theologies:

1. The FMWs' understanding of their relationships with God and who God is.
2. Their conceptions of suffering in light of the abuses and exploitations in their daily lives, and in view of an omnipotent and omnibenevolent God.
3. Their embodied religious practices that take place in diaspora.

It is within the framework of border theologies that I analyze the FMWs' elaborations on evil in this chapter. Thus, in this project, I argue that the Christian and Islamic theologies that are constructed from the lives of Indonesian FMWs cannot be simply regarded as a reflection of the traditional Christian and Islamic theologies, but rather need to be understood as theological knowledge and praxes on their own.

In a WhatsApp text conversation, Elsa told me that she began to hold on to Psalm 23:2-6 as a reminder of God's mercy from the day she left Indonesia ten years before to work as a domestic helper overseas.[1] Her experience with previous employers had been extremely negative. She was denied off-days and had no access to any forms of communication. In her current employment, Elsa could only use her phone after a long day of work, and even then, sometimes her employers would be angry when they found her talking on the phone too loudly after hours. In fact, the conversation I referred to here had to be conducted via text because she was scared that her employers would find her talking on the phone.

Elsa's faith in God's love is unshakable. She believes that God would not let her linger in suffering for too long, and that every suffering is actually a path that leads to a better plan that God has in store for her:

> I was once in despair. But then, I felt that that [her despair] was a way for God to show me the best path. So, from problems, which of course made me in despair, eventually I can feel that that was the way that God has prepared for me; a way that brought me to another [plan]. So, after a while, I just realized that God already set the course for me.[2]

To understand the intertwining relationship between the exploitative global labor market, lived experiences in diaspora, and the ways the Indonesian FMWs think of, elaborate on, and practice their faith is the goal of border theologies as a conceptual framework.

A simplistic look at Elsa's reflection on the challenges that she faced would draw us into a conclusion that evades the complexity of Elsa's—and other FMWs'—perspectives on suffering. However, the framework of border theologies shows us that in the context

---

[1] Interview with Elsa, WhatsApp text messages, May 17, 2020.
[2] Interview with Elsa, WhatsApp call, May 24, 2020.

of the sustained violence and exploitation that Elsa lives in, the relationship between violence that is inflicted and the kind of spiritual responses it elicits is not clear cut. More than just a pragmatic take that sees suffering as a pedagogical moment, Elsa's reflection shows us the ways that Elsa navigates her faith, pain, and the imperative of survival in that specific moment.

This concrete mode of faith reflection is one of the primary ways in which border theologies differ from traditional Christian and Islamic theologies. Crafted in the lives of the diaspora, border theologies ebb and flow following the contours of the FMWs' lives and do not—as with Christian and Islamic systematic theologies—start from the permanence of doctrines. In border theologies, perspectives on who God is and the divine's relationship to humanity as a part of creation are inseparable from the FMWs' struggles against oppressions. Conceptions of God as the ultimate friend of the FMWs or as the protector against their abusive employers and as the avenger of their pain abound in border theologies. What's more is that forms of resistance and agentic expressions in the context of oppression are varied and not always in line with a liberal understanding of agency that emphasizes individual active resistance against oppressions. What can be interpreted as mere submission to the oppressors can actually be a means of survival for the FMWs.

Indeed, we would be amiss if we equated Elsa's full trust in God's providence as a non-agentic submission by which she lets herself drift in the ocean of destinies. Elsa couples her reliance on God's plans with a confidence in the efficacy of her actions to change her predicaments. When I asked her about what the word "work" meant to her, she responded:

> There are verses in the Bible that talk about work and prayers. So, we are not supposed to only pray, or just to sit around praying and waiting, but we also need to work. Before God shows us His miracles or guidance, His blessings,[3] She tells us to pray and to work. So, we pray, but we also need to work. Prayers alone does not make things happen. So, we also need to work.[4]

I have to admit that my first instinct upon hearing Elsa's reliance on God's providence was heavily influenced by my presumptions about faith that, in turn, have been affected by a liberal, patronizing understanding of agency. I assumed that Elsa's full trust in God was mutually exclusive with a willingness to change one's predicaments. What I wanted to see from Elsa was an explicit, effective refusal of her oppressions that might involve anger, and not pleasure, toward the paths that God had given to her. In addition, planted deep in my presumptions, I think was a liberal expectation in which I placed the burden of fixing the systemic oppressions on victimized individuals, rather than on the oppressive system and the few people who sustained it with their powers.

Elsa made it clear that the Lord is her shepherd who guides her to the best of plans. Following a shepherd is not like following an emperor, for following a shepherd leads

---

[3] I took the liberty to translate the genderless Indonesian pronoun of "Dia" to "She/Her/Hers" in this statement.
[4] Interview with Elsa, WhatsApp call, April 26, 2020.

one to safety, nutrition, and comfort. Following a shepherd also implies that one's submission to the shepherd does not mean that one has given up one's agency. The flock of a shepherd can go astray, and the shepherd will still lead them back home. Furthermore, instead of showing His flock the right way, Elsa's Lord shows her "the best path." The word "best," instead of "right," insinuates a spectrum of choices that leaves a space for human will to affect the ways of their lives.

In Elsa's explanation of her faith and the place of a human's effort within it, there is a creative tension between personal submission to God and Elsa's determination to change her predicaments, no matter how difficult it may be. In this context, Elsa's elaboration on the dynamics between "work," "prayer," and "submission" delivers a clear "no" to the question of whether Indonesian FMWs' theological insights require the presence of suffering in their lives. Suffering might serve as a setting for the Indonesian FMWs' theologies, but it does not function as its horizon.

Elsa's ability to stay steadfast in the face of systemic oppressions while holding on to a faithful hope for God's help is a strong example of the non-redemptive quality of suffering in a Christian context. Elsa embodied well what Elizabeth Johnson once argued about non-redemptive suffering:

> The depth of suffering Jesus experienced on the cross, the wretched suffering as such, is not in itself salvific.... Rather than being an act willed by a loving God, it is a strikingly clear index of sin in the world, a wrongful act committed by human beings. What may be considered salvific in such a situation is not the suffering endured but only the love poured out. The saving kernel in the midst of such negativity is not the pain and death as such but the mutually faithful love of Jesus and his God, not immediately evident.[5]

Elsa believes that there is a significant meaning in the oppressions that she suffered. But this does not mean that she believes that her suffering is justified. Her perspective on the obstacles that she faces are that she sees "a way" for God to bring her to the best plan must be understood in light of her viewpoint on "work" and "prayer." In this context, the suffering could only be a way to something better when Elsa does not succumb to it. It is a two-pronged approach to suffering in which one's effort to end one's suffering does not discount one's hope for God's mercy, and vice versa.

More importantly, Elsa's understanding of suffering represents a theodicy that is specific to the setting in which Indonesian FMWs live. Many of the Indonesian FMWs that I talked with believe that everything good in their lives comes from God, and evil and sufferings in their lives come from human's deeds. While they do not use terms such as "systemic oppression," the Indonesian FMWs have a strong and clear perception of the structural and historical characters of their sufferings. In addition, they show a deep understanding of the historical involvement of the divine in which God actively and creatively takes the side of the oppressed.

---

[5] Elizabeth A. Johnson quoted in: Nancy Pineda-Madrid, *Suffering and Salvation in Ciudad Juarez* (Minneapolis: Fortress Press, 2011), 125.

The divine involvement in human lives as seen from the perspectives of the Christian FMWs is not limited to the historical presence of Jesus Christ in the past but is extended to an understanding of the divine presence in the details of their everyday lives. For them, God is the One who accompanies them through the thick and thin of their lives, and the One who protects them against danger that comes in their way. In this perspective, the notion of miracle is significant in explaining the ways God intervenes in the everyday lives of the FMWs.

A story from another Catholic FMW named Elena on a miracle that happened to her illustrates this point very well:

This is the story. My previous employer was very cruel to me. Every work [in the house] must be done on that very same day. [They did not care] even though I had to work all night until morning. If I could not finish the job, they would be very mad at me. They are Chinese, [of] Buddhist [religion]. They pray differently [than she does]. They prohibit me to pray and to worship. But I always did my prayer when they went to sleep.

[Unbeknownst to her] they sometimes peeped at what I did, including when I prayed. After a while, they asked me, "why did you pray?" I responded, "I could not sleep if I did not pray." And then they said, "your God cannot go together with my God." I stayed quiet. I did not want to talk back to them. I only recited a prayer in my heart.

One day, they were mad at me. And then they ordered me to apologize in front of their god. They ordered me to kneel, and they gave me three broomsticks, and they asked me to bow and kneel in front of the statue of their god. I did what they asked because I did not want to oppose them, because it was not my house, and [because] I lived with them. I prayed in my heart, "dear Lord Jesus, please forgive me, I did this [bowing to the statue] because I was forced to do so."

A few days later, my employer was out of the house. When she was about to go back into the house, there were two people on motorcycle trying to attack her, but they failed because she got into the house first. The day after, the same thing happened, but the attackers failed again. However, in the third day, my employer could not avoid [her fate?]. She [was about to] went out with a neighbor, but before she arrived at the neighbor's house, there was a dumpster there [by the neighbor's house], the two people on motorcycle who tried to attack her came around, and this time they were successful. With their motorcycle, they stopped by her side and grabbed her necklace with a knife to her neck.

It was around 6 pm, we [other household members] were at home, but nobody saw the incident. Then she went back home, it looked like life had been drained out of her, and then she said, "I was robbed." I thought, "God, this must be how you paid her back [the employer's oppression]." "This is what you give to her because of what she did to me."

After that robbery, my employers got more and more problem. The house was never peaceful. I did nothing, I said nothing. I only prayed. Sometimes she would fight with her husband. She said to me, "I've married my husband for decades, and we never fought before. But we fought a lot these days. What happened? What did you do?" She then kneeled in front of me, and cried. That was her turn to kneel, apparently. She cried at my feet. I told her that I did not do anything. After that [incident], I asked for forgiveness to God, and to give her peace. After that [incident], they treated me better. I told them that I would like to quit and go back home [to Indonesia] after my contract is finished.[6]

Elena strongly believed that God punished her employers for the oppressions that they inflicted upon her. Though all forms of oppression that they practiced were unjust, Elena highlighted the religious oppression that she suffered as a backdrop for the problems that plagued her employers: they forced her to worship another God. This theological oppression (and forced betrayal) not only hurt Elena but also affected her relationship with God. In Elena's perspective, the relationship between injustices and God's preference for the oppressed was clearest in this specific experience: God was directly "victimized" in the oppression along with Elena as the oppressed, and thus God's punishment was swift.

More importantly, Elena's experience is also a vindication of a theodicy that locates evil within a historical, political, and economic context. As Emilie M. Townes contends, it is an evil that is culturally produced and supported by truncated narratives that are in turn parts of the "fantastic hegemonic imagination."[7] In Elena's and the other Indonesian FMWs' lives, the fantastic hegemonic imagination at work is "modernity" that, with its "order building" and "economic progress," produces wasted humans who were cast out of modernized and modernizing contexts.[8] In this fantastic hegemonic imagination, Elena and the other Indonesian FMWs are trying their best to stay within the modernized Singaporean context by taking over the domestic and care responsibilities of the main modern subjects, the upper-middle class Singaporeans. They do this, in turn, to give their Indonesian families a fighting chance to carve out a space within a modernizing Indonesia.

In Elena's life, evil takes form through her oppressive employers, and a whole system of global labor migration that does not leave her with any other options except to leave her homeland to clean up after someone else's family in Singapore. In other words, the systemic evil that plagues Elena's life is one that comes as a result of certain combinations of political and economic abuses of power, and a racial capitalism that places Elena's life at the bottom of the hierarchy of human "dignity." In her work on Early Modern women's theodicy, Jill Graper Hernandez uses the term, borrowed from Claudia Card, "atrocious harms" to refer to any systemic violence such as that from which Elena suffers. Following Card, they differentiate "atrocious harms" from

---

[6] Interview with Elena, WhatsApp call, April 11, 2020.
[7] Emilie M. Townes, *Womanist Ethics and the Cultural Production of Evil* (New York: Palgrave Macmillan, 2006), 162.
[8] Zygmunt Bauman writes about "order building" and "economic progress" in these ways: "order building (each order casts some parts of the extant population as 'out of place,' 'unfit' or 'undesirable') and of economic progress (that cannot proceed without degrading and devaluing the previously effective modes of 'making a living' and therefore cannot but deprive their practitioners of their livelihood)." Zygmunt Bauman, *Wasted Lives: Modernity and Its Outcasts* (Cambridge: Polity, 2004), 5.

"particular harms" by "the basis of whether the systemic denigration and intolerable harm stems from a human institution that is perpetuated and maintained culpably."[9]

In this chapter, evil is understood as the political, economic, and social systems that produce foreseeable atrocious harms to the lives of the Indonesian FMWs. These systems are located in Indonesia (economic inequality, structural poverty, and gender-based violence that push many Indonesian women to take the risk of becoming FMWs, and the absence of protection over their rights in the diaspora, which is the Indonesian government's responsibility), in Singapore (the absence of effective labor law that can protect the rights of the FMWs, racial, gendered, and class-based prejudices that place the FMWs at the lowest rung of social hierarchy in Singaporean society, and serve as justifications for their abuse and exploitations), and globally in the forms of feminization of poverty, and the gendered view on domestic work that classifies their profession as unskilled work.

Evil in this context has its roots in transnational and global settings with local and personal implications. Hence, Hernandez's notion of atrocious harms that are differentiated from interpersonal harms that happen in one's everyday life (particular harms) is useful in understanding the nature of evil in the lives of the FMWs. The atrocious harms that the FMWs suffer (physical and sexual abuses, exploitations, tortures, humiliation, lifelong trauma, and dehumanization) are the results of the evil that comes from the oppressive systems located at the national, transnational, and global levels. This is to say that though the abuse and exploitation that the FMWs suffer from takes place in their everyday lives, the structures that allow for and sustain those abuse and exploitation are located at the systemic level. Struggling against this evil does not only require a reckoning from the perpetrators of the harms but also a total elimination of the oppressive systems that allow the harms to happen in the first place.

Since atrocious harms are historical and political, and associated with human culpability, sufferings that come from these harms are non-redemptive: that is, there is no good that could come out of atrocious harms. Atrocious harms are not Divinely made, and thus can be deconstructed. Suffering and trauma that is caused by these harms are foreseeable and thus can and should be avoided. In other words, since the elements of intolerable pain and culpable wrongdoing can be found within these atrocious harms, the suffering that comes out of it is not salvific, the harms must be stopped, and the evildoers must take responsibility over the harms that they did. In talking about the femicide of women and girls in Ciudad Juarez, Nancy Pineda-Madrid writes, "We realize salvation not in suffering itself but rather in the context of our response to suffering."[10] Thus, in the context of atrocious harms such as one that engulfs Elena's life, the important theodical conversation is not actually located on how we reconcile the existence of an all-omnipotent, omnibenevolent God with the presence of evil, but rather on how we create goods on earth so that we can "mediate God's self-giving more intensively."[11]

---

[9] Jill Graper Hernandez, *Early Modern Women and the Problem of Evil: Atrocity and Theodicy* (London: Routledge, 2016), Kindle ed., loc. 246.
[10] Pineda-Madrid, *Suffering and Salvation*, 126
[11] Ibid., 128.

Emilie M. Townes gives us a clue on how to create goods in the face of evil. She writes that, first, a conversion (in the sense that Pineda-Madrid uses it)[12] from a vision of "winning and losing" to a vision of "justice and peace" is needed in the world.[13] Furthermore, she contends that the work of dismantling the cultural production of evil "must be a group project."[14] In the context of the lives of the FMWs, the first element means that the deconstruction of oppressive systems that comprise evil in their lives must not be founded on an assumption that the marginalized would just replace the powerful and sit on the top of the hierarchy, hence sustaining it. Rather, deconstruction means to completely eliminate the hierarchical structures that serve as contexts for abusive and exploitative power. This deconstruction is not about the FMWs taking over the place of the powerful, but rather is about constructing another way of life in which FMWs' professions and rights are respected, appreciated, and protected.

Meanwhile, the second element suggests that the responsibility for deconstructing the oppressive structures, and constructing a compassionate and just way of life, does not only fall on the shoulders of the FMWs, but on all of ours. Indeed, within their marginalized position, there is not much that the FMWs can do to deconstruct the global and transnational oppressive systems that exploit their labors. Global allyship of scholars, activists, and policymakers is needed to eliminate the FMWs' suffering and achieve justice.

That being said, there are two important elements that are involved in this creation of good on earth, namely: the makers, and the kinds of good that they make. Nancy Pineda-Madrid gave a definitive answer to the question of who the makers of the good are on earth, which is the community. As Pineda-Madrid defines it, "community" is "a body of people [that becomes a community] as a result of particular processes of interpretation. Interpretation is the way community is formed and sustained."[15] Indonesian FMWs as a community share points of interpretation that are rooted in the historical setting of domestic work in Singapore, and extend their hopes toward achieving better working conditions in the future.

One thing that I noticed during my fieldwork in Singapore is that the safety and well-being of many Indonesian FMWs are more dependent on the networks of friendship among them than on the institutionalized networks that are provided by governments and law enforcement bodies. When an FMW is being abused by her employer or agent, her first recourse is usually to contact another FMW who is being regarded as a senior in her immediate friendship circles. This senior FMW would then give her advice on how to face her employer or agent, and/or on where to go to escape from the abuse that she experienced. Oftentimes, institutions such as the Indonesian embassy and organizations that provide shelters for Indonesian FMWs get their information about cases of abuse and exploitation of the FMWs from these senior members of the community. Such networks of care among the Indonesian FMWs come from a long tradition of communal cooperation between *amahs* in the 1930s.

---

[12] "By 'conversion' I mean letting go of an old way of seeing the self, God, the world, and others and being open to a radically new way of seeing." Ibid., 130.
[13] Townes, *Womanist Ethics*, 159.
[14] Ibid., 160.
[15] Pineda-Madrid, *Suffering and Salvation*, 133.

Within history, the current presence of Indonesian FMWs in Singapore was preceded by the existence of *amahs* (Malay lit: maidservants, nannies) in the 1930s. These *amahs* are mostly comprised of female immigrants from Southeastern China provinces (Guangdong, Guangxi, Fujian) who, after the Kuomintang-Communist conflict, chose (or were forced by the unstable situation in China) to migrate to Malaya, especially to the British posts of Penang and Singapore.[16] In this time period, the *amah* profession—and other domestic helpers such as cooks and gardeners—had been employed to be responsible for the whole aspects of social reproduction that took place in the domestic spheres of the colonial society in British Singapore and Malaysia. While the predominantly male colonial officers dealt with the day-to-day operations of the colonial society in the public space, their capacities to work were made possible by a retinue of servants, including the *amahs* who cared for their families and the upkeep of their houses under the supervision of their wives, the European madams.[17] Considering the position of FMWs as the ones who care for the upkeep of the houses, and the rearing of the Singaporean families that in turn allow for modern Singaporean women to build their careers outside of the house, we can say that not much has changed since the colonial era in regard to the FMWs' position and function in Singaporean society.

There are two continuities from that historical context that we still can find in contemporary lives of the Indonesian FMWs in Singapore. The first of these is control over the domestic workers' sexualities that is rooted in the colonial Contagious Disease Ordinance in Singapore, which aimed to curb the infections of venereal diseases among the British troops stationed at the Straits Settlement. The Ordinance, and other forms of social control, was specifically enforced on prostitutes (who were also comprised of FMWs from China) and brothels, as well as communities of *mui tsai* (Cantonese lit: little younger sister)[18] who were exploited as domestic servants in affluent families.[19] The association between FMWs and venereal diseases in a historical context in which a notion of racist and gendered Victorian hygiene was propagated is very much still at play in contemporary Singapore, where Indonesian FMWs are labeled as being morally deficient and thus suffer from sexual and bodily surveillance by their employers, agencies, and Singaporean society in general.

---

[16] Ooi Keat Gin, "Domestic Servants Par Excellence: The Black and White *Amahs* of Malaya and Singapore, with Special Reference to Penang," *Journal of the Malaysian Branch of the Royal Asiatic Society* 65, no. 2 (1992): 72.

[17] Janice Loo, "Mem, Don't Mess with the Cook!" *Biblioasia*, July–September 2016, 13.

[18] "The term Mui Tsai is a Cantonese colloquial expression—Mui by itself means 'younger sister' while *tsai* (literally 'son') is a diminutive. The whole means 'little younger sister.' . . . The Hokkiens use the term *char boh kan* . . . in the Chinese written language the term used is *pei nui* . . . [it] refer[s] to a girl who has been transferred from her own family, either directly or through a third party, to another family with the intention that she shall be used as a domestic servant, not in receipt of regular wages and not at liberty to leave employer's family at her own free will or at the will of her parents. A document would be drawn up reciting the details of the transfer and the consideration passing." Purcell, the Chinese in Malaya, quoted in Gin, "Domestic Servants," 74.

[19] Maria Platt, "Foreign Domestic Workers in Singapore: Historical and Contemporary Reflections on the Colonial Politics of Intimacy," in *Colonization and Domestic Service: Historical and Contemporary Perspectives*, ed. Victoria K. Haskins, Claire Lowrie (New York: Routledge, 2015), 133.

As recently as July 2020, a Singaporean website for maid agencies and browsing for maids, housemaid.com.sg, wrote the following in their article on "Way to Deal with New Maid in Singapore":

> Allowing the maid to get in touch with her family members and friends periodically must be done so that she doesn't feel alone. Although calls should be allowed meticulously see that it is in moderation and does not hamper her during carrying out her tasks and chores or tending to babies and the elderly. Allow the maid to take a day off but do all the same she must be taught to carry them out in a responsible manner.[20]

This continuity ties the current Indonesian FMWs with their predecessors in terms of the systemic oppressions, and the sociopolitical places that they occupy in Singaporean society. While the current Indonesian FMWs certainly have more legal protections for their rights, their position within the Singaporean imagination has not changed much from the 1930s: care providers and cleaners whose morality must always be questioned and surveilled lest it pollute Singapore's national morality.

The second point of interpretation in the formation and sustenance of Indonesian FMW communities is also rooted in history but it extends toward a hope for the future. In the 1930s, when the first major streams of FMWs from China arrived in the Straits Settlement, those who wanted to work as an *amah* preferred to take job contracts that were recommended by their peers,[21] rather than the ones brokered by a *kongsi pang*.[22] More importantly, the sisterhood built among the *amahs* also materialized in the ways that allowed them to take care of each other, from finding a reliable employer to establishing *kongsi pang* together where they nursed anyone of them who was sick back to health, the *amahs* carved diasporic spaces of comfort amid the hard work that they did.

Such a network of solidarity and trust is kept alive by the current Indonesian FMWs, who, regardless of their presence or the absence of knowledge of the history of the *amahs*, help each other in finding safety, comfort, and dignity amid the dehumanization and systemic violence that they suffer. Both points of interpretation (oppressive moral–sexual surveillance and abuse, and solidarity network) characterize the Indonesian FMW communities.[23] Their similar grievances on the moral–sexual

---

[20] Eazymaid, "Way To Deal with New Maid in Singapore," July 3, 2020, https://www.housemaid.com.sg/eazy-maid-blogs/blogdetail/way-to-deal-with-new-maid-in-singapore.

[21] Gin, "Domestic Servants," 78.

[22] "lodging house. The kongsi pang was often managed by a female coolie head who would provide new arrivals with food and lodging for a fee." Gin, "Domestic Servants," 74.

[23] "First, a community exists when its members claim at least some identical events as significant for them. Even though all members agree that particular events are central, each member will interpret the meaning of the events differently. Second, a community comes into being when individual members extend their lives in time well into the past and the future so that each claims events as their own that exist beyond the span of their lifetimes. These ideally extended selves are not simply a collection of past and future events or experience but are an interpretation of those events and experiences. Third, a community comes into being through a time process whereby it bears a consciousness of its past, present, and future. It interprets its past toward the future in the present." Pineda-Madrid, *Suffering and Salvation*, 134.

surveillance and abuses tie them together with a hyperawareness of their social, moral, and political positions in the Singaporean imagination, while also providing a basis for their solidarity network that, in turn, strengthens their distinct shared identity within Singaporean society.

This community, through their solidarity and care for each other, creates what Jill Graper Hernandez calls "transmuted goods." While the presence of transmuted goods is not by any means dependent on the presence of systemic evil (i.e., that to have transmuted goods, the Indonesian FMWs must suffer first), its impacts are in direct opposition with the impacts of systemic evil. Hernandez defines "transmutation" as something that "alters the individual who has experienced a real harm, and brings about consequences other than what the atrocities should have generated (those that are essentially debilitating and degrading)."[24] Transmuted goods are what communities create in the face of systemic evil: it is the coming together of a community to nurture life and prevent death.

Early Sunday morning in Singapore is always a joyful occasion for many FMWs and those who are sympathetic toward their lives and struggles. Sunday is a day off for the FMWs whose employers have the decency to give it to them, as per the government's suggestion. These "lucky" FMWs would literally seize the day by going out of their employers' houses at 6:00 a.m. to meet up with their friends and participate in many FMW-led activities in churches, mosques, and other public spaces. As it is a precious occasion, many FMWs would wear their very best clothing during this time. Areas that are popular for the gatherings of the FMWs like Ang Mo Kio, Paya Lebar, and Toa Payoh would be covered with the colorful dresses and glimmering hijabs that the FMWs wear on that day.

The communal activities (religious activities, picnics, meetups with friends, classes for craft and hobbies, etc.) that the FMWs organized in churches, mosques, and public parks on Saturday mornings are spaces of love, compassion, and resistance that have been denied from them in their workplace and during their workdays. In these spaces, the FMWs regain their expressions of religiosity (communal prayer and worship, reading and studies of their scriptures, wearing hijab, accessories with crucifix and other religious attire, etc.) that are commonly prohibited from being worn or practiced in their employers' homes. They also nurture their community and friendships by sharing food together and telling each other of their experiences with their respective employers.

In general, the Sunday morning gathering of the FMWs in Singapore can be understood as a transmuted good that the FMWs create for their own lives. If only for one day in the week, the communal love and care that is expressed in these gatherings alter the traumas that are caused by the abuse and exploitation that the FMWs suffer in their workspace. However, the Sunday morning gatherings also serve as more than just a space for temporary respites. In addition to the spaces of caring and love, the gatherings act as a reminder for the FMWs of life beyond the abusive settings in which they live and work. In these gatherings, the FMWs are able to actualize and see themselves as an individual whole whose identity is not defined by their profession,

---

[24] Jill Graper Hernandez, *Early Modern Women Early Modern Women*, loc. 537.

and the abuse that they suffer. In this sense, these gatherings are subversive, transmuted goods that do not only alter the harms produced by the oppressive systems, but also provide context for resistance in which the FMWs defy the capitalist logic that tries to mold them into a perfect commodity.

Nevertheless, since systemic evil does not equally impact all of us, and since, as Townes astutely observes, "we are in a world that we have helped make" and so we cannot let the Indonesian FMWs be left all alone in creating transmuted goods for the survival and flourishing of the Indonesian FMWs in Singapore. Some nongovernmental organizations, such as the Humanitarian Organization for Migration Economics, have been providing resources and protection for FMWs in Singapore. Yet, injustices toward FMWs happen on a global scale and are supported by racial capitalism. In this context, it is our responsibility to create networks of care, protection, and advocacy for migrant domestic workers from all around the world.

As the scope of this project includes Christian and Muslim FMWs' views on the problem of evil, and on Christian and Islamic theologies in general, it is important for us to understand the specifics of the traditional Islamic perspective on the question of evil, and the ways Muslim FMWs in Singapore navigate their own predicaments through their reflections on evil and suffering. While Elsa and Elena bring us to understand the relationship between faith and suffering through their assignations of the divine as the ultimate friend who accompanies them in their everyday struggles, Muslim FMWs like Fatimah, who we will encounter below, reflect on the question of faith and suffering by interrogating their own culpability in creating their own suffering through a cosmic calculation of good deeds and bad deeds. Yet, as with the complexities of paradigms on evil provided by the Christian FMWs, it will be premature to associate the Muslim FMWs' perspectives on evil with a fatalistic point of view in which evil and suffering are understood as punishments for bad deeds in the past and not as a product of oppressive systems that can and must be deconstructed. What we will see instead is an elaboration of the relationship between evil, suffering, and faith that balances out the imperative of personal submission to God through the lens of divine predetermination with an assertion of personal efforts in the realization of a better future.

It is not as easy to gain a politically applicable theodicy from the Ash'arite paradigm in Islam.[25] As far as we understand "theodicy" as "the attempt to reconcile the presence of evil in the world with the existence of a God who is unlimited in both power and goodness,"[26] the complexity of placing any moral responsibility to a human agent for the production of evil is high, but not impossible. The term "kasb" (acquisition) represents the Ash'arite's main paradigm of theodicy where it locates "a narrow margin in which is inscribed the relationship between the act created by God and human responsibility."[27] This paradigm in turn is characterized by two ideas of *ḳudra ḥāditha* (the "contingent

---

[25] The Ash'arite perspective is chosen due to the fact that the majority of Indonesian Muslims are Sunnis.
[26] Sherman A. Jackson, *Islam and the Problem of Black Suffering* (Oxford and New York: Oxford University Press, 2014), 4.
[27] Louis Gardet, "Kasb," in the *Encyclopedia of Islam*, ed. C. E. Bosworth et al., 2nd ed. (Leiden: A. J. Brill, 1997), 692.

power" created by God) and *istiṭāʿa* (the ability to act). It is the interplay of these two elements that produce a specific position in which a moral responsibility can be attributed to the human agent.

Al-Ashʿarī's opinion on the location of evil was well elaborated by Binyamin Abrahamov when he wrote:

> Al-Ashʿarī is of the opinion that God not only creates man's action, but is also its only real agent. That God is the creator and the real agent of man's action lays al-Ashʿarī open to the charge that God is an evil-doer (*jāʾir*) when he creates evil in man. In order to meet this charge al-Ashʿarī states that God creates in man his action, be it an act of appropriation or an involuntary act. Concerning an involuntary movement, the meaning of "man moves" is that he is one in whom movement inheres (*maʿnā al-mutaḥarrik anna al-ḥaraka ḥallathu*), and this cannot be possible with regard to God, i.e., God cannot be spoken of as moving. The same holds true with reference to *kasb*; God creates it in man and is its real agent, but the act is performed in man, not in God. Man is called an appropriator (*muktasib*), because the act takes place through power created for him by God. Thus al-Ashʿarī deduces from analogy that just as God does not move when He creates movement, so He is not an evil-doer when He creates evil.[28]

The story of Fatimah, an Indonesian Muslima FMW in her early thirties, is pertinent here. Fatimah started working as a caregiver in Singapore since 2006. As with many other Indonesian FMWs, Fatimah left Indonesia at that time to support her then-husband and earn money for their child's education. Yet, a few years after she left for Singapore, her then-husband cheated on her and abandoned his responsibility to take care of their child. Here is how Fatimah explained her predicament:

> From the beginning, I entered Singapore since 2006. I was married and have a child, and I wanted to earn some money for our future. So, I decided to go to Singapore. At that time, I had been working in Singapore for two years . . . and it was probably also because we [her and her then-husband] were not "soulmates" [a rough translation of the word "*jodoh*" in Bahasa Indonesia]. My [ex] husband abandoned his responsibility to take care of our child, and he had a girlfriend. I decided to divorce him, but he refused to divorce me. So, I asked the court to divorce me from him.
>
> After that, I decided to go back to Singapore [after the divorce process], for my child. At that time, my child was only three and half years old. So, I left my child and worked in Singapore again until 2010, and then I went back home [to Indonesia]. I started a small business at home from my savings. I opened a construction material store. I took a loan to buy a truck. But it might also be that I was not lucky, for a few months after [she started the business], two of my employees got into [work related] accidents. One of them needed a kneecap surgery, another one

---

[28] Binyamin Abrahamov, "A Re-Examination of al-Ashʿarī's Theory of 'Kasb' according to 'Kitāb Al-Luma,'" *The Journal of the Royal Asiatic Society of Great Britain and Ireland*, no. 2 (1989): 217.

needed a brain surgery. I was very unlucky, and after that I took care of all their treatments, for about five months I had to bring them for regular check-ups at the hospital, I gave them money, everything. I sold my car, I sold everything I had, and I still had some loan to BRI (Bank Rakyat Indonesia/The People Bank of Indonesia. A bank that is known to give loans to small business and individuals in rural Indonesia). In the past, my investment was also a loan from BRI. After that, I need a new "energy" to get back on my feet. So, I went back to Singapore in 2012. And I stayed [in Singapore] up to today.[29]

If we were to take the basic tenet of Ash'arite theodicy and apply it to analyze Fatimah's story, we would come with an almost too easy answer that Fatimah sees what happened to her through the lens of an Ash'arite theodicy where the betrayal of her husband and the failure of her business were attributed to some concepts of divine determination (i.e., "soulmate," "lucky/unlucky") rather than to any human agents. However, such a reading cannot consider the creative acts that Fatimah has taken up (i.e., demanded the court to grant her divorce, and to go back to Singapore to earn resources to rebuild her life) in order to face those predicaments. In other words, though Fatimah might not completely attribute her family crisis to the acts of betrayal and recklessness of her ex-husband (by attributing it to the tenet that they were not created as soulmates), her personal yearning for justice for herself and her child led her to file for divorce from her ex-husband.

In the same vein, she associated her business failures with the absence of luck on her part, rather than on the absence of structural support that could have assisted her to succeed as a single-mother and first-time entrepreneur. Yet, she also did not hesitate to start everything all over again by going back to the dehumanizing work in Singapore in order to establish a new foundation for her and her child's life. Fatimah's non-attribution of evil acts to the human and systemic agencies that were accompanied by her creative responses to divine determination brings some nuances to the basic tenet of the Ash'arite theodicy.

In analyzing Fatimah's theodical statement, I rely on Mairaj Syed's observation of theories of human agency developed by Abū' l-Ma'ālī al-Juwaynī (d. 478/1085) and by Abū Ḥāmid al-Ghazālī (d. 505/1111). Syed contends that,

> In Ash'arī's theology, then, the volitional act accepts two ontological descriptions: it is a creation and an acquisition. It is, on the one hand, created by God, as it is impossible to apply the term creator nonmetaphorically to anything besides God. The human being who performs the act is not its creator, she is its acquirer. . . . The volitional act itself, though, is capable of receiving two descriptions. It is God's creation and the human agent's acquisition.[30]

---

[29] Interview with Fatimah, WhatsApp call, April 26, 2020.
[30] Mairaj Syed, *Coercion and Responsibility in Islam: A Study in Ethics and Law* (New York: Oxford University Press, 2017), 73.

This quotation is important because it shows a nuance in the theory of human action from the Ash'arīte's perspective. Contrary to many assumptions that equate the Islamic paradigm of human action with a totalitarian perspective on divine predetermination, Syed argues that human actions can be described as both the result of God's creation and of human's acquisition. This perspective has two implications on the discussion of faith and suffering in the lives of the FMWs. First, it actually opens up a space for us to talk about suffering not as unchangeable destiny but rather as an implication of an act that is acquired/performed by a human agent. Though the specific action that results in suffering is, theologically speaking, created by God, the iteration of that act in the world, and hence its implication, can be attributed to a human agent who must account for their actions in the world in front of God on the Day of Judgment.

Second, on the flip side of the analysis on suffering, this perspective also allows us to talk about resistance against oppression as agentic action that is taken by the FMWs: as suffering, and the oppression that caused it, can be attributed to human action, the resistance against oppression can also be attributed to human agency that chose to acquire actions that eliminate oppression. Based on this perspective, attributing the creation of acts (good and bad) to God does not cancel out the moral responsibility from the human agent since they acquired the acts. As long as there are two components of volitional acts, namely the "contingent power" that is created by God within humans at the moment of the act, and "the ability to act" that consists of required physical power and cognitive abilities, then the individual is subjected to God's commands, and the moral responsibility that comes with following and/or denying God's commands.[31]

In the context of Fatimah's life, while there is no apparent sanction suffered by her ex-husband for his betrayal and the abandonment of his familial duty, such a theodical perspective places the moral responsibility for those evil acts upon Fatimah's ex-husband. Considering that any sexual relationship outside of marriage ties is prohibited and that taking care of one's family is also an obligation, and considering that Fatimah's ex-husband has the capacity to not do both acts, then those evil acts were attributable to him.

On the other hand, in Fatimah's responses to the calamities that came one after another in her life, there is an ingenious tension between submitting oneself to divine determination and one's yearning for justice. Fatimah could have stayed in an abusive relationship with her ex-husband and turned a blind eye to his infidelity. However, she chose—as far as "choosing" is an acquired act that is created by God through the mediation of a contingent power in Fatimah's self—to end the abusive relationship for the sake of herself and her child.

Thus, while it is admittedly difficult to directly apply the Ash'arite theodicy to the problem of structural oppressions, the creative responses that some Indonesian FMWs have toward sufferings in their lives can offer insights into the dynamic between one's submission to divine determination and one's struggle for justice, which in turn is one of the loftiest expressions of one's faith. Most importantly, as with the feminist Christian theodical stance on suffering, Fatimah's commitment toward getting a better life for herself and her child is a testament in itself to the fact that suffering has to be

---

[31] Ibid., 74.

ended. In fact, all of the struggles of the Indonesian FMWs are attestation for two things: first, that evil is a product of individual, communal, and global actions and thus cannot be abstracted from its everyday manifestation; and second, that regardless of who the effective agents of good and bad acts are, systemic evil is something that must be eliminated.

Border theologies that are constructed from the lives of Christian and Muslim Indonesian FMWs in Singapore invite us to think of theodicies as individual and communal efforts to grapple with the existence of evil and suffering that cannot be separated from the politics of everyday lives. The lives of Elsa, Elena, and Fatimah show that the engagement with the problem of evil and suffering cannot be seen simply from a doctrinal point of view since believers, and especially those who are marginalized, continuously navigate the relationship between their faith and experiences of suffering on a daily basis. In addition, Elsa's, Elena's, and Fatimah's reflections tell us that struggles against evil can take many forms in which narratives of submission and/or belief in predestination cannot be equated with the absence of resistance. Thus, seen from the perspective of border theologies, both the creation and sustenance of evil, as well as resistance against it, can be attributed to human agency, albeit with different understandings of agentic effectivity in Christianity and Islam. In this context, oppressive systems that produce suffering in the lives of the FMWs ought to be deconstructed to achieve social justice as an expression of the divine's love and mercy.

9

Fieldnotes from the Gardens

Methods, Ethics, and Rants

Nicole Hoskins

In the middle of one of our interviews,[1] Cheryl received a phone call from a reporter asking her about environmental racism.[2] Far from being a rarity, that call, and the emails like it wanting to know what it was like to live in Altgeld Gardens, is commonplace for Cheryl. A historically Black housing project on the far south side of Chicago, Altgeld has long been plagued with land, water, and air pollution. Built in 1945 for Black veterans and war workers, the 190-acre community originally held about 1,500 housing units. Before Altgeld was a Black housing project, the city of Chicago had been using the land to dispose of the city's industrial waste. When the industrial sewage farm closed in 1907, there remained an estimated 700 million gallons of waste, most of which had been dumped into the nearby Calumet River, and the remaining sewage was leveled into the ground on which Altgeld currently sits. Even though they relocated the industrial sewage farm far away from residents, city waste management authorities proceeded to burn municipal trash along the housing community's perimeter.[3]

Cheryl has been bringing awareness to environmental injustice since her mother Hazel Johnson (1935–2011) founded People for Community Recovery (PCR), a nonprofit environmental justice organization located in the Altgeld Gardens. Johnson launched the organization in 1979 when she learned that 50 landfills and 382 industrial facilities, along with 250 leaking underground storage tanks, surround the housing community on all sides. In response, she famously coined Altgeld as the "the toxic doughnut," to illustrate how polluting industries circle the housing community on all sides. She then galvanized her community (most of whom were women) to fight against environmental injustice in Altgeld Gardens. Johnson was at the forefront of fighting for environmental justice even before the official movement began. And because of this,

---

[1] The interviewees are public leaders in the environmental justice movement in Chicago, IL, and nationwide. Their real names have not been changed in this chapter.
[2] Interview with Cheryl Johnson, January 27, 2020, People for Community Recovery, 13330 S. Corliss Ave, Chicago, IL 60827.
[3] Sylvia Hood Washington, *Packing Them in: An Archaeology of Environmental Racism in Chicago, 1865-1954* (New York: Lexington Books, 2005), 215–24.

Johnson is known by many as the mother of the environmental justice movement.[4] Now as director of PCR, Cheryl is not only responsible for carrying on her mother's legacy, but she is also responsible for leading the organization—this meant responding to the myriad phone calls and email inquiries about environmental racism in Altgeld Gardens.

Because Cheryl and a small group of women in Altgeld have been fighting against environmental racism in their housing community since 1979, they have become locally famous for it. Anytime something transpires in Chicago that involves environmental justice, reporters call Cheryl seeking a quotable sound bite or a full interview. She knows exactly what reporters will ask before they open their mouths: They want to know about the appalling nature of her environmental situation. They want to know how poor Black families are devastated by living in an area with land, water, and air pollution. They want her to say how hopeless it feels to live in a place like Altgeld Gardens. She's quite used to that line of questioning—about all the suffering and death that Altgeld residents have experienced.

Academics are no different. Sociologists have been visiting the Altgeld community since the late 1980s, and their reports have always followed the same pattern. They document the tragedies, the ruins, and the death toll. They focus on Black people's suffering or how white people consider them to be disposable[5]—what cultural geographer Katherine McKittrick calls the mathematics of Black life.[6] "Three out of five of the largest commercial hazardous waste landfills in the US were located in black communities," they reported. "Three out of five black people live in communities with uncontrolled toxic waste sites."[7] Whether it's three out of five or four out of five, the statistical iterations convey the same mortal calculus. Such sociological reports sum up Black life and transform it into numbers and figures that mirror the relentless, predictable "ditto" of the slave ships' ledgers. As poet NourbSe Philip explains, Africans were not given names; the crew lists one as a "Negro woman" and then "ditto" the rest of the page. Ratios and percentages work like dittos, simultaneously invisibilizing Black subjects, the sociohistorical systems that order their suffering, and the ways in which they resist them.

I have come to understand these methodical forms of anti-Blackness because the activists from Altgeld rant often about how academics who study marginalized communities always arrive at a death sentence. I ignored their rants at first, perhaps

---

[4] https://www.chipublib.org/blogs/post/hazel-m-johnson-mother-of-the-environmental-justice-movement/.

[5] See Carl A. Zimring, *Clean and White: A History of Environmental Racism in the United States* (New York: New York University Press, 2015); Robert D. Bullard, *Dumping in Dixie: Race, Class, and Environmental Quality*, 3rd ed. (Boulder: Westview Press, 2000); Charles W. Mills, "Black Trash," in *Faces of Environmental Racism: Confronting Issues of Global Justice*, ed. Laura Westra and Bill E. Lawson (Lanham: Rowman & Littlefield Publishers, 2001), 73–91; David N. Pellow, *Garbage Wars: The Struggle for Environmental Justice in Chicago*. Urban and Industrial Environments (Cambridge, MA: MIT Press, 2004).

[6] Katherine McKittrick, "Mathematics Black Life," *The Black Scholar: Journal of Black Studies and Research* 44, no. 2 (2014): 16.

[7] Commission for Racial Justice, *Toxic Wastes and Race in the United States: A National Report on the Racial and Socio-Economic Characteristics of communities with Hazardous Waste Sites* (New York: United Church of Christ, 1987), xiv.

because it was all too familiar. For I heard rants on the sidewalk when I passed men from the Nation of Islam selling bean pies and *The Final Call* in their black suits and bow ties under the viaduct on 75th in Stony Island. I heard it when I waited for my order at Harold's Chicken Shack on 95th or at Home of the Hoagy on 111th. I didn't give it a second thought because Black Chicagoans rant all the time. It's part of our DNA. But the longer I spend with environmental activists, the more I come to understand their rants as an important thought form for theology and ethics. Their rantings are an important form of ethical thought because they reveal that the persistence of Black life amid anti-Black environmental racism is a moral resource for ethically living on and with the earth.

For example, while talking to Veronica one afternoon, she explained that "If you look to academia to describe you, they'll say [that] you live in a food desert. I don't live in a food desert. That's not how I would describe how I grew up," Veronica ranted. "I didn't grow up starving and dying. We found ways to grow and preserve our food," she went on. "And when we didn't have enough of something, we exchanged goods with the people in our communities,"[8] she explained passionately. Despite the particularity of theological studies to affirm life over and against death-dealing state-sanctioned violence, we often focused our gaze upon the tomb, naturalized Blackness to it, and thus missed the ways in which Black communities had resisted and critiqued systematic injustices and composted a new way forward—an ethical way of living on and with the earth.

As an academic, how can I be sure not to replicate this violence in my ethnographic work? How can I be sure not to shape the narrative through a grammar of violence and disposability? Or become analytically tied to a pathway that begins with a dead end? One that naturalizes Blackness in a womb to tomb continuum? This concern to not reproduce such violence is at the heart of my work.

I went back to the recordings of interviews I had conducted for my dissertation research between 2018 and 2020 and listened deeply to the activists' rants. I listened for how they understood their situation and how they themselves described their way of living. What I found was that theology, ethics, thick description, thin description, critique, normative claims, and moral demands all blurred together in nonlinear impassioned narratives. To think of rants simply as a barrage of complaints misses the point. Their rants are a critical form of ethical thought.

This chapter explores how the Black environmental activists' rants, as forms of thought, can expand Christian social ethics and theological discourse, as well as traditional ethnographic processes. By blurring the boundaries between the descriptive and the normative, and poetically transgressing Western constructions of narrative linearity, those rants—those instances of impassioned speech—are important interventions in Christian social ethics and ethnographic practices and demand the way of Black life amid anti-Black environmental racism as an ethical resource for a more just future on this earth.

---

[8] Interview with Veronica Kyle, November 8, 2018, Faith in Place, 70 E Lake St #920, Chicago, IL 60601.

Descriptive and Normative Dimensions of Rants

Veronica's was the first of many rants I heard from environmental activists in Altgeld Gardens. After a few months of doing participant observations, I'd heard about how the broken promises of the Chicago housing authority mirrored broken promises America made to the Negro, the connection between the over-policing and the underfunding of Black communities. I'd heard about how they begged the city to clean up the neighboring Calumet River for five decades but were ignored—until white people saw the river as an opportunity to dock their boats on the cheap. I'd heard about the snaggletoothed blocks in their communities—blocks where every other house is torn down or boarded up, blocks where the pollution-filled gas clouds loomed over their homes, where white particles wafted from the street drains at night and covered their cars and lawns. I'd heard about how climate change is not about the weather but about an anti-Black atmosphere, and the importance of understanding the connections between the cancer alleys and toxic doughnuts of the world.

Hearing such rants, it was clear to me that ranting is one way that the activists express critical thought. For rants simultaneously describe and make normative judgments about what is, and what ought not to be: state-sanctioned environmental violence that orders their death; the racial capitalist systems that profit from their dispossession; the anti-Black climate change bubble in which they are living; the transformation of land and bodies into territories; and new forms of environmental racism, gentrification, and redlining. Their rants describe and make value judgments about "what is, but should not have to be": the ways in which they creatively survived and resisted that violence by locking arms with people in their community to prevent dump trucks from entering their neighborhood, by training community members how to remove asbestos, by teaching children why the majority of them are asthmatic, by showing adults how to use personal protective equipment in the event of another gas spill in their community, by lobbying congress for clean air and energy, by planting food gardens, by instituting community cleanup days, and by working with other environmentally marginalized communities to get their voices heard.

Their rants are full of incisive theological critiques. "Pollution don't go to heaven,"[9] Cheryl once lectured me. Indeed, Christianity has long gotten it wrong: having dominion over the earth as a form of "stewardship" is the sin that has been warming our earth and sending it burning into hell's fire. Cheryl is clear that her environmental situation at Altgeld Gardens is based on such warped theological notions that value above all else owning/stewarding land and bodies and exploiting them. She is clear that this toxicity does not evaporate into thin air, but that because of structural racism it becomes her task and that of other poor Black women to find ways to care for the earth and for each other that do not reproduce domination and disposability. And because she knows that such care for the earth cannot be based on the same behaviors and ethics that led to its destruction, her rants are often buoyed by moral claims about "what ought to be" in order to cultivate a more ethical relationship with the earth:

---

[9] Interview with Cheryl Johnson, January 27, 2020, People for Community Recovery, 13330 S. Corliss Ave, Chicago, IL 60827.

we ought to have Black cooperative societies, renewable energies, sustainable food gardens, reparations, an inclusive understanding of humans, a redefinition of care and stewardship, a rethinking of ownership, an ethic of staying, and an embracing of non-belonging.

Ethics pervade the activists' rants in the form of shoulds, oughts, should nots, and ought haves. But there are no clean lines between the descriptive and the normative in their rants. Living under environmental duress does not afford their thinking such clear divisions. Simplicity is the domain of researchers and scholars who write about them from afar. Solutions are easy, they say, when they're not. The activists understand that they must be masterful observers, astute environmental thinkers, artful interpreters of atmosphere and climate, insightful creators of space, and moral visionaries and theological ethicists all at once.

Much of what is expressed in the activists' rants is the pervasiveness of anti-Blackness. Particularly, the activists are articulating anti-Blackness as both co-relation and causation in their descriptive and normative claims. In environmental justice discourse, scholars distinguish between co-relation (impact) and causation (intention). Co-relational data reveal that Black communities are disproportionately burdened with toxic waste dumps while causational data show why it is that Black communities are targeted. But unfortunately, "the majority of empirical research on environmental justice (e.g. analyzing data on what racial communities live near toxic industrial facilities) is able to demonstrate *correlation* but not *causation*,"[10] note Richard Bohannon and Kevin O'Brien in *Grounding Religion: A Field Guide to the Study of Religion and Ecology*. In other words, much research has been done to show that Black communities are most impacted from living in close proximity to toxic industrial facilities, but scholars have been less inclined to observe why this is the case. Some scholars have even conjectured that intentionality or causation is not what matters, but what matters is that Black communities are impacted. Such analyses ignore evidence of anti-Blackness articulated by communities most impacted, and when anti-Blackness is acknowledged, it is often presented as happenstance and not as part of a larger system of anti-Black racism in the United States.

Gwen made this point clear during a strategic planning workshop at the Chicago Urban League office. I had been trying to interview Gwen for months, but she would often reschedule our interviews just hours before they were supposed to take place. She later told me that she was shy and that she did not think she had anything to say. But on one cold Saturday morning in February when members of PCR were asked to go around and share in one sentence why they were involved with environmental justice in Altgeld Gardens, Gwen could not contain herself. She ranted,

> When you think about it and really look at what's going on, it's like, they think black communities are just open for them to dispose whatever they want. That's racist! Because they don't do that in white communities. It's like they see us, especially black women, and think it's a natural thing to do. I'd hate to think that it

---

[10] Richard Bohannon and Kevin O'Brien, "Environmental Justice and Eco-Justice," in *Grounding Religion: A Field Guide to the Study of Religion and Ecology* (New York: Routledge, 2011), 169.

was intentional but after talking to some of these legislators and fighting with the sanitation department, I can't help but think that's what they think of us ... and so I don't see a choice but to get involved.[11]

Gwen's confident, impassioned, and indignant response describes how Black residents are impacted (they have become dumping grounds), while also revealing the undergirding reason (because Black people are seen as disposable). In this way, it is not happenstance that there are uneven outcomes for Black communities, but the reason Black communities are disproportionately affected is because of anti-Black racist logics that view them as disposable. Gwen's response offers data that not only reveal that Black communities are negatively impacted but she diagnoses the root cause of the problem as anti-Blackness.

Normative claims are also embedded in Gwen's descriptive analyses. She notes that disposing in Black communities ought to be understood as racist, and the practice of confining people in toxic environments is particular to the Black experience in the United States and especially Black women. Gwen's descriptive precision is important because not only is she naming the particularity of anti-Blackness, but she is also normalizing the necessity to name how anti-Black racism especially impacts Black women. Theologian Delores Williams's words ring true that the violence done to the earth through strip-mining—a modern technology used to extract coal from the earth for faster and larger profits—parallels the violence done to Black women's bodies through female slave breeding—a technology of enslavement that used Black women's reproductive capacities for faster and larger profit. She writes that, "Put simply, the assault upon the natural environment today is but an extension of the assault upon black women's bodies in the nineteenth century."[12] Cultural geographer Katherine McKittrick writes in a similar vein, explaining how the exploitation of Black women's bodies on the auction block were key mechanisms that not only naturalized Blackness and womanhood to carceral-like spaces but played a key role in the development, distribution, and organization of environmental space altogether. Thus, accounts of environmental injustice ought to consider how anti-Black environmental racism has, and continues to, impact Black women.

Gwen's impassioned speech also exposes an enduring challenge Black activists face with white logics that either oversimplify or minimize the particularity of Black struggle in the United States. For when they weren't using a grammar of disposability, scholars (and especially politicians) were always co-opting the language of Black struggle and resistance in order to promote their own cause or to conflate Black struggle with that of non-Black people of color and poor whites. Politicians would rhetorically ask: "What about poor white people who also live in environmentally compromised places?" or "You know that black people aren't the only group of color suffering from environmental pollution?" Black activists were used to these questions and the ways they dismissed a legacy of anti-Black environmental racism and evaded responsibility

---

[11] February 8, 2020, Chicago Urban League, 4510 Michigan Ave, Chicago, IL 60653.
[12] Delores Williams, "Sin, Nature, and Black Women's Bodies," in *Eco-Feminism and the Sacred*, ed. Carol Adams (New York: Continuum Publishing Company, 1993), 25.

and action. Indeed, a white supremacist logic pervades this kind of political argument but undergirding that logic is a foundation of anti-Blackness.

In many ways, Gwen is calling our attention to what theologian Katie Walker Grimes calls "antiblackness supremacy."[13] According to Walker Grimes, "Just as white supremacy describes the fact that white people, both as groups and as individuals, possess more power than people of color, both as groups and as individuals, the phrase 'anti-black supremacy' identifies the fact that non-black people, both as individuals and as a group, amass power because of this country's pervasive antiblackness."[14] Thus, the oversimplification or dismissal of the particularity of Black struggle in order to elevate "all struggle" reveals how being against Blackness is a social power that non-Black people of color accrue because anti-Blackness permeates our society. In other words, there is "power embodied in nonblackness"[15] where in "non-black people accrue power over and at the expense of blackness."[16] In this way, anti-Blackness itself becomes a kind of power status and political tool.

For Grimes, who is referencing Saidiya Hartman's work, we misunderstand anti-Blackness because we mischaracterize slavery as just another form of domination. Slavery was a form of total domination, alienation, and annihilation that uniquely marks Blackness. As such, it makes all Black experience of oppression a struggle against the stigma of the slave status which not only exists ideologically but is reproduced and maintained structurally, in the construction of places like Altgeld Gardens, for example. It is important to distinguish between the oppression that Blacks and poor whites and non-Black people of color experience then because, as Walker Grimes notes, "even if nonblack people of color do not occupy the ontological position of 'master,' they enjoy immunity from the ontological position of 'slave.'"[17] So, even if working class and impoverished whites are not insulated from the toxicity of environmental pollution, their immunity from the ontological position of slave (their non-Blackness) has protected them from the most egregious cases of environmental racism in the United States, and allows them greater mobility in accessing spaces Blacks continue to be excluded from. So, we cannot ignore racialized dynamics of environmental pollution because anti-Black supremacy is the defining factor in how states distribute its environmental burdens and it continues to be a tacit rule in whether Blacks are approved for homeownership or leasing agreements in "white spaces."[18]

Gwen's ranting, which blurs descriptive and normative claims, then is helpful since it names the particularity of Black struggle and the pervasiveness of anti-Black environmental racism in the face of those who would otherwise oversimplify or

---

[13] Katie Walker Grimes, "Black Exceptionalism: Anti-Blackness Supremacy in the Afterlife of Slavery," in *Anti-Blackness and Christian Ethics*, ed. Vincent W. Lloyd and Andrew Prevot (Maryknoll: Orbis Books, 2017), 41.
[14] Ibid.
[15] Ibid., 47.
[16] Ibid., 45.
[17] Ibid.
[18] For more information, please review the landmark study by Benjamin Chavis Jr. and Charles Lee, *Toxic Waste and Race in the United States: A National Report on the Racial and Socio-economic Characteristics of Communities with Hazardous Waste Sites* (New York: United Church of Christ, 1987).

dismiss it as an issue that all people struggle with. Gwen's ranting furthermore shows that our ethical frameworks ought to account for, or at the very least, acknowledge how slavery's afterlife directly impacts whether Black communities have access to clean air, water, and soil, and the ability to move into any residential space freely.

Wrestling with Writing Descriptive and Normative Claims

Traditional ethnographic writing clearly separates descriptive and normative claims. It neatly distinguishes "what is" from "what ought to be." In other words, descriptive claims in traditional forms of ethnographic writing do not make value judgments. The same is true for traditional forms of constructing Christian ethics. The descriptive and normative inform each other, but the two almost never collide. So what happens when you are handed the stories—the rants—with the descriptive and the normative aspects deeply entangled, with no clear line separating the two? When the activists have clearly shown me that the conflation of the two is important for the formation of their critical thoughts, wouldn't unblurring them and parsing them be an act of violence? When the activists have so clearly resisted the transparency and legibility academic discourse often demands of its marginalized subjects, when they have so clearly insisted on a different way of knowing and forming critical thought, wouldn't parsing the descriptive and the normative to make them readable for an academic audience be another kind of violence? I was compelled by such questions as I wrote about Altgeld Gardens. I had started writing with the intention not to replicate the violence that this community has already suffered, often at the hands of academics who shaped their narratives through a grammar of violence and disposability. In transcribing their rants, it occurred to me that I also needed to resist the violence of forcing transparency and categorization that ethnographic writing often demands. I needed an ethical practice of transcribing long before I described.

Poetic Contours of Rants

The goal of traditional ethnographic writing was to decentralize the anthropologist in order to highlight the reality of the subjects she was researching. But according to James Clifford and George Marcus in *Writing Culture: The Poetics and Politics of Ethnography*, "this ideology has crumbled,"[19] in order to reveal "that academic and literary genres interpenetrate and that the writing of cultural descriptions is properly experimental and ethical."[20] In other words, there is a poetic and inventive dimension to ethnographic writing since anthropologists themselves are constructing the world with the subjects they study, and not simply describing it scientifically. Said differently,

---

[19] James Clifford and George Marcus (eds.), *Writing Culture: The Poetics and Politics of Ethnography* (Berkeley: University of California Press, 1986), 2.
[20] Ibid.

they have "blurred the boundary separating art from science"[21] and thus understand themselves as "both anthropologists and literary artists."[22]

For Clifford and Marcus, anthropologists and ethnographers are not using literary dimensions so that their work can be considered "good writing" but rather to call attention to how literary processes "affect the ways cultural phenomenon are registered, from the first jotted 'observations,' to the completed book, to the ways these configurations 'make sense' in determined acts of reading."[23] By writing poetically, then, they expose that power is always already part of the writing and thus cannot be separated when research is said to be ethnographic. In other words, "the literary or rhetorical dimensions of ethnography can no longer be so easily compartmentalized."[24]

Theological discourse took a similar turn to the poetics. Theologians highlighted the metaphors (good and bad) for talking about the divine, the limitation of language to describe the transcendent, and the ways in which all theological language is an act of *poiesis*, of creative making.[25] While the poetic shift in theology helpfully points toward the limitations and potentiality of language in describing the divine, theologian Mayra Rivera's observation of Caribbean writers' poetics underscores how I think about the poetic nature of the environmental activists' rants. Rivera notes that for the Caribbean writers she engages, "poetics refers not only to styles of writing, but also to modes of knowing, being, and acting in the world."[26] In this way, poetics is not solely about our own facility with language but capturing the creative ways the communities we study know, be, and act in the world. Attention to the creative ways the activists orient themselves illuminates what is being resisted in their everyday struggle with anti-Black environmental racism and how they conceive of a more ethical way forward.

Thus, writing the environmental activists' rants illuminated for me their poetic dimensions: their metaphors, refrains, rhythms, cadence, and especially narrative nonlinearity. For example, Veronica talked about playing in the woods that is adjacent to Altgeld Gardens when she was younger. In her reflection, she held multiple times and spaces together revealing the persistence of Black life amid a history of environmental struggle. She exclaimed that,

> We had always been told "don't go in the woods. The woods [are] not our friend." Now, we know that's a contradiction because in some ways, the woods were our refuge and our escape. All of that, in the same woods. We ran from the same people and hid from [the] same people, in the same woods. So, you can hang from the tree, you can hide in a tree, you can eat from the tree. We're the only people in America who can really own that tree that way.[27]

---

[21] Ibid., 3.
[22] Ibid.
[23] Ibid., 4.
[24] Ibid.
[25] For a fuller genealogy of poetics in theology, see Mayra Rivera, "Poetics Ashore," *Literature & Theology* 33, no. 3 (2019): 241–7.
[26] Rivera, "Poetics Ashore," 242.
[27] Interview with Veronica Kyle, February 6, 2020, 1465 E 53rd St, Chicago IL 60615.

Veronica's rant poetically crosses space and time by transgressing its assumed linearity. At once, she was in the woods in Altgeld, she was in the woods with a maroon community, and she was in the woods in the Jim Crow south. There are no temporal or spatial boundaries, or a clear singular historical time frame tracing a lineage. The persistence of Black life from one generation to the next, from one tree to the next, required that narrative linearity be resisted.

Linearity conceals the various sociohistorical and political forces that made Altgeld a toxic doughnut and implied that it was happenstance. Linear thinking says there is no way that mass incarceration could invoke slave plantations, that slum and high-rise buildings could conjure slave ships, or that environmental racism could summon a connection to slaves thrown overboard. Linear thinking severs connections, conceals hegemonic powers, and simplifies the narratives. There is nothing linear about how Black people exist in the world. Who else went from subject, to object, and to subject again? Who else was forced to modulate between non-freedom, to freedom, and non-freedom again? And from enslavement, to emancipation, and then Jim Crow?

Veronica's ranting—her nonlinear voyage of critical thought—shows us the need for multiple points of relation—or how the past is always informed by and touches upon the present at multiple points. Her ranting thereby resists what philosopher Édouard Glissant calls totalizing narratives—stories that progress smoothly from a singular root origin, which suggests that the truth of the story has been grasped or understood in its totality. For Glissant, Western ethnography emerged out of this totalizing impulse to grasp *the* world or *the* truth of human beings. He writes,

> Since the beginning of this century the shrinking of unexplored regions on the map of the world has made minds less infatuated with adventure, or less sensitive to its beauty, inclining more toward a concern for the truth of human beings. Understanding cultures then became more gratifying than discovering new lands. Western ethnography was structured on the basis of this need. But we shall perhaps see that the verb *to understand* in the sense of "to grasp" [*comprende*] has a fearsome repressive meaning here.[28]

The writing of ethnography "is partly determined"[29] by a similar aim to understand, or (as Glissant suggests) to grasp violently, the communities we study, by forcing them and their thought into clear linear modes of thought.

A nonlinear approach acknowledges the multiple modes of truth and life taking place at once, across time and space. The moral demand, then that Veronica's rant makes on Christian social ethics and theology, is a demand to embrace and institute nonlinear ways of thinking as an ethical necessity for Black life . To be clear, the environmental activists' rants are not a random collection of aimless points: they resemble what Glissant calls errantry—sacred movement and motivation. He notes that "errantry follows neither an arrowlike trajectory nor one that is circular and

---

[28] Édouard Glissant. *Poetics of Relation* (Ann Arbor: University of Michigan Press, 1990), 26.
[29] Ibid., 23.

repetitive, nor is it mere wandering-idle roaming."[30] Rather, it reveals a network of relations taking place simultaneously. "In reality," he writes, "errant thinking is the postulation of an unyielding and unfading sacred."[31] Errant thinking that thus reflects the movement and motivation of the divine is a necessary intervention for Christian social ethics and theology.

Wrestling with Writing Linearly

Of all people, theologians should be comfortable with narratives that do not follow a linear progression. After all, isn't the biblical text our greatest example? The Gospels as presented do not follow a historical timeline. Even though Matthew is presented to us in the biblical text as the first Gospel, historically it was written second, Mark is the first or earliest, while Luke is third and John is last. In essence, the structure of the Gospels teaches scholars the value of multiplicity, and how to hold complexity. My theological training should have prepared me to understand and accept the environmental activists' rants in whatever rhizomatic formation they were presented. Nevertheless, my ingrained expectation of a clear and linear narrative progression persisted.

For example, when conducting my interviews, I began each the same way: I rolled out a 9×10 sheet of paper with a historical timeline of Altgeld Gardens housing project, and I asked the women when their families first came to the housing project. I wanted a method that would visibly ground them in a longer history of place and space in Chicago. Most of the women paused and had a perplexed look on their faces. They began reciting their histories, still with a confused look, as if they were not sure if that was what I was asking. But, as I nodded in affirmation, a confidence came over them and they more proudly and strongly talked about their parents and grandparents. From memory, they told me dates, cities, street names, expressions, and histories of tenement housing and racial unrest in Chicago. Some of it had a linear progression, but most of it did not. There were also gaps—not because of a loss of memory, but because of family displacements and forced migrations that left holes in their histories. Sometimes, when they came across a gap in their history, their voices became solemn, almost to signal they knew something terrible happened but that they were unwilling to go there. Other times, they imagined what had happened, thereby holding a history of local and national stories of migration and displacement together. Despite my ill-formed habit to capture a linear history, what opened up in their stories was poetics—a way in which the women were claiming space and forming knowledge across space and time. They filled in the gaps by making connections across time and space but in ways that held multiple relationalities together.

Interviewing the activists and diving deeply into theological studies made me question whether narrative linearity is possible. After all, isn't the Gospels one of our greatest examples to resist linearity? And, isn't it the case that Black people's experience

[30] Ibid., xvi.
[31] Ibid., 21.

in the middle passage, transatlantic slavery, and chattel slavery is also symbolic of the impossibility for narrative linearity? In what ways, then, can this way of being, knowing, and acting in the world inform our writing and reading practices?

Conclusion: A Stubborn Insistence on Black Life

When Cheryl ended her call with the reporter, I asked her why no one called upon her or the other Black women activists in Altgeld for the kinds of knowledge and practices that would actually help with their environmental situation. Her body language let me know that I had touched on a sensitive topic. As she inhaled, she shook her head in agreement and cleared the way for what she knew would require her whole breath. "Our voice has not been documented," Cheryl empathically declared as she exhaled. "You know . . . our struggle hasn't been documented. The *way* we care about where we live has not been documented. Our values . . . have not been documented," she went on.[32]

Cheryl's rant is not only a call for us ethnographers and theologians to collect and document Black women's environmental stories but also a call to value Black women's *way*. Thoroughly expressed in Black feminist and womanist thought, way-making[33] is how Black women creatively survive hegemonic structures and death-dealing situations. Womanist theologian Monica Coleman notes that the characteristics of "making a way" are multidimensional. When Black women talk about a way being made, she notes that they are often referring to one of four characteristics: "(1) God's presentation of unforeseen possibilities; (2) human agency; (3) the goal of justice, survival, and quality of life; and (4) a challenge to the existing order."[34]

Cheryl's response suggests the fourth characteristic: that Black women's environmental stories have not been documented because their particular way of caring for the earth challenges existing values and norms. Indeed, the kind of ethical relationship to the earth to which Cheryl and the other activists aspired challenges the fixed rules and existing norms that rendered them disposable and that normalized exploitation of the earth. The *way* in which they cared for the environment, as Cheryl put it, was outside the norm of what is considered care. For they practiced environmental care outside models of ownership, dominion, expansion, colonization, exploration, segregation, gentrification, urban renewal, redlining, mining, piping, extracting, disposing, and gutting. And they practiced environmental care outside modes of self-reliance, individualism, survival of the fittest, and the varieties of "bootstrap" politics.

---

[32] Interview with Cheryl Johnson, January 27, 2020, People for Community Recovery, 13330 S. Corliss Ave, Chicago, IL 60827.

[33] See Delores Williams's *Sisters in the Wilderness: The Challenge of Womanist God-Talk* (Maryknoll: Orbis Books, 1993), Katie Cannon's *Black Womanist Ethics* (Eugene: Wipf & Stock, 2006), Karen Baker-Fletcher's *A Singing Something: Womanist Reflections on Anna Julia Cooper* (New York: Crossroad, 1994), and Monica Coleman's *Making a Way out of No Way: A Womanist Theology* (Minneapolis: Fortress Press, 2008).

[34] Coleman, *Making a Way Out of No Way*, 33.

Echoing how Black women's way challenges the existing order, theologian Katie Cannon notes that "racism, gender discrimination and economic exploitation" are age-old inherited complexes which have required Black women "to create and cultivate values and virtues in their own terms so that they can prevail against the odds with moral integrity."[35] The values Black women create stem from moral wisdom in their real-lived context, Cannon explains, values and wisdom which do "not appeal to fixed rules or absolute principles of the white-oriented, male structured society."[36] Black women's environmental rants, then, challenge the existing order and analytical framework of Black environmental death and dying all the while caring for each other and for the earth outside of that violence—that is, in ways that do not reproduce domination and disposability, and other kinds of ideologies and behaviors that have led to earth's and Black women's exploitation. The activists' critical thoughts in the form of a screed, then, are their stubborn insistence on the persistence of Black life a as a way to be in ethical relationship with and on the earth.

Scholars in theology, ethics, and ethnography ought to take seriously Black women environmental activists' ranting as a form of critical thought that reveals moral resources for living a more ethical and antiracist future on this earth. Who better to describe the various workings of environmental racism than the people most affected by it? Who else has resisted state-sanctioned racialized environmental violence? Who else has survived the disavowed geographies of the world?[37] Who else has such an intimate relationship with toxic atmospheres and has spent their days resisting the violence of these institutions and dreaming of a better world, a better earth? Who else has not only planned how to survive the violence but ranted on about ways to be in the right relation with the earth? And what better way is there to communicate this than in the form of a rant—a screed?[38]

---

[35] Cannon, *Black Womanist Ethics*, 2.
[36] Ibid., 4.
[37] Saidiya Hartman, *Wayward Lives, Beautiful Experiments: Intimate Histories of Social Upheaval* (New York: W.W. Norton and Company, 2019), 347.
[38] Saidiya Hartman's work was incredibly important for helping me think about rants and screeds as a critical thought form.

10

The Curious Case of the Swedish Woman

Ethnographic Reflexivity and Accountability in Transnational Feminism

Sara A. Williams

The first time I heard of the Swedish woman, I was in a stuffy conference room atop Jerusalem's Gloria Hotel. We had begun the morning at the crest of the Mount of Olives, traversing down its steep slope to the Garden of Gethsemane before crossing into Jerusalem's Old City. Now after lunch, we found ourselves halfway through back-to-back panel sessions, seated in rows facing a long table in front of a wall of windows. The late afternoon sun streamed in, exposing dust particles dancing through the air and causing us to squint as we listened. The room's warmth and our fatigue from the day's activities competed with our desire to remain attentive. In my peripheral vision, an occasional head jerked up from an unintentional doze.

We were near the end of the second full day of the two-week "Mosaic of Peace Conference," a packaged Holy Land tour sponsored by the Peacemaking Program of the Presbyterian Church (USA). The Mosaic of Peace was one of six tours I joined in 2016 as part of the ethnographic fieldwork for my doctoral dissertation on progressive Christian engagement with packaged tourism as an ethical practice. My research had raised questions that gave me a particular interest in this final panel of the day. Its focus was Kairos Palestine, a Palestinian Christian social movement organization emerging from the Kairos Palestine Document. Modeled after the 1985 Kairos South Africa Document, the Kairos Palestine Document is a theological and political statement imploring the international community and the global church to stand with Palestinians in nonviolent resistance against the Israeli occupation.

The document's 2009 release significantly deepened the solidarity infrastructure between Palestinian Christians and Christians in the West. It produced a flurry of global conferences and Western-facing publications, and sparked renewed interest in Palestinian-led Holy Land pilgrimages like the one I was on. As I immersed myself in the document's productive aftermath, I noticed that consistently popping up at the periphery was Kairos Palestine's relationship to women. The Kairos Palestine Document nowhere mentions women specifically, yet such an omission hardly seems noteworthy. As with the Kairos South Africa Document—which also makes no mention of gender—the Kairos Palestine Document is primarily oriented on a call to repentance for political and religious complicity in state-sanctioned violence that sustains oppressive conditions. It also seeks to cast a theological vision for a just and equitable shared presence in the land. Palestinian intracommunity dynamics, such as the role of women, seem, if not unrelated, at least understandably absent in an approximately seven thousand-word document aiming to make a tight theological and political case related to the Israeli military occupation.

Despite this lack of mention of women specifically, prominent Palestinian Christian women were speaking and writing about Kairos Palestine in relationship to gender. For example, Nora Carmi, the original project coordinator for the Kairos Palestine organization, contributed an essay to an edited collection on Kairos Palestine discussing how the document's demands for justice apply specifically to women.[1] Similarly, in her recorded remarks at the Kairos for Global Justice Conference in Bethlehem in 2011, Jean Zaru noted, "It seems to me that the Kairos Palestine Document does not deal with women's issues. The pain of sexism is eclipsed by the lack of national liberation. I think it's crucial to remember, however, that all structures of violence and domination are tightly interwoven. We cannot become free if women are not free."[2] Comments like these signaled that at least some Palestinian women were thinking about Kairos Palestine in terms of gender. I was curious to know more.

When it was time to ask questions of the two panelists, George and Hanna,[3] both in leadership with Kairos Palestine, I asked: "I know that both [Palestinian Christian lay leaders] Jean Zaru and Nora Carmi have written about gender and the Kairos Document. I'm curious how that's been received, and how Kairos Palestine is focusing on gender issues."

"You know, Kairos Palestine is not handling all issues," Hanna responded. "I mean, even in the Palestinian context we struggle, we have so much struggle in front of us when our daily life is threatened, when our children's life is threatened, when we have so many anxieties. The main struggle we have is for political liberation because without that, believe me, nothing's gonna work." Hanna went on to offer a litany of threats and anxieties Palestinians face, concluding, "We are in too much trouble to worry only about women."[4]

After she finished, George interjected in a soft-spoken voice,

> I will say something very shortly. [Hanna] was talking about *destruction*, and [then] there is *distraction*. So these questions about gender in the Kairos Document [were] total distraction.... It was coming from Sweden, a Swedish lady started this thing of a gender problem in the Kairos Document. So instead of talking about destruction, she wanted to distract us.[5]

---

[1] Nora Carmi, "Kairos: Exploring the Idea of Justice in Palestine From a Woman's Perspective," *Theologies and Cultures* 11, no. 1 (June 2014): 32–41.
[2] Jean Zaru, "Introduction: To Hold the Sky and Identify with Jesus: Abstracts from A Gender Analysis of the Kairos Palestine Document," in *Kairos for Global Justice*, ed. Robin Meyers, 74–8 (Bethlehem: Kairos Palestine, 2011), 74.
[3] Both are pseudonyms. As I discuss later in the essay, George asked for a pseudonym. I was unable to reach Hanna to confirm use of her name.
[4] Hanna, Mosaic of Peace Kairos Palestine Panel, April 8, 2016.
[5] George, Mosaic of Peace Kairos Palestine Panel, April 8, 2016.

As we shuffled down to dinner following the panel, I felt perplexed as to why my question about gender had elicited such a strong response, particularly since two respected Palestinian Christian women leaders had themselves raised the issue in global publications and conferences. I had assumed I was asking about a subject that was sensitive but open for discussion. Confusing me further was George's assertion that the subject of gender and the Kairos document had come not from Palestine, but from Europe. Who was this Swedish woman? After that April 2016 panel, the Swedish woman became my white rabbit. I felt an irresistible curiosity to find out who she was and what exactly she had done, convinced that this piece of information would help me understand more about the subtle politics I had stumbled into around gender and the Kairos Document.

In this chapter, I chronicle my investigations into the Swedish woman and offer an analysis of their significance for positionality, reflexivity, and accountability in ethnographic fieldwork. By recounting these investigations more or less as they unfolded in my own experience, I hope to demonstrate how reflexive conscientization can happen in the field, particularly around power dynamics that may be obscured for the researcher because of her privileged social location.

Ethnographic Puzzles: Investigating the Swedish Woman Affair

Getting to the bottom of the Swedish woman affair proved to be a formidable task. Through interviews and informal conversations, it became evident that the Swedish woman had tried to insert her perspective into the proceedings of a 2011 Kairos conference a few years earlier. Memories of this conference often elicited strong reactions among the Palestinian women with whom I spoke. Yet no one seemed to remember all that much about who the Swedish woman was or why she had been at the conference. There was also no record of what exactly she said, though some did offer fragmented memories of her words. And, I could not figure out why she often came up in interviews before I mentioned her at all.

This was the case in my interview with Nora Kort, one of three women on the Kairos Palestine document authorship committee. Nora K.[6] is a prominent woman in Jerusalem's Orthodox Christian community. As president of the Arab Orthodox Society, she has founded numerous women's cooperatives and a Palestinian museum and cultural center, where she regularly hosts Western visitors. I interviewed Nora K. at one of her cooperatives, the Melia Art and Training Center, an unassuming storefront tucked into Jerusalem's Armenian Quarter. Affixed to Melia's glass entrance is a green and purple sticker that reads, "Women can do ... ANYTHING!" Inside, the little shop's ancient stone walls are adorned with embroidery and jewelry made by women from villages in the West Bank and Gaza.

---

[6] I refer to Nora Kort as Nora K. in order to differentiate her from Nora Carmi. Likewise, when not using her full name, I refer to Nora Carmi as Nora C.

I sat with Nora K. next to a desk in the back. She wore a long strand of pearls over a flowy black and white chiffon dress, her lips colored a deep glossy pink. Two other women working at the cooperative sat with us, occasionally interjecting to supplement what Nora K. was saying. After a while, we began talking about Nora K.'s experience participating in the Kairos document's writing process. Without my prompting, the conversation quickly shifted to the Swedish woman: "[The authorship committee] had long hours of discussion on one word and the way religious people [might] see it, what we say and what we do," she told me. "And there was a conference [in 2011] where one woman, I think she was a minister from—probably the Netherlands or from England—and she said Kairos is the voice of a man. It's not the voice of women."

I asked Nora K. if the woman could have been from Sweden. "I think so," she replied. "She's a feminist, and their understanding of feminism is not like ours." Nora K. continued:

> In one of the [Kairos Palestine] conferences, I argued with her. She wanted to speak about Kairos from a woman's perspective, and what it's lacking. . . . I said, "I'm a Palestinian and I don't see that there is [patriarchal] language." [And] she said, "The language is more manly. [It does not say] there are women there [in Palestine]." I said, "We don't see that." . . . It's very strange how people, you know, analyze and split the areas that they want and want to argue about. [But] we silenced her. Me and another woman, we silenced her.[7]

It was evident that Nora K. had felt disrespected by a woman who did not understand her cultural context. As someone who had spent her life creating economic opportunities for other Palestinian women, one could understand that Nora K. would be offended by the suggestion that the Kairos authorship committee—including the women on it— had not pushed hard enough to include women's issues in the document explicitly. Yet why did Nora K. gravitate to this isolated incident at a conference five years earlier when describing her participation in the authorship of the Kairos document? We had not been discussing gender explicitly. I felt puzzled that the Swedish woman had come up at all. And, if Palestinian Christian women like Jean Zaru and Nora Carmi were writing about gender and the Kairos document, why discuss the topic of women in reference to this Swedish woman? Why not focus on the ideas emerging from women within the Palestinian community?

With these questions in mind, I interviewed another woman on the Kairos authorship committee, Cedar Duaybis. Cedar was one of a small group of Palestinian Christian laypeople who, under the leadership of Palestinian Anglican priest and liberation theologian Naim Ateek, helped found the Sabeel Ecumenical Liberation Theology Center twenty-five years earlier. Cedar told me that one of her contributions to the Kairos Palestine writing process was the idea to structure the document by the three theological virtues of faith, hope, and love. She had also noticed that an early draft of the document used exclusively masculine pronouns. One evening she stayed up all night revising it to be gender neutral. Cedar's robust contributions to the document,

---

[7] Nora Kort, Interview with the Author, July 29, 2016.

including its gendered dimensions, made me interested to get her take on the Swedish woman incident. As our interview was wrapping up, I broached the subject with her. Cedar became visibly uncomfortable. Her eyes diverted down to the table and she began to squirm in her seat. "Yeah, there's this woman who said that there should be a section about women," Cedar told me. She continued,

> I did not think that, because if there's a section about women, there should be a section about youth, there should be a section about the disabled . . . but then [some others] insisted [that] there has to be a section about women. . . . I don't know what happened, but I was entangled in something I didn't want to [be in].[8]

Cedar trailed off, remarking that she should probably not be talking about this with me. We switched subjects, but her unease spoke as loudly as her words might have.

Not all Palestinian women disagreed with the substance of the Swedish woman's critiques. "When I saw the [Kairos] Document, and some people asked me about [it], I said, 'It's important that we cover also the role of women in the churches,'" Jean Zaru told me. "Not as a point of criticism," she continued, "and some of the church leaders took it as criticism. But if we want to empower women, we have to feed their role and we have to feed their contribution and we have to be both part of the decision-making process of society and of the church."[9] Jean seemed to be echoing the essence of the Swedish woman's critique, namely that the Kairos Document should have explicitly addressed the subjugation of women in Palestinian society. When I brought up the Swedish woman in our interview a few minutes later, however, Jean, like Cedar, became uncomfortable. She asked me to turn off the recorder as she shared her recollection of the conference, and stopped a number of times mid-sentence to emphasize that she did not want this part quoted. Even as Jean expressed affection for the Swedish woman, she was concerned about reawakening the divisions that had resulted from her comments.

Through a number of interviews, conversations, and some fairly extensive internet sleuthing, I was finally able to piece together that the Swedish woman was a clergy person in the Church of Sweden and a longtime advocate for Palestinian rights. She had attended the 2011 Kairos for Global Justice Conference, and there she publicly critiqued the document's lack of mention of women. Though her exact words had been lost, it was apparent they had caused deep pain, even trauma, among the Palestinian women present at the conference. Her words had forced the women there to take a public stance in front of powerful male religious leaders on whether the Kairos Palestine document adequately addressed justice for women, something about which they were not in full agreement among themselves. This had created internal divisions among them that even five years later were still healing. Though I had pieced these facts of the puzzle together, I continued to grapple with the significance of the Swedish woman. Why did her presence loom so large in my interviews with Palestinian women? The "Swedish Woman Affair" seemed to point to something beyond the incident itself and the Swedish woman at the center of it.

---

[8] Cedar Duaybis, Interview with the Author, August 18, 2016.
[9] Jean Zaru, Interview with the Author, August 24, 2016.

It was Nora Carmi who helped me begin to understand the larger dynamics at stake. Nora C. is a woman of some prominence in the Palestinian Christian community, having spent a long career working in community development with women in East Jerusalem and the West Bank. This work had earned her the nickname "Mama Nora," a term of reverence and affection. Though not on the Kairos authorship committee, Nora C. was the original project coordinator for the Kairos Palestine organization after the document's publication. In this role, Nora C. had been intimately involved in the early work of developing the Kairos Document's mandate into a global movement. I interviewed Nora C. three times during my fieldwork because we just never seemed to finish our conversation. I came to know her as generous and warm, her ethic of care palpable to those around her.

It was in the context of one of our extended conversations that I brought up my questions about the significance of the Swedish woman. I recounted to her that first experience at the Kairos panel, in which George had accused the Swedish woman of using gender as a "distraction" from the justice issues at stake for Palestinians. "Well, no problem, I mean you can ask me anything you want," Nora C. replied. She continued:

> I don't think gender distracts. I don't think that was the correct word. . . . I think [George] should have told you that we have three women who were there who wrote [the Kairos Palestine Document]. And not anything else, you know? But with the focus coming from a Western community, especially Sweden, [asking] "why don't we have women?" . . . I don't feel bad, even as I have worked for women all my life, I know how I defend women's rights. But in the Kairos Document I really did not feel that we should have been pointed on women.[10]

Nora C.'s comments got to the heart of the matter. They synthesized what I head learned in my interviews: though the Kairos document does not name women specifically, women had played an integral role in the creation of the Kairos Palestine document. By calling the Kairos Palestine document androcentric simply because it did not contain an explicit section questioning patriarchy in Palestinian society, the Swedish woman was erasing the multitude of women's agential expressions at play. In the end, the "Swedish Woman Affair" turned out to be quite a familiar story. A Western feminist with the best of intentions had imparted deep harm through unreflexive complicity in cultural colonialism.

Ethnographic Reflexivity: Western Feminism and Palestinian Women's Agency

As I mulled over my field notes and interviews related to the Swedish woman, I continued to return to Nora Kort's lack of recollection as to which European country the Swedish woman came from. One might attribute this to fading memory over time, yet she

---

[10] Nora Carmi, Interview with the Author, May 3, 2016.

recalled the rest of the details so clearly. It did not seem to me the fallibility of memory was at issue here. Rather, it seemed more likely that Nora K. did not remember where the Swedish woman came from because it simply did not matter to her. It was insignificant to the importance Nora K. placed on the incident: that she won the debate over whose feminism would define the terms of the discourse, that of the West or that of Palestinian women.

In addition, there appeared to be divergent constructions of agency among Western and Palestinian women, a tension that reaches beyond the Palestinian Territories and Israel. Since the 1980s, racially minoritized women scholars and women scholars from the majority world have been exposing the whiteness and ethnocentrism at play in Western feminisms. The resulting body of work points to how white Western feminists define what is and is not agential on their own terms, using "third world women" as tropes to support an agenda centrally focused on liberation from patriarchy: "the veiled woman, the powerful mother, the chaste virgin, the obedient wife."[11] As Women's Studies scholar Chandra Mohanty writes, "These images exist in universal, ahistorical splendor, setting in motion a colonialist discourse which exercises a very specific power in defining, coding, and maintaining existing first/third world connections."[12] While white women have come to define global feminist discourses, Black and Brown women have been rendered silent and passive objects used to prove the point that white Western feminists want to make. Women from the majority world are stylized to represent the most egregious forms of patriarchal oppression from which women should be liberated.

With the terms of engagement structured this way, claims to agential action for ends other than liberation from patriarchy are often unintelligible to white Western feminists. They either remain invisible or are dismissed as a product of internalized oppression. In the terms of influential feminist literary scholar Gayatri Spivak,[13] white Western feminists have created a framework for feminism in which subaltern women cannot speak. Yet as Anthropologist Saba Mahmood[14] has argued, confining women's agency only to the disruption of patriarchal norms erases women's agential practices as they relate to an expansive constellation of other cultural goods within their lifeworlds. It reduces the complexity of women's subjectivities to Western cultural constructions, thereby rendering feminism a colonial project. The Swedish woman, it seems, had unreflexively internalized such a white Western feminist epistemology, unwittingly doing violence to Palestinian women she clearly cared deeply about.

My initial hunch had been right: investigating the Swedish woman *did* offer me insight into the gender politics of Kairos Palestine. Quite unexpectedly, however, this insight was as much about me as it was about Palestinian women. I began to recognize that in my conversations with Palestinian women, the "Swedish Woman"

---

[11] Chandra Talpade Mohanty, *Feminism without Borders: Decolonizing Theory, Practicing Solidarity* (Durham: Duke University Press, 2003), 41.
[12] Ibid.
[13] Gayatri Chakravorty Spivak, "Can the Subaltern Speak?" in *The Post-Colonial Studies Reader*, ed. Bill Ashcroft, Gareth Griffiths, and Helen Tiffin (New York: Routledge, 2006), 28–37.
[14] Saba Mahmood, *Politics of Piety: The Islamic Revival and the Feminist Subject* (Princeton: Princeton University Press, 2011).

was functioning as a kind of shorthand signal. My white skin, blue eyes, and Western passport represented the same colonial danger that was present in the "Swedish Woman Affair." These women were taking a risk by opening up to me. Naming the "Swedish Woman" placed her presence in the air between us. It was a plea, in some cases even a warning, not to do violence to Palestinian women's ways of knowing and advocating for themselves, and it indicated a suspicion that I might.

My investigations into the "Swedish Woman Affair" offered me a new lens for reflection on how, for those of us in the West, even solidarity is vulnerable to our worst colonial impulses. How was it that a woman who by all accounts was not only a dedicated activist for Palestinians, but also a personal friend of a number of Palestinian women leaders, reproduced the kind of hegemonic logics she was trying to disrupt? And how could I avoid making her mistakes? Honoring the Palestinian women I had come to know required me to hold open the possibility that I *am* the "Swedish Woman," and vigilantly doing the reflexive work to try not to be. The Swedish woman's transgressions made clear that I had a responsibility to analyze my data against the grain of my own Western feminist epistemological assumptions, to hear and understand more clearly how Palestinian women think about their own agency.

While some of the Palestinian women I interviewed did bemoan patriarchal aspects of their culture, most did not understand overturning patriarchy to be the primary way they exercised agency in their everyday lives. Rather, interviews revealed a diverse repertoire of strategies Palestinian women employ to advocate for themselves and other women. Specifically, I identified three broad categories in which the Palestinian women I interviewed articulated their agency: (1) leveraging cultural assets and social capital, (2) strategic use of "patriarchal bargains,"[15] and (3) direct confrontation of patriarchy. The recognition of difference in feminisms makes it important to note that these three categories should not be construed as universalizable to all Palestinian women, but rather as illustrative of the multiplicity of women's agency in subaltern communities. Palestinian Christians living in Israel and the West Bank generally have greater access to education and class mobility than their Muslim counterparts due to more direct ties with the West.[16] Certainly not every Palestinian Christian benefits from these arrangements equally, but it is important to keep in mind that the women I interviewed were all relatively privileged in Palestinian society.

In what follows, I offer illustrative ethnographic vignettes representing how each of these categories was present in the time I spent with Palestinian women in the field.

Leveraging Cultural Assets and Social Capital

"In 1990, we had our first bazaar at the YMCA East Jerusalem. [The YMCA director] did not charge us for anything," Nora Kort told me as we sipped Turkish coffee in the

---

[15] Deniz Kandiyoti, "Bargaining with Patriarchy," *Gender & Society* 2, no. 3 (September 1, 1988): 274–90.
[16] Bård Kårtveit, *Dilemmas of Attachment: Identity and Belonging Among Palestinian Christians* (Leiden: Brill, 2014), 5–6.

back of the Melia Art and Training Center. "The bazaar was a success because we were proximal to St. George's Cathedral, and they had tourists. Everything more or less sold out." She continued,

> So that was the beginning, and then we started women, we started with 15, they doubled in the second year and they tripled and this is how—when I was the country representative of the International Orthodox Charities, it's an American faith-based organization, I got a USAID grant, and partly I included the training of women in skills. And we took the teachers from here to the West Bank to train them. We trained 250 women. Now they have their own cottage industries and they're selling in the city of Nablus.[17]

Nora K. was recalling the origin story of the complex of women's cooperatives she had founded since her first bazaar in 1990, during the height of the First Intifada.[18] Nora K. was not the only one starting a women's cooperative at the time. During the First Intifada, Palestinians practiced myriad forms of nonviolent resistance to the Israeli occupation, from tax boycotts to the use of "victory gardens" to facilitate boycotts of Israeli agriculture.[19] Women's cooperatives gained popularity during this time as a way to conscientize Palestinian women and get them involved in political action, while also economically empowering them on an individual level.[20]

The period that followed the end of the First Intifada saw an influx of international development money, prompted by the Oslo Accords and its creation of the Palestinian Territories. While most of these monies were more directly focused on the peace process, increased attention from the West also opened up new funding streams for smaller projects, particularly those that might build capacity for a stable Palestinian state.[21] Nora K. leveraged her social capital with a Western organization to benefit from this favorable funding climate, securing not only the USAID grant she mentions above, but also funding from a number of other international agencies. She made strategic use of the Palestinian tourism market as well, which was newly expanded by the creation of the Palestinian Ministry of Tourism and Antiquities.

While such reliance on the West for development funds and tourism markets can be read as capitulating to colonial structures and the tourist gaze, it can also be read as savvy tactical use of available resources and existing political conditions. Nora K. not only created economic opportunities for women through her cooperatives, but she also made opportunities for them to participate in the export of Palestinian perspectives

---

[17] Nora Kort, Interview with the Author, July 29, 2016.
[18] The First Intifada was a period of Palestinian popular uprising in the West Bank and Gaza in response to Israeli military crackdowns. Palestinian resistance during this period was characterized by a mix of violent tactics and nonviolent strategies of civil disobedience such as strikes and boycotts. Both violent and nonviolent resistors were met with Israeli military force and mass arrests (Charles D. Smith, *Palestine and the Arab-Israeli Conflict: A History with Documents*, 8th ed. [Boston: Bedford/St. Martin's, 2007], 401–12).
[19] Jennifer Lynn Kelly, "Asymmetrical Itineraries: Militarism, Tourism, and Solidarity in Occupied Palestine," *American Quarterly* 68, no. 3 (2016): 723–45.
[20] Eileen Kuttab, "Empowerment as Resistance: Conceptualizing Palestinian Women's Empowerment," *Development* 53, no. 2 (June 1, 2010): 247–53.
[21] Ibid., 248–9.

and culture to the West. Souvenirs have afterlives that follow travelers back home as containers for narratives. Whether given away as gifts or displayed in an office or a home, travelers use souvenirs to convey meaning they made from their trip with family, friends, colleagues, and others. The handicrafts sold in Nora K.'s cooperatives became "vehicles of values" in service of cultivating ties of solidarity with the West.[22]

Nora Kort extended this work when she established Wujood, a Palestinian museum and cultural center in the Armenian Quarter of Jerusalem's Old City. When she was renovating the ancient building that houses the museum, a few owners of nearby souvenir shops tried to intimidate her into dropping the project because they were afraid it would bring them competition. They burned Nora K.'s home, destroyed her car, and stabbed two of her construction workers. But, Nora K. told me, "they did not know that I was resilient."[23] She pressed on. At Wujood, which means "existence," Nora now regularly hosts Western groups to share her story and those of women in her cooperatives, and to sell goods the women have made.

Nora K. bristles at forms of feminism predicated on direct confrontation with patriarchy. Yet as with all of the women I interviewed, she has dedicated her life to empowering other Palestinian women. Through leveraging cultural assets and her own social capital, at moments risking her own safety to do so, Nora K. creates opportunities for women to contest their economic and political subjugation through the making and selling of handicraft souvenirs.

Strategic Use of Patriarchal Bargains

For our final interview, Nora C. invited me to her apartment in East Jerusalem's Beit Hanina neighborhood. She greeted me at her door in a powder blue T-shirt, a simple skirt, and flip flops. She wore no makeup on her face. Over the course of several hours, we ate chicken with traditional Arab salads, drank tea, and washed dishes as we talked. Nora C.'s uncharacteristically casual appearance and our sharing in ordinary domestic rhythms in her home created a sense of intimacy. I felt honored to be invited a little further into Nora C.'s world.

Nora C. regaled me with stories of her long tenure working with women in East Jerusalem, first with the YWCA and then with the Sabeel Ecumenical Liberation Theology Center, and about how she became the project coordinator for Kairos Palestine. As she spoke, here and there Nora C. would throw in a small detail about how she influenced powerful men behind the scenes, as if it were inconsequential. Describing her early advocacy for Sabeel's legitimacy as an ecumenical but Protestant-led convener among the historical churches of Jerusalem, she commented,

---

[22] Jackie Feldman, "Vehicles of Values: Souvenirs and the Moralities of Exchange in Christian Holy Land Pilgrimage," in *Toward an Anthropology of Nation Building and Unbuilding in Israel*, ed. Fran Markowitz, Stephen Sharot, and Moshe Shokeid (Omaha: University of Nebraska Press, 2015), 259–75.

[23] Nora Kort, Interview with the Author, July 29, 2016.

When you speak to the other churches, of course they say, "the Protestants." Okay. But having said that, I tell them—because I argue a lot with the bishops and so on—I say, "Let's look at who has been really doing more studies, more biblical studies, among all the four [church] families, okay?" . . . Because Patriarch [Michel] Sabbah and I are very close. He's my mentor and we help each other.[24]

Nora C. also told me of moments in which she would debate or advise Naim Ateek, Sabeel's founder and prominent Palestinian liberation theologian, during crucial organizational decision points at Sabeel and while he served on the Kairos authorship committee.

For Nora C., arguing with the bishops or advising Ateek seemed so commonplace as to simply blend in with the rest of her stories. For me, these details popped out. Nora C. had clearly played an instrumental role behind the scenes regarding the churches' theological and political responses to the occupation, in ways that would be taboo for a woman to do publicly. Nora C. did not demand that women have a place among the patriarchs of the thirteen recognized churches in Jerusalem. While she does quite a lot of public speaking, she maintains deference to the male heads of churches. Nora C. had instead developed close friendships with many of the patriarchs and other powerful religious leaders. She had their ear, and this allowed her to influence their decision-making while leaving their public authority intact.

Nora C.'s strategies relate to what Middle East and Gender Studies scholar Deniz Kandiyoti describes as "patriarchal bargains": ways in which women effectively negotiate patriarchy within culturally specific "rules of the game."[25] While "bargaining with patriarchy" may seem categorically antithetical to feminist commitments, it is only so if we take Western feminist epistemologies as normative. Nora C.'s backdoor debates with bishops and Cedar Duaybis's quiet advocacy for gender-inclusive language in the Kairos Document did not center the dismantling of church patriarchies because such an outcome was simply not their focus. They were both more concerned with fostering the work of the churches as it relates to the welfare of Palestinians. This is not to suggest that their friendships with male religious leaders have been purely instrumental. It is rather to say that to advance the projects about which they care most deeply, they find it better to work within those relationships than to challenge their terms.

Direct Confrontation of Patriarchy

Jean Zaru was traveling abroad for the bulk of my nine months in the field, and consequently I did not get to know her well. We were finally able to connect a week before my departure. By that point, Jean's presence had already loomed large in my research, at least in regard to gender, and it felt important to speak with her directly. I was thrilled she was willing to speak with me even though we had not had the opportunity

---

[24] Nora Carmi, Interview with the Author, August 23, 2016.
[25] Kandiyoti, "Bargaining with Patriarchy," 274.

to build rapport, though it is important to note that what she shared was limited by our lack of relationship.

Jean is the former presiding clerk for the Ramallah Friends Meeting, one of the only Palestinian women to hold an official religious office in Israel and the Palestinian Territories. Her public critiques of patriarchy had also been more direct than those of the other women I spoke with. When I asked Jean about this, she responded,

> I had been the first woman elected for the executive committee [of the] World Conference on Religion and Peace. I was also the first woman from the Middle East serving on the Central Committee of the World Council of Churches. At the beginning it wasn't easy. . . . The patriarchs would ask me, "Are you married?" And [they would say], "Oh, why do you bother with these issues? Do you have children?" [I would answer], "Yes." [They would respond], "Why don't you go back and take care of your husband and children?" So, you know, religion, it was not part of women's work. . . . It put more pressure on me to behave in ways that I cannot run away from communication with my community. Not in a rebellious way, but in a way that they can understand, that it's not for me personally but it's in general for our community.[26]

Jean's positions in formal religious leadership had given her a different set of experiences than the other women I interviewed. She was the first woman in the room not only among Palestinian religious leaders in her role as presiding clerk for the Quakers but also in global religious bodies. Jean's feminism had been formed in the crucible of breaking barriers in public ways, and in navigating the pushback she received from men who felt threatened by her presence at the table. Her way of advocating for Palestinian women was reflective of her experience of patriarchy as a force that would need to be totally dismantled for women to become true coequal partners in Palestinian society.

In her book *Occupied with Nonviolence*, Jean writes,

> We Palestinian women live and work in a very traditional society where the dos and don'ts for women are made very clear. Often our effectiveness in leadership depends on how well we follow the expectations of our own people. If we don't meet their expectations, our work may not be validated or even taken seriously. . . . I constantly live life in my traditional society on the one hand and in the ever-changing world on the other hand.[27]

Jean captures the tension in which Palestinian women in leadership must live. They inhabit a community with traditional gender expectations, while simultaneously seeking to articulate themselves to an increasingly postfeminist Western world that recognizes the concept of gender itself as a social construction. As with any community, there is plurality as to how Palestinian women negotiate this tension. When such a plurality

---

[26] Jean Zaru, Interview with the Author, August 24, 2016.
[27] Jean Zaru, *Occupied with Nonviolence: A Palestinian Woman Speaks*, ed. Diana L. Eck and Marla Schrader (Minneapolis: Fortress Press, 2008), 110.

is erased by flattening "the other," possibilities for genuine cross-cultural solidarities are diminished, as are opportunities for the conscientization that arises from reflexive interrogation of Western epistemological assumptions.

A Coda on Ethnographic Accountability

Five years after conducting my ethnographic fieldwork, I sat down to write this chapter. The "Swedish Woman" remained in the back of my mind, an experience from the field that felt important to write about reflexively rather than at academic remove. She represented a colonial shadow self whose possibility caused me great concern. Yet to write about the "Swedish Woman" at all also felt dangerous. What I wanted to say—that those of us in the West should look to her as a cautionary tale of the harms that can result from our unexamined neocolonial impulses—risked reproducing that same insidious coloniality. If I did not write with care, I could end up reawakening or exacerbating conflict within the Palestinian Christian community, the very thing George had accused the Swedish woman of doing.

As a matter of accountability, I emailed my first draft of this chapter to everyone it mentioned by name. Within thirty minutes, a response from George appeared in my inbox:

> You got got [sic] it all wrong dear. This is not what I meant. I did not mean that Women's equal rights and role were a distraction to our struggle I meant that people who do not want to deal with the real question of how to end the occupation might want to destract [sic] the discussion into any other issue. Exactly like what you are trying to do now. Instead of talking about the document, it's [sic] calls, and its vision your [sic] are chosing [sic] to distract any audience just to show a hole in the basket.[28]

George concluded by asking that I not use his real name in the piece because he felt I was using his words in a misleading way.

My first reaction to George's email was panic, followed by shame. It was possible my worst fear had come to pass: I had become the "Swedish Woman." This almost made me scrap the piece altogether. Then I received responses from the women in the chapter, some of whom were effusively supportive and affirming, and others who said that they think my analysis of the whole affair is a good one, but they would rather be done with it and did not want to offer me further feedback. All but one of the women in the latter category told me they were fine with being named in the piece; one woman said though she liked my analysis she just wanted to put the Swedish Woman Affair behind her and did not want to be in the piece. As requested, I took her out.

I grappled with what it means for ethnographic accountability when there is a strong divergence of opinion among research participants as to the accuracy of the analysis.

---

[28] George, Email to the Author, September 28, 2021.

In the end, I concluded that in this case it seemed right to privilege the women's feedback because their positionality gave them epistemological authority regarding women's perspectives. I sensed that one dimension of the divergence between their responses and George's has to do with the fact that while George has the privilege to put gender aside as a distraction, Palestinian women do not. Gender is literally always bodily present for them. They must negotiate it one way or another; it is never totally peripheral to their experience. Yet in making the choice to move forward with the piece, I do not mean to dismiss George's point. By raising the question of gender as I did at that 2016 Kairos Palestine panel, I unwittingly struck a nerve. In that moment, in my body, asking that question, I became the "Swedish Woman." Her potential is, in fact, always with me.

My investigations did eventually lead me to discover the name and whereabouts of the Swedish woman. By the time I did, I learned she was dying of cancer. I did not think it right to contact her in her final stages of life. But I also realized that I did not really need to. It hardly mattered exactly what she said or who she was. More important was her symbolic presence in the field, not only as a warning but also an invitation. The practice of ethnography can—and *ought to*—invite Western subjects into the reflexive work of recognizing our own complicity in the colonial rupture. In doing so, we open possibilities for the work of repair.

11

Qualitatively Studying Evangelical Whiteness

Excerpts and Experiences

Nicole Symmonds

Introduction

For the last thirty years, white evangelical Christians have been one of the most prominent groups in the North American anti-trafficking movement. They advocate for policy changes in commercial sex work, interact with populations vulnerable to sexual exploitation, or stage rescues. These moral actors use Christian religious practices and values to respond to trafficking and commercial sex work. Whether they are marketing sexual exploitation victims as defenseless white women on billboards around cities such as Atlanta or narrating white Christian missionaries as saviors, white evangelicals toggle between victim and victor with great aplomb. They captivate the public sphere with harrowing tales of victimhood as well as victory. In this way, anti-trafficking work is always coded by evangelical whiteness which uses the norms of sexual purity and racialization[1] in their interactions with and recovery of trafficking victims and survivors. My research explores how evangelical whiteness works behind the scenes and how these actors understand themselves as moral actors in the fight against so-called modern slavery.

I conducted my research at Atlanta-based New Daughters and Sons[2] (NDS), an evangelical anti-trafficking organization that ministers to, rescues, and recovers victims of commercial sexual exploitation. I explored the motives for NDS's work, especially as it was concentrated in predominantly Black communities in Atlanta. This research

---

[1] I use the definition of racialization established by activist and organizer Steve Martinot: that racialization precedes racism by establishing race as that which is produced and bestowed upon subjects by institutional social actions. "Racialization means that race is something people do, rather than what they are," says Martinot. Therefore, race is defined by what the individual does. In the context of white slavery and racializing sex, this meant that reformers often fell—or crawled—into the trap of emphasizing differences between native-born white women, immigrants, and Black men.

[2] The name of the organization, components of their social outreach, and volunteers and staff are pseudonymous. The organization agreed to participate in the case study under the condition that it could remain anonymous so that it can protect itself and the women whom it serves in the Atlanta area.

started as a general inquiry of the organization's understanding of their Christian faith in relation to the organization's mission and the epidemic of trafficking.

Over the course of the nine months of research where I conducted eight in-depth interviews with staff and volunteers, attended staff and related meetings, and engaged in two months of weekly participation observation, I discovered a thread of evangelical whiteness that ran through their work. Whether it was how they oriented prospective volunteers through contemporary evangelical worship, the rhetoric used in meetings, or the methods of outreach, the normative assumption that forwarded the work was that white evangelical faith and values were the standard and telos. One of the ways that this thread became clear to me was during my participant observation or what I call "observant participation" work. As both an observer and full participant in the organization's work, I fully inculcated myself in their mission. Consequently, I became keenly aware of their whiteness, my otherness, and how that translated to how they perceived their work.

This chapter details my observant participation work with NDS and works toward a phenomenological account of evangelical whiteness through the excerpts and experiences of the research. In producing a phenomenology of evangelical whiteness, I attempt to narrate the effect of evangelical whiteness among the NDS workers and how that whiteness affected me. What follows are excerpts that demonstrate how evangelical Christianity functions to orient subjects to itself, how it judges bodies outside of itself, and finally how it understands the dynamics of race in relation to itself. Interspersed within the excerpts are my autoethnographic notes that narrate the impact of evangelical whiteness and how I perceive the ease with which it is transferred from body to body to continue its mission. I share these excerpts and experiences to hone in on the matter of ethnography as Christian theology and ethics. I take a definition of theology as the study of the lived experience of the Christian faith and, as such, ethnography can aid in understanding how that Christian faith plays out when it is used to address social issues. It puts flesh on the bones of our theological-ethical inquiries by inviting us into an incarnational moment where our words and the words of our research subjects become flesh and we dwell among the flesh.

A Brief History of Anti-Trafficking Work

Evangelical Christian social reform efforts from the eighteenth-century white slavery panic (Grittner 1990; Donovan 2006), the nineteenth-century anti-vice, temperance, and prohibition campaigns (Thompson 2013); to the twentieth- and twenty-first-century anti-trafficking campaigns (Campbell and Zimmerman 2014; Lobasz 2019), have coded white women as the primary subject. Whether the white woman appears as virtuous, vulnerable, or victorious, she has occupied a central position that propels the evangelical imagination and catalyzes the evangelical to act on behalf of a particular type of woman. As the white woman moves and morphs, she displaces women of color and makes them subjects of and subject to white evangelical Christian values. That is, to be read as properly recovered and properly woman, the Black woman and all nonwhite subjects must be formed in evangelical Christian notions of purity and piety.

Therefore, while recovery from sexual exploitation is the explicit concern of faith-based anti-trafficking ministries, how recovery is offered in anti-trafficking interventions is charged by a trend of racialization.

The response to sex trafficking is often organized by evangelical Christians who have a storied history with sex, purity, and missions. In exploring this history, I discovered a thread that connected several iterations of social outreach work in Christian missional history. From anti-white slavery campaigns and anti-vice work to prohibition and anti-trafficking, these movements were all connected by what historian H. Paul Thompson Jr. calls the "evangelical reform nexus."[3] The evangelical reform nexus is the intersection of religious practices, theologies, and ideologies that rooted the efforts of eighteenth- and nineteenth-century evangelical social reform movements. Thompson suggests that northern evangelicals in the eighteenth and nineteenth centuries attached their Christian beliefs of what was morally permissible and expedient to southern Blacks to obtain their obedience to temperance and prohibition measures. I follow Thompson by claiming that contemporary evangelical anti-trafficking movements continue the evangelical reform nexus by centering white evangelical religious practice, theology, and ideology as the concern and catalyst for saving work. In doing so, evangelicals create a moral social order in which women of color in the commercial sex trade are exposed to and have imposed upon them mores and values steeped in the practices and politics of evangelical whiteness.

Once I saw the thread and understood the historical dimensions of white evangelicals in social outreach work, I studied how this history repeats itself in the contemporary practice of anti-trafficking work through my qualitative research. I conducted my qualitative research with an eye on the appearance of old habits embedded in the new missional frame of evangelical whiteness and sought to create a phenomenology of evangelical whiteness. I focus on evangelical Christians and their missionary interventions because they are prevalent in anti-commercial sexual exploitation efforts. For example, Atlanta-based Passion City Church holds an annual conference named Passion that attracts 60,000 young Christians to worship and raises millions of dollars to assist in the fight against human trafficking and its resulting effects such as homelessness and joblessness. I also focus on this brand of Christian because numerous presidents from Bill Clinton to Donald J. Trump, who identified as Christians or are swayed by their conservative Christian constituents, launched anti-trafficking programs during their administrations.[4] Finally, I chose to study an evangelical anti-trafficking organization in response to American anthropologist Laura Nader's encouragement to anthropologists and other social scientists to "study up." "Studying up" in this case refers to studying a faith-based organization that wields power for better and for worse, their power having as much capacity to form as it does

---

[3] H. Paul Thompson, *A Most Stirring and Significant Episode: Religion and the Rise and Fall of Prohibition in Black Atlanta, 1865-1887* (DeKalb: Northern Illinois University Press, 2013), 16.

[4] Bill Clinton was the first president to issue a directive about the trafficking in women and girls. The Bush administration, for example, contributed $50 million to combating human trafficking and signed into law the Trafficking in Victims Protection Act; Barack Obama signed the Strengthening Protections Against Trafficking in Persons in Federal Contracts; and the Trump administration contributed $35 million to trafficking victims and signed the Fighting Online Sex Trafficking Act into legislation.

to deform. Though this is a study of a single organization, it is complicated by the fact that the organization is part of a network of faith-based trafficking efforts that typically function by advocating for Christian ideological commitments to remedy social ills. Such productive power warrants critical evaluation.

Encountering NDS

I initially encountered NDS in 2013 as a prospective volunteer. I, like many in attendance, was looking for a way to help with Atlanta's alleged trafficking problem.[5] Like so many anti-trafficking organizations in Atlanta, the mission of NDS is to reach, rescue, and restore women affected by the presence and pervasive nature of the commercial sex trade in Atlanta. Members of the NDS understand themselves as ambassadors of Christ who, through God, are responsible for reconciling people to God. They go about this reconciling work by visiting neighborhoods where commercial sex trades such as prostitution, stripping, brothels, escorts, and trafficking are most pervasive, and engaging women thought to work in these areas through casual conversation, prayer, and the distribution of goods such as cards and flowers. Every week, the organization loads volunteers into an unmarked van and takes to the streets and the strip clubs to build relationships with women and men.

NDS orients prospective volunteers using two different vignettes: pimped and prostituted young Black girls in one frame and white women who escaped trafficking in the other. I was startled by the visual contrast between the hapless young Black girl who could not escape the grips of street prostitution and the well-coiffed white women who testified to being redeemed from escort services and strip clubs. That visual image startled and stayed with me. In 2018, I attended another orientation and found the same script was running. Furthermore, between the first orientation and the second one I attended, I noticed how white evangelicals were operative in the anti-trafficking movement,[15] and I wanted to understand the logic of that dominance.

Qualitatively Studying Evangelical Whiteness

What I intend by the term evangelical is not just a descriptor of a Christian-identifying person whose mission is to spread the Gospel of Jesus through their works and deeds. Instead, the term contends with how that Gospel mission becomes a way of extending theological and political power into society. Religion scholar Anthea Butler suggests that evangelicals are concerned with maintaining the cultural and racial whiteness that they have transmitted to the public.[6] Therefore, evangelical power exerts its

---

[5]   I say alleged because details are scant regarding how and to what extent trafficking is unfolding in Atlanta. Part of why the statistical details are scant is because trafficking victims and suspects are hard to trace, let alone codify in a statistical data set.

[6]   Anthea D. Butler, "White Evangelical Racism: The Politics of Morality in America," in *White Evangelical Racism: The Politics of Morality in America* (Chapel Hill: The University of North Carolina Press, 2021), 11–12.

authority in broad social contexts, dictating the norms not only for social action but social behavior. The moniker "white evangelical" is in recognition of two things, the first being the demographic whiteness of evangelical Christianity as demonstrated by a 2018 Pew Forum survey that shows 76 percent of evangelical Protestants in the United States are white.[7] "White evangelical" also signifies a mode of evangelicalism that privileges whiteness. It signifies the biopower of white evangelicals whose ideologies around morality and purity—racial, sexual, and social—bolster their ranks while deforming anyone who falls outside of the ranks. It is that whiteness operating under the banner of Christian humanitarianism that is the site of contestation this chapter engages and attempts to uncover through qualitative research methods such as participant observation.

Whiteness, then, functions as a racial, cultural, and political category that shapes social behavior, both that of its host and of its guests. In the context of evangelicalism, whiteness positions itself as the face of moral movements that protect and defend the supremacy of pure white womanhood by establishing norms such as sexual purity and social respectability as viral qualities. The transmission of evangelical whiteness ensures that the center of white Christian evangelicalism that establishes the boundaries of purity and embodiment holds. While evangelical whiteness initially needs a white body to exist, it can transmit its culture, beliefs, values, and practices to nonwhite bodies. This process of transmission is the content of the phenomenology of evangelical whiteness I constructed from my qualitative research. It uses the evangelical reform nexus to verify the common strains of Christian mission work through participation observation that provides evidence of how the religious practice, theology, and values of NDS were bodily performed.

Observing the evangelical reform nexus at work was not only about what NDS workers verbally articulated but what their embodiment communicated when they encountered Black women in commercial sex work. The idea of providing a phenomenological account of evangelical whiteness explores how whiteness is distributed under the guise of well-intentioned Christianity and how one might read and interpret that movement. The phenomenology of white evangelicalism exposes the social behavior, habits, and religious practices that are inseparable from evangelical action in the world. Feminist scholar Sara Ahmed suggests that the phenomenology of whiteness helps us to notice institutional habits and brings to the surface what is hidden or "behind."[8] What is behind for Ahmed is whiteness that trails behind actions. She suggests that white people "do not get 'stressed' in their encounters with objects or others, as their whiteness goes unnoticed."[9] Ahmed argues that white bodies do not typically face their whiteness, and that they are not typically oriented toward their whiteness because they dwell in a world where whiteness is the norm. When other bodies lag behind, the body of whiteness extends its reach to impart whiteness to the

---

[7] David Masci and Gregory A. Smith, "Following Rev. Billy Graham's Death, 5 Facts about U.S. Evangelical Protestants," *Pew Research Center*, July 27, 2020, https://www.pewresearch.org/fact-tank/2018/03/01/5-facts-about-u-s-evangelical-protestants/#:~:text=As%20of%202014%2C%202011%25%20of,U.S.%20public%20as%20a%20whole.

[8] Sara Ahmed, "A Phenomenology of Whiteness," *Feminist Theory* 8, no. 2 (2007): 149–68, 149.

[9] Ibid., 156.

other. In doing so, the other becomes legible and can be absorbed into a preexisting system of production.

Orienting Whiteness

An NDS prospective volunteer's first encounter with the organization is through the worshipful atmosphere of orientation. During my research, I attended three orientations that took place over the course of a year in 2019. Although worship and prayer may seem like innocuous practices, a critical reflection of their usage in the organization reveals that a significant part of NDS's work is in orienting the individual to the organization's ethos of evangelical whiteness transmitted through those spiritual practices. In adhering to these spiritual practices, the volunteer is formed to will themselves to do good through worship and prayer. In this way, I begin to shape the phenomenology of evangelical whiteness by following Ahmed's claim that whiteness involves a form of orientation.[10] Of this, she says, "The starting point for orientation is the point from which the world unfolds: the 'here' of the body, and the 'where' of its dwelling. Given this, orientations are about the intimacy of bodies and their dwelling places. If orientations are about how we begin from 'here,' then they involve unfolding."[11] I suggest that the "here" of the body that informs the NDS orientation is that of the white body and how it moves in obedience to its conception of God.

As prospective and current volunteers and staff mill about the orientation room, the sounds of Cory Asbury, Hillsong, and other Contemporary Christian Music (CCM) artists singing about God's love and saving grace bid them to settle into the space. A person attending an NDS orientation is quite likely to encounter Cory Asbury's song "Reckless Love" because the song's main theme is rescue. The popular CCM song is used during the worship segment of orientation, and the swelling bridge, "There's no shadow you won't light up, mountain you won't climb up, coming after me," encapsulates the affective nature of the work of NDS.[12] The organization is in hot pursuit of women entangled in the commercial sex trade in Atlanta. They are also in pursuit of people whose hearts are moved by the harrowing tales of the trafficking in women. "Reckless Love" and similar songs that demonstrate God's interest in and hot pursuit of people who have gone astray set the tone for what prospective volunteers feel, hear, and see during orientation.[13] This is the affective work of NDS because it creates spaces that remind people of their conversion experience or of the presence of God and sweeps them up in that emotion to move them to action. This sweeping often gathers individuals in a fit of emotions and moves them to act.

---

[10] Ibid., 150.
[11] Ibid., 151.
[12] Cory Asbury, *Reckless Love* (Jason Ingram, Paul Mabury, 2017).
[13] The length of the orientation varies based on the location. I attended the two-day orientation and the one-day orientation, both packing in the same amount of orientation content and materials for prospective volunteers to consider.

The 2022 documentary "Hillsong: A Megachurch Exposed" demonstrates how the chord progression in CCM is composed to sweep people up in emotionalism because they confuse a modulation with the move of the Spirit. Journalist Kelsey McKinney says, "It's easy to mistake emotional manipulation for a movement of God. Are you crying because the Lord is staging some sort of intervention in your life or are you crying because the chord structure is built to make you cry?"[14] Similarly in orientation, NDS sets the atmosphere to make bodies feel as much as they make minds understand. This begins with the bodies in worship:

> Before I spoke a word, You were singing over me/You have been so, so good to me
> Before I took a breath, You breathed Your life in me/You have been so so kind to me

My first time hearing "Reckless Love" was during an NDS orientation, and I found myself both moved and confused. I was moved by the notion of God being so persistent about recovering one who had gone astray, a notion affirmed by the Gospel parable of the Lost Sheep, which tells of God (as shepherd) leaving ninety-nine sheep to track down the one who is lost, and once recovered, throwing a party to celebrate that one's return. It is difficult not to be moved by the idea as captured in scripture and Asbury's iteration where one might imagine God shining a flashlight down dark alleys, climbing mountains, and kicking down doors. I took note of how effective this orientation worship was on me. I found myself caught up as tears rolled down my face, and I placed the image of helpless women alongside the image of a valiant savior cutting through darkness to save her.

I felt a pang of embarrassment at my emotional reaction as I stood in the room as a researcher but in that moment, I also understood what was afoot. I looked around the room full of predominantly white women, some white men, and a handful of Black people, and saw most of them with eyes closed, tears streaming down their faces, and fully committed to the moment. This was a centering moment. This practice ensures that volunteers and workers are continually entranced by a feeling of being called by God to save people. This feeling empowers workers and volunteers to work under the aegis of the white savior complex which moves people to action through emotion.

A critical look at "Reckless Love" in relation to anti-trafficking work upsets the unequivocal notion of God as redeemer. How redemption occurs in this song is intricately bound to how women in trafficking experience boundedness and captivity. This can be easily overlooked by those who approach the song and the idea of anti-trafficking interventions as categorically good work that requires no critical intervention, only good intention. These people are often motivated by individual ideas of what constitutes goodness and good work. The wave of emotion that "Reckless Love" elicits in those who attend the NDS orientation piques their interest, and thus motivated they begin the process of becoming a volunteer with the organization. The process of becoming an NDS volunteer immerses participants in the religious practices of worship through music and prayer that the organization uses to orient and prepare

---

[14] *Hillsong: A Megachurch Exposed* (United States: Breaklight Pictures).

people for the work. While the type of music NDS engages to set the atmosphere for the orientations may seem innocuous, I believe that the choice of CCM not only communicates a message about the posture of those desiring to rescue women, it also reinforces the productive power of evangelical Christian whiteness.

As Larry Eskridge notes in a study of evangelical Christian worship, the stock image of evangelical worship is so recognizable that it is a visual cliché. Its practitioners are usually middle class and white, and appear in corporate-looking auditoriums or sanctuaries, swaying to the electrified music of "praise bands," their eyes closed, their enraptured faces tilted heavenward, a hand (or hands) raised to the sky.[15] In her study of prayer in evangelical churches, anthropologist Tanya Luhrmann describes CCM in detail when she says,

> Here in these songs, the remarkable God of this kind of church shines forth. Rarely do you hear of his judgment; always you are aware of his love; never, ever, does a song suggest you fear his anger. He is a person: lover, father, of course, but more remarkably, friend. Best friend. One song begins with breathless amazement that God pays attention to the singer, that he hears the singer, thinks of the singer, loves him or her. Then the chorus, clean, simple and repetitive, as these songs tend to be.[16]

Luhrmann describes the general tone of worship via CCM, a tone that effectively draws listeners closer to God through the notion that God is a friend who sticks closer than a brother and is not punitive. Rather, God is always present with open arms, and as such, listeners (in this case participants in NDS's orientation) are emboldened to play God in their own effort to mimic the radical hospitality illustrated in the songs they sing. Empowered by motivating lyrics, this is the white savior complex in action. This is also whiteness in action because it is transported through a musical genre that is almost exclusively white.

In a 2015 study, Omotayo O. Banjo and Kesha Morant Williams explored attitudes toward Gospel and CCM that demonstrated how these genres of Christian music are racialized.[17] The racialization is demonstrated in the way that the Christian music that white artists create is labeled as Christian, while the Christian music that Black artists create is labeled as "other" or Gospel. While one could argue that Black Christian music's label as "Gospel" is affirmative because Gospel means "good news," Gospel music is often segregated from the broader Christian music industry and is not offered robust marketing or distribution deals. Furthermore, Banjo and Williams's study demonstrates that CCM, unlike Gospel, is dominant in themes about personal motivation and perseverance; therefore, it empowers those in places of privilege more than it signals them to pay attention to the world around them.

[15] Larry Eskridge, "Slain by the Music," *Religion Online*, February 25, 2021, https://www.religion-online.org/article/slain-by-the-music/.
[16] T. M. Luhrmann, *When God Talks Back: Understanding the American Evangelical Relationship with God* (New York: Alfred A. Knopf, 2012), 4–5.
[17] Omotayo O. Banjo and Kesha Morant Williams, "A House Divided? Christian Music in Black and White," *Journal of Media and Religion* 10, no. 3 (2011): 115–37.

CCM nurtures listeners' personal relationship with God and satisfies their craving to be seen by God.

What the racialization of CCM and Gospel marks is a perceptual difference about the concerns of white and Black listeners. Banjo and William draw out a startling claim that indicates white Christians focus on themselves and their salvation, while Black Christians focus on more communal notions of salvation. This necessarily troubles how one reads the utilization of CCM in organizations such as NDS because it doubles down on white Christian culture that dominates the space. The worship during orientation disarms the prospective volunteers with its impassioned plea for people to come out of the dark places of life and bids the listener to come out of the dark to save others from a similar fate. Worship likewise marks the time of preparation before going into outreach. Time is of the essence on outreach nights, so getting lost in worship is not possible. Yet the leaders ensure there is an opportunity to listen or sing along to a CCM song during the ride into the neighborhoods where outreach takes place.

Reckoning with Race

NDS has conducted outreach work for over a decade, driving into neighborhoods with the same van and, mostly, with the same demographic of volunteers—predominantly white women. The leaders often talk about how people recognize the organization when they come out to do outreach. The van, which they call the "Jesus van," is unremarkable except for the fact that it is large and white, and on the nights when there are many volunteers, there are multiple Jesus vans canvassing the area, with predominantly white people (women and men) hopping out to encounter the women on the streets. On most nights, I was either the only Black person in outreach or one of less than a handful, always outnumbered by young, white, and female volunteers.

During the initial nights of attending outreach, I observed an interesting pattern: though I was a regular fixture among the volunteers because of my research, the volunteers came on a rotating basis and therefore it was uncommon to see the same person two weeks in a row. I never learned the reason for this but speculate that few people are interested in spending back-to-back weekends praying in a van or out on the streets with women with varying levels of need.

On several occasions when we stepped out of the van to speak with a woman on the street, she would look at one of these new young white woman volunteers and say, "Oh, I remember you from the last time, do you remember me?" The girl would often say that she is sure she is not who the woman is thinking of, but after a while she would concede to the woman's recognition of her. All the while I stood beside these white girls/women and went unacknowledged. I couldn't say, "Hey, I was here last week," because that would be jockeying for unnecessary attention, and to what end could I state my presence among these women? Do the women need to see me as a Black woman like them or, simply, a woman there to help? Does this question of race even matter in the face of such precarity?

After a few weeks of being a phantom in the streets compared to the young white women, I segued into observing the racial reconciliation meetings that the NDS higher-ups organized. These weekly meetings started around the same time as my research with the organization, and I was invited to attend to gain insight into how the organization thinks about race. The executive director and her supervisor excitedly spoke to me about the potential of these meetings in relation to my presence in the organization because they believed that "now is the time." As someone who has a "heart for"[18] the work of NDS and who is Black and paying attention to race in ways that they weren't, my arrival was perceived as a gift. The goals of the racial reconciliation meetings as listed in the weekly agendas were to "create a safe space to discuss issues of race, justice and unity and how they affect one's Christian walk and work"; "to educate and inform ourselves on the issues of racism in the world and in the church"; and to "better equip us to pray into this issue." These meetings took place over the course of three months and were usually sparsely attended by staff. Even the incentive of providing lunch did not compel a critical mass of the staff of thirteen to attend the meeting.

Week after week, the small dispensation of attendees discussed YouTube videos, documentaries, and current events regarding race and shared their perspectives. Their method reminded me of an activity to which I've been party in numerous church settings: the "lemon squeeze." In the lemon squeeze, people gather to air their grievances with one another so that they can wipe the slate clean and start over. The racial reconciliation meetings mirrored the lemon squeeze in that the majority of what happened was people airing their grievances about how Christianity, broadly construed, constructed their views around race and how they feel bereft of the capacity to resolve it. During one meeting, they appealed to the work of Dr. Soong-Chan Rah whose 2017 keynote speech at NEXT Church[19] introduced them to the concept of the "pet or threat." This concept suggests that the white gaze upon Black people, Black men in particular, places them in two closed categories, pet or threat. At Rah's words, the meeting participants nodded and moaned in agreement, and for twenty-five minutes, he had their rapt attention. After Rah finished his excursus on pets or threats, the leader of the meeting turned off the video and invited everyone to share their reactions. Three of the five people in the room shared from their vantage points. A white woman married to a Black man marveled at how she became convicted about the verbiage she used to talk about Black people—whether it is appropriate to use "Black" or "African American"—and how that has shifted her understanding. The other two respondents, both white men, shared that they understand they must "put down their power" and "be open to hearing from different perspective . . . even from the upper class." I sat on the other end of the table rather awkwardly and thankful that I, as a researcher, could bypass the moment. But that was not to be.

"Nicole, what do you think about the pet or threat concept?"

I looked up from my notebook and laughed nervously. "Technically," I said, "as a researcher I am here but not here, and I don't want to muddy things by injecting my

---

[18] "Heart for" is an evangelical vernacular for demonstrating passion for a person, place, or thing.
[19] Soong-Chan Rah, "National Gathering Keynote," *Next Church*, April 6, 2017, https://www.youtube.com/watch?v=RgHCJ3eu6IA (accessed March 31, 2021).

perspective." They all nodded in agreement and let me off the hook while I went back to writing my notes. It was at that moment that it became clear to me that though I came in as a researcher, I represented something more to them. I was the Black woman who could speak for Black people in general and might be able to assuage any guilt they had about doing the right thing the wrong way. I learned as much during my in-depth interviews when one volunteer disclosed that the executive director was struck and "super burdened" by our conversations because "I'm just now realizing the harm that we could have been doing by not talking about these things and by not training people on these things." Yet, from my vantage point, the racial reconciliation meetings, my meetings with the executive director, and the interviews barely scratched the surface of what NDS needed to reckon with. I came to grips with just how much they were only scratching the surface when I continued to watch Rah on my own and was led to his dissertation to find a line that the group skipped over in the racial reconciliation meeting. While Rah spoke about the ability of the gaze to determine the worth of people, which was his prerequisite statement before his pet or threat excursus, he said, "Salvific viability oftentimes is connected to a proximation to whiteness."[20] No one in the room reacted to this statement. But maybe they would have reacted to the full statement from his dissertation which says, "White supremacy results in the assumption that salvific viability is rooted in approximation to whiteness. With the assertion of Jesus as a white male, approximation to a white Jesus becomes the expression of redemption. The normative value of whiteness generates a narrative of white triumphalism."[21] Rah spared NEXT Church the true weight of his statement and thus NDS was spared as well. Given this, NDS could continue to major in the minor issues of their dealings with race and pat themselves on the back for doing just enough.

During my in-depth interviews which occurred during the summer of 2020, I posed the question of how racial and cultural awareness informs how the volunteers encounter women. One after another, volunteers responded that it was not a matter of Black and white, but a matter of helping people. Jenny, a volunteer with the jail ministry, pointedly said,

> I've always seen it as we are just helping women. I haven't noticed anyone talking about different things, about different races, and I probably wouldn't like it if I did. Obviously, I'm going to notice if someone's Black or white, that's a part of who they are, but I feel like we should be more about just helping these women regardless of whatever race they are.

I was struck by her comment for a variety of reasons, the most significant being that I conducted these interviews during the height of the protests in response to the murders of Ahmaud Arbery, Breonna Taylor, and George Floyd. I, as a Black researcher, contended with my all-white-identifying interviewees bristling at questions around race as if race were an expletive. Bodies squirmed and tensed up, speech was defensive

---

[20] Soong-Chan Rah, "In Whose Image: The Emergence, Development, and Challenge of African-American Evangelicalism" (dissertation, 2016), 143.
[21] Rah, "National Gathering Keynote."

at times, and in general, it felt as though I ought to rush through the questions for fear of interviewees deciding to opt out of the process. Generally, volunteers said that NDS leaders encouraged them toward their work and the belief that NDS stands in solidarity with Black lives.

I was troubled by the interview responses and by NDS's response at a pivotal moment in public awareness of the harms of systemic racism. I began to question whether my pursuit of the question of race and racialization in this work was necessary. Was I overstating its significance because of my positionality? I wondered whether social ethicists could afford to jettison concern about race in faith-based work because the fact that the work is being done (albeit by someone else) should count for something? Yet, when I reflected on NDS's work through the lens of the participant observation work and the in-depth interviews, I realized that my questions and concerns were not unfounded. My questions, concerns, and critiques about the ongoing racialization of anti-trafficking work are grounded in the insidious history of Christian reform movements. NDS operates within a history it does not know, deploying racialized practices it does not see.

Thinking about Qualitatively Studying Evangelical Whiteness

I have described NDS work and their perception of it. I have also shared my experience with the powerful lure of their orientation, their affect in encountering Black women, and their process around acknowledging and processing race. It was important to me in this project to, as anthropologist Laura Nader suggested in the 1960s, "study up" which is to include the "study of the colonizers rather than the colonized, the culture of power rather than the culture of the powerless, the culture of affluence rather than the perceived culture of poverty." The white evangelical culture of anti-trafficking work and activism is a culture of affluence and power. Given this, my role as a researcher was not only to conduct research but to cut through that power. My observant participation work resulted in my presence challenging the organization's understanding of their work along cultural and race lines. Placing my Black woman body in the way of their work reversed the gaze and the notion of intervention. I did this to think of the work of studying up in the twenty-first century as an embodied way of poking at the stronghold of whiteness and what might be the problems and promises therein.

As a researcher driven by qualitative methods, it was important to distill the data into a narrative form for two reasons. The first was to let the data speak for itself through a presentation of stories that show the reader what I observed with little to no theoretical interference. I attempted to let the data speak for itself through story and only after the story is told, to respond with analysis. Second, I distilled the data into a narrative form to reflect how Christianity and its attendant practices are guided by stories. Whether it is from scripture or living out Christian faith, the Christian life is oriented by stories, the stories Christians tell about God or about themselves and others in relation to God.

As a Christian ethicist whose work is informed by the womanist method of granting experience epistemic privilege, I use phenomenology to plumb the depth of my embodied experience within NDS as well as to explore the phenomena of evangelical whiteness as it is dispensed through the organization's body. In so doing, I extract what is discernible through vision about the contours of evangelical whiteness. What behavior do white evangelicals exhibit in social outreach that can be patternized and even traced to the evangelical reform nexus? To obtain the preliminary answers, Maurice Merleau-Ponty's notion of vision as not just a neutral recording of the visible but vision as a consequence of learning to see was instructive. Given this, I argue that white evangelicals learn to see themselves in relation to those raced as nonwhite and not discernibly Christian or pure as those that require Christian intervention. As philosopher Alia Al-Saji suggests, "vision not only *makes* visible, but it does so *differentially* according to sedimented habits of seeing according to the tacit ways our bodies relate to and move in the world, allowing certain aspects of that world to be foregrounded."[22] My observations of NDS's work in orientation, outreach, and organizational meeting reflected how their vision, despite their good intentions, calcified beyond repair, making them unable to perceive how their social outreach practices sustain the problem of evangelical whiteness.

---

[22] Emily S. Lee and Alia Al-Saji, "A Phenomenology of Hesitation," Essay. *In Living Alterities: Phenomenology, Embodiment, and Race* (Albany: SUNY Press, 2015), 133–72.

12

Inhabiting the Aftermath of Firearm-Caused Violence

Guns and the Practice of Vigil Keeping

Michael Grigoni

Ruth Behar, in *The Vulnerable Observer: Anthropology That Breaks Your Heart*, uses a simple but illuminative set of metaphors to describe anthropological inquiry. "For me," she writes, "anthropology is about embarking on . . . a voyage through a long tunnel. Always, as an anthropologist, you go elsewhere, but the voyage is never simply about making a trip."[1] Rather, as she goes on to describe, it involves something more fraught and complicated: the attempt to enter a lifeworld not your own, and the struggle to write about it in the form of field notes, write-ups, and—eventually—full-fledged prose. For Behar, these efforts, characterized by varying fits and starts, constitute "the stopping places along the way." Yet, anthropological inquiry holds out a certain promise of culmination: "At the end of the voyage, if you are lucky, you catch a glimpse of a lighthouse, and you are grateful."[2]

In 2017, I embarked on an ethnographic voyage into the world of evangelical Christian handgun culture in Durham, North Carolina, and its environs. I sought to develop a Christian ethics of handguns, and to do so I was compelled to begin with the experience of those who claim to follow a crucified savior and yet feel the need to have a gun in their lives. Growing up on the west coast in a home in which my father, a Roman Catholic, kept a gun did not temper the "strangeness" I felt as I visited gun shops, attended church security seminars, and spent time on the range with my interlocutors. Yet I sought to make these experiences "familiar"—or at the very least, less "strange"—through my use of ethnographic methods.[3] To ensure I was a participant as much as an observer, I purchased a semiautomatic handgun and brought it into my home.

---

[1] Ruth Behar, *The Vulnerable Observer: Anthropology that Breaks Your Heart* (Boston: Beacon Press, 1996), 2–3.
[2] Ibid., 3.
[3] The language of "strange" and "familiar" derives from the adage that anthropological inquiry renders the strange familiar and the familiar strange. See Matthew Engelke, *How to Think Like an Anthropologist* (Princeton: Princeton University Press, 2018), 6.

I carried out my fieldwork under the shadow of two devastating church shootings, the Charleston church shooting of 2015 and the Sutherland Springs church shooting of 2017, both of which, I came to find, shaped the imaginary of my interlocutors in profound ways. Through participant observation and qualitative interviews, I learned that my interlocutors use guns to secure those bodies that present as vulnerable to them—their body, their family's bodies, and their church's body—which I describe as taking up a posture of care with a tool of violence.[4]

Toward the end of my first year of fieldwork, I was invited by a friend who was familiar with my project to attend a vigil for a young African American man who had been killed by gunfire earlier that year in Durham. There I was introduced to the vigil ministry of the Religious Coalition for a Nonviolent Durham (RCND), where I encountered a new community and new set of interlocutors that would not only become part of my study but would radically reorient my reflections. And there I found something that appeared to me as Behar's lighthouse—a different orientation to guns by persons of Christian faith, an orientation that attempts to enact a form of care in the aftermath of firearm-caused violence rather than in its anticipation.

This chapter offers a thick description of the vigil ministry of the RCND. Through ethnographic vignettes and an analysis of the vigil, I display how the RCND engages in a form of care in response to the tragic and enduring presence of violent death—much of it firearm-caused—in Durham. I consider how the vigil ministry and other key practices of the RCND do not simply mark and memorialize the impact of guns on Durham's common life but seek to foster new forms of relationality among those who gather at the vigil and among those who participate in the broader set of practices facilitated by the Coalition.

Further, I describe how keeping vigil discloses the world in a particular way. Through engagement with James Cone and Kelly Brown Douglas, I argue that the vigil discloses the presence of crucified persons in our common life—the victims of firearm-caused homicide, the majority of whom are young men of color. In doing so, I render a contrast between my Christian handgun-owning interlocutors and vigil keepers. If the first, like Peter in the Garden of Gethsemane, adopt an armed posture in the anticipation of violence, the latter, like Joseph of Arimathea, emplace themselves in its aftermath to care for the crucified body. I conclude by naming the invitation issued by the vigil for Christian handgun owners, arguing that a Christian ethical response to the place of the gun in the United States requires that they—and we—begin to keep vigil.

---

[4] During my fieldwork, which I carried out from 2017 to 2019, I engaged in participant observation and conducted qualitative interviews with twenty-five male Christian handgun owners, the majority of whom identifies as white evangelical Protestants.

The Vigil

As I prepared to attend a vigil for the first time, I found myself preoccupied by questions I had not asked since beginning my fieldwork:[5] What should I wear? Will I stand out? Can I take notes in my field notebook? And the most burning of all: Will my presence be tolerated? I tortured myself with these questions during my initial visits to gun sites. With time, their intensity faded, but as I prepared for the vigil they rushed forcefully back into view, reminding me that I was, in a sense, beginning again, setting foot on new Malinowskian shores.

My intensity of feeling likewise had something to do with the site itself. Unlike gun shops and shooting ranges, I was approaching the literal site of a "wound."[6] The vigil was being held for a young African American man who had been killed earlier in the year at the age of thirty-five. Further, it was being held on what would have been his thirty-sixth birthday, and in the neighborhood where he had been killed. I was preparing to inhabit a space that had been violently broken. What would it mean for me to do so? How would I, a stranger and outsider, inhabit this space sensitively, but also in a way that would enable me to advance my research? I did not know how to answer these questions, and I am not sure I can answer them now. All I knew was that this would require a kind of inhabitance different from that to which I had become accustomed thus far.

As I crossed into east Durham from its west side, it began to rain. Exiting the freeway, I found myself in a neighborhood where I had never been before. Small, run-down, rectangular brick homes in tiny lots lined the street. Turning a corner, I saw a cluster of umbrellas hovering above a line of cars along the side of the road. I parked and fished an umbrella from my trunk, clear vinyl with pink polka dots. Perfect, just perfect, I thought. I opened the umbrella and walked toward the gathering, deciding at the last minute to leave my field notebook behind.

As I neared, I took in my surroundings further. A school of blue balloons floated above the mass of umbrellas. Nearly everyone walking toward the gathering was African American, and some appeared to be coming to the vigil from their own homes in the neighborhood. Many of the attendees wore light blue shirts with the photo and name of the deceased. Others wore matching, crimson-colored shirts with the name of a local Baptist church. There were about seventy-five people present, seven or eight of whom appeared to be white, the rest African American. Everyone stood in damp dirt, in a set of concentric rings beneath a grove of trees, trying to avoid the rain. There were three rings in total, a tightly formed inner ring that contained, I would later determine, family and friends of the deceased; then a looser ring of people; and a broadened-out ring of people standing outside of the grove. I decided to stand under a tree, somewhere between the second and third rings, somewhere between foreground and background, participant and observer.

---

[5] This section originally appeared in Michael Grigoni, "Worlds of Sound," *Comment* 39, no. 2 (Summer 2021): 69–76. *Comment* (www.comment.org) is a publication of Cardus (www.cardus.ca).

[6] See Mary McClintock Fulkerson, *Places of Redemption: Theology for a Worldly Church* (Oxford and New York: Oxford University Press, 2007), 12–18.

The vigil began with a call to prayer. I lowered my head and closed my eyes but found myself unable to quiet my mind. I was trying—perhaps too hard—to acclimate myself while also making mental notes about what I was hearing and observing. The vigil raised some uncomfortable questions: Did the absence of the field notebook alter my subject position? Was I still an ethnographer, in other words? Or had I morphed into something else? Perhaps I was present as a Christian and nothing more, one who was wrestling with the challenges and confusions of the issues I was studying, and who needed a place to listen, discern, and pray. Or maybe, as one who had brought a gun into his life, my subject position was closer to my interlocutors—a thought that made me more than a little uncomfortable. Maybe I was acting as a proxy for my interlocutors. Maybe, in a play on Loïc Wacquant's phrase, I had, in some sense, "go[ne] native armed."[7] And in joining the circle, I sought to discover what, if anything, could be done about the gun in my life, as well as the guns in their lives.

As the prayer ended, those wearing the crimson-colored shirts began to sway and sing an acapella hymn in a call-and-response style. I later learned they were choir members of the local Baptist church identified on their shirts. There were references to "Exodus" and "Pharaoh," and I thought if I could remember enough of the lyrics, I could perhaps identify the hymn later at home. But these thoughts soon dissipated. As I listened, concerns about my subject position—whether ethnographer, Christian, or handgun owner—dropped away. The impulse to capture and inscribe experience gave way to a desire to quietly listen—simply to inhabit experience. I was becoming what Charles Briggs and Clara Mantini-Briggs term an "overhearer," one who, in listening to a mourning community, finds themselves on the edge of "a conversation that is not for them."[8] In overhearing these sung laments, I became "interpellated by their sensory, ethical, affective, and bodily demands."[9] Listening in this register shifted my attention from myself to the gathered, mourning community, and to the individual being memorialized, locating me in an "affective and ethical soundscape" that began to make demands of me.[10]

After the hymn, a female African American minister entered the space enclosed by the inner ring and read from Psalm 34: "The Lord is close to the brokenhearted," she intoned, "and saves those who are crushed in spirit." She gave a reflection on the deceased's life, emphasizing the importance of the community standing together, gathered in vigil. Persons in the inner ring wept while she spoke.

She then asked if anyone wanted to share a reflection about the deceased. An African American woman spoke about her experience of losing a child to gun violence and extended her love and support to the family of the deceased. Others spoke: a representative of the Baptist church pledged the support of the church for the family and the neighborhood; a younger African American man from the neighborhood voiced his admiration for the deceased; and a cousin of the deceased spoke of how she saw him as her "little brother."

---

[7] Loïc Wacquant, "The Body, the Ghetto, and the Penal State," *Qualitative Sociology* 32 (2009): 119.
[8] Charles Briggs and Clara Mantini-Briggs, *Tell Me Why My Children Died: Rabies, Indigenous Knowledge, and Communicative Justice* (Durham: Duke University Press, 2016), 207.
[9] Briggs and Mantini-Briggs, *Tell Me Why My Children Died*, 220.
[10] Ibid.

After the minister's reflection and the sharing of thoughts by family and community members, the director of the RCND, a young white man in jeans and a light green polo, came into the center of the circle and read the "death resolution." I would later learn this was done toward the conclusion of every vigil. The death resolution is a statement prepared by the RCND that is both archived in the Coalition's records and given to the family members of the deceased. The resolution honors and recognizes the life of the deceased and commits them to God.

The choir then sang another hymn in call-and-response style. Lastly, an older African American woman spoke, identifying the space beneath the small grove of trees as a "brush harbor." "Our ancestors used to pray in places like this," she said in a slow, gravelly voice, "in brush harbors. Maybe we need to return to having church like that, out here in the open." Brush harbors were places where enslaved Africans assembled and worshipped away from the eyes of the master; they were secret, concealed places.[11] Upon hearing her words, I realized that in all of my efforts to understand the place of the gun in US American life, this particular site had been out of view. In my movement from gun shops, ranges, and churches with armed security, I had never entered this neighborhood. The vigil remained a brush harbor, a hidden place, obscured from the eyes of the master; a manifestation of how guns and race in the United States condition ways not only of seeing but of not seeing—a recognition that emerged for me in the "overhearing."[12]

The vigil ended with gatherers turning from the grove toward the side of the road. As they did so, they released the balloons into the air, shouting "Happy birthday!" and cheering. I stood on the periphery and watched.

The Religious Coalition for a Nonviolent Durham

Founded in 1992 by Leslie Dunbar and Reverend Mel Williams, the RCND has remained, over the course of nearly three decades, a steady fixture in a changing Southern city. As with any social organization, the RCND has evolved over time: its leadership has changed, and the practices in which it engages have both expanded in number and shifted in emphasis. Its impact has even inspired a book-length account of its ministry and mission.[13] For my purposes, however, the significance of the RCND lies in how it embodies a particular orientation to the place of guns in US American life—one that takes as its point of departure the tragic effect of gun violence on the common life of Durham, North Carolina.

Against the backdrop of a revitalized downtown and rapidly gentrifying neighborhoods, twenty-five to forty-five people are murdered with guns each year in

---

[11] For an influential treatment of the brush harbor (also referred to as "hush harbor" or "brush arbor"), see Albert J. Raboteau, *Slave Religion: The "Invisible Institution" in the Antebellum South* (New York: Oxford University Press, 1978), 212–19.
[12] Briggs and Mantini-Briggs, *Tell Me Why My Children Died*, 207.
[13] Samuel Wells and Marcia A. Owen, *Living Without Enemies: Being Present in the Midst of Violence* (Downers Grove: IVP Books, 2011).

Durham.[14] In keeping with national trends, most victims of firearm-caused homicide in Durham are young African American men.[15] The numbers, considered in and of themselves, are staggering. But these losses indicate the presence of a broader environment of insecurity and precarity in Durham. In 2022, for example, in addition to forty-one firearm-caused homicides, 770 shootings were reported to the Durham Police Department, and 206 people were struck by nonfatal gunfire.[16] It is precisely this state of affairs to which the RCND attempts to fashion a response—the myriad everyday forms of firearm-caused violence in the city of Durham.

The nature of this response has shifted over the course of the Coalition's existence. In its early years, the RCND focused on pursuing legislative changes on the municipal level regarding guns. In keeping with the orientation of many organizations seeking to reduce gun violence, the RCND initially believed that the solution to gun violence lay in passing and strengthening municipal ordinances that would reduce the number of guns in Durham. The RCND assumed, in other words, "that what it needed to do was create policy."[17] Among its earliest efforts was to rally support for the passage of the 1994 Federal Assault Weapons Ban, as well as local firearms-related ordinances for Durham.[18] Yet soon thereafter, as a result of NRA organizing, the North Carolina General Assembly passed a state preemption law that prevented local municipalities from passing ordinances that would restrict what state law permits regarding firearms.[19] Its efforts to curb gun violence through policy change invalidated, the RCND was forced to rethink its approach.

What emerged was an approach to the issue of gun violence in Durham characterized by "being with" rather than "working for," as Samuel Wells and Marcia A. Owen name it in their book, *Living Without Enemies: Being Present in the Midst of Violence*. Given its focus on policy, the earlier, "working for" approach, reinforced a benefactor–client relationship between the RCND and those it aimed to serve, one in which both parties could ultimately remain "strangers to one another" as the Coalition pursued legislative change.[20] Wells and Owen describe the "working for" model as:

> the conventional model of engagement across class and race boundaries. One person has a need, while the other person has skills, availability and willingness to help. This latter person conventionally spends a lot of time working those skills up to a very high standard and consequently makes those skills available in specific circumstances under strict rules. This is what is known as being a professional.[21]

---

[14] Philip J. Cook and Audrey Vila, "Gun Violence in Durham, NC, 2017–2021: Investigation and Court Processing of Fatal and Nonfatal Shootings," Sanford School of Public Policy and Wilson Center for Science and Justice at Duke Law, Duke University, February 2023, 6, www.law.duke.edu/sites/default/files/images/centers/wcsj/Durham_Shootings.pdf; "Durham Police Department Shooting Data: Year-to-Date through December 31, 2022," *City of Durham*, www.durhamnc.gov/ArchiveCenter/ViewFile/Item/6111 (accessed September 30, 2023).

[15] Cook and Vila, "Gun Violence in Durham, NC, 2017–2021," 7.

[16] "Durham Police Department Shooting Data."

[17] Wells and Owen, *Living Without Enemies*, 55.

[18] Ibid., 56.

[19] Ibid.

[20] Ibid., 33.

[21] Ibid., 26–7.

Oriented as such, the RCND's work remained at arm's length from those most affected by gun violence in Durham. It pursued legislative change, but it did so without considering the quality and character of relationships in Durham's common life.

"Being with," in contrast, offers a radically different form of social engagement. If "working for" centers on finding solutions to distressing issues, "being with" centers on building relationships across communities of difference. With regard to the myriad dimensions of a problem like gun violence, a "being with" approach begins with the conviction that "working for" efforts are likely too top-down in orientation, too divorced from the everyday realities of those living on the margins, and too vulnerable to paternalistic forms of advocacy and care. "Being with" approaches try instead to draw near to the "wound" of gun violence—not simply in terms of building relationships with the persons and communities suffering from such marginalization and oppression, but in terms of uncovering one's relationship to, and complicity with, the conditions that render persons and communities vulnerable to such marginalization and oppression. According to Wells and Owen,

> The approach of *being with* is less given to programs and movements, and is more to be found in piecemeal initiatives and small-scale relationships. This is because *being with* is not fundamentally about finding solutions, but about companionship amid struggle and distress.[22]

While this approach does not eschew the pursuit of solutions, it claims that "the obsession with findings solutions can get in the way of forming profound relationships of mutual understanding, and sometimes those relationships are more significant than solutions."[23] It is within this context that the RCND turned to the practice of vigil keeping at the sites of firearm-caused death in Durham. As a practice that embodies a "being with" approach to the tragic and enduring presence of gun violence in Durham, vigil keeping provides a basis upon which to describe an alternative approach to guns in US American life by persons of Christian faith—that of the vigil keeper.

The Vigil Keeper

To situate the vigil keeper, first let me more fully describe the orientation to guns I encountered while carrying out fieldwork with evangelical Christian handgun owners. For these interlocutors, guns serve as a means of defending particular bodies— their own bodies and their family's and church's bodies. For them, guns enable taking up a posture of care in the anticipation of violence, one that enhances and extends their ability to defend against potential threats in a firearms-saturated society. They see practices like concealed carry and armed church security as amenable to, and expressive

---

[22] Ibid., 30.
[23] Ibid.

of, Christian discipleship rather than as in conflict with it. Taken together, I name this particular posture the Christian-protector orientation to guns in US American life.[24]

Given this, how might we contrast the role of the vigil keeper? First and foremost, like Christian-protectors, the orientation of the vigil keeper to the place of guns in US American life is an embodied one. Keeping vigil is an embodied practice, as the vigil is, most fundamentally, an assembly of bodies. Vigil keepers gather at the site of firearm-caused death to mourn and memorialize the loss of "our brother" or "our sister," as the deceased is often referred to by vigil officiants. Vigil keepers assemble around the memory of the deceased body and those bodies within the deceased's kinship and ecclesial networks, enacting a practice of being present to, or "being with," these bodies.

With regard to space, the vigil is not geographically fixed but rather follows the path of firearm-caused death throughout Durham. Compared to the fixity of those sites Christian-protectors seek to secure—namely, their homes and their churches—vigil keepers inhabit a broad and ever changing range of sites in their effort to remain accountable to the place of firearm-caused death in their municipality. Unlike Christian-protectors, whose care is inward directed, and whose practices of protection are attuned to the various environmental characteristics of their homes and churches, vigil keepers identify the entirety of their city as a milieu in which to enact care. Where the narrow spatial focus of Christian-protectors generates a desire for mastery and precision with regard to their practices of protection, vigil keepers adopt a more improvisational, ad hoc posture with regard to their practices of "being with."

With regard to time, vigil keepers operate within a temporality of aftermath. Rather than take up a posture in the anticipation of violence, they follow the pathways of an already enacted violence. In contrast to Christian-protectors, for whom guns facilitate a posture of care, vigil keepers know guns primarily as a tool of violence, one with an incomparable ability to "*intensify* violence" in interpersonal contexts.[25] Further, vigil keepers understand that, with respect to firearm-caused homicide, this intensification disproportionately affects young men of color. The aftermath in which they enact their work of care is therefore a racialized one. Cognizant of and convicted by the racialized nature of gun violence, vigil keepers purposely situate themselves within this aftermath.

The care enacted at the site of the vigil has inspired and generated other practices of care within the RCND. Over lunch, a longtime volunteer of the Coalition, an older white woman, told me, "The Coalition is learning. We don't have answers. We know we can't fix it."[26] I had just spent several hours with her at the Durham County Courthouse, where she was accompanying an African American family who was testifying at the hearing of the young African American man who had killed their son. A component of the Coalition's vigil ministry, court accompaniment serves as another way of "being with" families as they traverse the aftermath of gun violence, extending this practice

---

[24] For a fuller discussion, see Michael R. Grigoni, "The Christian Handgun Owner and Just War," *Journal of Moral Theology* 12, special issue no. 2 (2023): 108–32.

[25] See Philip J. Cook and Kristin A. Goss, *The Gun Debate: What Everyone Needs to Know*, 2nd ed. (Oxford: Oxford University Press, 2020), 1–2.

[26] Interview with the author, Durham, March 18, 2019.

of presence beyond the vigil itself. "We focus on relationships," she said, "a phone call, a note, a cup of coffee, or what you saw today in the courtroom," the point being to "bring someone from the community other than family into this circle of loss."

During an interview in February 2019, another Coalition member, a middle-aged white male, expressed frustration with traditional approaches to addressing gun violence. Just weeks earlier, in response to a string of firearm-caused homicides in the first weeks of 2019, Durham city officials had held a press conference that called for the passage of "common-sense gun laws" by the North Carolina General Assembly.[27] "What's that going to accomplish?" he asked, his voice full of exasperation.[28] "It won't make a difference. Nothing will get passed, and they know it." He continued: "Any approach to this issue that strictly focuses on making it more difficult to get a gun is out of touch. Something else is needed."

As we continued to talk, he didn't point to any single thing as constituting that "something else," and I slowly understood that he didn't think any single thing would actually suffice; rather, something more complex and grounded was required. "We need a language, or a logic," he said, "something that can account for the intersection of spaces. We need stories that will help us see this isn't just about guns but about fear and racism and income inequality. We need a way of getting at the root of the problem instead of simply a law that will make it harder to get a gun."[29]

He then asked: "Do we really want to be healed?" Here he cited the words of Ruby Sales, an elder of the civil rights movement, to say that he did not think most people in Durham, despite their liberal progressive commitments, want to do the work of connecting in concrete and embodied ways with the communities that suffer under the burden of gun violence.[30] "We want to have a program or a press meeting or sit around a table and brainstorm," he said. "We don't really want to be healed."[31]

What my interlocutor averred, and what the vigil ministry of the RCND upholds, is that the "slow violence" of firearm-caused homicide will not cease apart from the slow work of building relationships across communities of difference. The phrase "slow violence," coined by Rob Nixon, refers to "a violence that occurs gradually and out of sight, a violence of delayed destruction that is dispersed across time and space, an attritional violence that is typically not viewed as violence at all."[32] While Nixon here refers to the slow violence of environmental racism, we should likewise see gun violence—its racialized nature, its geographic concentration in certain parts of cities and not in others, its generational effect on low-income communities of color—as a form of slow violence, albeit one that can erupt in a dramatic, spectacular form.

---

[27] Thomasi McDonald, "After 6 Homicides in 11 Days, Durham Officials Call for 'Common-Sense Gun Laws' in NC," *The News & Observer*, January 17, 2019, www.newsobserver.com/news/local/article224673440.html.
[28] Interview with the author, Durham, February 7, 2019.
[29] Ibid.
[30] Ruby Sales, "How We Can Start to Heal the Pain of Racial Division," *TED Salon*, filmed September 2018, www.ted.com/talks/ruby_sales_how_we_can_start_to_heal_the_pain_of_racial_division.
[31] Interview with the author, Durham, February 7, 2019.
[32] Rob Nixon, *Slow Violence and the Environmentalism of the Poor* (London: Harvard University Press, 2011), 2.

The value of keeping vigil lies precisely in its facilitation of this slow work. At the vigil, whether in expressing lament, in helping to facilitate its expression, or being drawn in by its expression, vigil keepers become placed within a different network of relationships, one in which the deceased becomes "brother" or "sister," and one in which gun violence becomes a scourge to be addressed in common. The vigil invites its participants into a new form of life, reconfiguring relationships of church and kin, bridging communities of difference in order to foster a genuinely common life. This reconfigured relationality provides a basis upon which a communal form of care aimed at curbing gun violence might emerge. In this way, keeping vigil stands among the most crucial practices of the Coalition given the relational foundation it cultivates and sustains. It recognizes that, in order to carry out this reconfiguration of relationships, people must come before policy and program.

In its posture of "being with," the vigil also presses its participants toward forms of care beyond the vigil's work of mourning and memorialization. In 2003, the Coalition began the Reconciliation and Reentry Ministry, which pairs congregational teams with newly released incarcerated persons to provide accompaniment and assistance in the transition to post-incarcerated life. And in 2017, the RCND began Restorative Justice Durham in partnership with various city and county offices to facilitate a restorative justice process within Durham's criminal justice system. Combined with the vigil ministry, which began in 1997, and a monthly luncheon roundtable that has been held since the Coalition's inception, these constitute the Coalition's four core practices. As such, they represent the fruit of a decades-long journey in discerning how an interfaith community might foster and sustain a response to gun violence in a city in the American South. Together these practices constitute a grassroots form of care, one that has organically emerged over time, and one that seeks to cultivate solidarity with the persons and communities who most directly suffer the effects of gun violence in Durham.

As my fieldwork brought into view, the Coalition's core practices serve as the animating center of a broader hive of relationality among persons, families, communities, and places in Durham. This rich sociality of relationships and connection emerges from and orbits around its core practices. Whether in late-night phone calls with emergency requests, morning conversations over coffee, or unexpected collaborations in writing,[33] the relationships the Coalition fosters extend beyond the spatial and temporal boundaries of its formal practices. This, I believe, is also important to attend to in giving an account of the alternative orientation to guns modeled by the RCND, as the Coalition's formal practices can be understood as spreading seed that arises in unexpected and unanticipated forms of sociality—in what *mujerista* theologian Ada María Isasi-Díaz refers to as *lo cotidiano* (which translates as "the quotidian" or "the everyday").[34] This perspective reflects the Coalition's commitment to cultivate the possibility of a genuinely common life for the inhabitants of Durham. Having characterized the vigil and the vigil keeper, I turn now to display

---

[33] See, for example, Simon Partner and Emma Johnston, *Bull City Survivor: Standing Up to a Hard Life in a Southern City* (Jefferson: McFarland, 2013).

[34] See Ada María Isasi-Díaz, *En la Lucha / In the Struggle: A Hispanic Women's Liberation Theology* (Minneapolis: Fortress Press, 1993).

the improvisatory nature of these relationships, and in doing so extend my account of what the vigil discloses.

The Quilt

I arrived at 9:00 a.m. to help Sidney Brodie set up the Durham Homicide and Victims of Violent Death Memorial Quilt. The quilt was going to be on display for the weekend as part of a community arts fair. I found Sidney in his silver sedan in front of the building where the quilt would be housed. He greeted me warmly, wearing jeans and a T-shirt that read "Black Dad Magic."

After chatting, we started setting up. Robert, his brother, had parked the covered trailer containing the materials used for the quilt's display near the building's stairwell, and he had already begun moving items outside the trailer for us to carry inside. Sidney started carrying pieces up the stairwell, directing me to do the same. We carried some pieces on our own and others together, depending on their size. The sky threatened rain, so we moved quickly.

Once we had moved enough of the display inside, Sidney began arranging the pieces of the quilt's platform until they stretched nearly fifty feet along a side of the hall. These were large, rectangular-shaped wooden frames that stand a foot off the ground, the width of which matches that of the quilt so that, once assembled, the quilt can lie lengthwise along the platform—what Sidney calls "the runway." As I carried in other pieces of the display, I watched Sidney as he aligned the frames and drilled them together with screws. He then unrolled a lengthy piece of quilted ruby-colored fabric for adorning the sides of the platform—what Sidney calls the "skirt." As he walked slowly around the runway, using one hand to line the runway's edge with the skirt, and the other to secure it with pushpins, I realized that he was engaging in a work of care.

How might the assembly of the runway and the display of the quilt constitute "a species of activity [by which we] maintain, contain, and repair our 'world' so that we can live in it as well as possible"?[35] While the assembly of the display—an hours-long endeavor—provides some insight into this question, properly answering it requires consideration of the quilt itself, an effort that has been years in the making. A Durham native, Sidney began the Durham Homicide and Victims of Violent Death Memorial Quilt in 1996 in response to the shooting and killing of two-year-old Shaquana Atwater. Feeling that the public outcry to Atwater's death was not strong enough, Sidney became compelled to create something that would more directly bring attention to the presence of violent death in Durham. Now over eighty feet long, the quilt contains nearly eight hundred squares, each of which features the name and death date of a victim of murder in Durham. As such, it memorializes and accounts for every murder victim in Durham County since 1994, the majority of whom, like Sidney, are African American men.

---

[35] Joan C. Tronto, *Moral Boundaries: A Political Argument for an Ethics of Care* (New York: Routledge, 1993), 103.

The quilt itself is a patchwork of variegated fabric, each square bearing a name inscribed with fabric paint, shiny letters that gleam against a myriad of colors and patterns: greens, yellows, reds, and blues; different plaids and stripes; leopard patterns, patterns of leaves and fruit. It is a material form that grows spatially over time. "Every stitch does something to me," he told me one afternoon over coffee. "When I sew on a new square, I open up the border of the quilt, but once we get that square installed, we actually close the border again in hope that the quilt is finished."[36]

Sidney began bringing the quilt to Coalition vigils in 2017, and it has become a regular feature of the vigils ever since. That was where, several months earlier, I first encountered the quilt—at a vigil being held in Durham's Hayti District. From the 1880s onward, the Hayti District served as a thriving community for Durham's African American residents, but it was dismantled in the 1960s as part of a federally subsidized "urban renewal" effort. What was left of Hayti was eventually bisected by the construction of the Durham Freeway in 1970.[37] As I drove to the vigil, I passed the Hayti Heritage Center before turning into a neighborhood of mostly disheveled homes. One was elevated by planks with water pooled underneath, and yet another appeared to have been newly remodeled and was on the market—evidence of an uneven but emergent gentrification.

A large crowd of about forty people was already present, many of whom had gathered around the quilt, which was set up in front of a small blue home with a red door that appeared to have dents in it. One end of the quilt was propped up by a table, the end containing the newly stitched square that memorialized the deceased. The rest of the quilt was draped along the sidewalk—"the vigil setup," Sidney later told me. It was early evening and the sun was still out. Walking from my car to the gathering, I was struck by how the quilt served as a material form around which the crowd drew itself together. I noted the assemblage of bodies, objects, and environment: the quilt on the sidewalk in the dust, the warmth of the air despite the approaching evening, cars that sometimes honked as they passed, and a light buzz of energy among those gathered.

Sidney came over to say hello, looking at me through aviator sunglasses. I asked him about various features of the quilt—the presence of a button on some squares and not others. "I always put a small black button on the patches of young victims, of children twelve years old or younger," he told me. A series of white squares had shirt cuffs sewed into them. I asked him why. "I felt like the quilt needed more color," he said, before concluding, "It's art, man." He then led me to the end of the quilt that was propped up by the table where he had placed a glass half dome over the square bearing the name of the deceased individual for whom the vigil was being held. "He was killed in that house, right there," Sidney told me, pointing to the home with the dented red door just a few yards away.

The vigil soon began with a gathering prayer. Cars passed constantly, the engine and tire sounds blending into the sound of song, scripture reading, and spoken testimony from the gathered community. Two African American individuals from the neighborhood spoke about their experiences with poverty, one admonishing us to "come and visit when we don't have the quilt." A volunteer with the Coalition produced

---

[36] Sidney Brodie, Interview with the author, Durham, May 22, 2019.
[37] Partner and Johnston describe this history in "Dreams and Realities," in Partner and Johnston, *Bull City Survivor*, 95–119.

three large paper bags full of McDonald's hamburgers, and the vigil ended with those assembled sharing a small meal. Afterward, I watched as Sidney and two others began to put the quilt away. Since the quilt had been placed directly on the sidewalk, Sidney held a portion of it upright first, striking it with a plastic broom to pummel out the dust it had absorbed. Those helping him then rolled up that portion of the quilt as he moved to the next part, repeating the process.

That night as I typed up my notes, I could not help but think that the vigil somehow resembled Golgotha, where Christ was crucified and where a small band gathered around the cross as he died, the quilt resembling Christ's crucified body. Watching Sidney care for the quilt, removing the accumulated dust and carefully rolling it up before placing it in a large, white mattress cover, I could not help but see him as caring for those crucified by the gun in our common life.

The Crucified Body

The quilt at the vigil raises questions: What might it mean to associate Christ crucified with the victims of gun violence in our common life? How might we characterize the work of vigil keepers and persons like Sidney as a mode of care for the crucified among us? Resources for thinking through these questions appear in both twentieth-century Latin American and North American liberation theologies in which the presence and significance of "crucified peoples" has a been a key thematic and concern.[38] In particular, this theme has featured in recent work by James Cone, the father of Black liberation theology.

In *The Cross and the Lynching Tree*, Cone wrestles with one of the most appalling and tragic features of US American history in the "afterlife of slavery"—the forms of mob violence and torture that culminated in the lynching of nearly five thousand Black persons from 1880 to 1940 in the United States.[39] Cone turns to the lynching tree and the cross in tandem, affirming that we must reflect on them together in order to draw near to "the deep wounds lynching has inflicted upon us" and confront the legacy and continued presence of white supremacy in US American life.[40]

For Cone, seeing the cross and the lynching tree together enables us to identify the crucified Christ with the black lynched body. This, in turn, serves as a way of countering antiseptic accounts of the cross in white US American Christianity. Both Jesus and the victims of lynching were victims of mob violence and torture; both were hung upon a tree. Seen from the underside of history, the cross in the US American context embodies God's identification and solidarity with the black lynched body. This identification renders the cross a critique of the lynching tree and the broader white

---

[38] See, for example, Ignacio Ellacuría, "The Crucified People," in *Mysterium Liberationis: Fundamental Concepts of Liberation Theology*, ed. Ignacio Ellacuría, SJ and Jon Sobrino, SJ (Maryknoll: Orbis Books, 1993), 580–603.

[39] James Cone, *The Cross and the Lynching Tree* (Maryknoll: Orbis Books, 2011). For the phrase "afterlife of slavery," see Saidiya V. Hartman, *Lose Your Mother: A Journey along the Atlantic Slave Route* (New York: Farrar, Straus and Giroux, 2007), 6.

[40] Cone, *The Cross and the Lynching Tree*, xix.

supremacist structures that underwrote and animated its practice. To identify Christ crucified as such prevents the cross from being sanitized of the "dangerous memories" it holds, and US American history of the "dangerous memories" it contains, while likewise exposing the machinations of white supremacy in the afterlife of slavery.[41] Further, it announces God's message of liberation to those who are being crucified in the present.

As we turn to those crucifixions, we should begin by noting what lynching and gun violence have in common. Both are expressions of violence that many do not wish to face. Just as many "would prefer to forget" the memory of lynching in the history of the United States, everyday forms of gun violence—particularly in contrast to mass shootings—often take on an amnestic quality in the communities in which they occur.[42] Both also reflect the legacy and continued presence of white supremacy in the United States. The lynching tree, which worked hand in glove with Jim Crow as a means of terrorizing and controlling African Americans, reflects the embeddedness of white supremacy in post-emancipation US American life. Firearm-caused homicide constitutes a crisis that disproportionately affects young men of color, which is all too easily ignored in cities that are concerned with preserving an image of affluence and social ascent. Reflecting on these realities and bringing them into view is painful and difficult. Yet, as Cone instructs, "Until we can see the cross and the lynching tree together, until we can identify Christ with a 'recrucified' black body hanging from a lynching tree, there can be no genuine understanding of Christian identity in America, and no deliverance from the brutal legacy of slavery and white supremacy."[43] The same applies to the countless victims of gun violence.

No theologian has done more to advance this effort than Kelly Brown Douglas. Also working within the tradition of Black liberation theology, Douglas's *Stand Your Ground: Black Bodies and the Justice of God* develops a critique of Stand Your Ground legislation and what she names as "stand-your-ground culture."[44] Taking the 2012 fatal shooting of Trayvon Martin as her point of departure, Douglas argues that Stand Your Ground laws represent a contemporary expression of a broader "stand-your-ground culture" that has characterized life in North America since the introduction of chattel slavery in the American colonies, extending from slavery to "Black Codes, Jim Crow, lynching, and other forms of racialized violence against black bodies."[45] In narrating the history and logics of this culture, Douglas avers that, "in the stand-your-ground war today, crucifixion comes in the form of gun violence."[46]

In characterizing gun violence as a form of crucifixion, Douglas draws from Cone's assertion that Christ's crucifixion expresses God's identification with the lynched but reframes it with reference to the gated community in which Trayvon Martin was

---

[41] On "dangerous memory," see Johann Baptist Metz, *Faith in History and Society: Toward a Practical Fundamental Theology*, trans. David Smith (New York: Seabury Press, 1980).
[42] Cone, *The Cross and the Lynching Tree*, xiv.
[43] Ibid., xv.
[44] Kelly Brown Douglas, *Stand Your Ground: Black Bodies and the Justice of God* (Maryknoll: Orbis Books, 2015).
[45] Ibid., xiv, xiii.
[46] Ibid., 179.

pursued, shot, and killed by a member of the community's neighborhood watch. In doing so, she reorients what she names as the "Matthean question":

> "But Lord, where did we see you dying and on the cross?" And Jesus would answer, "On a Florida sidewalk, at a Florida gas station, on a Michigan porch, on a street in North Carolina. As you did it to one of these young black bodies, you did it to me."[47]

Douglas finds, and admonishes her readers to find, the face of Christ in the face of Trayvon Martin as he died on a "Florida sidewalk." Pressing further, because the crucifixion of Christ represents God's solidarity with the oppressed, it provides a basis upon which to name Stand Your Ground laws, and the culture that sustains it, as "a culture of sin," one that manifests on both individual and structural levels.[48] Upon this basis, Douglas concludes that Stand Your Ground laws should be condemned by persons of Christian faith.

How might we extend Douglas's critique to Christian-protectors who view guns as a means for securing their bodies, their family's bodies, and their church's bodies—even those who might reject Stand Your Ground laws but still feel it necessary to have a gun in their lives? How might we assess this mode of armed embodiment with reference to the quilt and what is disclosed at the site of the vigil? If, as Cone and Douglas suggest, we find Christ crucified on the lynching tree and on the neighborhood watch, then we also find him at the vigil and among the countless victims of firearm-caused homicide throughout the United States today.

As men who engage in a mode of care on behalf of those bodies that present to them as vulnerable, and who require a tool of violence—a gun—in order to enact this care, Christian-protectors fail to recognize how the vast presence of guns in our common life, and the ease with which they can be procured, generates security for themselves while increasing precarity for others (i.e., for the victims of gun violence). Encountering the crucified body at the vigil brings this into view, as crucified peoples are revelatory of the structures of power and oppression that lead to their crucifixion. The Christian-protector, who lives, moves, and has his being in the anticipation of violence, remains blind to this reality. If Christian handgun owners feel they cannot give up their guns, they—and the church more broadly—should engage in practices of solidarity with the victims of gun violence, the crucified members of Christ's body in the place of the gun in US American life. Like Joseph of Arimathea, they must place themselves in the aftermath of violence to care for the crucified body. They can begin by keeping vigil.

---

[47] Ibid., 179–80. Douglas here refers to Jesus' words in Matthew 25:31-46.
[48] Ibid., 193.

13

Making Lemonade with Substitute Sugar

Toward an Ethics of Receptivity

AnneMarie Mingo

On the evening of Friday, August 26, 2005, Shannon went to a restaurant and jazz club in New Orleans East with coworkers to celebrate with a colleague who had recently received his master's degree. As she left the restaurant, she noticed that it was anything but a normal Friday night in her hometown. It was empty, the sights and sounds of New Orleans night life were absent, and she described the place looking scarce, almost like a ghost town. That night, as she drove toward where her family was gathered, the gas station she normally frequented was closed. She later reflected that should have been a red flag that the storm was more serious than others, but she simply drove around until she found a gas station that was open. Once she arrived at the house Shannon turned on the news and listened to the trusted voice of weatherman Bob Breck; it was then she realized the storm had become a hurricane and it was headed directly toward New Orleans. The more she listened to the television, Shannon decided that she would have to leave.[1]

In this chapter, I use oral histories, ethnographic research, governmental reports, church newsletters, and supplemental local and national media reports to construct an understanding of what happened when persons left New Orleans and found themselves in cities and towns throughout the United States. For many who left, their lives were completely disrupted as they were forced to make their way to new places while experiencing some of the most devastating losses imaginable. As they entered new communities, some stayed for a temporary period until they were able to return to New Orleans while others made their initially unplanned move more permanent. The bitter losses were lemons that had been handed to them. The ability to look at what they had been given and connect to a life-giving substance within them marks the beginning of a construction of an ethics of receptivity, experienced through faith and mutual openness to change. Beyond the generally shorter-termed obligations of hospitality, this ethics of receptivity enabled resiliency for displaced Katrina survivors as they reestablished their lives in communities outside of the south.

---

[1] A version of this chapter was originally published in Practical Matters (2018:11) used here by permission. Interview by author with Shannon, November 4, 2015 and July 22, 2016.

More specifically, this chapter analyzes the experiences of families who made the small town of State College, Pennsylvania, and a specific church, their home after Katrina. I began regularly attending Albright-Bethune United Methodist Church in the fall of 2013 as a postdoctoral fellow at Penn State University and continued when I began teaching there full-time. As a result, I was not only a participant observer in the church-based fellowships that characterized the ethics of receptivity I offer here, I also built and maintained trusted relationships with those who shared their experiences with me for this research. As a native Southerner in a small predominantly white central Pennsylvania town, I was drawn to the population of Black women and men from New Orleans clustered at this particular church, including some who were not interviewed for this research. The ethics of receptivity put forth in this chapter honors the faith these families relied on to take their bitter realities after massive destruction and make lemonade. It also recognizes individual and institutional commitments to creating communities with mutual openness for something and someone new.

Like many throughout the United States and around the world, I sat glued to my television set in late August 2005 watching the devastation that followed the breaching of levees in New Orleans. The storm, winds, and rains uncovered the class differences at the center of the division between those who could leave and those who could not, those who could rebuild and those who could not even return.[2] As historian Peniel E. Joseph wrote shortly after the devastation,

> Despite the ferocious rage, Katrina is not solely responsible for the untold devastation that was visited on the poor people of New Orleans and the Gulf Coast region. She is only guilty of exposing the cynicism of an American political system that allows masses of the poor, especially the black poor, to endure lives of quiet desperation amid a land of plenty.

He continued, noting that "in addition to inflicting incalculable horrors on the region in the form of death and misery, [Hurricane Katrina] opened up the vortex of race, class, and citizenship that provides a backdrop to this unfolding national crisis."[3]

Many scholars like Carolyn Yoder emphasize the structural violence that reinforces the inequities, stating, "The ongoing violence of poverty and systems that make people unable to meet basic needs such as healthcare is called *structural violence* and is a cause of trauma. Often these structural-induced traumas go unnoticed until an event such as Hurricane Katrina graphically exposes what has existed all along."[4] Largely the result of policies that confined poor households to areas with limited educational and economic opportunities, there was little prospect of upward mobility and socioeconomic change.

---

[2] For a more comprehensive exploration of the realities of race and class in New Orleans before Katrina, see Chester Hartman and Gregory D. Squires (eds.), *There is No Such Thing as a Natural Disaster: Race, Class, and Hurricane Katrina* (New York: Routledge, 2006) and James R. Elliott and Jeremy Pais, "Race, Class, and Hurricane Katrina: Social Differences in Human Responses to Disaster," *Social Science Research* 32, no. 2 (2006): 295–321.

[3] Peniel E. Joseph, "Left Behind: Backdrop to a National Crisis," in *The Sky is Crying: Race, Class, and Natural Disaster*, ed. Cheryl A. Kirk-Duggan (Nashville: Abingdon Press, 2006), 125.

[4] Carolyn Yoder, *The Little Book of Trauma Healing: When Violence Strikes and Community Security Is Threatened* (Intercourse: Good Books, 2005), 12.

Poverty was concentrated in extremely poor neighborhoods, such as the lower Ninth Ward, which did not receive infrastructural investments that would protect those living there if the predicted destruction happened. Geographically relegated to the shadows of the levees, most families could not afford expensive flood insurance, therefore anchoring the most economically vulnerable to the most physically vulnerable land.[5] The dismal Orleans Parish school systems, which boasted the second-lowest math and reading scores in Louisiana, were filled with students from impoverished families who could not place them in the higher-performing private schools. Many of these students left school unprepared to attend college or obtain a job that would enable them to move out of the poverty that held a firm hold on them.

Hurricane Katrina has a lot to teach us not only about preparing for natural disasters, but also about directly addressing the policies and practices which continue to exert structural violence among those who are the most vulnerable within our nation. The catastrophic event forced the United States to critically analyze our response to difference (especially racial and class differences) as well as our response to forced geographical change.

Recalculating: Changing Course while Evacuating

For those of us who rely on GPS navigation systems to guide us to our destination, we've become accustomed to hearing a voice tell us when we are off course: "Recalculating." The real-time course correction helps us reach the destination efficiently as possible. State College, Pennsylvania, was not the initial destination for any of the persons with whom I conducted oral histories.[6] Albert was born in 1923, and he had lived in New Orleans for all of his life. He had lived through Hurricanes Betsy and Camille and others that impacted the city. However, as Hurricane Katrina approached, at the prodding of his family, he along with his wife Azalea, his niece and her daughter made hotel arrangements in Tallahassee, Florida. Albert and Azalea were planning to drive the six hours to Tallahassee the day before the hurricane hit, when their son, a surgeon in State College, Pennsylvania, told him to turn around and drive to Georgia where Albert's nephew lived. While resting after the long drive, Albert's nephew told him to look at the television. When he saw the St. Bernard Market, a landmark not far from his house completely under water, the massive destruction by flooding made it clear that the one- to two-day trip he packed for would become much longer.[7] Recalculating.

Lydia was also born in New Orleans and had lived in the city for all of her life. When Hurricane Betsy hit in 1965, she and her family lived in an area of the city where they were not impacted by the breach of the levees. As Hurricane Katrina was making its way toward New Orleans, Lydia along with two daughters, a son-in-law,

---

[5] This was especially true for families who owned their homes and did not have to adhere to the expensive flood insurance requirements of mortgage companies. This was also expressed by Lydia, a Katrina survivor I interviewed.
[6] The first names of research participants are used in this chapter. Pennsylvania State University, IRB # 44705.
[7] Interview by author with Albert, December 6, 2016.

and granddaughter started driving toward Texas. The roads were packed as thousands tried to leave the city at the same time, so they turned around and drove to Mississippi where they watched the news in horror as 80 percent of the city they loved was flooded by water when the levees that were supposed to protect the city were breached. After spending four days in Mississippi and realizing that they would not be able to go back to New Orleans any time soon, they headed north to State College where Lydia's daughter Michelle was in a PhD program at Penn State University through a partnership with Xavier University in New Orleans. When they left New Orleans, none of them would have imagined that they would live in State College for seven months before they could return home to assess the damage and determine when or if they could return for good.[8] Recalculating.

Shannon decided that she would leave in advance of the hurricane hitting land, and she struggled to convince her mother, who did not want to leave her cat, to go with them. Shannon's sister was working as a dormitory monitor at Xavier University and planned to stay with the students to make sure they were okay. However, when the administrators at Xavier told her to try to evacuate with her family, she called Shannon who was just about to join the caravan of family members on their way out of New Orleans. After turning around to pick up her sister, the family began the drive to a cousin's home just outside of Memphis, Tennessee. Along the drive, Shannon and her family experienced people exploiting the devastating situation, including businesses charging $10.00 for a bag of ice. When they finally arrived in Tennessee eighteen hours later (normally the drive is five hours long), there were nearly fifty family members under one roof. They gathered around televisions and watched the massive destruction unfold in their beloved city, realizing that the one- to two-day evacuation they expected would not turn out like planned. Recalculating.

Recalculations operate as a tool of survival by keeping track of where the person is, even if they are not on the initially designated route. Built within the feature of literal and figurative recalculations is the understanding that there may be more than one route to the destination when intentional or unintentional detours happen. For Global Positioning Systems with live updates that capture accidents, road construction, and other hazards, it also acknowledges when the destination is no longer a possibility and may provide another end goal.

For those who were able to leave ahead of Hurricane Katrina as well as those who were trapped in New Orleans and other areas of the gulf region and left when they were able to, most found their way to big cities, including Houston, Texas, which received nearly 250,000 evacuees, and Atlanta, Georgia, where nearly one hundred thousand evacuees traveled.[9] However, the displacement data generated through the support payments provided through FEMA shows that the women, men, and children from Louisiana, Mississippi, Alabama, and Florida who survived Hurricane Katrina

---

[8] Interview by author with Lydia, October 30, 2015.
[9] Maria Godoy, "Tracking the Katrina Diaspora: A Tricky Task," *NPR—Katrina One Year Later*, August 2006, http://www.npr.org/news/specials/katrina/oneyearlater/diaspora/ (accessed February 9, 2017).

were spread throughout every state within the nation.[10] For many, there had been an unexpected recalculation of their destinations, and they found themselves in small towns without the cultural connections they were accustomed to.

The question for me is not *why* did the people I interviewed go to State College, a small central Pennsylvania town with 40,000 residents, over 47,000 students, and even more white-tailed deer. The why of State College is a logical answer. Like many who migrate to other locations in times of turmoil, each person I interviewed had a connection to someone living in State College, the majority as graduate students at Penn State.[11] Many who evacuated from New Orleans and other areas impacted in the Gulf region went to State College and stayed for a week, a few months, or up to three years in order to complete a degree after transferring to Penn State. The people who I interviewed have been away from New Orleans and in State College for over ten years after Hurricane Katrina, with the majority congregating at Albright-Bethune United Methodist Church, even after there were opportunities to leave and move back south. The real question for me is, why did they choose to *stay*?

Being Open to Receive: Small Towns and Big Hearts

A naturally hard worker who valued her independence, Shannon found that she had to be open to receiving from a community that she did not know and had not planned to find herself in.

She began to make a home in Cordova, Tennessee, until the FEMA support for Hurricane Katrina survivors was removed. After unsuccessfully trying to find something that would allow her to return to work in New Orleans, she too made her way toward State College, Pennsylvania, upon the invitation of a friend who was in graduate school at Penn State.

State College and the Penn State Community

In the fall of 2005, there were seven students, Lydia's daughter among them, participating in a collaborative program with Xavier University and Penn State University's College of Education.[12] Within days of the hurricane's destruction, graduate student family members like Lydia made their way toward State College. Arrangements were made to

---

[10] Many residents from the poorest areas were most likely to be transported to some of the most distant larger receiving communities. See Narayan Sastry and Jesse Gregory, "The Location of Displaced New Orleans Residents in the Year After Hurricane Katrina," *Demography* 51, no. 3 (2014): 753–75.

[11] While there are similarities, this form of migration within the United States does not relate completely to theories of refugees who are forced into exile and resettlement in different countries. See Egon F. Kunz, "Exile and Resettlement: Refugee Theory," *The International Migration Review* 15, no. 1/2, Refugees Today (Spring–Summer 1981): 42–51, and Sreeram Sundar Chaulia, "The Politics of Refugee Hosting in Tanzania: From Open Door to Unsustainability, Insecurity, and Receding Receptivity," *Journal of Refugee Studies* 16, no. 2 (2003): 147–66.

[12] In addition to the seven graduate students from New Orleans who were a part of the collaborative doctoral program, Penn State identified over sixty students with hometowns in the areas of Louisiana, Mississippi, and Alabama that were impacted by Katrina.

enroll children in State College Area District schools, provide free or prorated housing, furniture, clothing, and other resources to help acclimate them to a new community as quickly as possible. Penn State's president at the time, Graham B. Spanier, announced they were opening the twenty-four campuses of Penn State to students primarily from Tulane University who had been impacted by Katrina. As he explained, many of the students had previously applied and been accepted to Penn State but chose to go to a southern school, so it was easy to access the records of about fifty students who would join Penn State as undergraduates. In the press releases from that time, it is interesting to note that Spanier did not mention helping undergraduate students from New Orleans' Historically Black Universities of Xavier and Dillard minimize the disruption to their education even though Penn State already had a relationship with Xavier to recruit more Black graduate students to the field of Education.

Unlike many who left their homes quickly to evacuate in advance of the hurricane, Lydia grabbed medicine and important paperwork before she left for what she thought would be a few days. She could not explain why she took those items because she had never done it in previous evacuations. It was seven months before they could return to New Orleans, so those documents helped her begin the claim process with FEMA and her insurance company from almost 1,200 miles away.

Albright-Bethune United Methodist Church

Albright-Bethune United Methodist Church is a relatively new congregation that finds its origins as the result of the need to build cultural community in the small predominantly white town of State College, Pennsylvania. The church began in 1988 as the United Black Fellowship, drawing primarily from faculty and staff members of the Forum on Black Affairs at Penn State under their first pastor, Rev. Cecil Gray. The second pastor, Rev. Bernice Stevens, named the church Bethune Memorial after Black educator, political leader, and Methodist, Mary McLeod Bethune. Through blending the congregation with St. John United Methodist, the church was renamed for Pennsylvania evangelical Methodist Jacob Albright and Bethune and formally welcomed into the United Methodist denomination.

Persons who were a part of the early congregation describe being drawn to the people and familiar Black church practices and not any particular denominational attributes. As a result, Baptists, Methodists, and Pentecostals worshipped and fellowshipped together in a Black church tradition where they could hear the preaching, teaching, and singing to which they felt connected. From July 2002 until June 2007, Reverend Marion J. Roddy-Hart served as the pastor of Albright-Bethune. She is described as being a strong older Black woman who had a heart for people and knew how to get along with the young and the old members equally.

Jennifer joined Albright-Bethune when her youngest daughter was one year old, and over twenty-five years later, she is still a member of the church. She described Rev. Roddy-Hart as a powerful, praying, Bible-based preacher who could make the connections between the text and the current environment using her "divine imagination." Pastoral care was also central to Roddy-Hart, who often "adopted" and nurtured graduate students who were part of the congregation. It was under Roddy-

Hart's leadership that Jennifer began to serve as one of the primary liturgists for the church. When she reflected on the church during the time Katrina survivors arrived, she noted they were welcomed without making a big deal about how or why they were there. She said, "When we saw a new group of people arrive, we just loved on them."[13]

One name that three of the Katrina survivors I interviewed mentioned as a person who was openly receptive to them when they arrived was Carla, a member of Albright-Bethune since the late 1980s. Carla, a white woman from Pennsylvania, began attending the church as it formed because she wanted her Black husband and biracial children to have a place where they could be comfortable with both cultures they had to navigate. She described the church during the time it was forming as primarily Black, but "very welcoming to everyone."

This welcoming spirit continued to be a characteristic of the church when it became a spiritual gathering place for Black people arriving after Hurricane Katrina.[14] Carla does not recall any special preparations being made by the church, but because many of the graduate students within the congregation had familial roots in Louisiana, the church leadership, including her husband Terrell, and members said, "Just come and we'll do what we can." The members of the church took on a role the Penn State community could not, that of spiritual stability for those whose lives had been shaken to the core. For most, there was a need to make State College a home for at least a year, while others were open and receptive to making a more permanent move. As Carla reflected on what that period was like for those who arrived after Katrina, she said, "I am just in prayer every time I think about them and what they must have endured and come through it with such grace and such love. They are just amazing people."[15]

Another church couple, mentioned by three of the Katrina survivors, Blannie and Cathy joined what would become Albright-Bethune around 1989 shortly after moving to State College. Blannie started the monthly church newsletter, which has now been published over twenty-five years. In it, he captures a letter from the "Pastor's Desk," birthday and wedding anniversary announcements, local church events, community events, denominational news, and more. The monthly "A-B Newsletter" is distributed beginning the first Sunday of the month, so an issue was compiled and printed only days after the devastation took place on August 28, 2005. In the September 2005 issue, Rev. Roddy-Hart's letter began and ended with a focus on the impact of Hurricane Katrina and the need to pray and act. She wrote,

GREETINGS IN THE NAME OF OUR LORD AND SAVIOR JESUS CHRIST!

HURRICANE KATRINA is our burden that we must take to the Lord in Prayer. He said, "Rest all your care upon me, for my yoke is easy and my burden is light." We must pray, pray, pray. We must do all that we can to share in this horrible disaster left by Katrina.

. . .

---

[13] Interview by author with Jennifer, March 7, 2018.
[14] A small number of white men and women also arrived in State College after Hurricane Katrina; however, my research only identified one woman who did not return to the south before the ten-year anniversary.
[15] Interview by author with Carla, January 1, 2017.

> I AM GRIEVED and heart-broken that people were left, ignored, or whatever, for five (5) days without food, medication, or water until the news reporters made it public. Just in plain sight, nothing was moving in or out until September 2. This is a sad time for all. God is not pleased with this world. We must pray and give until it hurts. Please bring your gifts and food supplies to Albright-Bethune and we will take them to Mt. Nittany UMC, which is our pick-up site. Place all money designated for the disaster victims in the envelopes provided. I love you. Your Pastor, Rev. Marion Roddy-Hart.[16]

In comparison to the style and voice in subsequent letters from the pastor in newsletters I received access to, Rev. Roddy-Hart's transparency, urgency, and frustration are felt in this rushed missive to the congregation and is likely an indication of the types of messages she shared verbally during worship services at that time. Her reference to a lack of action until September 2, 2005, the Friday before the Sunday that the newsletter was distributed, indicates that this letter was not crafted leisurely, but in the moment as lives still hung in the balance. We are able to hear the pain and cry for help from the pastor as she also criticized the global society, not simply local, state, and federal government's lack of action, for the citizens in the gulf region.

Lessons

As a part of my interview process with survivors, I asked each participant to tell me what lessons they learned from Katrina as they reflected from their homes in State College, Pennsylvania, ten years later. Lydia's lessons included her conviction that she has truly learned to trust in God with all her heart, and although she misses her home in New Orleans, after Katrina she learned to be content wherever she finds herself.[17] Family has always been important and as the oldest person in her family, Lydia relishes time with the next generations. Although no longer in the south where most of the family has returned, she spends Thanksgiving through New Year's Day in Louisiana or Texas to be present with her grand and great grandchildren. Lydia also now talks to her children every day and relishes the simple joy of living.

Lydia's home was in the Ninth Ward and despite being built on four-foot pillars it was not saved from flooding. When I asked about her home, Lydia's response was, "It's just things." Although she misses the pictures and videos from her daughters' weddings, she prayed about the losses and did not let it upset or consume her. As a result of her experience, like many others who experience great tragedies of physical loss, she does not keep as many material things now.

Albert said after Hurricane Katrina he realized that with so much devastation you have to learn how to both act and react. A key to moving forward is knowing how to get along with people. He said, "If you can get along with people you can go where you want. People know you are in town for the holidays and they want you to be around." I have observed this with Albert and Azalea with families from Albright-Bethune who

---

[16] Blannie Bowen (ed.), "A-B Newsletter," 12, no. 9 (September 2005): 1.
[17] Her response reflected the scriptures Proverbs 3:5 and Philippians 4:11 (NRSV).

make sure that they have places to go for holidays from Easter to Thanksgiving. He admonished me to remember to get along with others, particularly if you want to live a comfortable life, which reflected the posture he took enabling him and his wife to be received in the State College community as long-term members.

Shannon's journey continues to require adjustments as she makes and remakes a home for herself and her daughters in State College. She shared three lessons from Katrina that reflected the journey to where she is today:

1. Home essentially is within me. Because after everything else has been destroyed, after I've lost all . . . all I have left is what's within.
2. No matter what I go through, I always look for the lesson in the message . . . sometimes you don't get a chance to experience the lesson, sometimes you *are* the lesson.
3. "When life serves you lemons, find a way to make lemonade, even if you have to use substitute sugar." First you acknowledge the reality that you are dealing with lemons—loss of life, loved ones, dealing with change. But lemonade is your hope, faith, and perseverance—the inner motivation to keep going.

As she continued to reflect on her journey and her memories of home, Shannon was very descriptive about the foods she missed from New Orleans including specific brands. When she first arrived in State College, there were brands from home that she could not easily find, including spices and sugars, but her resilience was connected to her ability to make a substitution to create something similar to home. It was this response from Shannon, "When life serves you lemons, find a way to make lemonade, even if you have to use substitute sugar," that opened my understanding of an ethics of receptivity. It is one where the person must be open to receiving what the new person or place has to offer, even if adjustments have to be made to obtain a new sense of normalcy. An ethics of receptivity requires improvisation where the person becomes open to accepting a close approximation utilizing the resources available in the new location, such that lemonade made from the bitter lemons of life may be sweetened with Stevia instead of Domino sugar.

Receptivity versus Hospitality

Scholars such as Christine D. Pohl, Arthur Sutherland, N. Lynne Westfield, and Letty M. Russell have written about the theological constructions of hospitality as a Christian practice.[18] Pohl's act of recovery traces hospitality as a Christian tradition and argues that hospitality was a moral practice in ancient times. It "addressed the physical needs of strangers for food, shelter, and protection, but also included recognition of their

---

[18] Christine D. Pohl, *Making Room: Recovering Hospitality as a Christian Tradition* (Grand Rapids: William B. Eerdmans Publishing Company, 1999); N. Lynne Westfield, *Dear Sisters: A Womanist Practice of Hospitality* (Cleveland: Pilgrim Press, 2001); Arthur Sutherland, *I Was a Stranger: A Christian Theology of Hospitality* (Nashville: Abingdon Press, 2006); and Letty M. Russell, *Just Hospitality: God's Welcome in a World of Difference* (Louisville: Westminster John Knox, 2009).

worth and common humanity."[19] Hospitality was also marked by boundaries involving "some space into which people are welcomed, a place where unless the invitation is given, the stranger would not feel free to enter."[20] Pohl's requirement of an invitation to allow the stranger to feel welcome is possible in individual settings, but more challenging in communal ones where boundaries and corresponding calls to cross them may not be clear.

Sutherland defines Christian hospitality as "the intentional, responsible, and caring act of welcoming or visiting, in either public or private places, those who are strangers, enemies, or distressed, without regard for reciprocation."[21] Like Pohl, for Sutherland there are thresholds and boundaries associated with hospitality such that "the offer and acceptance of hospitality can take place anywhere there is space to share and the authority to share it."[22] The welcome, however, does not require reciprocation and therefore can produce an unarticulated dependency associated with actual or perceived imbalances of power. While there may be a sense of extending a welcome, it does not necessarily result in an equitable sense of belonging.

Westfield's hospitality is understood through the practices of Black women and the use of "concealed gatherings" as womanist spaces of resilience and not simply survival. For Westfield, this communal space reflects a deep sense of both being and belonging.[23] This womanist practice of hospitality among Black women consists of giving and receiving through shared intimacy, reciprocity, and safety.[24] This intra-group hospitality may not fully apply in mixed encounters.

Russell's concept of just hospitality explores "the practice of God's welcome by reaching out across difference to participate in God's actions bringing justice and healing in our world of crisis and fear of ones we call 'other.'" Just hospitality requires the recognition of the "other," the stranger, and not simply an embrace of the neighbor.[25] Using a feminist hermeneutic of hospitality clarifies in God's sight that no one is the "other."[26] Hospitality, as God's welcome, can reflect unity in Christ without uniformity.[27]

These practices of hospitality are often linked to biblical constructions and admonitions to show hospitality to strangers because in doing so you may entertain angels.[28] However, it is not only angels who may be in your midst while providing for strangers, but it may actually be an unrecognizable Jesus with whom you share when you feed, clothe, and care for the stranger you encounter.[29] Among Jesus' many teachings in Matthew 25, he includes the practice of hospitality toward those who are in need but are not recognized as a part of the community in verses 36-40. This practice focuses on the person who had the resources to provide to the person in need.

---

[19] Christine D. Pohl, "Hospitality, a Practice and a Way of Life," *Vision* (Spring 2002): 35.
[20] Ibid., 39.
[21] Sutherland, *I Was a Stranger*, xiii.
[22] Ibid., 41.
[23] Westfield, *Dear Sisters*, 7.
[24] Ibid., 49–52.
[25] Russell, *Just Hospitality*, 101–2.
[26] Ibid., 43.
[27] Ibid., 80.
[28] Hebrews 13:2 (NRSV)
[29] Matthew 25:31-46 (NRSV)

Nothing is noted about the posture and position of the person to whom the services are provided and whose needs are met; the evaluation and judgment are on the giving and not the receiving. Jesus' teaching also suggests a much broader family system that includes persons who may live in the greatest physical and social need.

As Pohl argues, today the activities associated with historic and biblical hospitality often fall within the realm of separate institutions where professionals are paid to provide services, including protection, education, care for the sick and aging, and meeting the physical needs of strangers.[30] Within modern hospitality that is extended in personal versus professional spaces, there is a giving and receiving component for the host and the guest, for which there is a clear distinction between a person who is in a position of authority to provide and another who is in a position to receive. Personal hospitality also implies preparation and catering toward the desire of others such that a good host will know if their guest prefers orange juice or apple juice, coffee or tea, and will have that available for the morning beverage. This preparation is a result of a knowledge of preferences and "comforts of home," which is best ascertained through relationships.

Receptivity requires the reciprocal openness to receive, where even those who are in perceived positions of power or authority must not only give provisions but also welcome in and receive individuals with different cultural experiences and expectations for perhaps an extended period of time. Risk, vulnerability, and openness are required on both sides for receptivity of others to enable a mutual strengthening of the expanded community. There is also a temporal element where receptivity requires a potentially permanent change for the future long-standing member of the community, compared to the shorter-termed welcome of hospitality toward an accepted visitor. The person on the traditional receiving end must also be open to being received by a new community that may not meet their actual needs or be aware of their preferences. Receptivity implies a radical welcome that actively reaches out toward persons to welcome them in and makes adjustments in their own cultural society to ensure that the initial openness has the potential to become permanent, not temporary until the visitors leave and things "get back to normal." Receptivity requires adjustments for multiple sides of the community over time.

Receptivity, therefore, is also encountered from a place of empathy from both sides: one for the giver and the other for the receiver; one for the person in perceived power and the other for the person who does not appear to have power. Carla reflects on what it must have been like for those who arrived in State College from New Orleans and said, "To think about transferring from one area. . . . If I were the person going to Louisiana, basically leaving everything that [was] Pennsylvania behind; I would not nearly handle it as well as they have all handled it."[31]

Despite not having Mardi Gras balls to attend or the opportunity to join a second line as a brass band parades down the street, when a person is open to different experiences, from athletic games, concerts, plays, and lectures, there are things to do in State College. Blannie often takes Albert to events at the university and in the

---

[30] Pohl, *Making Room*, 56–7.
[31] Interview by author with Carla, January 1, 2017.

community, which provide access to interactions with leaders including the mayor and university president. These types of interactions slightly replicate positions Albert found himself in as an elder statesman in his area of New Orleans. Because the town is small, Albert has become known throughout State College and can walk into places and be greeted with familiarity and respect, something he cherished about his role as an active leader in social clubs and political arenas in his hometown.[32] He proudly shares how he and his wife were sought after for newspaper interviews when they arrived in State College, and a decade later he is still invited to local schools to share his life experiences with students. Albert's receptivity to the new town has been met by the town's receptivity to him.

Once they could no longer drive, Cathy began taking Albert and Azalea places including the store, the post office, or the weekly senior social at Albright-Bethune. While still quite vibrant, Albert and Azalea are now in their nineties, and Cathy, a native of North Carolina, expressed that growing up in the south you were taught to respect your elders. She described the nonagenarians as "good people to be around.... He helps you to have fun and see things differently." In the spirit of the biblical reaping what you sow, Cathy said, "Respect elders. Do what you can. Learn from them. Put yourself on the receiving end."[33] Even as she gives, she too is open to receive what they have to offer. Receptivity is not simply a matter of openness. It requires an ability to *be* in ways that have possibly not been considered or offered before. Receptivity involves a process of becoming, where the person responds to and may be transformed by what is encountered and the encounter is itself unique because of the persons involved.

Gathering for Gumbo and Making Lemonade with Substitute Sugar

Gumbo

One of the most consistent things missed about New Orleans that the individuals I interviewed noted was the communal aspect of their city represented by the coming together of family and friends around a large pot of gumbo. When I entered the State College residence of Albert and Azalea, he gave me a tour of their townhouse and showed me pictures of his family and those who were like family. All but a couple of the pictures were recent moments captured within the last ten years, but a few were of older family members now deceased, which he was able to save as a result of their high placement on the walls of the twenty-room house he owned in New Orleans. As we walked through the kitchen, he paused to show me his "seasonings" of herbs that he was chopping and preparing, and he opened the refrigerator to pull out a large jar of garlic cloves that were central to his cooking. He showed me the large freezer where he stored shrimp and other items until he was ready to prepare his gumbo. He was

---

[32] Interview by author with Blannie, March 4, 2018.
[33] Interview by author with Cathy, March 4, 2018.

not able to find all of the ingredients as readily as he could in New Orleans, but he found a way to adjust and make things work.

Gumbo brings many layered flavors together to create a warm and inviting meal that can be shared with whomever comes to the home. There is no headcount associated with gumbo. There is no need to purchase a particular number of filleted fish or know whether a guest will like the drumstick or the chicken breast. A good pot of gumbo, prepared with love, welcomes everyone and easily stretches to meet the needs as its warmth comforts while it is consumed.

In my first interview with Shannon, I asked her to describe life in New Orleans prior to Hurricane Katrina, and almost all of her descriptions centered on food. She remembered fried fish, fried pork chops, collard greens, macaroni and cheese, and candied yams after church on Sunday, and anyone was welcome to come by to eat. There were red beans and rice with chicken on Monday, and similar meals throughout the week. She recalled many food-related memories from the typical crawfish boils, with corn, potatoes, gumbo, and shrimp jambalaya; to the specific Patton's hot sausage in the "red and white container"; and Huck-a-bucks (frozen cups of juice) on a hot day that older women would sell to make a little money to supplement their fixed income. Desserts, made using locally processed Domino sugar,[34] ranged from sweet potato pone, homemade pound cake, and bread pudding with raisins. Eggnog, made from scratch in the big gumbo pot, was always a favorite, and cakes with delicious icing from McKenzie's Pastry Shoppes were special treats for birthdays.[35] Food, and gumbo in particular, had a special place in family and communal life in New Orleans.

Christine Pohl describes table fellowship as "historically an important way of acknowledging the equal value and dignity of people."[36] Each person that I interviewed reflected on the ways large intergenerational groups of family would come together in New Orleans around a shared meal. Communal celebrations involved large pots and open tables where everyone was welcome. Those New Orleanians who have remained in State College have opened their table in order to share with others in the community. Food contributions for a culture day fund-raiser at the local high school that I attended included jambalaya prepared by Shannon so her daughters could share food from New Orleans. I also experienced this at church potlucks at Albright-Bethune where contributions of jambalaya and étouffée have become the norm.

During the annual Souper Bowl of Caring[37] fellowship at Albright-Bethune on Super Bowl Sunday, for over three years, I observed not only the inclusion of gumbo as one of the "soup" options, but also a table located in a place of prominence in the fellowship hall decorated for the New Orleans Saints even when they have not made it to the big game. The presence of the Saints tablecloths, napkins, cups, and table decorations in central Pennsylvania has become normalized in what is more readily Pittsburgh

---

[34] The Domino Sugar's Chalmette refinery in the St. Bernard Parish of New Orleans has been in existence since 1909.
[35] Interview by author with Shannon, November 4, 2015.
[36] Pohl, "Hospitality," 35.
[37] In partnership with the local food bank, the church collects soup to donate throughout the month in collaboration with Souper Bowl of Caring, https://souperbowl.org/welcome. In celebration after worship, congregants join in fellowship with homemade soups.

Steelers and Philadelphia Eagles territory. During the annual Men Who Cook fundraiser held on March 19, 2006, the "A-B Newsletter" announced a gumbo cook-off between Albert and Carla's husband Terrell, with references to Albert moving to State College with his wife the previous year after losing their home of sixty-five years in New Orleans.[38] The welcome table has literally been extended and incorporated into the social life of the congregation.

Acknowledging Lemons and Making Lemonade

Some of the losses that were faced after Hurricane Katrina are still incalculable more than ten years later. Friends and family members died as a result of the lack of preparation and delayed actions by the city, state, and federal government that left thousands trapped in flooded areas without adequate resources. Even for those who evacuated early, many of their homes and treasured possessions were destroyed. Sociohistorical loss and lack were experienced in the immediate aftermath when those who attempted to return home quickly found that the grounding spirit of their communities had been displaced along with the people. A bitter reality for many was the feeling of abandonment by the nation, President George W. Bush, and the president's administration. Individuals, families, and other kinship groups who lived through the devastating destruction of the hurricane experienced real sour and bitter moments of life. They recognized they had been given lemons, and many chose to do something with them.

Months before Beyoncé Knowles Carter released her visual album "Lemonade," Shannon described the concept to me that led to the main insight for this ethics.[39] There is an act of receiving what is available in the place where you find yourself, and an act of acceptance that you will find a way to make things work even if you have to use something that is not a part of your normal experiences. As Shannon asserted toward the end of our first interview, "Lemonade will be my outcome!" It gives substance to the "go-through," she said. Lemonade is flexible—sometimes sour, sometimes sweet, and sometimes tart. But when bitter lemons are what you have been handed, in order to make those experiences have productive meaning, make lemonade, even if, as Shannon concluded, you have to use substitute sugar when the brands/cultural elements you are accustomed to are no longer readily available. The practice of making lemonade can be a healing process requiring a willingness to not hold onto what has been given in its original form but to break and squeeze the essence out while finding the right balance of sweetness and replenishing water to create something new. An ethics of receptivity as evidenced by making lemonade with substitute sugar is a Romans 8:28 type of ethics that openly sees all things, including initially distasteful things, working together for the good of those who love God.

---

[38] Blannie Bowen (ed.), "A-B Newsletter," 13, no. 2 (February 2006): 3.
[39] Beyoncé's "Lemonade" was filmed in New Orleans and other areas of Louisiana. Her grandmother Agnéz Deréon and her husband Shawn Carter's grandmother, Hattie White, both inspired the wisdom of lemonade that has been passed from generation to generation.

Unlike larger cities such as Houston where over one hundred thousand former New Orleans residents have stayed for over a decade, created homes, and formed organizations such as the New Orleans Association of Houston,[40] life in State College is different. State College does not offer formal networks and support systems that have been able to be maintained beyond the initial year after Katrina.[41] Yet people like Shannon, Albert, Azalea, and Lydia choose to remain there.

Albright-Bethune has been a central place of community for these four New Orleanians. The transition has not been without challenges along the way, but those who have stayed in State College reflect that their faith was central to their lives in New Orleans, and it informs their ability to adjust through the recalculations of migration and the re-appropriation of something bitter into something better. In church, at least there were songs that could remind them of home; there was a place for fellowship and the coming together around a table, both sacramental and social; and there were people whose radical welcome extended beyond the media-focused window of the migration of Katrina survivors throughout the country to the current moment. Despite the itinerant nature of the pastoral leaders who have served at Albright-Bethune since 2005, the receptivity of the congregants has been consistent, and their support has enabled Shannon, Albert, Azalea, and Lydia to be receptive to making State College home.

Over fifteen years ago, the United States witnessed a national crisis unfold right before our eyes. The crisis uncovered through Hurricane Katrina has not been addressed, and unfortunately it has been revealed yet again through the racialized, gendered, and classed rhetoric and reasoning of many during and following the 2016 US Presidential election, the massive destruction from more frequent and intense Hurricanes, for example, Harvey, Irma, and Maria (among others) in Texas, Florida, the US Virgin Islands, Puerto Rico. And this problematic reasoning and rhetoric also permeates our nation's continued racial conflict, our experiences of the global COVID-19 pandemic, and the defense of the January 2021 assault on the nation's capital.

Today, many US inhabitants believe we have been given sour lemons, and although not all are migrating to new physical communities, many are being forced out of places, policies, and perspectives where we have been comfortable. Even more, all of us—whether positioned "in the eye of the storm" or not—must do the critical work of justice that creates the mutual respect and risk necessary to create a more ethical society. Our challenge is to become more receptive to the positive possibilities of difference by taking lessons from persons who literally lost everything, yet still found a way to gather various ingredients from their new environments and bring others together across differences. An ethics of receptivity as lived by the New Orleanians

---

[40] See http://jessemuhammad.blogs.finalcall.com/2012/08/the-new-orleans-association-of-houston.html (accessed January 3, 2017) and Tracy Jan and Brittney Martin, "Houston Took Them in After Katrina," *Then Harvey Hit*, August 29, 2017, https://www.washingtonpost.com/news/wonk/wp/2017/08/29/houston-took-them-in-after-katrina-then-harvey-hit/?noredirect=on&utm_term=.95344046ed9d (accessed May 29, 2018).

[41] Houston, Texas, has more Hurricane Katrina survivors than State College has with the town and university communities combined.

in State College reminds us that even when you have to discover alternative ways to add spice and sweetness to challenging moments, you can gather at a communal table where a warm bowl of gumbo filled with the spices of life can be shared from a large inclusive pot. You can also actively squeeze the lemons tossed at you by life and make lemonade to transform the bitter into the sweet and replenish you for the next phase of life's journey.[42]

---

[42] A longer version of this essay was originally published in the *Practical Matters* journal.

Part III

Method

14

Benedictions

For Those Willing to Give Ethnography a Try

Collectively, the chapters in Part I explore important histories, debates, and methods related to ethnography and theology. However, the methodological discussion is more on the analytical side than practical. Part II offers thought-provoking, concrete examples of theological ethnography and, along the way, points to some specific, continually evolving, methodological designs and issues. You might be the sort of diligent reader who has plowed through the chapters from start to finish. But you may also be the sort of person who has, either by choice or by assignment, turned straight away to this last section that focuses on the "nitty-gritty" pragmatic discussion of methods. However you got to this point, we now offer some benedictions for those wishing to take up, or deepen their practice of, ethnographic research. Benedictions are good words, words of sending for those transformed by the Word and Sacrament present for them at the heart of Christian worship. Here, we hope to send those inspired by the powerful and compelling witness embodied especially in the exemplar chapters found in Part II. Our "good words" for sending you highlight the basic outline of a research project, along with commentary and references to additional reading you may find helpful.

Formulation of a Research Question

At a number of points along the way we have discussed differences between qualitative and quantitative research, and their divergence begins here, at the outset, when one begins formulating a question that the process of research might answer. As mentioned in Chapter 1, Robert P. Jones, a contributor to the 2011 edition, is founder and president of *Public Religion Research Institute* (PRRI), a nonprofit and nonpartisan organization that conducts independent quantitative surveys on myriad topics related to religion, culture, public policy, and American perceptions.[1] For instance, a 2023 PRRI study features comparative data on American Jewish and Christian views of climate change

---

[1] See https://www.prri.org/. For another prominent example of quantitative research in the areas of religion, public opinion, politics, and various demographics, see the Pew Research Center: http://pewresearch.org/.

and environmental policy across denominations and the political spectrum.[2] The report gives a broad snapshot of how American Christians and Jews at a moment in time report on personal convictions. The report found, for example, that:

> three-fourths of Hispanic Catholics and religiously unaffiliated Americans (76 percent) believe climate change is caused by human activity, as do the majority of other non-Christians (70 percent), Jewish Americans (67 percent), Hispanic Protestants (61 percent), Black Protestants (59 percent), other Protestants of color (59 percent), white Catholics (56 percent), white mainline/non-evangelical Protestants (54 percent), and about half of Latter-day Saints (48 percent). However, just three in ten white evangelical Protestants (31 percent) believe that climate change is caused by humans.[3]

Yet, to understand *how* people come to their convictions regarding climate change and their faith, and *what* people do on the basis of those beliefs, one would need, at a minimum, to conduct interviews or focus groups. Spending additional time participating in the lives of specific faith communities would likely yield even richer understanding.

Dawne Moon did just this in her book *God, Sex and Politics* to get at *why* Christians think whatever they do about LGBTQAI+ people. Whereas survey research can find out what people admit to believing, Moon took a classically ethnographic approach. "I ask," Moon writes, "given that members of these congregations believe in God, what do they do with that belief? How is it that members can purport to believe in the same God and yet have such very different theologies" when it comes to homosexuality?[4] Ethnographic studies go beyond reporting the facts of "what is" found through research to paint a fuller picture of what these facts mean in the lives of a person or community. In other words, they are better at getting at "how" and "why" kinds of questions that shape individual and social decisions, activities, and practices.

In terms of practical counsel, we would advise that while some—or even just one—orienting research question is needed at the outset in an ethnographic project, that it should be fairly open-ended, or at least open to revision, as the learning process in the field progresses. Mindy Fullilove explains that ethnographic research is a "feel-forward" approach, meaning that the researcher cannot know or identify all of the relevant questions or issues at the inception. Instead, they need to be open to the possibility that the initial questions turn out to be not the most helpful ones for learning from the field.[5] In summary, it is good to identify a basic question or set of questions that one brings to the study. Doing so is vital for crafting a cogent and manageable focus. Yet, this framework should not be heavy-handed or overdetermined. There is a necessary

---

[2] https://www.prri.org/research/the-faith-factor-in-climate-change-how-religion-impacts-american-attitudes-on-climate-and-environmental-policy/ (accessed October 4, 2023).
[3] See https://www.prri.org/research/the-faith-factor-in-climate-change-how-religion-impacts-american-attitudes-on-climate-and-environmental-policy/ (accessed October 4, 2023).
[4] Dawne Moon, *God, Sex and Politics: Homosexuality and Everyday Theologies* (Chicago: University of Chicago Press, 2004), 4.
[5] Fullilove, *The Little Handbook*, unpublished guide for her graduate students, 9.

fluidity at work—the central research questions may shift as the ethnographer immerses themself in the context and learns from it.

Finally, before the formal ethnographic work begins, we think it is worthwhile to take time to discern what the most pressing issues are for a given place or people. Again, this understanding may indeed shift once the ethnographic portion begins or deepens—the researcher may be decidedly mistaken in what they think these needs are. Yet, whenever possible and appropriate, there is real merit in attempting to align one's research with the actual needs of others from the outset.

Research Design

The orienting question one begins with, then, sets in motion choices about each of the aspects of the research process that follow. The questions imply, if you will, the kinds of evidence required in order to find answers, and therefore set a direction toward particular kinds of research. This volume, in advocating ethnography, imagines the fruitfulness for theology and ethics of following the sorts of "how" questions asked by Dawne Moon. To illustrate the point: to ask about clergy beliefs regarding queer communities, one need not leave the office. Constructing a survey to email to pastors *does* require layers of work, but it does not actually require speaking with any pastors or visiting any congregations. However, if one seeks to see *how* people's lives in community are shaped by shared belief in God while holding divergent views of sexual and gender identities, one needs to actually go and be with people.

While research designs vary widely, a common thread pulls together the various things we include under the term ethnography. That thread might honestly be named "mucking around." To be clear, we do *not* suggest that researchers carelessly gallop out "into the field" without sufficient preparation, introspection, and needed skills. Indeed, the chapters by Grigoni, Hoskins, and Williams in Part II all show distinct dimensions of rigorous and self-reflective engagement. Yet, while this quite pedestrian term may not immediately strike you as helpful, it points to the inescapably difficult, often messy, work of joining in the lives of people where they live. This might, as with Whitmore's work, require learning the tribal language of the people and living in difficult circumstances in a large Ugandan refugee camp. Vivid description and close to the bone reflection about the theological and moral issues at stake arise from the messiness of his fieldwork in the midst of these particular people. Such "mucking around" might also, as with Fitriyah, require long hours of careful listening to Indonesian migrant women's lives. This kind of listening cannot simply be structured by a narrow set of predetermined questions. Instead, it requires a more open-ended approach that enables questions to emerge in response to the salient points raised by the persons interviewed. Often such interviews take narrative form, allowing the multilayered unfolding of lives as they are lived.

Certainly, the basics of research design can be unpacked in more detail. One must, for example, choose a research site and topic that balances the researcher's need for access with the need to do sufficient groundwork that helps expand opportunities to encounter rich, multi-facted experiences and insights. One must plan with some flexibility the duration and details of the research, and contemplate its potentially complex effects for those studied. Specific plans for use of core techniques of research must be thought through: participating and observing what, how, for how long; what methods of recording to use; interviewing which sorts of people and with which central questions; combining focus groups with individual interviews or not; using any kind of visual or autoethnographic methods or not; employing a participatory action model or not; how much, and what kind of, historical, sociological, or other kinds of contextual data are needed to supplement the ethnographic materials, and so on.

In general, the rule of triangulating data is important to consider. This means one has at least three overlapping but distinct angles of vision on a given project, each offered by virtue of a different method (interviews, observation, participation, document analysis). It also means that as a whole, a research endeavor often relates ethnographic data to relevant quantitative sources of information (e.g., census data, health/healthcare statistics, poverty indexes, historical documents or narratives of a community, nation, or place). Resourcing relevant quantitative sources of information can help to contextualize what one hears and sees through the ethnographic study. As Paul Farmer so powerfully embodied in Haiti, if one wants to understand fully the challenges and realities that Haitians describe, one needs to know a good deal about the legacy of US foreign (political and economic) policy in Haiti.[6]

In summary, in choosing a research design for your project, the research question plays a key role. You might ask yourself questions such as: "How does my basic question inform how I organize my study? How can I best learn what I hope to learn? What kinds of information do I need? How might the design process offer a plan for helping me and those participating in the research explore the question?" In sum, "form follows function"—the form of the study should correlate with the kinds of questions one hopes to pursue.

Site Selection and Sampling

Obviously, choosing where and with whom to do your "mucking around" is crucial to the overall outcome of the research process. Yet, the truth is that even this process is often a great deal messier than some tidy, after-the-fact reports show. For starters, as noted above research site selection (where the research is carried out) and sampling (a way to talk about who one recruits for interviews, for example) are often shaped by central questions that sometimes evolve or change completely during the course or research. Furthermore, the 2011 edition did not sufficiently unpack the complexities that come with researchers often identifying in various ways as "insiders" and "outsiders" to the communities from and with whom they aim to learn. At times, researchers share significant parts of the social locations of those who inhabit the site of study, such as Park's study of the one-man protest in her community in Seoul, South Korea. At other times, they stand afar but see themselves as sharing some of the same values and concerns; still other times, they choose to study groups, affinities, and places

---

[6] See Paul Farmer, *Pathologies of Power* (Berkeley: University of California Press, 2005) and also Tracy Kidder, *Mountains Beyond Mountains* (New York: Random House, 2003).

that are rather different from their own. Often, the reality is that it is a complicated combination of resonances and dissonances.

Symmonds's work illustrates this point well. Concerned about the realities of commercialized sexual exploitation, she sought to learn from a major anti-trafficking ministry in Atlanta. Given her own positionality and research interests, the choice of NDS, a well-established white evangelical ministry focused primarily on Black and Brown women who have been trafficked, was straightforward. To get her bearings, she first took stock of the spiritual and cultural landscape of NDS and the design of their orientations for new volunteers. From there, she worked toward meeting and conducting interviews with NDS leaders and participants. She also participated in and observed their van outreach efforts.

It is important to underscore the care she took in having preliminary conversations in order to discern with whom she ought to seek interviews and how best to learn from, and engage with, the NDS organization. As a Black woman, Symmonds was acutely aware that this study would entail "studying up" in terms of focusing on a predominately white evangelical Christian organization with significantly more power than the Black and Brown women it seeks to reach. Thus, Symmonds occupied the uncomfortable place of resonating with some of their aims and assumptions while being disquieted by others. In a related vein, Grigoni embarked upon a study of both predominately white, evangelical Christian gun owners and others, predominantly Black and Brown people, keeping vigil for their loved ones who had died from gun violence. He did so out of respect for his own family's complicated relationship to guns and out of his deep desire to understand and describe—in all their fullness—the faith and values that motivate each community.

For her part, Hoskins grew up in close proximity to Altgeld Gardens. Her relationships to environmental justice advocates there exposed her both to the community's agency and also to the narrow, problematic representations of them by outside interviewers and journalists. Thus, Hoskins turned to ethnography as a disciplined means to understand their perspectives, efforts, and lives in their own terms, refusing to dissect artificially their laments and critiques; their descriptive and prescriptive rants.

In contrast, sometimes the site selection and research question pop up in response to unanticipated events. For example, in Williams's case, her ethnographic study of predominately white/Western/Presbyterian Holy Land tours serendipitously led to an encounter at a conference that spurred an additional research question aimed to learn about "the Swedish woman." This search led Williams through a series of discoveries related to her own positionality as a white, Western Christian and to the complexity of strategies and agency embodied by Palestinian women.

To be sure, one cannot simply "count" or "justify" one's daily life or social location in this or that context as ethnography. Nor ought one jump too quickly to capitalize on an unexpected opportunity. Indeed, as so many of the chapters in Part II illustrate, there are complex dynamics to consider when one identifies in significant ways as "insiders" of a community one wishes to study. For starters, one has specific ethical responsibilities when moving from ordinary life to the role of a researcher, whether one is part of an institution in which qualitative research is regularly carried out or not. Even more, robust self-reflexivity regarding one's own values, assumptions, and positionality is vital, especially when one resonates with, or wants to be in solidarity with, the people inhabiting the research site(s). It is dangerous, and often dehumanizing, to take one's good intentions and affinities as evidence of "belonging" to a community or as authentic solidarity.

Proposals/Ethics/Institutional Review Boards (IRBs)

Once the research question, design, site selection, and sampling characteristics are clearly in mind, a pause is in order before plunging into the work. A process of ethical accountability generally includes a formal IRB that requires clear acknowledgment of one's plans from start to finish. This step includes asking questions about the risks and benefits for participants in the study. It can be a touchy question, especially when the researcher hopes to learn from people who live with various kinds of vulnerability. For example, IRBs raise eyebrows when researchers propose to study people who are living with acute or chronic illness; who occupy minoritized or marginalized social positions; those who have more to lose from careless, simplistic exposure than researchers with greater social capital.

IRB approval is also a moment to gain outside feedback and perspective on a research plan, a process that may raise ethical concerns or may simply provide wisdom for the process from others who have experience. In all, we urge prospective qualitative researchers to engage with the IRB early and often—to build clear lines of communication and mutual understanding of the research project and potential concerns that must be navigated. In certain situations, as alluded to by Hankela and Nishimwe, having an established qualitative scholar mentor a newer one, and advocate for them, can be of great help during the research process, including navigating IRBs.

Moreover, responsibility *only begins* with formal IRB approval. Beyond having any requisite permissions in place from authorizing bodies, researchers are profoundly accountable to those from and with whom they learn. Even with IRB certification in hand, it is entirely possible to act in ways which disrespect, and even obscure, the realities and people the ethnographer hopes to illuminate. As discussed in several places in Part I, ongoing, critical self-reflection about assumptions, descriptions, and what one does with the research (and how one benefits) are crucial dimensions to any study. We need ways to "check ourselves" again and again throughout the process. And we need to demonstrate a kind of accountability that continues well beyond the period of ethnographic study itself.

A challenging question in this regard has to do with the question of benefit. Who benefits from the research, and how? In some cases, the candor of participants in qualitative interviews mirrors what they have already stated in other public forums. Yet, even in these situations where the stakes are fairly low, it is nonetheless vital to—whenever possible—close loops with participants, checking with them before presenting or publishing materials from interviews so that each person will hopefully feel accurately represented.

Moreover, as the exemplars in Part II make clear, for theologians and ethicists engaging in qualitative research, there are nearly always deeply theological and ethical aims undergirding the work. It is important to be transparent and reflective about this fact. Put simply, there is generally at least a spark of hope that the research might have positive rippling effects in relation to its chosen topic. Such aspirations often constitute a key aspect of what motivates people to undertake such study in the first place. Indeed, Boopalan and Jongte urge potential researchers to create ethnographies that embody genuine solidarity with "crucified bodies."

Certainly, there are no guarantees. As Boopalan and Jongte also point out, without robust articulation of nuanced social locations, false equivalences and superficial alliances can deftly mask layers of oppression. Groups that possess certain power in one context can hide this power in another. For her part, Fitriyah cannot claim that the Indonesian migrant workers in Singapore fare any better because of her research. Instead, she hopes to show the strength these women derive from their network of relationships while urging readers to recognize the multidimensionality of their theologies and moral agency so they/we might be motivated to find ways to support their quests for better lives. In short, profound tensions around questions of who benefits and how from the work do not go away and are not easily resolved.

Entry/Permission/Reflexivity

To be sure, tensions are part and parcel of the plunge into research. As one moves from the stage of fully fleshing out the proposal and getting various formal approvals, entering the research site looms. In order to gain entry, even entry within a familiar world of context and competence for which one already has affinity, formal permission ought to be sought for the sake of transparency. Consider the example of Mingo, a Southerner and ordained Elder in the African Methodist Episcopal Church, who set out to learn about an ethic of receptivity from a United Methodist congregation populated by many individuals who had fled New Orleans in the wake of Hurricane Katrina. Before embarking upon her research, she first sought the guidance of the leadership in the congregation. They in turn helped her meet others she wished to include in the study.

Permission is often not straightforward and can fluctuate. Thus, researchers need to prepared to adapt to situations as they evolve and never take peoples' permission for granted. For example, Williams noticed how some of the interview participants were reticent to speak on the record or asked her to avoid certain lines of questioning. Even more, as one heeds Boopalan and Jongte's call to attend to "crucified bodies," one's face-to-face encounters with acutely vulnerable people necessitate that one reflects on the complexity of the privilege the researcher inhabits and the responsibilities for the relationships that develop during the course of one's research. At one point or other, the formal research project will end. To varying degrees, even if one is somewhat a part of the community who participates in the study, the researcher "leaves" the site. The "outsider–insider" dynamic continues to evolve. How does one both "move on" and yet not abandon the people to whom so much learning is owed?

Participant Observation

Participant observation, a key element of almost every ethnographic research project, might also be described as "going to see for oneself." But it is more than this, for one can go and see for oneself as a curiosity-seeker, with no intention of doing more than fulfilling a voyeuristic desire. One can, as well, be a journalist who investigates, often traveling to a specific scene, with an aim to share relatively quickly what one has found with the wider public. But participant observation as part of ethnographic research is, as we discuss in Part I, "untimely." Not captive to personal whim or the latest news cycle, this sort of participation can take time to dwell, listen carefully, and wait, if necessary, for the insights and experiences that help make sense of people's lives in a particular place and moment. As Hoskins' rich connections to the Altgeld Gardens community illustrate, her investment and long-term relationships give her much deeper and more careful information about the lives and perspectives of the community than any casual visitor or reporter calling for comment on a deadline manages to accomplish.

A fundamental aspect of such participant observation is, not surprisingly, recording one's thoughts, reactions, observations, wonderings, and so on. This is often done through what many call "field notes." While this is mostly a background facet in the research process, it is absolutely essential. It is, in a way, a memory aid. While of course one might use photography, video and audio recording, or other techniques, nothing really replaces the discipline of notes. It is often very helpful if one is able to jot some notes during the midst of any given event or experience. But regardless, within a few hours of finishing for the day, one ought to spend the time to recount the experiences as fully as possible. The key here is robust, narrative detail. If a reactive judgment arises, it can be placed in a margin and set aside so that the narrative focuses on giving as disciplined and as full a picture of what transpired as possible. Throughout his years of immersion in the Chicago boxing gym, Loïc Wacquant returned every night and sat up at his desk writing about the day.[7]

However, this is not to say one must adhere to the classical model of ethnography—living in an unfamiliar culture for a year or more—as Wacquant's and other similar studies suggest. The chapters in Part II portray quite a variety of of on-the-ground research, from relatively brief visits to longer immersions in local contexts. All of them required patient, empathetic listening and guided, but open-ended interviewing.

Interviewing

As we've already begun to describe, interviewing often plays a pivotal role in ethnographic research. When one "goes to see for oneself," part of that work is asking prepared questions of those one goes to see. Of course, in the process, one might have many kinds of informal conversations and all of these encounters are of value. Indeed,

---

[7] Loïc Wacquant, *Body and Soul: Notebooks of an Apprentice Boxer* (Oxford: Oxford University Press, 2003). Also see the excellent "how-to" by Robert Emerson, Rachel Fretz, and Linda Shaw, *Writing Ethnographic Fieldnotes* (Chicago: University of Chicago Press, 1995).

some of the most important learning happens in the unanticipated, unexpected moments. Yet interviewing in a formal sense is also often essential. It delineates the overall questions or topic areas about which one especially wants to know. These questions, and well-chosen follow-up questions that ask for further detail or clarity, represent the heart of the process, allowing for focus and care in hearing fully those from whom one seeks to learn. While one-on-one interviews are most typical, group interviews are not uncommon. They are not synonymous with focus groups, however, which are more like an opinion survey done in person. They are also at more depth than the typical phone, internet, or online survey questionnaire.

To be sure, interviews are difficult and can feel intimidating, not least because they require both careful listening and very effective modes of asking questions—opening questions and various sorts of follow-ups. Even more, attempting them can bring to the surface one's inner insecurities and awkwardness. Odd as it may sound here in a discussion of how to do research, having a handle on one's own issues, and being spiritually grounded oneself, is of great help in the process of research generally and interviewing particularly.

A common mistake: slipping into either judgment or attempts at fixing (which incidentally amount to the same thing). While such intention might be the aim in conversation with a friend, here the goal is to hold at bay one's own judgments and temptations to "solve" problems without being cold or unapproachable. Indeed, a person feeling strong emotions might not need to hear the next question on your list, but rather a momentary pause and supportive presence before continuing. Attentive study of qualitative methods and apprenticing work with mentors, as illustrated by Hankela and Nishimwe in their chapter, do indeed help develop interviewing strategies. The best "teacher" is self-reflexive practice, interviewing over and over and over, with critical evaluation of one's efforts via the transcript and dialogue with mentors and colleagues.

Since 2011, most pointedly starting in the Spring of 2020, millions across the globe have learned how much we can accomplish, including qualitative research, via Zoom and other online platforms. Since travel was impossible, Fitriyah conducted a bulk of her interviews using WhatsApp during the height of the COVID-19 pandemic. These interview technologies open up potential new avenues, and roadblocks, to ethnographic research. On the positive side, they can, as they did in Fitriyah's case, make it possible to speak with people who would otherwise be far out of reach. On the downside, such remote communications can make it harder to build genuine trust and rapport. People may be uncomfortable on camera or connected by technologies; the reception may falter; people may be more hesitant to open up or may worry more about being overheard than they otherwise would. And it is often harder to accurately understand/interpret facial expressions and nonverbal cues when communicating via phone, tablet, or computer. In short, early on, intentional planning about how/if to use the abundance of interview technologies available is essential.

In addition, increasing numbers of projects are incorporating visual ethnographic methods[8] adding to the more established modes of interviews, participant observation, and focus groups. Sociologists of religion, Nancy Ammerman and Roman Williams,

---

[8] See Sarah Pink, *Doing Visual Ethnography*, 4th ed. (London: Sage Publications, 2012).

were among the front-runners to do so.[9] In visual ethnography, participants might be invited to use cameras to document and describe their own lives. Or they may use digital media, paintings, or other visual art forms to depict their experiences and perspectives.

Sarah Dunlop's work illustrates how visual ethnographies can reveal layers of meaning that are generally untapped by an overreliance on words and texts. For example, in her studies of the spiritualities of Ukrainian, Russian, Hungarian, Slovakian, and Polish youth, Dunlop showed existent images (from pop culture, religion, sports, art, etc.) and asked participants to respond to them. She also invited participants to take their own photos for a period of time, after which she interviewed them. Dunlop puts the significance of this visual approach this way: "These studies combined revealed that the core values of young people, such as self-expression, freedom, and fun were at odds with their perceptions of the values of Christianity. . . . I literally saw their life values in action as they showed me their pictures and told their stories."[10]

Equipment

In order to have a transcript of an interview, one must either have a fantastic memory and write as much as can be remembered down immediately after or record the interview and transcribe it. Neither is foolproof, naturally, but the requisite ethos in either case is rooted in deep respect for what the other has to say. The equipment that allows one to record the event or interview—whether a recorder or an old-fashioned pen and notebook—allows that respect for the other's words and experience. We recommend doing both—writing a lot after interviews, focus groups, observations, *and* using some kind of digital recorder. If one is recording, getting permission ahead of time, and offering clarity about how the interview will be used, is important. One might do this when recruiting someone to the research project, or do it just before the interview. Some IRBs generally require a formal consent form that all participants sign.

The use of video and photography equipment is complicated. Certainly using them can provide stunning visuals to accompany printed text and/or oral presentations. They can provide helpful context—what the area looks like or what the dynamics of daily life appear to be just from seeing the place. They can similarly add greater dimension by putting faces and names to statistics—showing how various issues play out in embodied people's lives.

Moreover, as works by theological scholars such as Ammerman, Dunlop, and Ward demonstrate, the use of images is not limited to the recording of participant faces or voices. In addition to stories and narratives, ethnographers increasingly incorporate other mediums—including the use of the visual arts and original works created by

---

[9] See Nancy T. Ammerman, *Sacred Stories, Spiritual Tribes: Finding Religion in Everyday Life* (Oxford: Oxford University Press, 2013) and Roman Williams, *Seeing Religion: Toward a Visual Sociology of Religion* (London: Routledge, 2015).

[10] Sarah Dunlop, "Visual Ethnography," in *The Wiley Blackwell Companion to Theology and Qualitative Research*, ed. Pete Ward and Knut Tveitereid (Hoboken: John Wiley & Sons, Ltd, 2022), 418–19.

participants to elucidate meaning that is ineffable. As Sarah Dunlop notes, "Theology is more than listening, reading and speaking. It is seeing and being seen."[11]

Indeed, such photographic or video portrayals, especially of those who feel ignored or invisible, can be a means to affirm their dignity and identity. João Biehl's beautiful ethnography *Vita: Life in a Zone of Social Abandonment* includes stunning photography by Biehl's colleague, Torben Eskerod, that has an ethical argument in some ways parallel to the text itself.[12] In a similar fashion, Barbara Myerhoff's short documentary *Number Our Days*, accompanying her book of the same name, captured and publicized the beautiful but fragile life of a community of very elderly Jewish immigrants in Santa Barbara.[13]

Yet, as the Preface and other places in Part I indicate, images and video are also often a tool in commodification—turning a human subject into an object for consumption by others. Paul Farmer notes that graphic images do not always lead to meaningful intervention and cites the genocides in Rwanda and Sudan as cases in point.[14] Indeed, when such violent and shocking images are coupled with fleeting, "rubber-necking" attention and long-term apathy, they can become, in a sense, pornographic.

Similarly problematic and discussed in Part I, sometimes readers conflate the image with a more complex reality and person. Images can reveal part, but never the whole, truth. Thus, the use of images and video merit serious reflection. Why does the researcher want to video or take photographs? What purpose do they serve? How might they enhance or inhibit the research? What are the dangers of using them? How might collaborators be affected by their use?

In a pragmatic vein, setting up and using a camera can be off-putting to those interviewed. Fears about publicity or confidentiality can arise. Moreover, when a researcher uses and publishes the image of another, it can raise questions again about benefits. In all, we would caution against the use of video and film equipment unless the researcher is both highly self-aware about such use and is wholly confident that doing so will not get in the way of building trust and rapport. Asking people if they mind being photographed or filmed can help relationships grow, but is not a guarantee. Sometimes people are timid about indicating their true feelings or reservations to someone they do not know well or have only just met.

Analysis

Typically, one does not wait until the research is over to begin analysis. In fact, when one enters into a research project with one's question(s) in mind, the analysis begins right away.

---

[11] Ibid., 422.
[12] João Biehl, *Vita: Life in a Zone of Social Abandonment* (Berkeley: University of California Press, 2013), 42.
[13] Barbara Myerhoff, *Number our Days: A Triumph of Continuity and Culture among Jewish Old People in an Urban Ghetto* (New York: Touchstone, 1980).
[14] Farmer discusses both the powerful place and limits of the use of images in Paul Farmer, *Never Again? Reflections on Human Values and Human Rights* (University of Utah: The Tanner Lectures on Human Values, 2005), see especially 161-4. "The Rwandan genocide was among the world's most reported and photographed of mass killings. But abundant documentation, visual or otherwise, had virtually no role in halting that genocide." Ibid., 164.

This happens informally as questions arise as to what this or that comment or observation shows about the situation. There are disciplined methods of identifying themes (e.g.coding) that can assist in noticing emerging patterns across multiple interviews. Yet even before coding, simply attending to the discipline of research often leads one to begin to see core issues andpatterns. When such initial observations begin to unfold, it is important to note them and begin to test how these insights hold up as subsequent interviews, participant observation experiences, or other dimensions of study progress.

Some approaches argue for deriving themes directly from the participants' own words and lives. Other times the themes derive from the research question itself or from the theoretical frameworks one is exploring within a particular context. Whatever specific method one chooses or creates for tracking relevant themes and insights, it is crucial that a spirit of openness to surprise be continually present. As noted above with the initial research question, there needs to be a room for taking stock of how what one thought would be the central themes or findings turned out to be off-base or in need of substantive revision. Learning inductively from the field is an integral commitment of ethnographic study.

Moreover, while this thematic analysis is certainly important to do in relation to one's accumulating data, it is also a place forgenuine collaboration so that the reseracher is methodologically compelled to to present their findings to others and hear their reactions. One traditional opportunity for this kind of exchange is the student thesis or dissertation defense with a faculty committee. However, a potentially more interesting (and possibly more fruitful) avenue would be to design a thoroughly collaborative research project from the outset. This kind of endeavor is common in the natural and social sciences. We would like to see it become more standard in theology and ethics as well. The complexity of the world today—and the accessibility of so much information—makes the limits of any one researcher so very pronounced. Paul Rabinow and George Marcus, in their book on an anthropology of the contemporary, commend a "co-laboratory" or "studio" model in which the whole process—from generating concepts and questions through publication—is shared.[15]

In a related vein, Hankela and Nishimwe offer an illuminating, concrete example of collaborative, team research. Their chapter illustrates the rich conversations and thoughtful negotiations that are possible when more senior researchers are committed to the learning and growth of those who are assisting the research. As they make plain, the research assistant often has vital knowledge and insight that the other researcher may likely miss on their own. There are times when the apprenticing researcher needs the opportunity to lead; there are other times when it is more appropriate for the more senior scholar to step up to offer support or do the heavy lifting. The overall point is that collaborative work requires honest, self-reflective dialogue among the team members. Together, they need to explore the power dynamics, assumptions of the team members, and differing perceptions and experiences in the field. This shared reflexivity is an integral part of the overall research process and analysis.

---

[15] Paul Rabinow, George E. Marcus, James D. Faubion, and Tobias Rees, *Design for an Anthropology of the Contemporary* (Durham: Duke University Press, 2008), 83.

Publication

Finally, ethnography—writing culture, literally—must inevitably turn to the task of showing and sharing what one has learned. In what we have written thus far, we hope it is clear we do not endorse the privileged position of the scholar who studies and then writes an authoritative study of another's experience or culture. Ours is a more humble and self-critical stance, and in moving to writing, this complexity rushes to the forefront. Perhaps the chapters by Hoskins and Williams in this volume grapple most vividly with the complicated politics and privilege of moving from listening through research to writing.[16] Writing about the research ought not to leave the participants behind but holds them in its horizon as essential stakeholders in the dissemination of knowledge gained through the process. Said differently, ethnographically-informed writing must continually circle back to attend seriously both to the ethics of research and to one's accountability to those with whom the research was carried out.

Moreover, we want to push, perhaps more than we did in 2011, those pondering embarking upon a qualitative research project to expand the avenues for publication that they consider. Traditionally, scholars prize articles, chapters, and monographs in peer-reviewed academic journals and presses. And for good reason. Oftentimes, academic jobs, not to mention promotion and the job security of tenure, are in play. Yet, in addition to sharing the work in these circles, we urge creativity and collaboration in imagining ways to make it available to additional constituencies and communities. For example, if there are visual images or recordings, perhaps they could be, with the permission and involvement of participants, featured in public—online, in an art exhibit, in a short film or photographic series, and so on. Dunlop has done just this and describes her experience and the underlining ethic inspiring it this way:

> As we create exhibitions and websites to share our visual findings, others are invited to join in the interpretation of the data. . . . Just as visual research methods are highly participative, so too, these communications of findings are also democratized, extending beyond the limited audience of a paper given at an academic conference or the readers of an article in an academic journal. Just as visual material expands our theology, it also should expand how we communicate our theology.[17]

Dunlop calls academics to ground ourselves in approaches that democratize both our methods of research and interpretation of findings. We need to expand our understanding of the networks of communities to whom scholars are accountable. Doing so further uproots buried, but nonetheless alive, hierarchies in which academics presume to know more than those from/with whom they learn.

---

[16] Todd Whitmore's important book, *Imitating Christ in Magwi*, openly wrestles with these questions in the context of ethnography as a form of theology. Specifically, this work shows how writing can function both as an instance of one's own discipleship and also as a witness to the suffering of others.

[17] Dunlop, "Visual Ethnography," 422.

Collaborative qualitative methods such as participatory action research and community action models have been around for decades, and the number of projects continues to increase.[18] They offer compelling, concrete ways to put these platitudes into actual practice. And precisely here it merits highlighting again the pathbreaking work and vocation of the Rev. Dr. Melissa D. Browning. Even as her life was cut far too short, as Parsitau and Reimer-Barry vividly describe in their poignant tribute, the commitments and ethos undergirding Melissa Browning's qualitative studies remain at the forefront of creative, responsible, and participant-oriented approaches. Echoing Melissa's incisive convictions, we are convinced that, given the myriad—dire and fraught—challenges facing humanity in the twenty-first century, qualitative work ought not settle for being only "recognizably real." It ought to also strive to be as relevant to the wider society and as collaborative as possible. We can no longer afford the luxury (if we ever could) of writing and thinking with/for select and scholarly peers. The world is too fragile, and the need for meaningful interventions is too great. Formal theologians and ethicists have a responsibility to involve participants in ways that align with their interests and availability in as many research stages as feasible—from design to data analysis to dissemination. These hard, complex times yearn for more scholars to partner, create, and publish with individuals from a dazzling array of vocations, areas of expertise and positionalities.

Ethnography as theology and Christian ethics stays close to the ground, telling the stories and sharing the wisdom of those with whom one has done the research. Undeniably, putting such diverse fields as ethnography, theology, and ethics into conversation is a complicated task. The lines and boundaries blur. Often the research goes into unanticipated directions and takes surprising, even unsettling turns. As the writing progresses, the narrative can read like a textual cacophony, rather than a well-orchestrated symphony. Such complexity and even moments of chaos can lead some to lose heart—to give up on the process and go back to more familiar ways of doing, and conceiving of, theology and ethics. As Danish theologian Kirstine Helboe Johansen wryly observes, qualitative research can be overwhelming work that induces needling self-doubt:

> Every empirical researcher knows the drill. First, you are in the intense phase of gathering data. Insecure about whether you will be able to generate the necessary amount of and quality in your data to answer the research questions you set out to explore. You are interviewing and transcribing, doing observations and writing field reports, sorting pictures, handouts, and other types of material gathered in the field. Then, suddenly, you feel like you are drowning in data. There is so much to keep in mind, so much to delve into and a myriad new possible research questions arise.[19]

Qualitative research is hard, complicated, time-consuming work. If done well, self-scrutiny is a part of the process. And yes, it can shake one's confidence. To be sure, there

---

[18] See, for example, the chapters by Jonas Idestrom, Henk de Roest, and Angela Cowser on action, collaborative, and community action research in *The Wiley Blackwell Companion to Theology and Qualitative Research*, ed. Pete Ward and Knut Tveitereid (Hoboken: John Wiley & Sons, Ltd, 2022), 425–58.

[19] Kirstine Helboe Johansen, "Analytical Strategies," in *The Wiley Blackwell Companion to Theology and Qualitative Research*, 393.

are ways to remain grounded amid the unexpected and tumultuous. Even more, we vigorously contend that qualitative study is well worth the struggle, risks, vulnerability, and effort. This book represents an attempt to bolster courage and to equip people with both a rationale for going forward and with helpful guideposts that might help to navigate the terrain.

Even more, we are bold enough to suggest that some of the best work comes from "messy" projects where the relevant categories are not overly predetermined; when the researcher feels awkward and, at times, even ill-prepared; when even a conflicting and raucous collection of voices is heard in the narrative. The noted political scientist, Iris Marion Young, has called for attending fully to such differences rather than glossing over them. She contends that democracy depends on such wide-ranging participation where all are respected in their unique identities and communities.[20] In a similar vein, bell hooks observes that cultural studies—and we would add ethnography, Christian theology, and ethics—must be committed to "a 'politics of difference' that recognizes the importance of making space" where the sort of mutually respectful listening can overcome traditional divides between us. hooks continues,

> Drawing from a new ethnography, we are challenged to celebrate the polyphonic nature of critical discourse, to—as it happens in traditional African-American religious experience—hear one another "speak in tongues," bear witness, and patiently wait for revelation.[21]

These references to religious experience—and even revelation—lead us to conclude with the conviction that our efforts to both respect and listen to difference within a polyphonic dialogue are rooted in our very understanding of God. Trinitarian theologians have shown us that such relationality—self-giving communion within difference—is the essence of God's own life, and the core therefore of our lives in this wild and precious creation.[22] May it be so for us and for the readers of this volume. May we find the tenacity, humility, hope, and courage to attend to the complexity and richness of particularity and to trust—patiently and even impatiently at times—that revelation will come and dwell among us.

---

[20] Iris Marion Young, *Justice and the Politics of Difference* (Princeton: Princeton University Press, 1990).
[21] bell hooks, *Yearning: Race, Gender, and Cultural Politics* (Boston: South End Press, 1990), 133.
[22] See especially Catherine Mowry LaCugna, *God for Us: The Trinity and Christian Life* (San Francisco: Harper, 1991); John D. Zizioulas, *Being as Communion: Studies in Personhood and the Church* (Crestwood: St. Vladimir's Seminary Press, 1985); John D. Zizioulas, *Communion and Otherness: Further Studies in Personhood and the Church* (New York: T & T Clark, 2007).

Bibliography

Abrahamov, Binyamin. "A Re-examination of al-Ash'arī's Theory of 'Kasb' According to 'Kitāb Al-Luma.'" *The Journal of the Royal Asiatic Society of Great Britain and Ireland*, no. 2 (1989): 210–21.
Adams, Nicholas and Charles Elliott. "Ethnography is Dogmatics: Making Description Central to Systematic Theology." *Scottish Journal of Theology* 53 (Autumn 2000): 339–64.
Advocacy, Legislation & Issues. "Banned & Challenged Books." *Text*, July 28, 2017. https://www.ala.org/advocacy/bbooks.
Ahmed, Sara. "A Phenomenology of Whiteness." *Feminist Theory* 8, no. 2 (2007): 149–68.
Aloysius, G. "Trajectory of Hindutva." *Economic and Political Weekly* 29, no. 24 (1994): 1450–2.
Aloysius, G. *Nationalism without a Nation in India*. New Delhi: Oxford University Press, 1997.
American Civil Liberties Union. "Mapping Attacks on LGBTQ Rights in U.S. State Legislatures in 2023." https://www.aclu.org/legislative-attacks-on-lgbtq-rights-2023 (accessed January 10, 2024).
Ammerman, Nancy T. *Congregation and Community*. New Brunswick: Rutgers University Press, 1997.
Ammerman, Nancy T. *Sacred Stories, Spiritual Tribes: Finding Religion in Everyday Life*. New York: Oxford University Press, 2013.
Anwar, Nausheen H. and Sarwat Viqar. "Research Assistants, Reflexivity and the Politics of Fieldwork in Urban Pakistan." *Area* 49, no. 1 (2017): 114.
Anzaldúa, Gloria. *Borderlands La Frontera: A New Mestiza*. San Francisco: Aunt Lute Books, 1987.
Asad, Talal (ed.). *Anthropology & the Colonial Encounter*. Atlantic Highlands: Humanities Press, 1973.
Asad, Talal. *Formations of the Secular: Christianity, Islam, Modernity*. Stanford: Stanford University Press, 2003.
Bachelard, Gaston. *Le Nouvel Espirit Scientifque*. Paris: PUF, 1949.
Baker-Fletcher, Karen. *A Singing Something: Womanist Reflections on Anna Julia Cooper*. New York: Crossroad, 1994.
Banjo, Omotayo O. and Kesha Morant Williams. "A House Divided? Christian Music in Black and White." *Journal of Media and Religion* 10, no. 3 (2011): 115–37.
Barad, Karen Michelle. *Meeting the Universe Halfway: Quantum Physics and the Entanglement of Matter and Meaning*. Durham: Duke University Press, 2007.
Barnes, Michael H. (ed.). *Theology and the Social Sciences*. Maryknoll: Orbis, 2001.
Barth, Frederik, Andre Gingrich, Robert Parkin, and Sydel Silverman. *One Discipline, Four Ways: British, German, French, and American Anthropology*. Chicago: University of Chicago Press, 2005.
Baruah, Sanjib. "The Mongolian Fringe." *Himal Southasian* 26, no. 1 (2013): 82–6.
Bauman, Zygmunt. *Wasted Lives: Modernity and Its Outcasts*. Cambridge: Polity, 2004.

Beauchamp, Tom L. and James F. Childress. *The Principles of Biomedical Ethics*. 8th ed. New York: Oxford University Press, 2019.

Becker, Penny. *Congregations in Conflict: Cultural Models of Local Religious Life*. New York: Cambridge University Press, 1999.

Behar, Ruth. *The Vulnerable Observer: Anthropology that Breaks Your Heart*. Boston: Beacon Press, 1996.

Behar, Ruth and Deborah A. Gordon (eds.). *Women Writing Culture*. Berkeley: University of California Press, 1995.

Bell, Catherine. *Ritual Theory, Ritual Practice*. New York: Oxford University Press, 1992.

Bellah, Robert N. *Tokugawa Religion: The Cultural Roots of Modern Japan*. New York: The Free Press, 1957.

Bellah, Robert N. *Beyond Belief: Essays in Post-Traditional Religion*. New York: Harper, 1970.

Bellah, Robert N. "The Ethical Aims of Social Inquiry." In *Social Science as Moral Inquiry*, eds. Norma Haan, Robert Bellah, Paul Rabinow, and William Sullivan, 360–81. New York: Columbia University Press, 1983.

Bellah, Robert N. *Religion in Human Evolution: From the Paleolithic to the Axial Age*. Cambridge: Harvard University Press, 2011.

Bellah, Robert N., Richard Madsen, William M. Sullivan, Ann Swidler, and Steven M. Tipton. *Habits of the Heart: Individualism and Commitment in American Life*. Berkeley: University of California Press, 1985.

Biehl, João. *Vita: Life in a Zone of Social Abandonment*. Berkeley: University of California Press, 2005.

"BJP MP Pragya Thakur Refers to Nathuram Godse as a 'Patriot', Yet Again." *The Hindu*. https://www.thehindu.com/news/national/other-states/bjp-mp-pragya-thakur-refers-to-godse-as-patriot/article33568997.ece (accessed February 1, 2022).

Block, Jennie Weiss and Michael Griffin. "'Introduction,' in Paul Farmer, Reimagining Accompaniment: A Doctor's Tribute to Gustavo Gutierrez." In *In the Company of the Poor: A Conversation between Dr. Paul Farmer and Fr. Gustavo Gutierrez*, eds. Michael Griffin and Jennie Weiss Block, x–x. Maryknoll: Orbis Books, 2013.

Boas, Franz. *The Mind of Primitive Man*. New York: The Macmillan Company, 1911.

Boas, Franz. *Anthropology and Modern Life*. New York: W. W. Norton, 1928.

Boas, Franz. *Race, Language, and Culture*. New York: The Macmillan Company, 1940.

Boas, Norman. *Franz Boas 1858-1942: An Illustrated Biography*. Mystic: Seaport Autographs Press, 2004.

Bohannon, Richard and Kevin O'Brien. "Environmental Justice and Eco-Justice." In *Grounding Religion: A Field Guide to the Study of Religion and Ecology*. New York: Routledge, 2011.

Boopalan, Sunder John. *Memory, Grief, and Agency: A Political Theological Account of Wrongs and Rites*. New York: Palgrave Macmillan, 2017.

Boopalan, Sunder John. "Transnational Solidarities." *Conrad Grebel Review* 39, no. 1 (2021): 15.

Bourdieu, Pierre. *Outline of a Theory of Practice*. New York: Cambridge University Press, 1977.

Bourdieu, Pierre. *Language and Symbolic Power*. Stanford: Stanford University Press, 1991.

Bourdieu, Pierre and Loïc Wacquant. *An Invitation to Reflexive Sociology*. Chicago: University of Chicago Press, 1992.

Bowen, Blannie (ed.). "A-B Newsletter." 12, no. 9 (September 2005): 1.

Bowen, Blannie. "*A-B Newsletter*." 13, no. 2 (February 2006): 3.
Briggs, Charles and Clara Mantini-Briggs. *Tell Me Why My Children Died: Rabies, Indigenous Knowledge, and Communicative Justice*. Durham: Duke University Press, 2016.
Brown, Delwin, Sheila Greeve Davaney, and Kathryn Tanner. *Converging on Culture: Theologians in Dialogue with Cultural Analysis and Criticism*. New York: Oxford University Press, 2001.
Brown Douglas, Kelly. *Stand Your Ground: Black Bodies and the Justice of God*. Maryknoll: Orbis Books, 2015.
Browning, Don. *A Fundamental Practical Theology*. Minneapolis: Fortress Press, 1996.
Bullard, Robert D. *Dumping in Dixie: Race, Class, and Environmental Quality*. 3rd ed. Boulder, CO: Westview Press, 2000.
Bunzl, Matti. "Boas, Foucault, and the 'Native Anthropologist.'" *American Anthropologist* 106, no. 3 (2004): 435–42.
Butler, Anthea D. "White Evangelical Racism: The Politics of Morality in America." In *White Evangelical Racism: The Politics of Morality in America*. Chapel Hill: The University of North Carolina Press, 2021.
Butler, Judith. "Performativity, Precarity and Sexual Politics." *AIBR. Revista de Antopologia Iberoamericanan* 4, no. 3 (2009): i–xiii.
Butler, Judith. *Notes Toward a Performative Theory of Assembly*. Cambridge, MA: Harvard University Press, 2015.
Cahill, L. Sowle. *Theological Bioethics: Participation, Justice, and Change*. Washington: Georgetown University Press, 2005.
Cameron, Helen, Deborah Bhatti, Catherine Duce, James Sweeney, and Clare Watkins. *Talking about God in Practice: Theological Action Research and Practical Theology*. London: SCM Press, 2010.
Cannon, Katie G. *Black Womanist Ethics*. Eugene: Wipf & Stock, 2006.
Caretta, Martina Angela. "Situated Knowledge in Cross-Cultural, Cross-Language Research: A Collaborative Reflexive Analysis of Researcher, Assistant and Participant Subjectivities." *Qualitative Research* 15, no. 4 (2015): 489–505.
Carmi, Nora. "Kairos: Exploring the Idea of Justice in Palestine from a Woman's Perspective." *Theologies and Cultures* 11, no. 1 (June 2014): 32–41.
Cavanaugh, William. *Torture and Eucharist*. Oxford: Blackwell, 1998.
Chaulia, Sreeram Sundar. "The Politics of Refugee Hosting in Tanzania: From Open Door to Unsustainability, Insecurity, and Receding Receptivity." *Journal of Refugee Studies* 16, no. 2 (2003): 147–66.
Chavis, Benjamin Jr. and Charles Lee. *Toxic Waste and Race in the United States: A National Report on the Racial and Socio-economic Characteristics of Communities with Hazardous Waste Sites*. New York: United Church of Christ, 1987.
Choe, Sang-Hun. "'My Last Stand:' In South Korea, A Protester's Lone Fight Against Samsung." *The New York Times*, April 19, 2020. https://www.nytimes.com/2020/04/19/world/asia/samsung-tower-protest.html.
Clarke, Sathianathan. "Hindutva, Religious and Ethnocultural Minorities, and Indian-Christian Theology." *The Harvard Theological Review* 95, no. 2 (April 1, 2002): 197–226.
Clifford, James and George E. Marcus (eds.). *Writing Culture: The Poetics and Politics of Ethnography*. Berkeley: University of California Press, 1986.
Cole, Douglas. *Franz Boas: The Early Years 1858-1906*. Seattle: University of Washington Press, 1999.

Coleman, Monica A. *Making a Way out of No Way: A Womanist Theology*. Minneapolis: Fortress Press, 2008.

Commission for Racial Justice. *Toxic Wastes and Race in the United States: A National Report on the Racial and Socio-Economic Characteristics of Communities with Hazardous Waste Sites*. New York: United Church of Christ, 1987.

Commonwealth Fund Report. *Racial and Ethnic Disparities in U.S. Health Care: A Chartbook*. New York: Commonwealth Fund, 2008.

Cone, James. *A Black Theology of Liberation*. 40th Anniversary ed. Maryknoll: Orbis, 2010.

Cone, James. *The Cross and the Lynching Tree*. Maryknoll: Orbis Books, 2011.

Cook, Philip J. and Kristin A. Goss. *The Gun Debate: What Everyone Needs to Know*. 2nd ed. Oxford: Oxford University Press, 2020.

Cook, Philip J. and Audrey Vila. *Gun Violence in Durham, NC, 2017–2021: Investigation and Court Processing of Fatal and Nonfatal Shootings*. Durham: Sanford School of Public Policy and Wilson Center for Science and Justice at Duke Law, Duke University, February 2023. www.law.duke.edu/sites/default/files/images/centers/wcsj/Durham_Shootings.pdf, 6

Copeland, M. Shawn. "The New Anthropological Subject at the Heart of the Mystical Body of Christ." *CTSA Proceedings* 53 (1998): 25–47.

Copeland, M. Shawn. *Enfleshing Freedom: Body, Race, and Being*. Minneapolis: Fortress Press, 2009.

Cose, Ellis. *Color-Blind: Seeing Beyond Race in a Race-Obsessed World*. New York: HarperPerennial, 1997.

Cowser, Angela. "Ethnography as Community Action." In *The Wiley Blackwell Companion to Theology and Qualitative Research*, eds. Pete Ward and Knut Tveitereid, 446–58. Hoboken: John Wiley & Sons, Ltd, 2022.

Cuddeback-Gedeon, Lorraine. *The Work of Inclusion: An Ethnography of Grace, Sin, and Intellectual Disabilities*. London: TT Clark, 2022.

Darnell, Regna. *And Along Came Boas: Continuity and Revolution in Americanist Anthropology*. Amsterdam: John Benjamins, 1998.

de Roest, Henk. *Collaborative Practical Theology: Engaging Practitioners in Research on Christian Practices*. Leiden and Boston: Brill, 2019.

de Roest, Henk. "Collaborative Research." In *The Wiley Blackwell Companion to Theology and Qualitative Research*, 435–45. Hoboken: John Wiley & Sons, Ltd, 2022.

Deane, Kevin and Sara Stevano. "Towards a Political Economy of the Use of Research Assistants: Reflections from Fieldwork in Tanzania and Mozambique." *Qualitative Research* 16, no. 2 (2016): 214.

Desai, Ashwin and Goolem Vahed. *The South African Gandhi: Stretcher-Bearer of Empire*. Stanford: Stanford University Press, 2015.

Dunlop, Sarah. "Visual Ethnography." In *The Wiley Blackwell Companion to Theology and Qualitative Research*, eds. Pete Ward and Knut Tveitereid, 415–24. Hoboken: John Wiley & Sons, Ltd, 2022.

"Durham Police Department Shooting Data: Year-to-Date through December 31, 2022." *City of Durham*. www.durhamnc.gov/ArchiveCenter/ViewFile/Item/6111 (accessed September 30, 2023).

Eazymaid. "Way To deal with New Maid in Singapore." July 3, 2020. https://www.housemaid.com.sg/eazy-maid-blogs/blogdetail/way-to-deal-with-new-maid-in-singapore.

Eiesland, Nancy. *The Disabled God*. Nashville: Abingdon Press, 1994.

Ellacuría, Ignacio. "The Crucified People." In *Mysterium Liberationis: Fundamental Concepts of Liberation Theology*, eds. Ignacio Ellacuria and Jon Sobrino, 580–603. Maryknoll: Orbis Books, 1993.

Elliott, James R. and Jeremy Pais. "Race, Class, and Hurricane Katrina: Social Differences in Human Responses to Disaster." *Social Science Research* 32, no. 2 (2006): 295–321.

Emerson, Michael and Christian Smith. *Divided by Faith: Evangelical Religion and the Problem of Race in America*. New York: Oxford University Press, 2000.

Emerson, Robert, Rachel Fretz, and Linda Shaw. *Writing Ethnographic Fieldnotes*. Chicago: University of Chicago Press, 1995.

Engelke, Matthew. *How to Think Like an Anthropologist*. Princeton: Princeton University Press, 2018.

Eskridge, Larry. "Slain by the Music." *Religion Online*. https://www.religion-online.org/article/slain-by-the-music/ (accessed February 25, 2021).

Fals-Borda, O. "The Application of Participatory Action-Research in Latin America." *International Sociology* 2, no. 4 (1987): 329–47.

Farley, Margaret. *Just Love: A Framework for Christian Sexual Ethics*. New York: Continuum, 2006.

Farmer, Paul. "New Malaise: Bioethics and Human Rights in the Global Era." *Journal of Law, Medicine, and Ethics* 32 (2004): 243–51.

Farmer, Paul. *Pathologies of Power: Health, Human Rights, and the New War on the Poor*. Berkeley: University of California, 2005.

Farmer, Paul. *Never Again? Reflections on Human Values and Human Rights*. The Tanner Lectures on Human Values. Salt Lake: The University of Utah, 2006.

Farmer, Paul. "Reimagining Accompaniment: A Doctor's Tribute to Gustavo Gutierrez." In *In the Company of the Poor: Conversations between Dr. Paul Farmer and Fr. Gustavo Gutierrez*, eds. Michael P. Griffin and Jennie Weiss Block. Maryknoll: ORBIS, 2013.

Feldman, Jackie. "Vehicles of Values: Souvenirs and the Moralities of Exchange in Christian Holy Land Pilgrimage." In *Toward an Anthropology of Nation Building and Unbuilding in Israel*, eds. Fran Markowitz, Stephen Sharot, and Moshe Shokeid, 259–75. Omaha: University of Nebraska Press, 2015.

Fiddes, Paul. *Participating in God. A Pastoral Doctrine of the Trinity*. London: Darton, Longman and Todd, 2000.

Fiddes, Paul. *Seeing the World and Knowing God. Hebrew Wisdom and Christian Doctrine in a Late-Modern Context*. Oxford: Oxford University Press, 2013.

Fiddes, Paul. "Revelation and Normativity." In *The Wiley Blackwell Companion to Theology and Qualitative Research*, eds. Pete Ward and Knut Tveitereid, 121–30. Hoboken: John Wiley & Sons, Ltd, 2022.

Flyvberg, Bent. *Making Social Science Matter: Why Social Inquiry Fails and How It Can Succeed Again*. Translated by Steven Sampson. New York: Cambridge University Press, 2001.

Ford, David F. *Self and Salvation: Being Transformed*. New York: Cambridge University Press, 1999.

Frank, Arthur. *The Wounded Storyteller: Body, Illness, and Ethics*. Chicago: University of Chicago Press, 1995.

Fulkerson, Mary McClintock. *Changing the Subject: Women's Discourses and Feminist Theology*. Minneapolis: Fortress Press, 1994.

Fulkerson, Mary McClintock. *Places of Redemption: Theology for a Worldly Church*. New York: Oxford University Press, 2007.

Fullilove, Mindy. Unpublished handbook for qualitative research for classroom use, *The Little Handbook*, Edited by Mindy Thompson Fullilove, created for the use of the Qualitative Research Methods (QRM) 101 class, Mailman School of Public Health, Columbia University, New York, 2001.

Gardet, Louis. "Kasb." In *The Encyclopedia of Islam*, eds. C. E. Bosworth et al. 2nd ed. Leiden: A. J. Brill, 1997.

Garland-Thomson, Rosemary. *Extraordinary Bodies*. New York: Columbia University Press, 2017.

Gill, Robin. "Churchgoing and Christian Ethics." In *New Studies in Christian Ethics*, ed. Robin Gill, Vol. 15. New York: Cambridge University Press, 1999.

Gin, Ooi Keat. "Domestic Servants Par Excellence: The Black and White Amahs of Malaya and Singapore, with Special Reference to Penang." *Journal of the Malaysian Branch of the Royal Asiatic Society* 65, no. 2 (1992): 69–84.

Glissant, Édouard. *Poetics of Relation*. Ann Arbor: University of Michigan Press, 1990.

Godoy, Maria. "Tracking the Katrina Diaspora: A Tricky Task." *NPR—Katrina One Year Later*.

González-Justiniano, Yara and Christopher P. Ney. "Contextual Theology." In *The Wiley Blackwell Companion to Theology and Qualitative Research*, eds. Pete Ward and Knut Tveitereid, 185–94. Hoboken: John Wiley & Sons, Ltd, 2022.

Gordon, Deborah A. "Writing Culture, Writing Feminism: The Poetics and Politics of Experimental Ethnography." *Inscriptions* 3/4 (1988): 7–24.

Gossett, Thomas. *Race: The History of an Idea in America*. New York: Oxford University Press, 1963.

Goto, Courtney T. "Writing in Compliance with the Racialized 'Zoo' of Practical Theology." In *Conundrums in Practical Theology*, eds. Joyce Ann Mercer and Bonnie Miller-McLemore, 110–33. Leiden: Brill, 2017 .

Goto, Courtney T. *Taking on Practical Theology: The Idolization of Context and the Hope of Community*. Leiden: Brill, 2018.

Green, Rachelle. "Ethnography as Critical Pedagogy: Prisons, Pedagogy, and Theological Education." In *The Wiley Blackwell Companion to Theology and Qualitative Research*, eds. Pete Ward and Knut Tveitereid. 38–9. Hoboken: John Wiley & Sons, Ltd, 2022.

Grigoni, Michael R. "The Christian Handgun Owner and Just War." *Journal of Moral Theology* 12, special issue no. 2 (2023): 108–32.

Groopman, Jerome. *How Doctors Think*. Boston: Houghton Mifflin, 2007.

Gustafson, James M. "The Sectarian Temptation: Reflections on Theology, the Church, and the University." *Catholic Theological Society of American Proceedings* 40 (1985): 83–94.

Gutierrez, Gustavo. *A Theology of Liberation: History, Politics, and Salvation*. Translated by Caridad Inda and John Eagleson. 15th Anniversary ed. Maryknoll: Orbis Books, 1988.

Gutierrez, Gustavo. *The Power of the Poor in History*. Translated by Robert R. Barr. Eugene: Wipf Stock, 2004.

Haddad, Beverley. "The South African Women's Theological Project: Practices of Solidarity and Degrees of Separation in the Context of the HIV Epidemic." *Religion & Theology* 20, no. 1–2 (2013): 2–18.

Haggard, Dana L., et al. "Who Is a Mentor? A Review of Evolving Definitions and Implications for Research." *Journal of Management* 37, no. 1 (2011): 289–90.

Hall, Budd. "In from the Cold? Reflections on Participatory Research from 1970-2005." *Convergence* 38 (2005): 5–24.

Hamel, Liz, Lunna Lopes, Cailey Muñana, Samantha Artiga, and Mollyann Brodie. "The Undefeated Survey on Race and Health." https://www.kff.org/report-section/kff-the-undefeated-survey-on-race-and-health-main-findings/

Hancock, Ange-Marie. *Solidarity Politics for Millennials: A Guide to Ending the Oppression Olympics.* New York: Palgrave Macmillan, 2011.

Harding, Susan. *The Book of Jerry Falwell: Fundamentalist Language and Politics.* Princeton: Princeton University Press, 2001.

Hartman, Chester and Gregory D. Squires (eds.). *There is No Such Thing as a Natural Disaster: Race, Class, and Hurricane Katrina.* New York: Routledge, 2006.

Hartman, Saidiya V. *Lose Your Mother: A Journey along the Atlantic Slave Route.* New York: Farrar, Straus and Giroux, 2007.

Hartman, Saidiya V. *Wayward Lives, Beautiful Experiments: Intimate Histories of Social Upheaval.* New York: W.W. Norton and Company, 2019.

Hartocollis, Anemona and Eliza Fawcett. "The College Board Strips Down Its A.P. Curriculum for African American Studies." *The New York Times*, February 1, 2023, sec. U.S. https://www.nytimes.com/2023/02/01/us/college-board-advanced-placement-african-american-studies.html.

Harvey, Jennifer. *Whiteness and Morality: Pursuing Racial Justice through Reparations and Sovereignty.* New York: Palgrave Macmillan, 2007.

Harvey, Jennifer. *Dear White Christians.* 2nd ed. Grand Rapids: Eerdmans, 2020.

Harvey, Jennifer, Karin Case, and Robin Hawledy Gorsline (eds.). *Disrupting White Supremacy from Within: White People on What We Need to Do.* Cleveland: The Pilgrim Press, 2004.

Hauerwas, Stanley. *The Peaceable Kingdom: A Primer in Christian Ethics.* Notre Dame: University of Notre Dame Press, 1983.

Hauerwas, Stanley. *Christian Existence Today: On Church, World and Living In-Between.* Durham: Labyrinth Press, 1988.

Hauerwas, Stanley. "The Testament of Friends." *The Christian Century* 107, no. 7 (February 28, 1990): 213–16.

Hauerwas, Stanley. *In Good Company: The Church as Polis.* Notre Dame: University of Notre Dame Press, 1995.

Hauerwas, Stanley. *Sanctify Them in Truth: Holiness Exemplified.* Nashville: Abingdon Press, 1998.

Hauerwas, Stanley and Charles Pinches. *Christians among the Virtues: Theological Conversations with Ancient and Modern Ethics.* Notre Dame: University of Notre Dame Press, 1997.

Hazel M. Johnson. "Mother of the Environmental Justice Movement." October 6, 2018. https://www.chipublib.org/blogs/post/hazel-m-johnson-mother-of-the-environmental-justice-movement.

Healy, Nicholas M. *Church, Word, and the Christian Life: Practical-Prophetic Ecclesiology.* New York: Cambridge University Press, 2000.

Hernandez, Jill Graper. *Early Modern Women and the Problem of Evil: Atrocity and Theodicy*, 246. Kindle ed. New York: Routledge, 2016.

Heyward, Carter. *Touching Our Strength: The Erotic as Power and the Love of God.* San Francisco: Harper and Row, 1989.

Hobson, Jane, Gar Jones, and Elizabeth Deane. "The Research Assistant: Silenced Partner in Australia's Knowledge Production?" *Journal of Higher Education Policy and Management* 27, no. 3 (2005): 357–66.

Holmes, Seth M. *Fresh Fruit, Broken Bodies: Migrant Farmworkers in the United States.* Berkeley: University of CA Press, 2013.

hooks, bell. *Yearning: Race, Gender and Culture Politics.* Boston: South End Press, 1990.

Hunter-Bowman, Janna L. "Representation and Intersectionality." In *The Wiley Blackwell Companion to Theology and Qualitative Research*, eds. Pete Ward and Knut Tveitereid. 141–50. Hoboken: John Wiley & Sons, Ltd, 2022.

Hunter-Bowman, Janna L. *Witnessing Peace: Becoming Agents under Duress in Colombia.* New York: Routledge, 2022.

Ideström, Jonas. "Action Research and Theology." In *The Wiley Blackwell Companion to Theology and Qualitative Research*, eds. Pete Ward and Knut Tveitereid, 425–34. Hoboken: John Wiley & Sons, Ltd, 2022.

Isasi-Díaz, Ada María. *En la Lucha / In the Struggle: A Hispanic Women's Liberation Theology* Minneapolis, MN: Fortress Press, 1993.

Jackson, Sherman A. *Islam and the Problem of Black Suffering.* Oxford and New York: Oxford University Press, 2014.

Jaffrelot, Christophe. *Modi's India.* Princeton: Princeton University Press, 2022.

Jan, Tracy and Brittney Martin. "Houston Took Them in After Katrina." *Then Harvey Hit*, August 29, 2017. https://www.washingtonpost.com/news/wonk/wp/2017/08/29/houston-took-them-in-after-katrina-then-harvey-hit/?noredirect=on&utm_term=.95344046ed9d (accessed May 29, 2018).

Jenkins, Timothy. "Fieldwork and the Perception of Everyday Life." *Man, New Series* 20, no. 2 (1994): 433–55.

Jenkins, Timothy. *Religion in English Everyday Life: An Ethnographic Approach. Methodology and History in Anthropology*, Vol. 5. Oxford: Berghahn Books, 1999.

Jha, Dhirendra K. *Gandhi's Assassin: The making of Nathuram Godse and His Idea of India.* New Delhi: Penguin, 2022.

Johansen, Kirstine Helboe. "Analytical Strategies." In *The Wiley Blackwell Companion to Theology and Qualitative Research,* eds. Pete Ward and Knut Tveitereid, 393–402. Hoboken: John Wiley & Sons, Ltd, 2022.

Johnstone, Dan, Producer. *Hillsong: A Megachurch Exposed,* Breaklight Pictures, released on Discovery+, March 2022.

Jŏng, Daehi. "X sibŏk madahako kokkikkŭnŭn Namcha 'Kŭkakmudohan ilŭl Kyŏkŏtta. (The man who stop eating after refusing 100 million won from [Company X], 'I experienced extreme atrocity')." *OhmyNews*, July 9, 2019. http://m.ohmynews.com/NWS_Web/Mobile/at_pg.aspx?CNTN_CD=A0002552302.

Joseph, Peniel E. "Left Behind: Backdrop to a National Crisis." In *The Sky is Crying: Race, Class, and Natural Disaster*, eds. Cheryl A. Kirk-Duggan. Nashville: Abingdon Press, 2006.

Journal of World Christianity 2020 special issue, "The Ethnographic Method in World Christianity: A Conversation among Emerging and Seasoned Scholars."

Jung, Patricia Beattie and Aana Marie Vigen (eds.). *God, Science, Sex, Gender*. Urbana: University of Illinois Press, 2010.

Kaiser Family Foundation, Fact Sheet, December 2022 (updated March 2023). "Healthcare and Coverage of Immigrants." https://www.kff.org/racial-equity-and-health-policy/fact-sheet/health-coverage-and-care-of-immigrants/ (accessed June 20, 2020).

Kandiyoti, Deniz. "Bargaining with Patriarchy." *Gender & Society* 2, no. 3 (September 1, 1988): 274–90.

Kanyoro, Musimbi. "Engendered Communal Theology: African Women's Contribution to Theology in the Twenty-First Century." *Feminist Theology* 9, no. 27 (2001): 36–56.

Kårtveit, Bård. *Dilemmas of Attachment: Identity and Belonging Among Palestinian Christians*. Leiden: Brill, 2014.

Kaufman, Tone Stangeland. "Practicing Reflexivity: Becoming Aware of One's Default Mode and Developing an Epistemic Advantage." In *The Wiley Blackwell Companion to Theology and Qualitative Research*, eds. Pete Ward and Knut Tveitereid, 111–20. Hoboken: John Wiley & Sons, Ltd, 2022.

Kelly, Jennifer Lynn. "Asymmetrical Itineraries: Militarism, Tourism, and Solidarity in Occupied Palestine." *American Quarterly* 68, no. 3 (2016): 723–45.

Kerr, Fergus. "Simplicity Itself: Milbank's Thesis." *New Blackfriars* 73 (June 1992): 306–10.

Kiboko, K "Sharing Power: An Autobiographical View." In *Talitha Cum! Theologies of African Women*, eds. Musa W. Dube and Nyambura Njoroge, 207–21. Pietermaritzburg: Cluster Publications, 2001.

Kidder, Tracy. *Mountains Beyond Mountains: The Quest of Dr. Paul Farmer, a Man Who Would Cure the World*. New York: Random House, 2004.

Kikon, Dolly. "Dirty Food: Racism and Casteism in India." *Ethnic and Racial Studies* 45, no. 2 (2022): 279.

Kim, Myeong Soo. "Yesu humanismkwa Naŭi Sinhakŭi Kil (Jesus Humanism and My Theological Path)." *Journal of the Christian Literature Society of Korea* 739 (2020): 127–38.

Kim, Sun-Chul. "The Trajectory of Protest Suicide in South Korea, 1970–2015." *Journal of Contemporary Asia* 51, no. 1 (2019): 38–63.

Kleinman, Arthur. *The Illness Narratives: Suffering, Healing, and the Human Condition*. New York: Basic Books, 1988.

Koh, SueJeanne. "Excavation, Interrogation, and Incommensurability: Navigating Theological Landscapes as an Asian American, Feminist Scholar." In *Christianity Next, Women and Biblical Traditions*, ed. Young Lee Hertig, 43–60. Winter 2020.

Kohut, Heinz. *The Analysis of the Self*. Chicago: University of Chicago Press, 1971.

Kohut, Heinz. *How Does Analysis Cure?* Edited by Arnold Goldberg with the collaboration of Paul Stephansky. Chicago: Chicago University Press, 1984.

Kolers, Avery. "Dynamics of Solidarity." *The Journal of Political Philosophy* 20, no. 4 (2012): 365–83.

Kunz, Egon F. "Exile and Resettlement: Refugee Theory." *The International Migration Review* 15, no. 1/2, Refugees Today (Spring–Summer 1981): 42–51.

Kuper, Adam. *The Invention of Primitive Society: Transformations of an Illusion*. London: Routledge Press, 1988.

Kuttab, Eileen. "Empowerment as Resistance: Conceptualizing Palestinian Women's Empowerment." *Development* 53, no. 2 (June 1, 2010): 247–53.

Kwangsun, Suh. "A Political History of Korean Christianity in Case of South Korea in the Early 1970s." *Sinhakkwa Kyohwe (Theology and the Church)* 5 (Summer 2016): 270–3.

Kyujin, Choi. "Dasi Dolaon Ch'ekongnyeowa Kuldduknamŭi Side (The Return of the Age of Ch'ekongnyeo and Kuldduknam)." *Ŭiryowa Sahwe (Medicine and Society)* 2 (2015): 131–5.

LaCugna, Catherin Mowry. *God for Us: The Trinity and Christian Life*. San Francisco: Harper, 1991.

Lazoroska, Daniela. "Hot Topics, Gringo Parties, and the Dependent Independence of Friendship in the Field." *Etnofoor* 31, no. 1 (2019): 63–78.

Lee, Emily S. and Alia Al-Saji. "A Phenomenology of Hesitation." In *Living Alterities: Phenomenology, Embodiment, and Race*, 133–72. Albany: SUNY Press, 2015.

Lee, Ŭnhye. "Kokongnongsŏng 57il Kssi: Hyanrin kongdongch'e Yebe Dŏkbune Maŭm Dachapa … Kkŭtkkachi Sara Ssauketta. "[K] on High-Altitude Protest day 57." *Nyusŭaenchoi*, May 8, 2019. http://www.newsnjoy.or.kr/news/articleView.html?id-xno=224684&fbclid=IwAR3GJE9Q0i4MqgdpRs448M7YEefed97REOgpCyoFHqRS6m DbcHmIYdM07cA (accessed June 20, 2024).

Lenclud, Gerard. "The Factual and the Normative in Ethnography: Do Cultural Differences Derive from Description?." *Anthropology Today* 12, no. 1 (1996): 7–11.

Lewis, Herbert. "Boas, Darwin, Science and Anthropology." *Current Anthropology* 42, no. 3 (2001): 381–406.

Lincoln, Yvonna S. and Norman K. Denzin. *Turning Points in Qualitative Research: Tying Knots in a Handkerchief*. Lanham: AltaMira Press, 2003.

Longkumer, Arkotong. "The Power of Persuasion: Hindutva, Christianity, and the Discourse of Religion and Culture in Northeast India." *Religion* 47, no. 2 (2017).

Longkumer, Arkotong. *The Greater India Experiment: Hindutva and the Northeast*. Stanford: Stanford University Press, 2021.

Loo, Janice. "Mem, Don't Mess with the Cook!" *Biblioasia* (July–September 2016): 13.

Loury, Glenn C. *The Anatomy of Racial Inequality*. Cambridge, MA: Harvard University Press, 2002.

Luhrmann, T. M. *When God Talks Back: Understanding the American Evangelical Relationship with God*. New York: Alfred A. Knopf, 2012.

Mahmood, Saba. *Politics of Piety: The Islamic Revival and the Feminist Subject*. Princeton: Princeton University Press, 2011.

Mairaj Syed, *Coercion and Responsibility in Islam: A Study in Ethics and Law*. New York: Oxford University Press, 2017.

Martí, Gerardo. "Ethnography as a Tool for Genuine Surprise: Found Theologies Versus Imposed Theologies." In *The Wiley Blackwell Companion to Theology and Qualitative Research*, eds. Knut Tveitereid and Pete Ward, 471–82. Malden: John Wiley & Sons 2022.

Masci, David and Gregory A. Smith. "Following Rev. Billy Graham's Death, 5 Facts about U.S. Evangelical Protestants." *Pew Research Center*, July 27, 2020. https://www.pewresearch.org/fact-tank/2018/03/01/5-facts-about-u-s-evangelical-protestants/#:~:text=As%20of%202014%2C%2011%25%20of,U.S.%20public%20as%20a%20whole.

Mascia-Lees, Frances et al. "The Postmodernist Turn in Anthropology: Cautions from a Feminist Perspective." *Signs* 15 (1989): 7–33.

McDonald, Thomasi. "After 6 Homicides in 11 Days, Durham Officials Call for 'Common-Sense Gun Laws' in NC." *The News & Observer*, January 17, 2019. www.newsobserver.com/news/local/article224673440.html.

McKittrick, Katherine. "Mathematics Black Life." *The Black Scholar: Journal of Black Studies and Research* 44, no. 2 (2014): 16.

Mellott, David. *I Was and I Am Dust: Penitent Practices as a Way of Knowing*. Collegeville: Liturgical Press, 2009.

Merleau-Ponty, M. *Phenomenology of Perception*. New York: Routledge, 1962.

Metz, Johann Baptist. *Faith in History and Society: Toward a Practical Fundamental Theology*. Translated by David Smith New York: Seabury Press, 1980.

Milbank, John. "Enclaves, or Where is the Church?" *New Blackfriars* 73 (June 1992): 341–52.
Milbank, John. *Theology and Social Theory: Beyond Secular Reason, Signposts in Theology*. Oxford: Blackwell, 1993.
Mills, Charles W. "Black Trash." In *Faces of Environmental Racism: Confronting Issues of Global Justice*, eds. Laura Westra and Bill E. Lawson, 73–91. Lanham: Rowman & Littlefield Publishers, 2001.
Mohanty, Chandra Talpade. *Feminism without Borders: Decolonizing Theory, Practicing Solidarity*. Durham: Duke University Press, 2003.
Mohrmann, Margaret E. *Attending Children: A Doctor's Education*. Washington, DC: Georgetown University Press, 2005.
Mombo, Esther. "Doing Theology from the Perspective of the Circle of Concerned African Women Theologians." *Journal of Anglican Studies* 1, no. 1 (2003): 91.
Moon, Dawn. *God, Sex and Politics: Homosexuality, and Everyday Theologies*. Chicago: University of Chicago Press, 2004.
Moreno, Francisco. *Moral Theology from the Poor*. Quezon City: Claretian Publications, 1988.
Morgan, Henry Lewis. *Ancient Society*. New York: Meridian Books, 1877/1963.
"Munocho X Chaebŏlŭi Ch'uakhan Manhaengŭl Makachuseyo (Please stop the ugly atrocities of labor union-less X Chaebŏl)." Chŏngwadae Kukminchŏngwŏn Kesipan (Online petition board of Chŏngwadae). https://www1.president.go.kr/petitions/152236.
Myerhoff, Barbara. *Number Our Days: A Triumph of Continuity and Culture among Jewish Old People in an Urban Ghetto*. New York: Touchstone, 1980.
Myŏnga, Kwon. "Sagŏn Ihuŭi Inganhak: Honŭi T'uchaenge Dehayŏ (Anthropology after Events: Regarding Spiritual Struggles)." In *P'aengmokhangesŏ Pulŏonŭn Param*, ed. Inmunhakhyŏpdongchohap. Seoul: Hyŏnsilmunhwa, 2015.
Nagel Institute. "African Theological Advance." https://nagelinstitute.org/project/african-theological-advance (accessed April 12, 2023).
Narendorf, Sarah Carter et al. "Managing and Mentoring: Experiences of Assistant Professors in Working with Research Assistants." *Social Work Research* 40, no. 1 (2016): 19–30.
Nichols, Aidan. "Non Tali Auxilio: John Milbank's Suasion to Orthodoxy." *New Blackfriars* 73 (June 1992): 326–32.
Nixon, Rob. *Slow Violence and the Environmentalism of the Poor*. London: Harvard University Press, 2011.
Njoroge, Nyambura J. "A New Way of Facilitating Leadership: Lessons from African Women Theologians." *Missiology: An International Review* 33, no. 1 (2005): 34–5.
Oduyoye, Mercy A. "The Search for a Two-Winged Theology: Women's Participation in the Development of Theology in Africa-The Inaugural Address." In *Talitha Qumi! Proceedings of the Convocation of African Women Theologians 1989*, eds. M. A. Oduyoye and M. Kanyoro, 27–48. Ibadan: Daystar Press, 1990.
Oduyoye, Mercy A. *Introducing African Women's Theology*. Sheffield: Sheffield Academic Press, 2001.
Oduyoye, Mercy A. "Transforming Power: Paradigms from the Novels of Buchi Emacheta." In *Talitha Cum! Theologies of African Women*, eds. Musa W. Dube and Nyambura Njoroge, 223–5. Pietermaritzburg: Cluster Publications, 2001.
Oredein, Oluwatomisin. "Interview with Mercy Amba Oduyoye: Mercy Amba Oduyoye in Her Own Words." *Journal of Feminist Studies in Religion* 32, no. 2 (2016): 160–1.

Ozano, Kim and Rose Khatri. "Reflexivity, Positionality and Power in Cross-Cultural Participatory Action Research with Research Assistants in Rural Cambodia." *Educational Action Research* 26, no. 2 (2018): 199–200.

Pachuau, Joy L. K. *Being Mizo: Identity and Belonging in Northeast India*. New Delhi: Oxford University Press, 2014.

Panikar, K. N. "Culture and Communalism." *Social Scientist* 21, no. 3/4 (1993): 24–31.

Park, Hee-Kyu Heidi. "Divine Jealousy, Human Zeal: Self-Psychology and the Kenotic Spirituality of קנאtin Numbers 25." In *Landscapes of Korean and Korean American Biblical Interpretation*, ed. John Ahn, 38–48. Atlanta, GA: SBL Press, 2019.

Partner, Simon and Emma Johnston. *Bull City Survivor: Standing Up to a Hard Life in a Southern City*. Jefferson: McFarland, 2013.

Pelaez-Diaz, Francisco. "Central American Migration as the Way of the Cross: Ignacio Ellacuría's Notion of the 'Crucified Peoples' for Theological Reframing of the Migrant Experience." In *Migration and Public Discourse in World Christianity*, eds. Afe Adogame, Raimundo Barreto, and Wanderly Pereira da Rosa, 229–46. Minneapolis: Fortress Press, 2019.

Pellow, David N. *Garbage Wars: The Struggle for Environmental Justice in Chicago. Urban and Industrial Environments*. Cambridge, MA: MIT Press, 2004.

Pineda-Madrid, Nancy. *Suffering and Salvation in Ciudad Juarez*. Minneapolis: Fortress Press, 2011.

Pink, Sarah. *Doing Visual Ethnography*. 4th ed. Thousand Oaks: Sage Publications, 2012.

Platt, Maria. "Foreign Domestic Workers in Singapore: Historical and Contemporary reflections on the Colonial Politics of Intimacy." In *Colonization and Domestic Service: Historical and Contemporary Perspectives*, eds. Victoria K. Haskins and Claire Lowrie, 131–48. New York: Routledge, 2015.

Pohl, Christine D. *Making Room: Recovering Hospitality as a Christian Tradition*. Grand Rapids: William B. Eerdmans Publishing Company, 1999.

Pohl, Christine D. "Hospitality, a Practice and a Way of Life." *Vision* 3, no. 1 (2002): 34–43.

Prevot, Andrew. "Mystical Bodies of Christ: Human, Crucified, and Beloved." In *Beyond the Doctrine of Man: Decolonial Visions of the Human*, eds. Joseph Drexler-Dreis and Kristien Justaert. New York: Fordham University Press, 2020.

PRRI. "The Faith Factor in Climate Change: How Religion Impacts American Attitudes on Climate and Environmental Policy." https://www.prri.org/research/the-faith-factor-in-climate-change-how-religion-impacts-american-attitudes-on-climate-and-environmental-policy/ (accessed October 4, 2023).

Rabinow, Paul (ed.). *The Foucault Reader*. New York: Vintage, 1984.

Rabinow, Paul. "Representations are Social Facts: Modernity and Post-Modernity in Anthropology." In *Writing Culture: The Poetics and Politics of Ethnography*, eds. George Marcus and James Clifford, 234–61. Berkeley: University of California Press, 1986.

Rabinow, Paul. *Making PCR: A Story of Biotechnology*. Chicago: University of Chicago Press, 1997.

Rabinow, Paul. *French DNA: Trouble in Purgatory*. Chicago: University of Chicago Press, 2002.

Rabinow, Paul, Hubert L. Dreyfus, and Michel Foucault. *Michel Foucault: Beyond Structuralism and Hermeneutics*. Chicago: University of Chicago Press, 1983.

Rabinow, Paul George E. Marcus, James D. Faubion, and Tobias Rees. *Designs for an Anthropology of the Contemporary*. Durham: Duke University Press, 2008.

Raboteau, Albert. *Slave Religion: The "Invisible Institution" in the Antebellum South*, 212–19. New York: Oxford University Press, 1978.

Rah, Soong-Chan. "In Whose Image: The Emergence, Development, and Challenge of African- American Evangelicalism." (Dissertation, 2016), 143.

Rah, Soong-Chan. "National Gathering Keynote." *Next Church*, April 6, 2017. https://www.youtube.com/watch?v=RgHCJ3eu6IA (accessed March 31, 2021).

Rasmussen, Larry L. *Earth Community Earth Ethics*. Maryknoll: Orbis Books, 1996.

Rasmussen, Larry L. *The Planet You Inherit: Letters to My Grandchildren When Uncertainty's a Sure Thing*. Minneapolis: Broadleaf Books, 2022.

Rivera, Mayra. "Thinking Bodies: The Spirit of a Latina Incarnational Imagination." In *Decolonizing Epistemologies: Latina/o Theology and Philosophy*, eds. Ada Maria Isasi-Diaz and Eduardo Mendieta. Fordham: Fordham University Press, 2011.

Rivera, Mayra. "Poetics Ashore." *Literature & Theology* 33, no. 3 (2019): 241–7.

Robbins, Joel. "Anthropology and Theology: An Awkward Relationship?" *Anthropological Quarterly* 79, no. 2 (Spring 2006): 285–94.

Rosaldo, Renato. "Grief and a Headhunter's Rage: On the Cultural Force of Emotions." In *Text Play, and Story: The Construction and Reconstruction of Self and Society*, 178–95. Long Grove: Waveland Press, 1988.

Rosenbaum, Art. *Shout Because You're Free: The African-American Ring Shout Tradition in Coastal Georgia*. Athens: The University of Georgia Press, 1995.

Ross, Susan. "Like a Fish Without a Bicycle?" *America* 181, no. 17 (November 17, 1999): 10–13.

Ross, Susan. "Liturgy and Ethics: Feminist Perspectives." *Annual of the Society of Christian Ethics* 20 (2000): 263–74.

Russell, Letty M. *Just Hospitality: God's Welcome in a World of Difference*. Louisville: Westminster John Knox, 2009.

Sales, Ruby. "How We Can Start to Heal the Pain of Racial Division." Filmed, *TED Salon*, September 2018. www.ted.com/talks/ruby_sales_how_we_can_start_to_heal_the_pain_of_racial_division.

Sastry, Narayan and Jesse Gregory. "The Location of Displaced New Orleans Residents in the Year After Hurricane Katrina." *Demography* 51, no. 3 (June 2014): 753–75.

Saunt, Claudio. *Unworthy Republic: The Dispossession of Native Americans and the Road to Indian Territory*. New York: W. W. Norton & Company, 2020.

Scarry, Elaine. *The Body in Pain: The Making and Unmaking of the World*. Oxford: Oxford University Press, 1985.

Scharen, Christian. "Lois, Liturgy, and Ethics." *The Annual of the Society of Christian Ethics* 20 (2000): 275–305.

Scharen, Christian. *Public Worship, Public Works: Character and Commitment in Local Congregational Life*. Collegeville: The Liturgical Press, 2004.

Scharen, Christian. "Experiencing the Body: Sexuality and Conflict in American Lutheranism." In *Sexuality and the Sacred*, eds. Marvin Ellison and Kelly Brown Douglas, 2nd ed. Louisville: Westminster John Knox, 2010.

Scharen, Christian. "Interviewing Interpreted as Spiritual Exercise and Social Protest." *Ecclesial Practices* 4, no. 2 (2017): 218–36.

Scharen, Christian. "Fieldwork in White Theology." In *The Wiley Blackwell Companion to Theology and Qualitative Research*, eds. Knut Tveitereid and Pete Ward, 91–100. Malden: John Wiley & Sons, 2022.

Secker, Susan L. "Human Experience and Women's Experience." In *Dialogue about Catholic Sexual Teaching: Readings in Moral Theology*, eds. Charles E. Curran and Richard A. McCormick, Vol. 8, 577–99. Mahwah, NJ: Paulist Press, 1993.

Segundo, Juan Luis. *The Liberation of Theology*. Translated by John Drury. Eugene: Wipf and Stock, 1976.

Sharma, Supriya. "10,000 People Charged with Sedition in One Jharkhand District: What Does Democracy Mean Here?" *Scroll.* https://scroll.in/article/944116/10000-people-charged-with-sedition-in-one-jharkhand-district-what-does-democracy-mean-here; (accessed February 1, 2022).

Simpson, Audra. "Why White People Love Franz Boas; or The Grammar of Indigenous Dispossession." In *Indigenous Visions: Rediscovering the World of Franz Boas*, eds. Ned Blackhawk and Isaiah Lorado Wilner, 166–81. New Haven: Yale University Press, 2018.

Singh, Devin. "Liberation Theology." In *The Oxford Handbook of the Epistemology of Theology*, eds. William J. Abraham and Frederick D. Aquino, 551–63. New York: Oxford University Press, 2017.

Smith, Charles D. *Palestine and the Arab-Israeli Conflict: A History with Documents.* 8th ed. Boston: Bedford/St. Martin's, 2007.

Snyder, Timothy K. "Theological Ethnography: Embodied." *The Other Journal: An Intersection of Theology and Culture* (2014). https://theotherjournal.com/2014/05/theological-ethnography-embodied/.

Sobrino, Jon. *The True Church and the Poor.* Maryknoll: Orbis, 1984.

Sontag, Susan. *Regarding the Pain of Others.* New York: Picador, 2004.

"South Korean Ends Yearlong Tower Protest After Samsung Apologizes." *The New York Times*, May 29, 2020. https://www.nytimes.com/2020/05/29/world/asia/south-korea-protest-tower-samsung.html.

Spivak, Gayatri Chakravorty. "Can the Subaltern Speak?" In *The Post-Colonial Studies Reader*, eds. Bill Ashcroft, Gareth Griffiths, and Helen Tiffin, 28–37. New York: Routledge, 2006.

Spradley, James P. *The Ethnographic Interview.* New York: Holt, Rinehart, and Winston, 1979.

Spurrier, Rebecca. *The Disabled Church.* New York: Fordham University Press, 2019.

Stevano, Sara and Kevin Deane. "The Role of Research Assistants in Qualitative and Cross-Cultural Social Science Research." In *Handbook of Research Methods in Health Social Sciences*, eds. Pranee Liamputtong, 1–16. Singapore: Springer, 2017.

Stevens, James H. S. *Worship in the Spirit: Charismatic Worship in the Church of England.* Studies in Evangelical History and Thought. Carlisle and Waynesboro: Paternoster Press, 2002.

Stocking, Geroge W., Jr. *Race, Culture, and Evolution: Essays in the History of Anthropology.* New York: The Free Press, 1968.

Stocking, George W. Jr. (ed.). *A Franz Boas Reader: The Shaping of American Anthropology, 1883-1911.* Chicago: University of Chicago Press, 1974.

Stringer, Martin D. *On the Perception of Worship: The Ethnography of Worship in Four Christian Congregations in Manchester.* Birmingham: The University of Birmingham Press, 1999.

Sutherland, Arthur. *I Was a Stranger: A Christian Theology of Hospitality.* Nashville: Abingdon Press, 2006.

Tanner, Kathryn. *Theories of Culture: An Agenda for Theology.* Minneapolis: Fortress Press, 1997.

Tertullian, *De Spectaculis.* Translated by T. R. Glover, Loeb Classical Library 250. Cambridge: Harvard University Press, 1931.

The Civil Rights Project at Harvard University Report. *Race in American Public Schools: Rapidly Resegregating School Districts*, 2002.

Thompson, H. Paul. *A Most Stirring and Significant Episode: Religion and the Rise and Fall of Prohibition in Black Atlanta, 1865-1887.* DeKalb, IL: Northern Illinois University Press, 2013.

Tilly, Charles. *Popular Contention in Great Britain, 1758-1834.* London: Paradigm Publisher, 1995.

Tipton, Steven. "A Response: Moral Languages and the Good Society." *Soundings* 69 (1986): 165-80.

Toulmin, Stephen. *Cosmopolis: The Hidden Agenda of Modernity.* New York: The Free Press, 1990.

Townes, Emilie. *Womanist Ethics and the Cultural Production of Evil.* New York: Palgrave Macmillan, 2006.

Trondman, Mats. "Taking Normative Sense Seriously: Ethnography in the Light of a Utopian Reference." *Ethnography* 18, no. 1 (2017): 10–23.

Tronto, Joan C. *Moral Boundaries: A Political Argument for an Ethics of Care.* New York: Routledge, 1993.

Turner, Sarah. "Research Note: The Silenced Assistant. Reflections of Invisible Interpreters and Research Assistants." *Asia Pacific Viewpoint* 51, no. 2 (2010): 206.

Tveitereid, Knut. "Lived Theology and Theology in the Lived." In *The Wiley Blackwell Companion to Theology and Qualitative Research*, eds. Pete Ward and Knut Tveitereid, 67–77. Hoboken: John Wiley & Sons, Ltd, 2022.

Verhey, Allen. *Reading the Bible in the Strange World of Medicine.* Grand Rapids: Eerdmans Press, 2003.

Vigen, Aana Marie. "To Hear and To Be Accountable Across Difference: An Ethic of White Listening." In *Disrupting White Supremacy from Within: White People on What WE Need to Do*, eds. Jennifer Harvey et al., 216–48. Cleveland: The Pilgrim Press, 2004.

Vigen, Aana Marie. *Women, Ethics, and Inequality in U.S. Healthcare: "To Count Among the Living".* New York: Palgrave Macmillan, 2006.

Vigen, Aana Marie. "Neglected Voices at the Beginning of Life: Prenatal Genetics and Reproductive Justice." In *Catholic Bioethics and Social Justice*, eds. M. Therese Lysaught and Michael McCarthy, 97–112. Collegeville: Liturgical Press, 2018.

Vigen, Aana Marie. "Prenatal Genetic Testing & the Complicated Quest for a Healthy Baby: Christian Ethics in Conversation with Genetic Counselors." In *Suffering in Medicine, Theology and Medical Ethics, Christof Mandry*, 160–78 Germany: Schoeningh Verlag (scientific imprint Brill International), 2021.

Villarosa, Linda. *Under the Skin: The Hidden Toll of Racism on American Lives and on the Health of our Nation.* New York: Doubleday, 2022.

Wacquant, Loïc. "Carnal Connections: On Embodiment, Apprenticeship, and Membership." *Qualitative Sociology* 28, no. 4 (Winter 2005): 445–74.

Wacquant, Loïc. "The Body, the Ghetto, and the Penal State." *Qualitative Sociology* 32 (2009): 119.

Wacquant, Loïc. "Habitus as Topic and Tool: Reflections on Becoming a Prizefighter." In *Ethnographies Revisited: Constructing Theory in the Field*, eds. William Shaffir, Antony Puddephatt, and Steven Kleinknecht, 137–51. New York: Routledge, 2009.

Walker Grimes, Katie. "Black Exceptionalism: Anti-Blackness Supremacy in the Afterlife of Slavery." In *Anti-Blackness and Christian Ethics*, eds. Vincent W. Lloyd and Andrew Prevot. Maryknoll: Orbis Books, 2017.

Washington, Sylvia Hood. *Packing Them in: An Archaeology of Environmental Racism in Chicago, 1865-1954,* 215–24. New York: Lexington Books, 2005.

Watkins, Clare. *Disclosing Church: An Ecclesiology Learned from Conversations in Practice*. New York: Routledge, 2020.

Watkins, Clare. "Qualitative Research in Theology: A Spiritual Turn?" In *The Wiley Blackwell Companion to Theology and Qualitative Research*, eds. Pete Ward and Knut Tveitereid. Hoboken: John Wiley & Sons, Ltd, 2022.

Weber, Shantelle. "Practical Theology Rooted in and from Africa: The Tide is Turning." In *The Wiley Blackwell Companion to Theology and Qualitative Research*, eds. Pete Ward and Knut Tveitereid, 58–66. Hoboken: John Wiley & Sons, 2022.

Wells, Samuel and Marcia A. Owen, *Living Without Enemies: Being Present in the Midst of Violence*. Downers Grove: IVP Books, 2011.

West, Traci, C. *Disruptive Christian Ethics: When Racism and Women's Lives Matter*. Louisville: Westminster John Knox Press, 2006.

West, Traci, C. *Solidarity and Defiant Spirituality: Africana Lessons on Religion, Racism, and Ending Gender Violence*. New York: NYU Press, 2019.

Westfield, N. Lynne. *Dear Sisters: A Womanist Practice of Hospitality*. Cleveland: Pilgrim Press, 2001.

Whitmore, Todd David. "Crossing the Road: The Case for Ethnographic Fieldwork in Christian Ethics." *Journal of the Society of Christian Ethics* 27, no. 2 (2007): 273–94.

Whitmore, Todd David. *Imitating Christ in Magwi: An Anthropological Theology*. New York: T&T Clark, 2019.

Whitmore, Todd David. "Bringing the Mess That is Life into Theology: The Representational Task of Ethnography." *Ecclesial Practices* 8, no. 2 (2021): 142–64.

WHO. "Child Mortality Under 5 Years." January 2022. https://www.who.int/news-room/fact-sheets/detail/levels-and-trends-in-child-under-5-mortality-in-2020 (accessed June 12, 2023).

WHO. "Climate Change." https://www.who.int/news-room/fact-sheets/detail/climate-change-and-health (accessed June 13, 2023).

WHO. "Covid 19 Dashboard." https://covid19.who.int/?adgroupsurvey={adgroupsurvey}&gclid=Cj0KCQjwnrmlBhDHARIsADJ5b_mLfk_cyl1UQDGZ47-iKmz0aZOId4cCTxv1KrV9i_XuDyLHM0JXwUcaAuwqEALw_wcB (accessed July 12, 2023).

Wigg-Stevenson, Natalie. *Ethnographic Theology: An Inquiry into the Production of Theological Knowledge*. New York: Palgrave Macmillan, 2014.

Wigg-Stevenson, Natalie. *Transgressive Devotion: Theology as Performance Art*. London: SCM Press, 2021.

Wilkerson, Isabel. *Caste: The Origins of Our Discontents*. New York: Random House, 2020.

Williams, Delores. "Sin, Nature, and Black Women's Bodies." In *Eco-Feminism and the Sacred*, ed. Carol Adams, 24–9. New York: Continuum Publishing Company, 1993.

Williams, Delores. *Sisters in the Wilderness: The Challenge of Womanist God-Talk*. Maryknoll: Orbis Books, 1993.

Williams, Rowan. "Saving Time: Thoughts on Practice, Patience, and Vision." *New Blackfriars* 73 (June 1992): 319–26.

Williams, Rowan. *Seeing Religion: Toward a Visual Sociology of Religion*. London: Routledge, 2015.

Williams, Sara. "From Disciplinary Transactions to Political Practice: Moving Past Theology and Anthropology 'in General.'" *Political Theology*, May 12, 2022. https://politicaltheology.com/from-disciplinary-transactions-to-political-practice-moving-past-theology-and-anthropology-in-general/ (accessed June 20, 2024).

Williams, Vernon. *Rethinking Race: Franz Boas and His Contemporaries*. Lexington: University of Kentucky Press, 1996.

Yoder, Carolyn. *The Little Book of Trauma Healing: When Violence Strikes and Community Security is Threatened*. Intercourse: Good Books, 2005.

Young, Iris Marion. *Justice and the Politics of Difference*. Princeton: Princeton University Press, 1990.

Young, Michael W. *Malinowski: Odyssey of an Anthropologist, 1884-1920*. New Haven: Yale University Press, 2004.

Young, Richard Fox and Sunder John Boopalan. "Studied Silences? Diasporic Nationalism, 'Kshatriya Intellectuals' and the Hindu American Critique of Dalit Christianity's Indianness." In *Constructing Indian Christianities: Culture, Conversion and Caste*, eds. Chad M. Bauman and Richard Fox Young, 215–38. New York: Routledge, 2014.

Zaru, Jean. *Occupied with Nonviolence: A Palestinian Woman Speaks*, eds. Diana L. Eck and Marla Schrader. Minneapolis: Fortress Press, 2008.

Zaru, Jean. "Introduction: To Hold the Sky and Identify with Jesus: Abstracts from A Gender Analysis of the Kairos Palestine Document." In *Kairos for Global Justice*, ed. Robin Meyers, 74–8. Bethlehem: Kairos Palestine, 2011.

Zerger, Suzanne, Caitlin Anne Newberry, and Naveed Ahmed. "Research Assistants Caught in Limbo: Considering Their Role in Quantitative, Longitudinal Research with Vulnerable Populations." *Journal of Health Care for the Poor and Underserved* 26, no. 4 (2015): 1391–400.

Zimring, Carl A. *Clean and White: A History of Environmental Racism in the United States*. New York: New York University Press, 2015.

Zizioulas, John D. *Being as Communion: Studies in Personhood and the Church*. Crestwood: St. Vladimir's Seminary Press, 1985.

Zizioulas, John D. *Communion and Otherness: Further Studies in Personhood and the Church*. New York: T & T Clark, 2007.

Zumwalt, Rosemary Lévy. *Franz Boas: Shaping Anthropology and Fostering Social Justice*. Lincoln: University of Nebraska Press, 2022. http://jessemuhammad.blogs.finalcall.com/2012/08/the-new-orleans-association-of-houston.html (accessed January 3, 2017).

Contributors

Sunder John Boopalan is Associate Professor of Biblical and Theological Studies at Canadian Mennonite University in Winnipeg, Canada. His book *Memory, Grief, and Agency* compares Indian and US contexts of casteism and racism to argue that wrongs today are better understood as rituals of humiliation which are socially conditioned practices of domination affected by discriminatory logics of the past enacted against people who move out of place.

Lailatul Fitriyah is an Indonesian, Muslima feminist scholar who focuses on comparative Muslim and Christian feminist theologies, decoloniality, gender, and religions in Southeast Asia, and feminist interreligious dialogue. She is Assistant Professor of Interreligious Education at the Claremont School of Theology in Los Angeles where she teaches courses in Feminist Interreligious Dialogue, Decolonial Theories and Religions, Racism and Islamophobia, and Ethnography and Theologies.

Michael Grigoni is Assistant Professor in the Department for the Study of Religions at Wake Forest University, where he teaches courses in religion, politics, and the history of Christianity. His current research explores the relationship of guns to American Christianity and is based on fieldwork he carried out with Christian handgun owners and Christian antigun violence activists in central North Carolina.

Elina Hankela serves as Associate Professor in the Department of Religion Studies at the University of Johannesburg, South Africa. Much of her research is connected to liberation theologies and questions related to social justice, and ethnographic methods have been her primary means of making sense of the faith and faith worlds of people.

Nicole Hoskins is Assistant Professor of Religion and Ecology at Harvard Divinity School. Her research attends to Christian histories of colonial, racial, and environmental domination and connects those histories with communities resisting imposed environmental constraint today. She is especially interested in how black communities (particularly black women) operate and think outside of normative modes of care for the earth that challenges models of Christian settler coloniality.

RC Jongte is a Mizo liberation theologian from the northeast region of India. He earned his PhD from Princeton Theological Seminary in 2023. In his dissertation, "The Being of the Electing God: The Relevance of Karl Barth's Doctrine of Election for a Liberationist Theological Ontology," he puts the central liberationist theological tenet of God's preferential option for the poor in conversation with Barth's conception of the doctrine of election. Jongte's areas of research interest include the intersection between dogmatic and liberation theologies, traditional theological loci like the doctrine of God and Christology, political theologies, and Indigenous theologies particularly of Northeast India.

AnneMarie Mingo is Associate Professor of Ethics, Culture, and Moral Leadership, and Director of the Metro-Urban Institute at Pittsburgh Theological Seminary. She is a member of the American Academy of Religion, where she serves on the steering committee for Womanist Approaches to Religion and Society. She is also on the Board of the Society of Christian Ethics. Mingo is the author of *Have You Got Good Religion?: Black Women's Faith, Courage, and Moral Imagination Leadershipvvin the Civil Rights Movement* (Univ. of IL Press, 2024).

Clementine Nishimwe is a Lecturer in the Department of Religion Studies at the University of Johannesburg. Her academic specialization lies in Christian studies, with her research focusing on migration, gender dynamics, the Anglican church, and Pentecostal churches. Her research framework is deeply influenced by Concerned African Women's Theologies, reflecting her commitment to exploring the voices and perspectives of African migrant women in theological discourse. Additionally, she maintains an interest in topics related to conflict resolution and interreligious dialogue. Her research approach encompasses empirical methodologies, with a specific emphasis on ethnographic theologies.

Hee-Kyu Heidi Park is Associate Professor of Practical Theology in the Christian Studies Department of Ewha Womans University, Seoul, South Korea. She previously taught at Xavier University, Claremont School of Theology, and Lexington Theological School. Her research focuses on collective/historical trauma and spirituality in the context of such trauma.

Damaris Parsitau is Associate Professor of Religion and Gender Studies and the Director of the Nagel Institute for the Study of World Christianity at Calvin University, Grand Rapids, Michigan. In 2018–19, she served as a research associate and Visiting Professor at Harvard University. She is also Professor Extra-Ordinaire at the University of South Africa and the University of the Western Cape, South Africa. Her teaching and research interests include African Pentecostal/Evangelical churches and their intersections with gender, politics, civic and public engagement, and sexuality.

Emily Reimer-Barry is Associate Professor in the Department of Theology and Religious Studies at the University of San Diego, where she teaches undergraduate courses in theological ethics. Publications that utilize qualitative research include *Catholic Theology of Marriage in an Era of HIV and AIDS* (2015) and "An Intersectional View of Love in Marriage," in *Sex, Love, and Families: Catholic Perspectives*, ed. Jason King and Julie Hanlon Rubio (Liturgical, 2020). Links to other publications can be found on her website: https://emilyreimerbarry.com/

Christian Scharen is Associate Professor and the Gordon Braatz Chair of Worship, The Lutheran School of Theology at Chicago, where he teaches worship and practical theology. A leading scholar working at the intersection of ethnography and theology, he writes in the areas of ministry, worship, social ethics, ecclesiology, and popular culture. He is the author of several books and scholarly articles, including the theological memoir, *After Laura Ingalls Wilder: Facing My Family's Pioneer History Amid the Battle Over the Story of America* (forthcoming 2025).

Nicole Symmonds is Assistant Professor of Christian Ethics at Columbia Theological Seminary. Her work sits at the intersection of Christian ethics and women, gender, and sexuality studies. She explores Black women's embodiment, particularly the practices of liberative embodiment they craft as a method of resistance to domination and as a simulation of freedom. Dr. Symmonds' research qualitatively engages issues around faith-based sex trafficking interventions and commercial sex work, Caribbean cultural practices such as Carnival masquerading and embodied celebration, and she theorizes how trends in popular culture around performances of race, sex, and sexuality reveal and/or conceal opportunity for ethical reflection.

Traci C. West is a scholar-activist who teaches Christian Social Ethics and African American Studies at Drew University Theological School (NJ). Her teaching, research, and activism focus on gender, racial, and sexuality justice, particularly related to gender violence. In addition to many other publications, her most recent book is *Solidarity and Defiant Spirituality: Africana Lessons on Religion, Racism, and Ending Gender Violence*.

Sara A. Williams is Assistant Professor of Religious Studies at Fairfield University in Fairfield, Connecticut, where she teaches religious ethics. Her scholarship examines possibilities for just relationships in lived contexts marked by asymmetries of power and privilege. Her work can be found in scholarly journals such as the *Journal of Religious Ethics*, the *Journal of the American Academy of Religion*, and *Ecclesial Practices*. She is writing her first monograph based on her ethnographic work with progressive American Christian Holy Land tours.

Aana Marie Vigen is Professor of Christian Social Ethics at Loyola University Chicago. Her scholarship brings ethnographic methods into conversation with medical ethics, feminist ethics, Protestant ethics, and white antiracism commitments. In addition to numerous articles and chapters, she is the author of *Women, Ethics, and Inequality in U.S. Healthcare* (revised edition, 2011) and coeditor of *God, Science, Sex, Gender* (2010).

Index

Page numbers followed by "n" refer to notes.

AASR, *see* African Association for the Study of Religions (AASR)
accountability
   ethical   222
   ethnographic   xv, xxviii, xxix, xxx, xxxii, 21–5, 74, 168–9, 229
Adams, Nicholas   49, 57–8
   "Ethnography is Dogmatics"   57
Africa Exchange   xv
African Association for the Study of Religions (AASR)   xv, xxii, xxiii
African Methodist Episcopal Church   223
African Theological Advance (ATA) initiative, Nagel Institute of Calvin University   82, 87
Ahmed, Sara   174
Albright, Jacob   203
Albright-Bethune United Methodist Church   199, 202–5
Ambedkar, B. R.   101
Amnesty International   xvi
anthropology   20, 36
   postmodern   33
antiblackness supremacy   149
anti-Black racism   147–9, 151
antidiscrimination   98
anti-trafficking work, brief history of   171–3
antiviolence activism   22
Anzaldúa, Gloria   61–2
Asad, Talal   58
Asbury, Cory
   "Reckless Love"   175, 176
Asian and Asian American Working Group   105
ATA, *see* African Theological Advance (ATA) initiative, Nagel Institute of Calvin University

atonement   63
atrocious harms   132–3
audacity   28–9
authorship   25–8

Banjo, Omotayo O.   177, 178
baptism   52, 60
Barth, Karl   85
   theology of the Word   69
Behar, Ruth   xxvii, xxix, 14–15, 23, 28–9, 37
   The Vulnerable Observer: Anthropology That Breaks Your Heart   183
Bellah, Robert N.   35
   Beyond Belief   36
   Habits of the Heart   36
Benedict, Ruth   11, 14
benedictions   217–31
Bethune, Mary McLeod   203
Biehl, João
   Vita: Life in a Zone of Social Abandonment   227
Big Bethel African Methodist Episcopal   38, 40–2
   Love Feast   42–4, 47
BIPOC   60, 104
Black Lives Matter   104
Black Panther Party   104
Black theology   69
Boas, Franz   ix, x, 10–12, 15, 60
body politics   111
Bohannon, Richard
   Grounding Religion: A Field Guide to the Study of Religion and Ecology   147
Bonhoeffer, Dietrich   70
border theologies   127–42
Bourdieu, Pierre   34, 36, 38
   on eucharistic self   40

on habitus   39, 75–6
on socially informed body   39
Briggs, Charles   186
British colonialism   102
British Household Panel Survey   55
Broadway United Methodist, Notre Dame, Indiana   52
Brodie, Sidney   193
Browning, Melissa Brown   xv–xxv, 29, 37, 230
    on abstinence among teenagers   xvii–xviii
    community engagement   xxiv–xxv
    engagement with African women   xxii–xxiii
    on HIV/AIDS   xvii, xxiii
    on listening   xxiii–xxiv
    Navigating Dystopia: How to Understand Injustice, and then Start Changing the World   xxii
    Risky Marriage: HIV and Intimate Relationships in Tanzania   xix–xxi
    scholarly publications   xvi–xxii
    on street children   xvi
Browning, Wes   xv
Butler, Anthea   173
Butler, Judith   111–12, 122
    Notes Toward Performative Theory of Assembly   111, 112

Cannon, Katie   xi, xiv, 155
    Black Womanist Ethics   x
capitalism   xix, xx, 77
    racial   132, 138
Card, Claudia   132
Carmi, Nora   157, 161, 165–6
carnal sociology   34, 46
Carter, Beyoncé Knowles
    "Lemonade"   211–13
caste-based discrimination   97, 105, 106
casteism   96, 100, 106
Cavanaugh, William   118–19, 122, 123
    Torture and Eucharist   113, 118
CCM, *see* Contemporary Christian Music (CCM)
Central Presbyterian   38
"charity" or "pity" mentality   xxxivn.18
Circle of Concerned African Women Theologians   xv, xix, xxii, 83–5, 90, 93, 94

Clarke, Sathianathan   106
Clifford, James   12–13, 17, 20, 25
    Writing Culture: The Poetics and Politics of Ethnography   150–1
coauthoring, as mentoring and sharing power   91–3
Coleman, Monica   154
collaborative writing   27
colonialism   xx, xxiv, 9, 12, 16, 25, 105, 106
    British   102
    cultural   161
    neocolonialism   xxxiv
    post-colonialism   32
    Western   xxii
colorism   105
community, definition of   134
Cone, James   109
    Black theology   69
    The Cross and the Lynching Tree   195
Consortium for Street Children   xvi
Contemporary Christian Music (CCM)   175–8
contingent power   141
Copeland, M. Shawn   71
copublishing   91–4
COVID-19 pandemic   4, 123, 127, 225
critical self-reflection   72–7
crucified bodies   xxix, xxiii, xxxvi, 17, 28, 95–110, 195–7, 223
Cuddeback-Gedeon, Lorraine V.   66, 67
cultural colonialism   161
cultural relativism   11
cultural stereotype   23
cultural theory   20, 55
Curtis, Kimberley   75

Dalferth, Ingolf   59
Dalit Panther Party   104
Davis, James   41–4
Deepak, Sai   106
Deloria, Ella   11
de Roest, Henk   27
descriptive claims, writing   150
discipleship
    ethnography and   xxxii–xxxv
discrimination   xiii, 99, 114
    antidiscrimination   98
    caste-based   97, 105, 106
    gender   x, 155

global 101, 103, 104
  racial x, 10
Douglas, Kelly Brown
  Stand Your Ground: Black Bodies and the Justice of God 196
Douglas, Mark xxiii
Duaybis, Cedar 159-60
DuBois, W. E. B. 60
Dunbar, Leslie 187
Dunlop, Sarah 227, 229
Durham Homicide and Victims of Violent Death Memorial Quilt 193

Ebenezer Baptist Church 41
ecclesiological ethnography 46
economic inequality xvii, 133
Ellacuría, Ignacio 107
Elliot, Charles 49, 57-8
  "Ethnography is Dogmatics" 57
embodied knowing 64-8
environmental racism xxxv, 143-6, 148, 149, 151, 152, 155, 191
equipment 226-7
eschatology xxxvi, 57-9, 113, 123-5
Eskerod, Torben 227
ethics 222-3
  ethnographic turn in 32-48
  medical 6, 71
  of receptivity 198-213
  "recognisably real" 68-72
  social science use, critiques of 49-60
  and theology, interconnection of xxviii-xxix
  virtue 37, 55, 56
ethnographic praxis
  researcher and research assistant on, conversation between 81-94
ethnography 3-31
  context 40-2
  of crucified bodies 107-10
  definition of 16-18
  and discipleship xxxii-xxxv
  evolution of 9-16
  as fitting tool for embodied theology xxxi-xxxii
  of local congregations 38-9
  meanings of 6-16
  origins of 6-16
  personal account of 6-9
  theological justifications for 61-78
  tools 18-29
  values of 18-29
eucharistic self 38-40, 44, 46
evangelical reform nexus 172
evangelical whiteness 170-82
  orienting 175-8
  quantitative study of 173-5, 181-2
  reckoning with race 178-81
Evans-Pritchard, E. E. 10, 12, 15

Farmer, Paul xxxiii, 109 n.41, 227
Federal Assault Weapons Ban (1994) 188
femicide 133
financial inequality 77
Ford, David 38-40
  Self and Salvation 38-9
Foucault, Michel 36, 57
Frazer, Sir James 10
Freyre, Gilberto 11, 14
Fulkerson, Mary McClintock 23-4, 45, 47, 69, 70
  Changing the Subject 33
  on critical self-reflection 73-6
  on embodied knowing 65-6
  Places of Redemption 33, 67
Fullilove, Mindy 218

Gamio, Manuel 11
Gasabile, Pauline xv
Geertz, Clifford xxxi, 15, 32, 36
gender 158
  discrimination x, 155
  inequality xvii
  violence xii, 22-3
gentrification 146, 187, 194
al-Ghazālī, Abū Ḥāmid 140
Gill, Robin 49, 55-7
  Churchgoing and Christian Ethics 55
Gissendaner, Kelly Renee xxii
Glissant, Édouard 152-3
global discrimination 101, 103, 104
González-Justiniano, Yara 69
Gordon, Deborah A. 14-16, 26-7, 29
Goto, Courtney T. 16, 23
Gras, Mardi 208
Gray, Cecil 203
Green, Rachelle 24, 26
gumbo 209-11
gun violence xxxvi, 17, 72, 183-97, 221

crucified body 195–7
    guilt 193–5
    nonviolent Durham, religious coalition
        for 187–9
    vigil keeper 189–93
    vigil keeping 185–7
Gutierrez, Gustavo 109 n.41

habitus 39, 75–6
Harvey, Jennifer xxx
Hauerwas, Stanley 37, 49, 51–60
Hayti Heritage Center 194
Healy, Nicholas 38
Healy, Nick 46
Hernandez, Jill Graper 132–3, 137
Hiheon, Kim 121–2, 124
"Hillsong: A Megachurch Exposed" (2022)
Hinduism 97, 101, 102
honor-killings 96
hooks, bell xxix–xxx, 14–16, 231
hospitality vs. receptivity 206–9
Humanitarian Organization for Migration
    Economics 138
Human Rights Watch xvi
humility xxxvii, 19–21, 28–30, 231
    intellectual xxiii, 73
    spiritual 73
Hunter-Bowman, Janna 21–2
Hurricane Betsy 200–1
Hurricane Katrina 47, 198–213
Hurston, Zora Neale ix–xi, xiv, 11, 14, 60
    conservative racial politics xi
    ethnographic folklore xi

imago dei (image of God) 76
imperialism 9
income inequality 191
Indonesian female migrant workers
    (FMWs), in Singapore 127–42
inequality xiii, xxxiv, 8, 14, 24, 27, 28, 62
    economic xvii, 133
    financial 77
    gender xvii
    income 191
    racial 11
    social xvii
    structural xxix, 71
Institutional Review Board (IRB) 19, 63,
    222–3

intellectual humility xxiii, 73
intercaste relationships 96
internalized oppression 162
interviewing 224–6
IRB, see Institutional Review Board (IRB)
Isasi-Díaz, Ada María 192

Jenkins, Timothy 38–9
Jim Crow racial segregation ix
Johansen, Kirstine Helboe 230
Johnson, Elizabeth 130
Johnson, Hazel 143
Jones, Robert P. 5, 217
Jones, Williams 11, 14
Joseph, Peniel E. 199
Juarez, Ciudad 133
Jung, Patricia Beattie xv
just hospitality 207
al-Juwayn, Abū' l-Ma'ālī 140

Kairos for Global Justice Conference
    (2011) 157, 160
Kairos Palestine 156, 157
    gender politics of 162
Kairos Palestine Document 156–8, 160,
    166
Kairos South Africa Document 156–7
Kanyoro, Musimbi 92
Kapferer, Bruce 59
Kaufman, Tone Stangeland 21
Kerr, Fergus 50
Kikon, Dolly 105
Kimaru, Kimathi xvi
Kimin, Choi 121
King, Martin Luther, Jr. 41, 61
Kohut, Heinz 117
Kolers, Avery 124–5
Kort, Nora 158–9, 161–2

liberationist–incarnational
    approach 95–110
liberative movements, hegemonic
    dominant co-options of 101–3
Lindbeck, George 37
linear writing 153–4
liturgy 118
    as ethics 54
    as social action 53
Longkumer, Arkotong 102–3

Love Feast, as communion   42–4, 47
Lowe, Walter   69
Lutheran Volunteer Corps (LVC)   35
LVC, *see* Lutheran Volunteer Corps (LVC)

MacIntyre, Alisdair   55, 75
McKinney, Kelsey   176
McKittrick, Katherine   144, 148
Mahmood, Saba   162
male infidelity   xx
Malinowski, Bronisław   10, 12, 15
Manjule, Nagraj   96
Mantini-Briggs, Clara   186
Marcus, George E.   15
   Writing Culture: The Poetics and Politics of Ethnography   150–1
marginalization   xxii, 16, 17, 71, 98, 99, 101–4, 134, 142, 144, 146, 150, 189, 222
Martí, Gerardo   18
Martin, Trayvon   196–7
Maryknoll Institute of African Studies   xvi
Mbiti, John
   African Religions and Philosophy   xx–xxi
Mead, Margaret   11, 14
medical ethics   6, 71
Merleau-Ponty, M.   34
Milbank, John   54–60
   critique of social theory   58
   Theology and Social Theory   49–51, 58, 69
Mohanty, Chandra   162
Moon, Dawne
   God, Sex and Politics   218
Moreno, Francisco   108
Morgan, Lewis Henry   10, 11
"Mosaic of Peace Conference"   156
Myerhoff, Barbara
   Number Our Days   227
Myŏnga, Kwon   121

Nader, Laura   172–3, 181
Nambura, Teresia   xvi
NDS, *see* New Daughters and Sons (NDS)
neocolonialism   xxxiv
neoliberalism   111, 113
neoliberal rationality   111
New Daughters and Sons (NDS)   170, 171, 174–82, 221
   encountering   173
New Negro movement   ix
New Orleans Association of Houston   212
non-redemptive suffering   130
nonviolent Durham, religious coalition for   187–9
normative claims, writing   150

O'Brien, Kevin
   Grounding Religion: A Field Guide to the Study of Religion and Ecology   147
"observant participation" work   171
Oduyoye, Mercy Amba   83, 90
ontology   58, 96, 97, 100, 140, 149
oppression   xix, xxxv, 92, 95, 97, 98, 100, 102–9, 128, 131–4, 138, 142, 149, 157, 189, 197, 223
   internalized   162
   intersectional forms of   xxix, xxx
   patriarchal   162
   religious   132
   social   59
   structural   141
   systematic   xxxvi
   systemic   129, 130, 136
   theological   132
Orientalism   100
Owen, Marcia A.   189
   Living Without Enemies: Being Present in the Midst of Violence   188

Pachuau, Joy   100
Palestinian women's agency   161–3
Parsitau, Damaris   xviii, xix, xxii, xxiv, 230
Parsons, Talcott   35–6
participant observation   10, 13, 19, 20 n.36, 44, 45, 113, 127, 146, 171, 174, 181, 184, 224, 225, 228
patriarchy
   direct confrontation of   166–8
   patriarchal bargains, strategic use of   165–6
   patriarchal oppression   162

PCR, *see* People for Community Recovery (PCR)
Penn State Community 202–3
People for Community Recovery (PCR) 143, 144, 147
Philip, NourbSe 144
Pineda-Madrid, Nancy 133, 134
Plato xxvi
Pohl, Christine D. 206–8, 210
pornography 23, 227
positivist theology 50
post-colonialism 32
postmodernism 32
Powell, Annie Ruth 7
pragmatic solidarity 28–9
Prevot, Andrew 109
Proposition 187 7
PRRI, *see* Public Religion Research Institute (PRRI)
publication 229–31
Public Religion Research Institute (PRRI) 5, 217
public square, eschatological imagination in 111–26

qualitative methods 4–5, 71
quantitative methods 4–5

Rabinow, Paul 24, 36–7
race, *see also* racial; racism
    and evangelical whiteness 178–81
    as transformative lens in ethnographic research team 88–91
racial
    capitalism 132, 138
    discrimination x, 10
    inequality 11
    inferiority 11
    prejudice 9
    stereotype 23
    superiority 11
racism xxxiv, 60, 70, 91, 96, 99–101, 105, 106, 170 n.1, 179
    anti-Black 147–9, 151
    environmental xxxv, 143–6, 148, 149, 151, 152, 155, 191
    structural 146
    systemic 181
    white ix

rants
    descriptive and normative dimensions of 146–50
    poetic contours of 150–3
RCND, *see* Religious Coalition for a Nonviolent Durham (RCND)
"Recalculating" 200–2
receptivity
    ethics of 198–213
    hospitality *vs.* 206–9
"recognisably real" theology and ethics 68–72
reflexivity 21–5, 72–7, 156–69, 223
relative privilege xxx, 17, 72
relativism 64
    cultural 11
Religious Coalition for a Nonviolent Durham (RCND) 184, 187–92
    Restorative Justice Durham 192
religious oppression 132
research design 219–20
researcher and research assistant on ethnographic praxis, conversation between 81–94
    coauthoring, as mentoring and sharing power 91–3
    hierarchical relationship 85–8
    race 88–91
    two-winged theology 83–4
Research Institute of World's Ancient Traditions Cultures and Heritage, Arunachal Pradesh 103
research question, formulation of 217–19
revelation 3, 28, 67, 68, 72, 74, 231
    self-revelation 30
Rivera, Mayra 151
Robbins, Joel 49, 58–60
    "Anthropology and Theology: An Awkward Relationship?" 58
Roddy-Hart, Marion J. 203–5
Ross, Susan xv
Russell, Letty M. 206, 207

Sabeel Ecumenical Liberation Theology Center 165
Said, Edward
    Orientalism 100
Sairat 96
Al-Saji, Alia 182

salvation 44, 133, 178
sampling 220–2
saviorism 28
  white xxxiv
Scarry, Elaine 118
SCE, *see* Society of Christian Ethics (SCE)
Scharen, Christian xxxi, 23, 33, 34, 47, 62
  on embodied knowing 66–7
  Ethnography as Christian Theology and Ethics, Second Edition xi–xii
  Public Worship and Public Work 40
Schillebeeckx, Edward xvi, xxv
Segundo, Juan Luis 108
self-critical awareness 8, 16, 21–5
shared subjectivity xii–xiv
The Shrine of the Immaculate Conception 38
sin xxiv, 6, 107, 146, 197
site selection 220–2
sites of privilege, confronting and contesting xxix–xxxi
slavery 149, 150
  afterlife of 195, 196
  chattel 22, 154
  transatlantic 154
  white 170 n.1, 171
Sobrino, Jon 107
social capital 104, 163–5, 222
social inequality xvii
social justice xix, 142
social oppression 59
social science usage in theology and ethics, critiques of 49–60
  Adams, Nicholas 57–8
  Elliot, Charles 57–8
  Hauerwas, Stanley 52–5
  Milbank, John 50–1
  Robbins, Joel 58–60
Society of Christian Ethics (SCE)
  'Ethnography and Normative Ethics' xxvi
socioeconomic stereotype 23
solidarity x, xi, xiii, xvii, xix, xxxiv, 35, 95, 103, 107, 163
  interracial 105
  pragmatic 28–9
  superficial pursuits of 104–6
Sontag, Susan
  Regarding the Pain of Others 117

Spanier, Graham B. 203
spiritual humility 73
Spivak, Gayatri 162
Spradley, James xxxii
State College, Pennsylvania 202–3, 206, 208, 209, 212, 213
stereotype 10, 77
  cultural 23
  racial 23
  socioeconomic 23
Stevens, James 45, 46, 203
street children xvi
structural inequality xxix, 71
structural injustice 97, 98
structural oppression 141
structural racism 146
structural violence xvi, xxxiii, 96, 199, 200
Sutherland, Arthur 206, 207
Swedish woman affair 158–61
Syed, Mairaj 140
systemic oppression 129, 130, 136
systemic racism 181

Tanner, Kathryn 48, 54
  Theories of Culture 37–8
tautology 23, 30
theodicy
  at the border 127–42
  definition of 138
theological oppression 132
theology
  from the body 44–7
  border 127–42
  and ethics, interconnection of xxviii–xxix
  ethnographic turn in 32–48
  ethnography as fitting tool for xxxi–xxxii
  "recognisably real" 68–72
  social science use, critiques of 49–60
theory of human action 141
thick description xxxi, xxxvi, 32, 98, 108, 145, 184
Thompson, H. Paul 172
Tipton, Steven 57
Townes, Emilie M. 134
transmuted goods 137

transnational feminism, ethnographic
    reflexivity and accountability
    in 156–69
  coda 168–9
  cultural assets 163–5
  Palestinian women's agency 161–3
  patriarchal bargains, strategic use
    of 165–6
  patriarchy, direct confrontation
    of 166–8
  social capital 163–5
  Swedish woman affair 158–61
  Western feminism 161–3
Turner, Sarah 81
Tveitereid, Knut 20
  *The Wiley Blackwell Companion
    to Theology and Qualitative
    Research* xxvi
two-winged theology 83–4

UN Declaration on the Rights
  of Indigenous Peoples
  (UNDRIP) 102, 103
UNDRIP, *see* UN Declaration on the
  Rights of Indigenous Peoples
  (UNDRIP)

Vigen, Aana Marie xv, xxx, xxxi, 4, 6
  *Ethnography as Christian Theology
    and Ethics, Second Edition* xi–xii
  on medical ethics 71
violence
  gender xii, 22–3
  gun xxxvi, 17, 72, 183–97, 221
  of Hippo 70
  ontology of 58
  state-sanctioned 157
  structural xvi, xxxiii, 96, 199, 200
  of structural injustice 98
virtue ethics 37, 55
  Aristotelian tradition of 56
Visweswaran, Kamala 25–6

Wacquant, Loïc 34, 44, 186
  Body and Soul 39
Walker Grimes, Katie 149
Wambui, Rose xvi
Ward, Peter

*The Wiley Blackwell Companion
  to Theology and Qualitative
  Research* xxvi
Watkins, Clare 68
Weber, Shantelle 9
Wells, Samuel 189
  *Living Without Enemies: Being Present
    in the Midst of Violence* 188
Western colonialism xxii
Western feminism 161–3
Westfield, N. Lynne 206, 207
white antiracism 9
white feminism 16
white privilege 14
white racism ix
white saviorism xxxiv
Whitmore, Todd 67, 76
WHO, *see* World Health Organization
  (WHO)
Wigg-Stevenson, Natalie xxxii, 45, 67
  *Transgressive Devotion: Theology as
    Performance Art* 62
  *The Wiley Blackwell Companion to Theology
    and Qualitative Research* (Ward and
    Tveitereid) xxvi, 4 n.3, 9 n.11,
    18 n.34, 20 n. 38, 21 n.39, 22 n.41,
    23 n.46, 24 n.50, 27 n.61, 68 n.16,
    69 n.18, 226 n.10, 230 nn.18, 19
Wilkerson, Isabel 101–2
  Caste 101
Williams, Delores 148
Williams, Kesha Morant 177, 178
Williams, Mel 187
Williams, Rowan 51, 55
Winquist, Charles 69
women's submission xx
Woodlawn Boxing Club 46
World Bank 58
World Health Organization
  (WHO) xxxiii
worshipping self 38, 44

Young, Iris Marion 231

Zaru, Jean 157, 160, 166–7
  Occupied with Nonviolence 167